The Beloved Son
as Tantalizing Teacher

The Beloved Son as Tantalizing Teacher

Jesus Encounters His World

CARL E. ROEMER

WIPF & STOCK · Eugene, Oregon

THE BELOVED SON AS TANTALIZING TEACHER
Jesus Encounters His World

Copyright © 2021 Carl E. Roemer. All rights reserved. Except for brief quotations in critical publications or reviews, no part of this book may be reproduced in any manner without prior written permission from the publisher. Write: Permissions, Wipf and Stock Publishers, 199 W. 8th Ave., Suite 3, Eugene, OR 97401.

Wipf & Stock
An Imprint of Wipf and Stock Publishers
199 W. 8th Ave., Suite 3
Eugene, OR 97401

www.wipfandstock.com

PAPERBACK ISBN: 978-1-7252-9553-7
HARDCOVER ISBN: 978-1-7252-9552-0
EBOOK ISBN: 978-1-7252-9554-4

08/17/21

To Dottie
my wife and companion for 57 years
and to
the Judaic Studies Department at
the State University of New York at Binghamton
where the contents of this book had its beginnings
and to
all the pastors and lay people who want to understand
what it would be like to hear
Jesus as he was understood by his contemporaries.

Contents

Preface	xi
Abbreviations	xiii
Introduction	xvii
Front Matter Endnotes	xxiii
1 | The Beloved Son: The Birth, Baptism, and Temptation of Jesus	1
2 | The Tantalizing Teacher: Biographical Pronouncement Stories	57
3 | The Tantalizing Teacher: Controversy and Scholastic Dialogues	109
4 | Summary and Analysis: The Beloved Son as Tantalizing Teacher	162
Epilogue: Retrospect and Prospect	211
Chapter Endnotes	215
Bibliography	287
Index	295

Preface

This study is the third volume in a series investigating the Jesus of history. It grew out of a course on the historical Jesus that I taught in the Department of Judaic Studies at the State University of New York at Binghamton during the 1990s. I named that course "Jesus in Context."

The field of historical Jesus research is, to put it somewhat mildly, extensive and voluminous (even my little library contains some sixty authors who have ventured forth on this journey with just as many views on whom they perceive to have been the "Jesus of history"). So why am I adding more words to this discussion? In my introduction to the previous volume I analyzed the work of several of the more prominent investigators. I found them coming up with insightful and illuminating insights into the person of Jesus and his ministry. Most did not particularly relate Jesus to his context nor to the church that arose from him.

My thesis is that to truly understand Jesus, one must take his historical context as foundational. First, I want to answer the question of whether his words and deeds relate to the Jewish milieu of the first century, and if so, how do they function in it? My purpose in writing these books grows out of that thesis. It became clear in the previous volume in this series that Jesus was engaging his world in the land of Israel and its historical situation. His dynamic relationship with the first-century Jewish environment speaks volubly for the authenticity of the materials we find in the Gospels.

Second, I want to help pastors and laypeople to see and understand how intimately Jesus was connected to his time and place. He did not just say and do things that had some spiritual and universal application. He did not just "float above history" handing down ideas and maxims that were meant for every time and place (even though they have applicability beyond the particular instances of his historical situation). He spoke and acted in a particular historical context—everything he said and did had to do with the people of his time and place, their attitudes, and how they were relating to their environment. One obvious reflection of that specificity of time and place is the opposition that he engendered and the personal attacks that he had to confront.

In the present study I initially take a long and hard look at the birth stories and the two incidents in his life that had a profound effect on him, his self-understanding, and the conduct of his ministry, namely the narratives of his baptism and the temptation. In them I discover that he encounters a designation for himself that bears ominous undertones. I follow up those investigations with the so-called pronouncement stories, in which we find Jesus engaging directly with his fellow Jews in the land of Israel. They are divided into biographical stories and controversy and scholastic dialogues. The former are biographical in the sense that they concern things Jesus said in relationship to his experiences, intimate encounters with individuals, and actions that he initiated that reveal something personal about himself. The latter deal with encounters with groups and individuals who challenge his words and behaviors.

As in the parables, we meet Jesus here again "on the ground." In this study you are invited to join the conversation with this tantalizing teacher but now in his direct encounter with individuals and groups.

Biblical quotations are excerpted from the Revised Standard Version of the Bible. Old Testament Section copyright 1952; New Testament Section, first edition, copyright 1946; the Apocrypha, copyright 1957 by Division of Christian Education of the National Council of Churches of Christ in the United States of America.

The cover art was designed and executed by the Rev'd Joel Nickel, a liturgical artist who lives in Salem, Oregon. He depicts Jesus whose pronouncements are a "spring of water welling up to eternal life" and who personally is a font of knowing, a knowing that is discernment, a process discovered in relationships.

Abbreviations

HEBREW BIBLE/OLD TESTAMENT

Gen	Genesis	Song	Song of Solomon
Exod	Exodus	Isa	Isaiah
Lev	Leviticus	Jer	Jeremiah
Num	Numbers	Lam	Lamentations
Deut	Deuteronomy	Ezek	Ezekiel
Josh	Joshua	Dan	Daniel
Judg	Judges	Hos	Hosea
Ruth	Ruth	Joel	Joel
1–2 Sam	1–2 Samuel	Amos	Amos
1–2 Kgs	1–2 Kings	Obad	Obadiah
1–2 Chr	1–2 Chronicles	Jonah	Jonah
Ezra	Ezra	Mic	Micah
Neh	Nehemiah	Nah	Nahum
Esth	Esther	Hab	Habbkuk
Job	Job	Zeph	Zephaniah
Ps / Pss	Psalms	Hag	Haggai
Prov	Proverbs	Zech	Zechariah
Eccl	Ecclesiastes	Mal	Malachi

NEW TESTAMENT

Matt	Matthew	Col	Colossians
Mark	Mark	1–2 Thess	1–2 Thessalonians
Luke	Luke	1–2 Tim	1–2 Timothy
John	John	Titus	Titus
Acts	Acts of the Apostles	Phlm	Philemon
Rom	Romans	Heb	Hebrews
1–2 Cor	1–2 Corinthians	1–2 Pet	1–2 Peter
Gal	Galatians	1–2–3 John	1–2–3 John
Eph	Ephesians	Jude	Jude
Phil	Philippians	Rev	Revelation

THE APOCRYPHA/DEUTEROCANONICAL BOOKS

Tob	Tobit	Ep Jer	Epistle of Jerimiah
Jdt	Judith	Sg Three	Song of the Tree Young Men
Add Esth	Additions to Esther	Sus	Susanna
Wis	Wisdom of Solomon	Bel	Bel and the Dragon
Sir	Sirach or Ecclesiastes	1–2 Macc	1–2 Maccabees
Bar	Baruch	Pr Man	Prayer of Manasseh
1–3 Esd	1–3 Esdras		

PSEUDEPIGRAPHA

Enoch	1 (Ethiopic Apocalypse of) Enoch
Testaments	Testaments of the Twelve Patriarchs
4 Macc	4 Maccabees
Pss of Sol	Psalms of Solomon

OTHER ANCIENT SOURCES

Flavius Josephus

Josephus, *War*	The Jewish War
Josephus, *Ant.*	Antiquities of the Jews
Josephus, *Life*	The Life of Flavius Josephus

Philo

Life of Moses	*De vita Mosis*
Embassy	*Legatio ad Gaium*
Special Laws	*De specialibus legibus*

The Dead Sea Scrolls

(The scrolls are designated by the cave they were found in, the initial number, followed by "Q" for Qumran, and by the type of literature using the initial letter of the Hebrew name for the scrolls. S="Serek" (rule); H=Hodayoth ("hymns"); p="pesher" ("interpretation" or "commentary").

The Community Rule	1QS
The Thanksgiving Hymns	1QH
Commentary on Habakkuk	1QpHab

The Mishnah

The various tractates of the Mishnah are preceded by "*m.*"
    The names of the tractates are always spelled out and translated in the endnotes.

The Talmuds

The tractates of the Talmuds are preceded by "*y*" for the *Jerusalem Talmud* and by "*b*" for the *Babylonian Talmud*.

Introduction

Dear Reader, this book is part of a projected series of studies on the life of Jesus. The first, *What Was the World of Jesus?*,[1] portrayed the context that formed Jesus and his life's work. I described that world in terms of six dynamics factors: the history of the Mediterranean world from Alexander to the destruction of the Temple, its economic, social, religious, and political structures, and its ecology. I described in detail the models of renewal that arose out of Israel's history by which the people of Israel chose to confront what many perceived as the corrosion of their society. In that study it became clear that the Jewish people of the first century, living in their patrimonial land of Israel, were embroiled in a crisis that threatened to overwhelm the nation. Their situation can be summed up in the pithy phrase, a people whose "backs were against the wall."[2]

The second book in this series, *Who in the World Was Jesus?*,[3] investigated the message of the parables of Jesus. I chose to start my study with the parables because most scholarship deems them the shortest path to hearing the authentic words of Jesus, revealing his message and his conception of the kingdom of God. What follows is a synopsis of the results of this investigation of the parables by which I mean to provide the framework in which to understand the pronouncement stories, the subject of the present study.

He spoke in parables because he was part of a storytelling culture (the Old Testament!). Stories have the greatest potential for getting people to look at a situation in a different way—that is, they enhance the possibility of transformation of the self. He recognized that stories could have a psychological effect that would alter the heart and mind of the people. His parables drew on the very stuff of life, particularly the milieu in which he lived. They connected directly with the experiences of the people and their encounter with their environment.

The parables reveal that Jesus was not just concerned with transcendental matters, one's eternal destiny, and the future, supernatural kingdom of God but with the historical fate of his people and the nation. He addressed a people, the majority of whom had their "backs against the wall," who lived their lives on the edge, and whose existence was fraught with anxiety about survival. The nation itself was interwoven with hatred of the Roman occupation, seething resentment for the affront of that occupation to God's majesty, and the revolutionary fervor aroused by the desecrating paganization of the Holy Land as a result of the presence of Roman polytheistic and idolatrous temples and their devotees. These negative forces divided the nation, pitted brother against brother, and created an environment of competition and antagonism. The burning issue for the society as a whole was God's kingdom and its establishment as variously as it was conceived.

Patriarchy, honor and shame, limited good, and cultic purity were bedrock values of this society. Furthermore, the society was structured on the basis of corporate personality and the patron-client relationship. These values and structures lent the society a certain rigidity that predisposed those who would effect a renewal to act within certain parameters, namely to see Israel's crisis totally in terms of the Roman occupation.[4]

Jesus saw clearly where these attitudes and postures would end, in the destruction of the nation. So his parables were told to bring the nation back to its roots: their God of steadfast love, faithfulness, forgiveness, and compassion, all of which characterized his true kingdom.[5] He concretized the life of the kingdom in his common meals with sinners. The kingdom involved corruption including sinners like leaven in a lump of dough. In his tantalizing parables he clothed the kingdom with flesh and blood stories calling on contemporary images from the culture but also rooted in Israel's Scripture. They were arousing stories that generated curiosity and thoughtful reflection. They, to the consternation of many a hearer, found the kingdom's presence in surprising and unexpected circumstances and human activity (Luke 10: 30–37, 18:1–8, 16:1–8). It was uncontrollably free and so could appear under whatever guise God would choose. His paradoxical proclamation of the kingdom of God was both summons and threat, warning and promise, consolation and challenge.

God's kingdom is a divine action and pure gift that comes without human striving but requires human activity. This paradoxical nature of the kingdom is graphically illustrated in the act of sowing: a person sows, but it is God who gives the growth (Mark 4:3–8). The kingdom meant the opposite of internalizing the dogma of limited good[6] and hoarding one's abundant harvest for oneself like the "Rich Fool" (Luke 12:16-21) or ignoring the poor and destitute whose presence was so obvious lying even before the gate of the rich (Luke 16:19-31). Nor did it mean the practice of a stringent application of justice but rather the generosity of the master who paid a day's wages even to those who worked only an hour (Matt 20:1-16).

The kingdom involves role reversal: the master will serve the slave (Luke 12:37). But Jesus does not only reverse the role of masters but also demands that the lowly peasant also forgive as he has been forgiven (Matt 18:23-35). The kingdom means competition ends, hatred of enemies ceases, and forgiveness of debts thrives. It means not sitting in judgment on others because true piety is not merely rejoicing in God's blessing of chosenness but the constant consciousness that when all is said and done the human being stands before God as a beggar (Luke 18-14). Jesus calls for solidarity between all levels of society. It is, of course, based on an inner revolution brought about by entering the kingdom of God.

The kingdom is a great treasure and a boundless joy when a person finds it or, rather, when it finds him or her (Matt 13:44). It is not to be kept for oneself but demands a sharing of the joy (Luke 15:4-7, 8-10). It places everything else in the world in its proper perspective because one now has "treasure in heaven" that is not subject to decay as are the treasures of this world (Mark 10:21). The kingdom is about an ardent concentration on God's passionate and merciful love of his people (Luke 15:11-32) and translating that into an outgoing mindfulness for the common weal (Luke 10:30-37) rather than plotting violence against Rome, which would never bring in the kingdom. It meant expanding that magnificent oriental and village value of hospitality to the world (Luke 11:5-8).

For Jesus the kingdom is double-sided. It is both present and future, expressing the reality that God is not part of the world but transcendent and so not an object of speculation. In this way he affirms the biblical and Jewish understanding of God. Jesus is no gnostic who transmits secret knowledge. Even a child can grasp the wonderful grace of the kingdom (Matt 11:25, cf., 10:26). Rather, his parables portray God as the One who lays claim upon a person. God, though transcendent, is not far away, withdrawn into some mythological, heavenly realm. He is present as his kingdom expands and grows. Through the agency of Jesus, his proclamations, healings, exorcisms, and parables, God is present, creating a new community of concord and reconciliation.

Nor is Jesus an apocalyptist with a focus only on a future redemption. His parables hold together in tension the present and the future. The kingdom is surely present now (Luke 17:21), but the fullness of its reality lies in the future (Luke 11:2). The parables make the kingdom present and reveal its presence in the oddest and even most perplexing circumstances and people: a mustard plant rendering a garden unclean visualizes the kingdom; a conniving steward evokes the Jubilee (Luke 16:1–8); a nagging widow limns the kingdom's justice (Luke 18:1–8).

The parables also give us an insight into Jesus's own self-understanding. The parable of the sower (Mark 4:3–8) reveals how he experienced the various ways his message was rejected or accepted. Jesus's patience in waiting for his message to be received and grow and blossom among his people was expressed in the story of the patient farmer (Mark 4:26–29). This story also reveals his compassion for his nation and his craving for a positive response. For him the kingdom was a joyous affair, especially when the seemingly lost members of his people were found and responded positively to the preaching of the kingdom and joined him at table (the parables of the lost sheep, Matt 18:12–14, and the lost coin, Luke 15:8–10). He identified with society's rejects as he encountered the pejorative judgments of the "insiders" (the parable of the great feast, Matt 11:1–10). In the parable of the prodigal son (Luke 15:11–32) the father who shames himself, inviting the contempt of his fellow villagers, reproduces some of Jesus's contemporaries' responses to him. In the parable of the two sons (Matt 21:28–32) he agrees with his detractors who accuse him of disobedience but asserts paradoxically that he is really God's obedient son who ultimately is serving God's will. In that rejection the cross is already intimated.

The kingdom is an urgent affair. When it dawns repentance will no longer be possible, and those who have rejected it will be consigned to judgment. Jesus makes the urgency in responding positively to the kingdom crucial in the parables of the fig tree (Mark 13:28–29, Matt 24:32–33, Luke 21:19–31), the fishnet (Matt 13:47–48), the talents (Luke 19:12–27), the ten virgins (Matt 25:1–13), and perhaps preeminently the thief (Luke 12:39–40). God's intervention is at the door, and people must reorient their lives now.

So Jesus does not adopt any apocalyptic scenarios nor, above all, the triumph of Israel over the Gentile world and its consequent consignment to everlasting perdition. Though his mission was primarily to his own people, his message embraced the inclusion of Gentiles in God's promises. It is my opinion that he envisioned their inclusion by means of God's prevenient grace, which prepared a place for them in the kingdom based on their behavior toward Israel. The son of man invites these residents of the Gentile nations to "inherit the kingdom prepared for you from the foundation of the world" (the parable of the great Assize, Matt 25:34).

The parable of the unjust steward is another deconstruction of popular apocalyptic. Everyone in the parable acts in a fraudulent way, but in the end everyone celebrates a Jubilee and delights in a partnership of joy. Jesus proclaims completely new standards of power, justice, and what defines insiders and outliers: the master abjures the use of power and lets his steward's swindle stand, and everyone reaps the harvest of debt forgiveness. With this parable Jesus calls on his auditors to give up their theology that wreaks divine vengeance on Israel's enemies and, contrariwise, to celebrate their God of mercy and compassion.

The parable of the returning demons (Matt 12:43–45) is a horrific indictment of a nation that had been invaded with the worst of seven demons; with so many people overemphasizing its separation from the rest of the world; the increasing belligerent attitude toward Rome; the exclusive concern for obedience to the exclusion of mercy (Matt 5:7, 9:13); the fantasizing about an apocalyptic divine intervention that didn't include a sense of also standing under God's judgment oneself; the rebuffing of the prophets that were sent to them; the sitting in judgment on one another rather than nurturing brotherly love. And then there was the penchant of some to accuse Jesus of demon possession when he was the one who was attacking Satan's kingdom and binding the "strong man" (Mark 3:27). Here Jesus stands out as one of the prophets of old who called the nation to account in their life before God. He wasn't characterizing everyone, but these attitudes and behaviors were general enough and had invaded enough minds that Jesus could with integrity characterize the nation as being demon possessed. This is a prophetic-like hyperbolic invective meant to arouse the consciousness of the people.[7]

Jesus inverted the character of the nation by establishing an alternative kingdom, the very kingdom that was the subject of his proclamation and ministry. He created a counter-Israel, as it were, headed by himself as king. His kingship, however, was one of servitude: a true shepherd of the people who sought for the lost and the outcasts who sat at his table (Luke 19:10, Matt 10:6). He called an inner core of disciples, the symbolic twelve in number representing the twelve tribes of Israel. In this counter-kingdom people served one another and were not to lord it over others. His kingship was universal. It extended through all the world including his "brethren" (i.e., the Jews) who hungered and thirsted, lived as strangers, were naked, sick, and imprisoned—and beyond to those who serve them by providing food in their want, clothe them in their need, and visit them when ill or imprisoned (the parable of the great Assize). This alternative kingdom did not mean that Jesus was turning away from or opposed to his own people; rather he made visible the kingdom to which he invited his nation to enter. It was like the desperate cry of the prophet yearning for his people to turn and avoid the disaster that hung like a sword of Damocles over their heads.

He wanted to save them from disaster. Jesus' words and actions were both an invitation to his people and like a lover's quarrel.

In what follows you will stand beside Jesus as he interacts with persons and situations in his milieu. These are not disembodied words of Jesus, but each pronouncement story provides a context into which the words were spoken, so your experience will not be only of Jesus himself but of those who were part of his world. However, I will first explore the birth, temptation, and baptismal stories. These stories are foundational to grasping how Jesus understood himself and his identity and therefore set the stage for his subsequent activity, teaching, and ministry.

One of the heated deliberations in the study of the historical Jesus is establishing criteria for determining the historical reliability of words and deeds of Jesus as they are reported in the Gospels. The contents of the Gospels are suspect because, it is argued, they are filtered through the oral tradition and retelling of the early church. In addition, the Gospels themselves were written some forty to seventy years removed from the life of Jesus. So scholars have many a suspicion about how authentically the materials of the Gospels were handed down by oral transmission.[8] My assumption is that these Gospel materials are trustworthy for the most part, and each unit of that Gospel tradition must be individually evaluated in terms of its relationship to Jesus.[9] I assume the basic accuracy of the traditions in the Gospels and that they reproduce faithfully the gist of what Jesus said or did. They are short, concise, and succinct, absent of obvious elaborations, and easily remembered.[10]

Front Matter Endnotes

1. Roemer, *What Was the World of Jesus?*
2. An expression from Thurman, *Jesus and the Disinherited*, describing both the situation of the Jews in the first century and African Americans in the early twentieth century. See chapter 4, in whose early pages I provide an outline of the results of this study.
3. Roemer, *Who in the World Was Jesus?* See especially the summary chapter, 365–87.
4. The Pharisees for the most part were not revolutionaries, although some participated in such activities. Their answer to the crisis was Israel's total dedication to fulfilling the Torah.
5. Of course, the people and the nation as a whole rejoiced in God's favor and in the gift of the Torah, which was the way of living in faithfulness to God. The Pharisees and Essenes proposed their own ways toward confronting this crisis in their society. The Pharisees by focusing on the Torah and the oral law as it was preserved among the population sought to fulfill faithfully the will of God and in this way engender a renewal of the nation's relationship with the divine to become a holy, egalitarian nation. The Essenes withdrew from society and called the nation to abandon the present corrupt world to live a holy life correctly ordered under priestly rule.
6. See Roemer, *What Was the World of Jesus?*, 560–1.
7. See, e.g., the invective of Isaiah chapter 1. The invective does not mean rejection but to waken the people to their dire circumstances as they face the judgment of God. When Isaiah accuses Israel as a "sinful nation, a people laden with iniquity, offspring of evildoers, sons who deal corruptly! They have forsaken the LORD, they have despised the Holy One of Israel, they are utterly estranged" (1:4), he is not utterly discarding Israel but calling the people to repentance and to faithfulness to the covenant.
8. For example, see *Journal for the Study of the Historical Jesus* 7, 1 (2009), which is devoted to Kenneth Bailey's theory of the integrity of oral transmission, what he calls "informal controlled oral tradition." Bailey propounded his theory in "Informal," 34–54, and in "Middle Eastern ," 363–7. See also *Journal for the Study of the Historical Jesus* 16, 2–3 (2018). This volume of the journal is dedicated to memory studies.
9. See my previous book *Who in the World Was Jesus?*, 65–78, which discusses the historicity of the Gospels and the criteria used to determine authenticity. Also see Rodriguez, "Authenticating Criteria." He questions the concepts of authentic and

inauthentic as a way of interpreting the Gospel materials and reconstructing the historical Jesus.

10. See *Journal for the Study of the Historical Jesus* 16, 2–3 (2018) on memory and memory studies. For the related topic of eyewitnesses, see *Journal for the Study of the Historical Jesus* 6, 2 (2208), which discusses Bauckham's *Jesus and the Eyewitnesses*.

1

The Beloved Son

The Birth, Baptism, and Temptation of Jesus

"In the beginning was the Word and
the Word dwelt among us."

INTRODUCTION

The usual methods for evaluating the authenticity of the traditions in the Gospels use the criteria of dissimilarity, multiple attestation, embarrassment, and congruence.[1] While I utilize these criteria, in addition to them I also implicitly employ a further criterion of historical plausibility. That is, does a given report about Jesus and his actions and words fit into the historical situation in which Jesus was active?[2] I find that an overwhelming number of the traditions in the Gospels fit the historical situation of Jesus' time and are congruent with one another.

Another methodology of determining authenticity has also recently been proposed and explicated, that of the "remembered Jesus." It is claimed that community memories, as opposed to individual memories, provide reliable access to the Jesus of history.³ Dale Allison became skeptical of the traditional criteria seeking to establish the authenticity of the Gospel materials and especially the idea of appealing to community memories. He set a path that explores a different way and takes into serious account recent psychological and sociological discussion of memory.⁴ For him these studies are unsettling for research into the historical Jesus because they have shown the deficiencies endemic to memories. So on this basis, the memories preserved in the Gospels can be muddled or just plain wrong.⁵ Memory does not offer the past itself but tools for living in the present. The new life situation of the community has affected the shape and content of what is remembered. So Allison recognizes that the tradition is also shaped by the impact of Jesus on those who remembered him.

Allison hopes to find the Jesus of history in the broader patterns of the tradition. Therefore, specific details, especially when there is less support for them, cannot claim reliability.⁶ Conversely, if the broader aspects of our sources, such as Jesus' apocalyptic expectations, his placing himself at the center of God's action, or his expecting a violent demise, are rejected, there is no hope of confirming individual sayings or events ascribed to Jesus. So he relies on what he calls "recurrent attestation," by which he means repeating patterns and themes that appear throughout the tradition such as the "kingdom of God."⁷ In this way he affirms that the early church often represented the traditions about Jesus correctly. He can go forward and reconstruct his understanding of the Jesus of history and affirm, for example, that Jesus held exalted thoughts about his person.⁸ And he can furthermore affirm that the evangelists were not inventing metaphorical tales but reconfiguring actual memories of Jesus.⁹ So the Gospels, according to Allison, present the broad picture of Jesus correctly, while the details cannot be trusted to be authentic.

But is his methodology a good way of understanding the Jesus of history?¹⁰ If we are to give greater weight to the themes that emerge from the Gospels and not the details, how does the interpreter identify these themes?¹¹ However, Allison has established that the Gospels as memories of Jesus' followers still bear a strong correlation to the Jesus of history. He has established the potential of memory studies for retrieving the historical Jesus.

Rafael Rodríguez finds in his own work with memory studies that they clarify only how people living in communities experience their past and employ those memories to understand their present. According to him, within such a milieu both true and false memories function in similar ways once they find general acceptance within the community.¹² So he concludes, "In the case of the Gospels and the historical Jesus, memory studies do not so much provide tools for assessing a tradition's authenticity as they enable the historian to glimpse how Jesus' early followers understood, communicated and generalized from the significance of Jesus of Nazareth in and for later contexts."[13] He does, though, recognize that Allison affirms that the remembered Jesus has a strong connection with the Jesus of history so that memory studies can produce that kind of historical knowledge, although in "broad strokes and general ideas."[14] But the historian must recognize that these memories are shaped by the present concerns of the community even while being under the influence of the historical Jesus.[15]

However, are human memories so utterly suspect as Allison portrays them? People who witness a traumatic situation will describe and attribute different details to an event. But this does not mean that all the details that are reported are wrong or imaginary or not accurately recalled. Without accurate memory, the human being, or for that matter animals, could not function. Of course, we forget things every day, so there is both a pliability and a permanency to our functioning as beings with memories. In addition, we remember things that we sometimes wish we could forget! Our memories can also be modified and corrected by others who recall the same events but with more accuracy.[16] This implies that the people who share a memory are more likely to recount such memories with greater precision as they are modified in that direction by the community that holds, nurtures, and repeats them.

I have proceeded with the presupposition that the traditions we have in the synoptic Gospels are, for the most part, reliable. First, the individual pericopae that make up the Gospels are short and easily remembered. We do not find in them grand elaborations or embellishments that exaggerate the person of Jesus or his deeds, and so they appear to be sober retellings of what actually happened or was said. The parables are also highly rememberable. These little stories are told with some detail but again soberly. Second, the details that we find in the Gospel materials, rather than pointing to later supplements, are precisely what we would expect to be remembered. Third, the political, religious, and social environment of both Jesus and the remembering community are the same. What Jesus did and said not only fit Jesus' time and place but also that of the community, and corresponded to its needs. So why would the tradition need to be changed to fit a nonexistent new situation? The only question here is what words and deeds of Jesus were left out. Fourth, memory in that ancient cultural situation was especially important, and people of that day were capable of prodigious memory feats. Fifth, Jesus himself no doubt said similar things over and over, and he frequently would have privately spoken at length with his disciples to impart his understanding and perspectives. Finally, as I show in the analysis of the pronouncement stories, they fit perfectly into the environment in which Jesus lived.[17]

This is not to say that the evangelists themselves did not adapt the traditions to their needs and even invent some of the material they included in their Gospels.[18] For example, comparing Mark with Matthew and Luke, we can see the hand of the latter two evangelists at work.[19] In addition, it is possible to detect the hand of Mark as he adapted the traditions that he wove into his Gospel narrative. This means that I endorse redaction criticism—that is, the ability to distinguish between the original tradition and how each evangelist adapted it as they incorporated it into their Gospel context.[20]

THE BIRTH OF JESUS

In this section I will not deal in detail with the birth narratives as they are found in Matthew 1–2 and Luke 1–2. For that you may refer to Raymond Brown's massive investigation *The Birth of the Messiah*, which is perhaps the definitive investigation of these narratives. However, it is important to recognize that, though these narratives are each distinctive in their own way and very different from each other, they do share some commonalities:

1. Mary is named as the mother of Jesus and Joseph her betrothed.
2. Mary and Joseph are legally engaged but have not yet lived together nor had sexual relations.
3. Mary was found to be pregnant before the two were married.
4. It is clear that Joseph was not the father of the child.
5. An angelic messenger announces the coming birth of Jesus.
6. Mary does not conceive the child by intercourse with her husband.
7. This same messenger directs that the name of the child is to be Jesus and declares that he will be the Savior.
8. The birth takes place after the couple come to live together.
9. The birth occurs in Bethlehem.
10. The birth takes place during the reign of Herod the Great.
11. The couple eventually settles in Nazareth.
12. Mary's conception was virginal and of the Holy Spirit.[21]

Other than these points of contact, the two versions are incapable of being harmonized even if one assumes that Matthew's story contains reminiscences of Joseph and Luke's that of Mary. For example, Matthew relates the coming of the magi and the flight into Egypt and Luke the census of Augustus. Matthew knows of no domicile in Nazareth until the reign of Archaelaus and represents Bethlehem as their home for at least two years. The two narratives thus contradict one another. But the agreements listed above give the core of both stories: the virginal conception, the name the child is to be given, the identity of Jesus' mother and reputed father, the historical circumstances and place of the birth, and the home of this family in Nazareth. The narratives took form and were constructed on these basic elements. At the root of the list is the recognition that Joseph was not Jesus' father and that, externally speaking, Jesus could have been thought of as the illegitimate son of Mary except that Joseph ultimately married her and accepted Jesus as his son, and so removed any possibility of having him regarded in that way.[22]

That is not to say that Jesus was not maligned. He was accused of being in league with Satan (Mark 3:22), of being a glutton and drunkard (Matt 11:19), which was tantamount to being labeled as a rebellious son (Deut 21:18–21) making him liable to the death penalty, of being blasphemous (Mark 2:7, 14:64), and of being a false prophet who leads Israel astray (Matt 27:62–64).

Did illegitimacy play a role in his ministry and self-consciousness?[23] The investigation into this question is predicated on the assumption that if there was a stigma attached to Jesus because of a supposed illegitimacy there would be stories that revealed his social status and whether it was likely he had such a reputation. The Hebrew word for "illegitimate" or "bastard" was *mamzer* (ממזר), which designated someone who was conceived out of wedlock or the son of someone other than the mother's husband. Stigma and dishonor were associated with such persons.[24] There also seem to have been prohibitions against marrying since they could have had Gentile parentage or married unknowingly within prohibited degrees of affiliation. The interest in the status of the *mamzer* beginning with Deuteronomy and continuing in Qumran and the Rabbis indicates the seriousness with which the concern was treated.[25]

However, merely labeling him a *mamzer* does not mean he was, since the word could be used as an insult between equals. What is at issue is the actual social status of an individual. Jesus was certainly called names. That name calling by important individuals, however, only underscores that he had status rather than he lacked it.[26] If he had been considered illegitimate, he would not have been criticized for consorting with outcasts and sinners.

In that case he would have been living up to expectations. As it is, people act with surprise, suggesting he is behaving contrary to his social status (e.g., Luke 7:39). And no one is scandalized for associating with him, least of all Pharisees. There is disdain for his Galilean origin and that he consorts with social outliers but not for his social status. Indeed, Pharisees seek him out to discuss points of the Torah (e.g., Mark 10:2–9). Social-scientific investigations demonstrate that one did not engage in controversy with someone beneath oneself in the honor pyramid.[27] Jesus is also constantly portrayed as teaching in the synagogues and therefore regarded as a recognized teacher, even though he apparently had no formal training (John 7:15, cf., Paul who did, Acts 23:6, Phil 3:5).

Contrariwise, Jesus was recognized as a descendant of David (Rom 1:3–4). Mark already regarded the appellation as inadequate (Mark 12:35–37), which implies a widely held and undisputed genealogy. If he had been thought to be illegitimate, he hardly would have been identified and known as a descendant of Israel's greatest king-messiah.[28] Jesus elicits surprise from people of status because he associates with sinners and tax collectors, which implies that Jesus is of higher status than those with whom he associates.

It is thought that the designation of Jesus as Son of David is older than the virgin birth traditions as we find them in Matthew and Luke. These narratives do unequivocally assert that Mary was pregnant before her marriage to Joseph, which implies Joseph was the father. Because of the subsequent marriage, which publicly acknowledges the child as Joseph's own, the out-of-wedlock pregnancy has no impact on the status of parents and child. He has safeguarded the honor of both Mary and Jesus, which supports exactly how Jesus was publicly regarded as an adult. Matthew asserts that Joseph graciously avoids a public scandal and so does not use the virginal conception as a way to counter the charge of illegitimacy, which would not be an effective stratagem anyway. Because he is made the child of the deity, he is inadvertently technically made a *mamzer*. Matthew heightens Jesus' status not from illegitimate to legitimate but from a legitimate Son of David to Son of God.[29] So virgin birth doesn't cover up shame but only increases Jesus' honor.

Jesus' status as an honorable member of society, and as a son of David,[30] makes his renunciation of status, family, and possessions (Mark 10:28–30, Luke 9:58) all the more striking.

Is the virgin conception, however, merely a later addition and stratagem designed to increase Jesus' honor and prestige? Paul writes:

> But when the time had fully come, God sent forth his Son, born of woman, born under the law (Gal 4:4).

The phrase "God sent" can refer to a historical sending of a person to undertake a particular mission (Gen 45:5) but more frequently to sending a supernatural being to earth (Judg 9:23, 1 Chr 21:15, Dan 6:22), which idea Paul is employing here because it precedes the words "born of woman," which implies the sending of a supernatural being.[31] In the story of Abraham and Isaac's birth, God overcomes nature itself, and a child is born to an ostensibly barren woman of very advanced age. Isaac is the promised son born of a supernatural plan to overcome a curse of nature and realize the promise to Abraham to make him a great nation.[32]

Paul quotes a hymn in Philippians 2:6–11. So the hymn was already in existence before Paul wrote this epistle perhaps in the AD 50s from Caesarea. It is indeed a very early formulation going back to within a few years of Jesus' earthly existence. Verses 10–11 also echo Isaiah 45:23 where the Lord declares every knee shall bow to him, claiming that Jesus himself exercises the unique divine sovereignty of God over all creation.[33] The opening verses 6–7 seem to assert at first blush the pre-existence of the Messiah Jesus who emptied himself of divinity to take historical form. However, in the light of the following analysis these verses also refer to the historical Jesus who humbled himself and interpreted his ministry as servanthood (Mark 10:45).

Verse 8 of the passage is an allusion to the story of Jesus' prayer in the Garden of Gethsemane.[34] Jesus calls God his "Abba" in the Gethsemane story in Mark 14:36, a word that is used twice by Paul in Gal 4:6 and Rom 8:15. Within these two epistles Paul also contrasts "flesh" and "Spirit," and Jesus does the same in his prayer in Gethsemane. Jesus also describes himself as "sorrowful unto death" (Mark 14:34), which corresponds to the phrase in Phil 2:8, "to the point of death." In addition, Jesus says he is "distressed" (Mark 14:33, Matt 26:37) (Gk., ἀδημονῶν, *hadēmonōn*), a word used elsewhere in the NT only in Phil 2:26 where the phrase in the following verse 30 "near to death" also occurs using the same words as in 2:8. Immediately preceding the Christ hymn in Phil 1:19–24, Paul writes about the alternative between life and death, prayers offered with the aid of the Spirit, as well as struggling with remaining "in the flesh" or departing to "be with Christ." These themes find parallels in the Gethsemane story. All of this strongly suggests that Paul was familiar with the Gethsemane story and had it in mind as he himself was facing death and as he composed his epistle.[35]

Hebrews 5:7–10 is an explicit reference to the Gethsemane story. The Hebrews passage shares with the Philippians passage the theme of obedience through suffering and Jesus' sonship. Furthermore, the Hebrews passage, Phil 2:8, and the Gethsemane story do not interpret the cross in salvific terms, although the writers do so in other parts of their writings.[36] None of them introduce elements of atonement. They all emphasize that Jesus' obedience is the means whereby Jesus is tested and having remained faithful to God's will is rewarded with exaltation. In this he is like that other "beloved son," Isaac, who, as he goes to the place of sacrifice, "carries his cross on his own shoulder."[37] That Jesus in Mark asks to be spared the suffering that lay before him, ostensibly seeking not to go through accomplishing the salvation of the world, is disconcerting, which suggests that the story is very early tradition indeed. It *seems* to swim against the current of a Christological understanding that interpreted the meaning of Jesus' suffering as redemptive. So the story's embarrassing character[38] in this regard also speaks for its authenticity to say nothing of its multiple attestation[39] by Mark, Paul, and the author of Hebrews.[40] As with Abraham, Jesus' submission to the will of God counteracts Adam's disobedience.

So in the Gethsemane narrative Jesus reveals his consciousness of being the Father's beloved son who struggles with obedience to the will of the Father to offer his son up as a sacrifice of God's love for the world.[41] I will deal with the resonance of Jesus as the "beloved son" and his submission to the Father's will with the story of the sacrifice of Isaac below. Jesus in Gethsemane limns Abraham and his obedience to God by his willingness to sacrifice his only son (Gen 22:2, 12).[42]

In other imagery Jesus is the paschal lamb, slain that those who are destined for death may live. He dies in their stead. This love of God then is not a romanticized notion but involves the killing of Jesus in the divine order of things so that God's elect might receive his blessing of life. In this way "all things work together for good for those who love God" (Rom 8:28).

Jesus' humbling in Phil 2:8 is also portrayed in the Gethsemane story as Jesus throws himself on the ground and pleads with his Abba.[43] The cup[44] that he wishes to bypass but which he finally accepts minimally means that Jesus' faith encompassed necessity for him to accept his suffering and death because his Abba would rescue him and inaugurate him, following his own proclamation, as the one who had fulfilled all of Israel's expectations, as the prophet, priest, and anointed one.[45] He had taught that the last shall be first (Luke 13:30) and those who abase themselves would be exalted (Luke 14:11). John portrays Jesus' humility as he washed the feet of the disciples (John 13:1–17). That teaching aligned itself with all the great leaders of the past. Moses and David were initially just lowly shepherds, but then they were called to lead God's people. Both were also involved with suffering. Indeed, David's *via dolorosa* was a type of Jesus' own.[46]

That Jesus struggled with accepting the "cup" that he perceived as the will of God and could have escaped those who marched from Jerusalem to arrest him does not mean that Jesus hadn't foreseen that fate as the Gospels report.[47] So the investigator has sound reasons to conclude that Jesus foresaw his death and did not flinch when the crucial time broke upon him.[48] Although the hymn does not mention the crucifixion of Jesus as an atoning sacrifice but rather his obedience, the former is implied in verse 8 by stressing that his death was by crucifixion. Luke 24:26–27 parallels this verse. The Torah and prophetic Scriptures interpret the death on a cross: the Scriptures in general are full of sacrificial language, and Isaiah 53 in particular portrays the servant's suffering as bearing the sins of the nation.

So the whole of the hymn reflects the person and ministry of the Jesus of history. When the hymn sings that Jesus was in the form of God and emptied himself of divinity (vss 6–7), those verses are intertwined with historical descriptions of Jesus in his earthly activity, specifically his struggle in Gethsemane (vs 8) and his resurrection/exaltation (vss 9–11). The hymn knows of no distinction between the world of the spirit and the natural world. Earthly history and divine reality are of a piece (as verse 10 explicitly implies).

This ancient hymn coordinates with the virgin birth of Jesus, which too is an ancient and very early understanding of Jesus' identity. It is not an add-on to his descent from David. Matthew and Luke have merely narrativized the reality of Jesus' supernatural pre-existence and his historical birth that were already known by them and given to them. What Matthew and Luke convey in narrative John puts in theological language, "the Word became flesh." The list above demonstrates, in spite of the differences between the narratives, how much they are in agreement with the basic events surrounding Jesus' conception and birth.

Of course, the incarnation—that is, the "infleshment" of the pre-existent Son of God—is an *unicum*—there is nothing comparable to it.[49] The reality of the incarnation might be used to explain what we know of the life and ministry of Jesus: his magisterial "but I say to you," his authoritative teaching "not as the scribes," his forgiving sin, his power over unclean spirits, and his claiming to be in a unique filial relationship with and having an exclusive knowledge of Israel's Father-God. However, taking the *kenosis* of Philippians 2 into consideration, those characteristics of Jesus' power and authority are not due to some divine origin. (More on this below.) It follows that the incarnation and the concomitant virgin birth are not some kind of late addendum to understanding the person of Jesus. They build on Jesus' own self-understanding, which I will now explicate.

So what was Jesus' understanding of his own person? To ask this question is to fly in the face of scholarship that has declared Jesus' self-consciousness verboten territory because the materials we have for the reconstruction of his person and activity were not written to answer such a question. However, that does not mean we cannot ask it.[50] A related dynamic is the question of a development of Jesus' consciousness. I have already made that case in the study of Jesus' parables regarding his attitude toward Gentiles and other outliers.[51] We must expect development in any real human being.[52] We can also expect to get a glimpse of the inner life of a person from their words. And we have a plethora of words of Jesus even though the evangelists are more interested in theology than psychology. And John's Gospel, which we have learned is no more "theological" than the other Gospels, asserts his deep humanity as much as his exalted divinity, and yet is thought out of hand to be incapable of giving us any historical information about his person. Would John have made up the accusation against Jesus that he "had a demon" because he claimed to be greater than Abraham, that he existed before Abraham (John 8:58, 10:20), and that he was a blasphemer because he claimed, according to his accusers, divinity (John 10:33)?

Just who is Jesus?[53] That question of identity is precisely what the gospels seek to answer. John A. T. Robinson appositely asserts that Jesus' self-consciousness "is the indispensable heart of the mystery: to regard it as a matter of indifference or as a 'no go' area is to leave a blank"[54] at the very heart of an investigation of the "historical Jesus." All four of the evangelists address this question, although the synoptists do so in a more oblique manner: in the baptism (see below), in his manner of speaking with authority, in his parables (particularly the wicked tenants and the lost sheep[55]), in his intimacy with God in prayer, and above all in his declaration that "no one knows[56] the Son except the Father, and no one knows the Father except the Son and any one to whom the Son chooses to reveal him" (Matt 11:27, Luke 10:22).

Here I want to take the time to summarize the conclusion Robinson comes to in his investigation of this question of Jesus' self-consciousness or self-understanding. The Gospels themselves put the question: "Who and from where comes this man?" (Mark 4:41, John 19:9). That Jesus is "known" by the Father (Matt 11:27) includes the love of the Father (Mark 1:11, 9:7, 12:6, Col 1:13). He is the son of love, and his life is a constant response to this relationship. The synoptics presuppose this relationship but do not expose "this umbilical cord of his life."[57] This reticence of the synoptics to make explicit Jesus' self-consciousness as John does reflects, says Robinson, Jesus' own reticence. For example, in Peter's confession of Jesus as the Messiah (Mark 8:29), Peter obviously has a completely different notion of what the Messiah is compared to the meaning it had for Jesus. The synoptics accurately portray the disciples as not understanding Jesus' true nature and the significance of what he said and did. However, John exposes the real nature of Jesus and his ministry. It is not a matter of reading back into the life of Jesus what was not there but that John sees Jesus as he really was and the way the disciples should have seen him. In this way the synoptists see Jesus and his words and deeds "from the outside" through the eyes of the disciples, whereas John reveals the mind of Jesus: he sees Jesus as the one who is governed by this consciousness of his messianic function as Son of God.[58]

The "I am" sayings in John are the evangelist's interpretive clues to Jesus' self-understanding. They correspond to the "I have come" sayings in the synoptics (Mark 1:38, Matt 5:17, 10:34-35).[59] This is the one to whom the Father has committed the words and deeds by which the kingdom is made present, the one who proclaims God's invitation in the name of divine Wisdom and sends forth God's emissaries, who is lord of the Sabbath, forgives sins, crushes the powers of demons, exercises proleptically the prerogatives of the final judgment, and bestows the Spirit of the Father.[60]

So in Jesus there is something greater than Solomon, Moses, or Abraham (Matt 12:42, John 8:58). These statements do not lift Jesus out of the ranks of humanity but assert his unconditional precedence. They are not "ego statements." His ego was no more pre-existent than that of any other human being. Robinson makes the important point that when Jesus announces that he speaks about what he has "seen with my Father" (Joh 8:38), he defines what that means two verses later when he identifies himself as "a man who had told you the truth which I have heard from God." Yet the word he speaks is the word that transcends time and space.[61]

Robinson sees two ways of misunderstanding Jesus' use of his "I" utterances: to interpret them on the level of the ego, which would destroy his humanity, or to see them as usurping the divine name and identifying him with YHWH. Those "I am" statements are meant to say, "Listen to me if you would know God." The absolute use of the phrase "I am he" confirms his identity, or, in the case of John 8:24, 28, 13:19, it means "I am what I am"— namely, "the Christ the Son of God." He correctly observes that "the Jews" in John's Gospel do not accuse him of arrogating to himself the divine name but that he made himself equal with God by calling God "his own Father."[62]

Robinson concludes that the "I" with which Jesus speaks means the totality of the self, the archetype of the divine image. Or it is like the "I" of the mystics who claim unity with God without claiming to be God. Quoting another scholar, he understands Jesus as the one who "knew himself in the depth of his spirit as one with the eternal ground of being."[63] Again he quotes Martin Buber's *I and Thou*, which says this of Jesus' "I" statements: "[I]t is the *I* of unconditional relation in which the man called his *Thou* Father in such a way that he is simply Son, and nothing else but Son. Whenever he says *I* he can only mean the *I* of the holy primary word that has been raised for him into unconditional being." That is, his whole being is simply determined by this relationship to his Father-God.⁶⁴ He "speaks only what he has heard" (John 8:40).

So Jesus did not do some things "as God" and some things "as man." He was an integrated human being who was totally one with the Father as he was with humanity. He was uniquely human in the sense that he was totally dependent on God and so could be a servant of all. His self-understanding was "total filial self-awareness" (Robinson's terminology) and so was the point of contact between God and humanity. It follows that a "mere man" Christology and a "heavenly visitant" Christology are false alternatives.

It is my conclusion that Robinson's interpretation is exactly right and fits my understanding of the historical Jesus based on the Christ hymn of Philippians 2: Jesus was indeed the God-man, both human and divine, but had emptied himself of all divinity and so was totally human, subject to all of what it meant to be human including human development. There can be no thought of some kind of special access to divinity in the human Jesus by which he acquired knowledge, insight, wisdom, or any so-called supernatural faculty. He was, to put it somewhat brusquely, "on his own."

It is within the parameters of these observations that we can understand how Jesus called God "Abba." This term of endearment reflects an inner consciousness of an intimate relationship with God and that his Father was God, not Joseph. In describing the multiplying entourage that will build from Jesus' ministry, Jesus says:

> Truly, I say to you, there is no one who has left house or brothers or sisters or mother or father or children or lands, for my sake and for the gospel, who will not receive a hundredfold now in this time, houses and brothers and sisters and mothers and children and lands, with persecutions, and in the age to come eternal life (Mark 10:29–30).

"Fathers" are omitted in what one will regain because it is God who is the real Father in the community of Jesus, which matches with his exhortation to "call no man your father on earth, for you have one Father, who is in heaven" (Matt 23:9). Over and over, Jesus calls God "Father." It comes across with such force that it resounds in such a way that it is not hyperbolic to think that he experienced and had the consciousness that God was his own "Abba" (Mark 14:36), his own "dear Father."⁶⁵

Jesus' self-understanding does not include some kind of consciousness that he is God incarnate but that he had a unique filial relationship with God. That consciousness is not a given, but it is something that developed within him as a human being. The circumstances of his birth coupled with this unique self-consciousness and above all his baptism and resurrection came together in the confession of his pre-existence and subsequent incarnation. It was the only deduction that could account for all the facts and adequately answer the question, "Who can this be?" (Mark 4:41). Jesus' self-consciousness, virgin birth, incarnation, baptism, and resurrection all harmoniously cohere in a unity. Without them, Jesus' identity, actions, and words are all incomprehensible.

So whence his filial self-understanding? The answer lies in his baptism, to which we now turn.

THE BAPTISM OF JESUS

John's Ministry

Before investigating Jesus' own baptism, it is important to place John, the one who baptized him, in his own theological and historical perspective.[66]

It has been suggested that John had been an Essene before he began to exercise his prophetic call because of the similarities of location and practice. He was in the "wilderness" just as the Essenes chose to be, to prepare for the eschaton (1QS 8, 14–16). They interpreted their residence there on the basis of Isaiah 40:3, the same basis for John's presence there (Mark 1:2). His water baptism corresponds to the practice of the Essenes, who emphasized ablutions and ritual bathing, which, Josephus tells us, were undertaken twice daily before meals.[67] Like the Essenes too was the gathering of a following who lived in community with him. The Gospels clearly indicate that John had an entourage of disciples gathered around him (Matt 9:14, 11:2, John 1:35). The majority of those baptized, however, returned to their everyday life and occupation (Luke 3:10–14).[68]

The Essenes, on the other hand, withdrew from the greater society of Israel and understood themselves as the "true Israel," while all others outside their community were the "sons of darkness" who would have no place in eschatological salvation.[69] In contradistinction, John's prophetic ministry was to all Israel even including perhaps Gentiles (Luke 3:14). But it is also possible that John was initially an Essene but there was a parting of the ways, John taking a much more universal approach toward the renewal of Israel.

That John was baptizing in the Jordan was not a haphazard or random choice. After all, he could have chosen any number of bodies of water: the Sea of Galilee or the rivers Nahaliel and Jabok (both within Perea, part of Herod Antipas's realm). The Jordan was redolent with Israel's holy history. The story of the entry into the land under the leadership of Joshua took place at the Jordan. It was a leaving of the past, the wandering in the wilderness of Sinai, and entering into the future and taking possession of the divinely promised land. It was leaving the dead and desert land and entering into the land "flowing with milk and honey." The old generation had died off, and now the new generation was entering the land of life. The priests stood in the Jordan with the Ark of the Covenant, and the river stopped flowing so that Israel could enter the land dry-shod. So John the priest calls Israel back to the Jordan to enter into, by these same waters through repentance and baptism, the new kingdom of God waiting to break into the world.

John's water baptism resonates with the use of water for cleansing required by the Torah. Sacrificial victims had to be washed (Exod 29:17), the priests had to wash before entering the Temple and conducting their sacrificial service (Exod 30:20–21), and a person who contracted corpse uncleanness had to wash (Lev 11:25–40). Leviticus 13–17 enumerates all the conditions that require cleansing by washing. Washing is also used metaphorically as ridding oneself of evil thoughts (Isa 1:16, Jer 4:14), reminding the people that real cleansing is the inward removal of spiritual defilement.[70] The exilic prophets looked forward to a renewed cleansing by waters proceeding from the Temple (Ezek 36:25, 47:1–12, Joel 3:18, Zech 14:8). Zechariah 13:1 refers to an eschatological fountain that opens up in Jerusalem and purifies sin and uncleanness, which will eliminate idols, prophets, and the "unclean spirit," all apparent allusions to the pre-exilic practices in Jerusalem. In this way, water and its cleansing properties were spiritualized from earliest times, and an eschatological cleansing, restoration, and renewal of the people were anticipated, symbolized in the prophetic announcement of a cleansing stream opening up in Jerusalem.[71] So John's baptism for the "repentance and the forgiveness of sins" (Mark 1:4) could well have been identified with this eschatological renewal. Even so, it is only a preparatory rite that fades in consequence in comparison with the baptism of the coming "mightier one" (Mark 1:7, Luke 3:16).[72]

The Gospels indicate people were flocking to the Jordan to participate in John's call for repentance and being baptized, seeing in him the way to participate in the longed-for restoration and the end of exile. His identification with Elijah underscores this eschatological interpretation.[73] His dress (Mark 1:6, cf., 2 Kgs 1:8) and the description of his death under Herod Antipas and his wife, Herodias, parallel the struggle of Elijah with the decadent Ahab and his pagan wife, Jezebel. John's proclamation of what constitutes a true descendant of Abraham recalls Elijah's struggle with the prophets of Baal on Mount Carmel (Luke 3:8 and 1 Kgs 18:20–40)—that is, the vacillation between two opinions and what constitutes being a true Israelite and child of Israel's God.[74] As with Elijah, John's ministry was a call to the whole of Israel (Mark 1:5): a national repentance was demanded in preparation for the end. The accounts of John identify him as the fulfillment of Malachi 4:5–6 that Elijah would return before the "coming of the great and dreadful day of the Lord."[75] Like Elijah, he too must pass on his mantle: a "mightier one" must come. John prepared the way for the one who would actually bring in the kingdom.

The anticipation of a cleansing stream that would purify the people and the expectation of a returning Elijah heralding the end-time are combined in John's ministry as it is described for us in the Gospels. So John announced the turning of the ages, the in-breaking of the kingdom of God, and the way to genuinely prepare for it. The new age is dawning, and to participate in it one must be truly repentant and be cleansed of one's sin in this eschatological washing of John.

This washing was evidently not conceived as merely symbolic. It was a required washing to enter into God's presence and a confirmation of one's inner renewal. Mere physical descent counts for nothing. His message is one of judgment, the consignment of the unrepentant to its fire (Luke 3:9), and the promise of salvation and inclusion in the kingdom when the Messiah arrives (Mark 1:7-8, Luke 3:16-17). John apparently interpreted his ministry also in terms of Malachi 3:1–5.[76] The "lord" in the passage is אדון ("ADON")—that is, "lord, master," which is not the covenant name of God, YHWH. So it may refer to the Messiah as in Psalm 110:1 where YHWH speaks to "my lord" ("ADONI," i.e., the Messiah). As in this psalm passage, YHWH is the subject of the proclamation in Malachi 3:1. Like the demand for personal morality and social justice in Malachi 1:5, John's preaching makes the same demands (Luke 3:10-14).

John was speaking to the crisis in which his society had fallen.[77] It was felt that the voice of God was silent since prophecy had not been heard for years. It seemed in days of old the God of Israel had spoken actively and mightily through the prophets. It is not surprising that among the Essenes the voice of God was restored by their Teacher of Righteousness, who opened up the Scripture and led his devotees to see how the ancient texts spoke directly to their circumstances.[78]

The Pharisees for the most part were calling the nation to faithfulness to Torah, emphasizing egalitarianism, and renewing the voice of God by updating the Torah so it could be obeyed in the changed circumstances of their contemporary world. They also divinized the oral Torah as the living voice of God in the present. The elite Sadducees only cared for accommodation with Rome and maintaining the status quo. Revolutionary fervor and groups were growing and mounting as well as prophets who predicted the imminent intervention of God to save and renew his people.[79] In short, the whole society seemed caught up in the longing for a return from the spiritual and political desert of exile that encumbered them and was embodied so graphically in the Roman occupation. Furthermore, that restoration included the hope that the twelve tribes—that is, the whole people—would be reestablished in the land.[80] In this way the end would recapitulate the beginning when Israel would once again be established as twelve tribes. Wholeness and completeness would characterize the new age.[81]

John must be seen within this highly charged atmosphere of expectation. God's intervention was at the door. So it is not surprising that even from the little we know of John's message, it was eschatologically oriented.[82] He proclaimed the in-breaking of the judgment to come, repentance, forgiveness, the call to order one's life in terms of that repentance and judgment on those who would not repent. That reordered life had to do with the long-familiar message of the prophets: the non-oppression of the underclass, the practice of social solidarity, and the concern for the poor by relieving their poverty. He called on the elites to end their exploitation of the people through their police actions. John also was fearless in addressing the nobility as in the case of Herod Antipas, who married his brother's wife, Herodias, while the brother was still alive, violating the Torah (Lev 18:16, 20:21). Perhaps he again was shaping his message on the basis of Malachi 2:14–16, which states that none "should deal treacherously with the wife of his youth" and that YHWH "hates divorce."

The Gospels also set John's ministry in the context of Isaiah 40, which suggests that John's message must be understood in terms of restoration and the return of the exiles.[83] In other words, John's movement was that of renewal and preparation for the dawn of God reestablishing his kingdom and the return of the twelve tribes so that the end resembles the beginning.[84] It is like a new exodus and conquest. Deuteronomy, a writing completed during the exile, ends with Moses's farewell speech promising a future ingathering of the people after the Lord has scattered them (30:1–5). The ingathering, however, depends on Israel's obedience to the covenant. That condition remains a dominant theme throughout the period. It is balanced on the other hand by the idea that it is God's prevenient grace of gathering that elicits Israel's turn to faithfulness to the divine ordinances (Ezek 11:17–19, 20:27–44).[85] Second Chronicles ended the Hebrew canon on the promising note of a return by reporting Cyrus's edict allowing the return of exiled peoples.[86]

Who will execute the return? Some witnesses such as Isaiah 49:5 say an exalted individual or Messiah will be involved in this eschatological ingathering of God's people. There is, however, a diversity in perception in the way the ingathering will be executed, whether by supernatural or political means.[87]

This little overview suggests that John, in calling for repentance, held that the return was conditioned on Israel's faithfulness to the covenant. However, judgment is coming, and only the repentant will be saved and reconstitute the new people of Israel. So was John, by proclaiming the forgiveness of sins, bypassing the Temple? More likely it has to do with his identification with the traditions surrounding the hopes of restoration of Israel. Isaiah 40 announces Israel's "penalty has been paid." Even more pointedly the Isaiah Targum paraphrases this declaration of remission with the more explicit "her sins have been forgiven her." Furthermore, Ezekiel 36:24-25 prophesizes water will cleanse the people from their uncleanness.[88] So the gathering of the people from the nations and their restoration are linked with inner cleansing, not just a ritual purification, by water. I've already referred to the connection of John's ministry with the Exodus-conquest tradition that involves a passing through water.[89]

John referred also to a "mightier one" who would succeed him and considered his baptism to be a preparation for this coming one who will "gather the wheat into his barn but the chaff he will burn with unquenchable fire"—that is, he will be the messianic agent of divine judgment (Pss of Song 17:21-23). A "mighty one" suggests this future figure is messianic (Isa 11:1-2). His baptizing with God's spirit also resonates with the description of the future Messiah of Isaiah 11:1-2. And John himself inquires of Jesus whether he is the expected one, which implies Jesus conformed enough with John's previous identification to elicit the query (Luke 7:18-23).[90]

John's activity and message were solidly within the biblical and postbiblical tradition of the ingathering of Israel and her restoration. His powerful presence indicates how real was the sense among the people that, though they were living in the land, they were still in exile subsisting, as they were, under Roman occupation, and that their present national existence was not the order that was according to God's will. John was preparing the people for the in-breaking of the kingdom that would come from that "mightier one" who would succeed him. This preparation consisted of a water baptism that meant a cleansing from sin and not a mere ritual washing. John was preparing the "wheat" that was now separated from the chaff by their repentance and being cleansed from sin. The mightier one would gather this "wheat" into the kingdom, while the "chaff" would be consigned to the fires of judgment. Finally, John's activity seemed to have a universal dimension, not directed exclusively to Israel.

Jesus' Baptism[91]

But first the new Joshua must come to lead the way. And Jesus (the Graecized form of the Hebrew name Joshua) comes, bringing the new covenant, and as Israel's representative, enters the waters of repentance on behalf of all Israel. The ministry of Jesus, according to the synoptic tradition, began with his baptism by John.[92] For Mark his baptism did not present a problem. But it was a source of embarrassment for Matthew and Luke. How could the sinless Son of God submit to a baptism of "repentance for the forgiveness of sins" (Mark 1:4)? Added to that contradiction is the inference that he then was inferior to John. Each evangelist deals with this problem in his own way. Matthew has John question the baptism's propriety, exclaiming that he should be baptized by Jesus. Jesus replies that he "had to fulfill all righteousness." This phrase is equivalent to God's will to save (Pss 70:2, 103:17), which accords with Matthew's theological schema of Jesus as the fulfiller of Israel's salvation history.[93] Luke rather obscures his baptism by John by having him imprisoned before he reports the baptism. This embarrassment underscores the authenticity of the event.

In Mark it is Jesus alone who sees "the heavens torn open and the Spirit descending upon him like a dove" (1:10). However, it is ambiguous whether the voice that then occurs was heard only by Jesus or also perceived by others. Matthew follows Mark in his presentation (3:16) except that it is not Jesus alone who sees the "heavens open," making the event public. Luke formulates the whole scene with his own favored syntax of infinitive constructions rendering the scene in an objective, observational report:

> And it happened while all the people were baptized also Jesus while being baptized and while he prayed the heaven opened and when the Holy Spirit descended in bodily form as a dove upon him, there was also a voice from heaven.[94]

John, however, does not report the event directly, but the Baptist himself recounts that he saw the Spirit "descending as a dove from heaven and remaining on him" (1:32), which implies that all the details were a public occurrence seen and heard by all those present.

The dove imagery limns the rabbinic reading of Genesis 1:2, which compares the Spirit of God "moving over the face of the waters" to a dove that broods over her young but does not touch them.[95] So the imagery would imply that just as the Spirit of God was at work in creation so now it is at work in his new creation that is being wrought in the life and work of Jesus. However, the place in which an actual dove appears is the story of Noah where the evidence that the waters had begun to dry up is signaled by a dove with an olive leaf in its beak. It was a sign that Noah and his family could disembark from the ark upon a fresh and new creation, like a new Adam and Eve. So the dove imagery evokes the presence of the new creation that has now begun in Jesus.

The theme of a "new creation" resonates everywhere in Jesus' words and deeds. In his understanding of marriage, he recalls the original divine intention in Gen 2:24; his exorcisms and healings were a restoration of the creation. The reuniting of all people within the kingdom, reversing the divisions of Babel (the parables of the mustard seed, leaven in a lump[96]), and the stories of his calming of the waters are like the creation story of bringing order out of the chaos; he places his ministry in terms of 2 Isaiah's theology of the new creation, especially the anointing with the Spirit (Isa 11:2). The triad of a man in the water, the heavens opening, and the appearance of a dove suggests the story of Noah, who, surviving the flood, enters upon a new and restored creation.[97]

Mark describes the heavens "splitting." The only other "rending of the heavens" occurs in Isa 64:1, which is connected with the Lord making his name known. Both Matthew and Luke say the heavens were "open," which is the word used in the LXX of Isa 64:1. There is also a "splitting" of the Jordan as the people enter the promised land (Josh 3:16). So Jesus in his baptism, as he stands in the Jordan, limns the entrance into a new "land"—that is, the kingdom of God, which is now present in Jesus' ministry. He also appears as the new "ark" of the presence of God (Josh 3:15–17) as he stands in the water with the priest John.

In the theophany described as attendant on the baptism, there is also a heavenly voice that declares "you are my beloved son in whom I am well pleased" (Mark 1:11, Matt 3:17, Luke 3:22).[98] The designation "beloved son" is pregnant with highly evocative associations, namely the sacrifice of Isaac in Gen 22:1–19, where Isaac is described as the one "whom you [Abraham] love."[99] So there is a dark side to the voice. His declaration to be the "beloved son" also announces the destiny of the one who stands in the river with John: he is to be sacrificed. "First fruits" (Deut 21:17) belong to God. God's portion must be the first and the best. In Exod 13:15 the firstborn belongs to God but can be redeemed by substitution and only in this way be gotten back. The theology here is that the life of the firstborn is not the father's by right but a gift. So the firstborn has an exalted status but a precarious position. He's marked for both humiliation and exaltation.[100] Isaac is the chosen one, not Ishmael. But to be chosen also means to be subject to God's absolute claim.[101]

Abraham loved God and his son Isaac (Gen 22:2). But his love of God took precedence over the love he had for his only son. So God respects and rewards uncompromising obedience, an obedience even unto death.[102] Paul also has this story in mind in Rom 8:32, where he poignantly contrasts God's act in Jesus with Abraham's willingness to offer up Isaac, whom God spared at the last minute. But God did not spare his own son![103] In the new offering God offers up his beloved son, which leads to his exaltation, his resurrection life. God remains faithful to the law that demands the life of the firstborn son.[104]

Again in John 3:16 God himself pursues the path of Abraham but actually follows through and "gives" his son ("*give* me your first born," Exod 22:28).[105] Jesus literally dies, but he is restored by resurrection (but "never to die again," Rom 6:9, unlike the others who are resurrected in biblical stories). In this way he is not like Ishmael, Isaac, and Jacob. None suffers actual death. Ishmael is saved from dying by lack of water (Gen 21:19), Jacob from the wrath of his brother Esau (Gen 32:11, 33:3–16), and Isaac, of course, by the staying hand of the angel (Gen 22:12).[106] John 3:16 reverses the old pattern and transforms the (earthly) father's gift to the gift of God the Father. But the gift of his son in sacrifice is not based on fear of calamity as was Mesha's offering of his son (2 Kgs 3:27) but rather on love as in the pattern of Abraham's love for God exceeding his love for his beloved son Isaac.[107]

Jesus as the "beloved son" places the cross in the background of the whole of his ministry and his own self-consciousness.[108] Jesus affirms his call in his baptism as the "beloved son" by describing himself as the "[beloved] son" in absolute terms (Mark 12:6, 13:32, Luke 10:22). His references to the "cup" he must drink and "the baptism" with which he must be baptized (Mark 10:38, 14:36, Luke 12:49–50)[109] parallel his baptismal experience and reveal how deep in his consciousness was his understanding of himself as the "beloved son." So there is a congruence between what is described as Jesus' baptismal experience and how he thought of himself.[110] This call experience of Jesus was an experience of the world of the spirit. However, the nature of his call places him in the context of Israel's prophetic tradition, not in the mold of a "mystic."[111]

Jesus' religious experience at his baptism did lead him to believe that he had direct, experiential knowledge of God and to share it with others and show them how to gain such knowledge. He also experienced God in prayer, the power of the Spirit in his healings and exorcisms, and the experience that the end-time was both present and future. Direct access to God meant not needing any formal structures such as temple, authoritative text, or concern for purity. So his new authority, based on his call and the revelation attendant on it, placed him in conflict with the normative observance of Jewish "covenantal nomism."[112] But Jesus didn't set his experience at the center of his proclamation any more than the prophets of old had. Rather, he was a pious Jew who was found to have the God of Israel within him in a final and unsurpassable way.[113] His baptismal experience was a prophetic call that led him to proclaim, not the nurturing of so-called mystic experiences like an adept. He did not set his experience at the center of his ministry nor found an esoteric sect.[114] His ministry was to all of Israel.

Jesus did exhibit so-called mystic characteristics:[115] instructing in revelatory/apocalyptic knowledge and his appeal to the order of creation and subordinating the Torah to it.[116] In this way Jesus intensified marital law and relaxed the Sabbath law. God's original purpose in this matter has priority over the Mosaic Law. Jesus was not particularly concerned with ritual purity. His real priority was discerning the will of God, so the proclamation of the kingdom was the bedrock of his teaching and proclamation. He also deviated from the cultural norms of family, marriage, and employment. He was transgressive of social and cultural boundaries and had a passionate concern to alter the attitudes of the peasant toward their social and economic anxieties. Above all he challenged the traditional and religious norms and conceptions of God. God was the nation's "Abba," an intimate and dear Father, who was concerned about even the fallen sparrow but whose concern for his people, whose worth far surpassed that of sparrows, was consequently so much greater.[117] These characteristics were also exhibited by the classical prophets. And as with the prophets his ministry was founded on and expressed the content of his call, the revelatory experience at his baptism.

The "beloved" terminology is also used of God's people Israel. In each case it is used absolutely and not as a modifier.[118] So Jesus incorporates and recapitulates[119] Israel, and, because he is the "beloved *Son*," he is anointed simultaneously as the royal messiah (Ps 2).

Jesus in his passion is a manifestation of God's love prefigured in Isaac. The "beloved son" designation is also resonant with Is 42:1 and 53:1–12, making of his suffering a vicarious atonement and accomplishing the cosmic transformation, which did not issue from his earthly ministry that proclaimed the nearness of the kingdom of God.[120] Is 53:7 also compares the suffering servant with a sheep. Jesus like Isaac accepts his fate and is obedient to death and replaces Isaac, who had such a prominent place in Judaism as the means of reconciliation with God.[121] The promises and blessings of God through Abraham and Isaac's sacrifice are now available in Jesus.[122]

Another aspect of sonship is its relationship to the Spirit in the baptismal narrative. That Jesus was anointed by the Spirit at his baptism results in the grounding of his whole ministry and his self-understanding in his experience of the world of the spirit.[123] This implies that Jesus was embedded in Israel's faith and life and believed himself to be a son of Israel's God as did every other Israelite (Exod 4:23, Hos 11:1). The Davidic kings were particularly understood as sons of God (Ps 2:7, 1 Chron 22:10). That he is now divinely pronounced to be "son" also identifies him as representative of Israel and her Davidic kings. The whole people are called the "beloved" in the lament of Ps 60:5 (cf., Ps 108:6). "Beloved" is used most frequently in the Song of Songs, which implies Israel as God's beloved people. It is used again and again in the Pauline corpus for the churches, the new people of God. Jesus is then designated preeminently as the representative of the people of God who is now "visiting and redeeming his people raising up a horn of salvation in the house of his servant David" (Luke 1:68–69).

The evangelists set the institutional narrative of the Lord's Supper within the celebration of Passover. The narrative itself supports that context, for body and blood are central to it. The eating of his body is in place of the consumption of the lamb, and his blood is consumed rather than sprinkled on the celebrants (Exod 24:8) in apparent contradiction to the Torah, which forbids the drinking of the blood (Lev 3:17) because "the life is in its blood" (Lev 17:14). In this way Jesus indicated that by reversing the old stricture his very life was to be ingested. Paul, affirming the Passover context of Jesus' final supper with his disciples and of his death, also describes the crucifixion in terms of the Passover sacrifice in 1 Cor 5:7–8. Here again we find the idea of Jesus as the recapitulation of Israel and her history.

Fourth Macc 13:10–12 makes Isaac an exemplar of fidelity and a prototype of the Jewish martyr and the martyr's death as sacrificial and redemptive. In 4 Macc 17:17–22 the martyrs are exalted to the divine throne and participate in the age to come. So the apparent defeat of the martyrs becomes a victory and their death a propitiation (ἱλαστήριον, *hilastērion*).[124]

In Exod 4:22 Israel is God's firstborn. The Exodus occurs not because of God's opposition to slavery but on the basis of this relationship.[125] So the Exodus is a story of the release of the firstborn to rejoin and serve his Father-God. This liberation occurs at the cost of all the firstborn in Egypt (cf., Hos 11:1–8, Gen 22:10–12, Jer 31:7–9). God brings back Israel, the beloved son, who had been taken off and almost vanished.[126] So Jesus is conceived of as the Passover lamb whose blood saves from the Destroyer, defeats demonic forces (cf., Rev 12:10–11, κατήγωρ, *katēgōr*, "accuser"), and brings life out of death.

In Dan 7:25–27 the suffering of the righteous precedes the eschatological age. In the language of Dan 7:13, the son of man is presented to the Ancient of Days. The word used there (*HaQeReBiUHY*) has the meaning of "offer" (Ezr 6:10), and the old Greek translates with παρίστημι (*paristēmi*, "present"), which is also used in sacrificial contexts.[127] The three passion predictions in Mark (8:31, 9:31, 10:33) are not the work of the church retrojected back into the ministry of Jesus but refer to the eschatological tribulation of Dan 7, where the son of man is representative of the saints who suffer at the hands of the fourth beast.[128] That Jesus was eschatologically oriented underscores that these predictions came from him.[129] Even using Allison's memory method of "recurrent attestation" affirms that Jesus knew and anticipated his death.[130]

It is certainly plausible that just as the Old Testament prophets recorded their call experiences so would Jesus and that the description of the baptism comes directly from him. To push off the description to a later Christian formulation assumes Jesus would not have had an understanding of himself in relationship to Israel's history and to Israel's God. And why would early Christianity choose to call him "son" except for the fact that this was how Jesus designated himself? Furthermore, it is not as Meier avers. There is nothing in the story that directly sets Jesus over against John, no more than any report of a prophet's call sets him or her against some other person in Israel. It's an embarrassment, for Christian faith underscores its authenticity. If the story was meant to present Jesus as superior to John, why does Matthew have to add the conversation justifying his baptism by John (3:14-15)?[131]

But even then Meier refers to Jesus' baptism as a "conversion," by which he means "his decision to dedicate himself totally to a religious mission to all Israel, a mission lacking any official sanction."[132] It was no "conversion." Jesus did not "convert," a word that implies going over to another, new religion or a nonbeliever taking up a religious faith. He remained a faithful Jew. Rather, his baptism was his prophetic call and the revelation of a special status before and with the God of Israel. It was a profound reordering of his existence. He is now no longer a *tektōn* (Mark 6:3),[133] nor even a prophet who proclaims "Thus saith the Lord," but one who speaks authoritatively (Mark 1:27, Luke 4:32, 36) and without intermediation by declaring, "But I say to you . . ." (Matt 5:22-44), —that is, he speaks as God's chosen Son. His sense of sonship derives directly from his experience and call at his baptism.

Was the event then a subjective experience of Jesus or an objective event experienced by all those present? Mark is obviously the original report, and the other evangelists depend on him. Mark says it was Jesus who saw the "heavens parting" and the descent of the Spirit. The occurrence of the voice from heaven is connected to the preceding by Mark with the simple copulative "and," which suggests also that the descent of the Spirit and the occurrence of the voice were coordinated and that both were experiences of Jesus alone. Just as the prophets recorded their call experiences so Jesus must have also related his experience to the disciples. A prophetic call was a public affair.

The spirit of God is everywhere present and active in the biblical world and texts. It is present and active at creation (Gen 1:2); God's spirit creates people who are called to lead the people of God (Judg 3:10); wisdom and perspicacity are special gifts of the spirit that can be shared with others (Num 11:25); it creates understanding (Sir 39:6). The spirit is particularly related to understanding and wisdom ("Who has learned your counsel, unless you had given wisdom and sent your holy Spirit from on high?" Wis 9:17).[134] This latter passage connects intimately with the text of Jesus' baptism in which the Holy Spirit descends from heaven.

The spirit is also intimately associated with prophecy.[135] In classical prophecy the old elements of the trance and clairvoyance disappear. The prophet is connected to the work of God in history; he speaks and writes intelligibly and rarely speaks of his own inspiration. The spirit of prophecy does not overwhelm the personality of the prophet. The inspired word is of highest importance and stands in the forefront of the prophet's activity. He certainly speaks to Israel as the holy nation bound to God by covenant, but the prophet also calls for repentance because it is an astonishingly disobedient people.

Jesus' baptism by John might suggest that he was one of his disciples until they parted ways. Such a suggestion is made by John 4:1–2 in that Jesus' disciples were baptizing and also by the continuing practice of the church, although it was understood differently by the church (Acts 1:22, 18:25).

Jesus' outlook and ministry shared a number of characteristics with John's. Both were eschatologically oriented. Both called for Israel's repentance: Israel had to have an interior change of heart and mind.[136] Both challenged the current understanding of what constituted a true member of God's elect people; they were celibate, addressed the sins of the ruling class, and no longer pursued a craft.[137] John saw a "mightier one" who was to follow him. Jesus considered John as a "great one," although those who entered the kingdom he declared to be greater than him (Luke 7:28). Of course, Jesus accepted John's baptism and underscored his continuity with John in that regard by practicing it in his own ministry (John 3:22–23).

Jesus' baptism and his practice of it demonstrate his identification with his people; he aligns himself with sinners, the marginalized, the rejected, and the unholy and so faces with them the impending judgment and salvation that both he and John proclaimed. However, this does not mean that Jesus thought of himself as a sinner. Rather, he is the one who had "emptied himself" and took on the form of a slave (Mark 10:43–45).[138] Like John, he considered it necessary to enter the kingdom. This is made clear by the following considerations.

"Sin" biblically means breaking the covenant. John seemed to have understood that the covenant was broken because of the lack of concern for the poor and their exploitation (Luke 3:10–14). The Torah and prophets are rife with evidence of how the poor were exploited and how Israel should take care not to participate in such attitudes and actions. The Torah demands both an inner repentance and a consequent change in external behavior toward the poor:

> If there is among you a poor man, one of your brethren, in any of your towns within your land which the Lord your God gives you, you shall not harden your heart or shut your hand against your poor brother, but you shall open your hand to him, and lend him sufficient for his need, whatever it may be. Take heed lest there be a base thought in your heart, and you say, "The seventh year, the year of release is near," and your eye be hostile to your poor brother, and you give him nothing, and he cry to the Lord against you, and it be sin in you. You shall give to him freely, and your heart shall not be grudging when you give to him; because for this the Lord your God will bless you in all your work and in all that you undertake. For the poor will never cease out of the land; therefore I command you, you shall open wide your hand to your brother, to the needy and to the poor, in the land (Deut 15:7–11).[139]

Indeed, the Messiah was to bring equity (i.e., justice) to the poor but judgment to the wicked—that is, those who oppress the poor. Note particularly the parallelism of Isa 11:4:

> . . . but with righteousness he shall judge the poor, and decide with equity for the meek of the earth; and he shall smite the earth with the rod of his mouth, and with the breath of his lips he shall slay the wicked.

My study of the parables makes it clear that it is precisely these people whom Jesus had in mind and exactly those to whom he extended the invitation to enter the kingdom of God in his actions and table fellowship.[140] So Jesus' own baptism does not mean he thought of himself as a sinner but rather that he was in solidarity with his "sinful" nation and represented and recapitulated the new Israel, as he comprehended in his ministry the outcasts, marginalized, poor, rejected, and ritually unclean.

So Jesus was not some kind of spiritualized antiritualist.[141] The coming kingdom demanded a new rite that was unconnected with the official liturgies of synagogue and temple just as he and his ministry were not particularly attached to those institutions.[142] The public washing of baptism was intimately connected by John with repentance and thus preparing for the coming judgment. Jesus, however, reversed the order of things as appears so vividly in his parables. Repentance for him followed entry into the kingdom, and therefore his baptism, prefiguring Christian baptism, must have enacted entry into the kingdom, sharing in the grace of acceptance from which the reordering of one's life followed. Like John, Jesus could say, it is not appealing to your physical descent from Abraham, a sort of complacent resting on mere externalities, but what counts toward God is the inner change of heart (Deut 15:7).[143]

Repentance and confession of sins in Israel were first of all an acknowledgment of betrayal of the precepts of Torah and that the individual stood in solidarity with Israel's forefathers who had broken the covenant. Daniel's prayer illuminates this communal aspect of confession and sin:

> O Lord, the great and terrible God, who keepest covenant and steadfast love with those who love him and keep his commandments, we have sinned and done wrong and acted wickedly and rebelled, turning aside from thy commandments and ordinances; we have not listened to thy servants the prophets, who spoke in thy name to our kings, our princes, and our fathers, and to all the people of the land. To thee, O Lord, belongs righteousness, but to us confusion of face . . . to our kings, to our princes, and to our fathers, because we have sinned against thee. To the Lord our God belong mercy and forgiveness; because we have rebelled against him, and have not obeyed the voice of the Lord our God by following his laws, which he set before us by his servants the prophets. All Israel has transgressed thy law and turned aside, refusing to obey thy voice. And the curse and oath which are written in the law of Moses the servant of God have been poured out upon us, because we have sinned against him (Dan 9:4-11).

When the individual confessed sin, it had to do with breaking the covenant, standing outside of faithful Israel. God and his covenant were at the center of the prayer of confession and the admission that the individual stood in solidarity with the people. That identification was acknowledged even when the individual was not personally involved in the apostasy that was being confessed.[144]

So Jesus in his baptism is identifying with Israel in its collective sins and apostasy. He does not stand above his people but along with them. In this identification, as his ministry makes clear, he has particularly in mind the outcasts and public sinners: he has come to save them, "the lost" (Matt 10:6, Luke 15:4, 24, 19:10).[145] Absent any other indication to the contrary, Jesus' baptism has to be seen in the light of his identification with sinners and not as a confession of personal sin. Rather, it was the sense of being bound up with Israel.

Jesus and John

Being baptized by John does not necessarily imply he became one of John's disciples any more than all those who came to be baptized by him became his students. After all, his call was to the nation to repent and be cleansed in the Jordan in preparation for the impending judgment. However, John 3:23 suggests that Jesus remained with John and was baptizing along with him and assisting him in his preaching and teaching. That a school of John existed from very early on is indicated by Luke 7:18–19.[146] In John's Gospel Jesus makes his first appearance in the environs where John is active (1:19–34). Two of John's disciples (Andrew is named as one of them, 1:40; 1:44 may indicate the other was Phillip) then follow Jesus. So John, in contradistinction to the synoptic gospels, reports that some of Jesus' earliest disciples came from the orbit of the Baptist. All of this implies that Jesus himself began his public ministry as part of the circle of close disciples gathered around John the Baptist.

Again, in John 3:22–24 Jesus alone is portrayed as baptizing (as also 4:1 affirms).[147] Immediately following this, John records a dispute "about purification" with "a Jew."[148] However, it has to do with Jesus baptizing and that "all are going to him." This text need not imply an allusion to competition between Jesus and John but rather only that Jesus began his ministry as a disciple of John and gathered his first disciples from among John's disciples.[149] The question of John in Luke 7:19 contradicts any thought of competition and demonstrates that John thought of him, at least initially, as "the coming one."

However, the call nature of Jesus' own baptism implies an independent prophetic ministry and not that Jesus would have become a disciple of John, at least not for an extended period of time. It meant, and was the grounds for, the initiation of his own ministry. The differences between the two men point in this direction. Furthermore, Jesus, according to John's Gospel, included baptism within his prophetic activity, although, other than coordinating his ministry with John's (Luke 7:31–35), there are no such indications in the synoptic gospels that he was a formal disciple of John. The fact that he did baptize is compelling given that his own baptism was constitutive of his ministry and his self-understanding, and so the church continued the practice.[150] Mark 6:14 implies that Jesus' public ministry began after John's death. So Twelftree's assumption is not unreasonable that Jesus remained in the wilderness with John but that this ended with John's arrest. At that point, it might be so that he interpreted that the in-breaking of the kingdom was near, thus impelling him to take the message of the kingdom to the populace.[151]

I've already alluded to the similarity of John's teaching and practice with Jesus' own. These traits embodied the life of the kingdom into which Jesus had entered by his baptism and to which he now began to call the people. Like John's insistence on repentance and baptism, Jesus' message demanded entrance into the kingdom to be included in the age to come.[152] Other verbal similarities between John and Jesus include "bearing fruit" (Luke 3:8, 6:43–45), cutting down the fruitless tree (Luke 3:9, 13:6–9), the fire of the judgment (Luke 3:9, Matt 13:40, Mark 9:47–50, John 15:1–16), and baptizing with fire (Luke 3:16, 12:49–50).[153] Jesus, also like John, worked miracles. Mark 6:14 reports that some thought of Jesus as John redivivus and "that is why these powers are at work in him." In other words, the report is saying that John worked miracles.[154] Another continuity with John is suggested by the disciples' request that Jesus teach them to pray as John did his disciples (Luke 11:1).

However, there were other eschatologically oriented individuals and movements, which also did not appeal to Gentiles, gathered followers, and called all Israel to repentance: prophets, messiahs, and bandit-judges.[155] Seen in this perspective, the similarities are not striking.

But the differences between them are striking: for Jesus, repentance followed one's entrance into the kingdom. Jesus was itinerant and relied on village hospitality for board and room; he practiced open commensality; he bound up the kingdom with himself and taught that it was already proleptically present in him and his ministry.[156] The twelve disciples who formed the inner circle of his ministry limned the beginning of the newly constituted Israel, witnessing also to the kingdom's contemporary presence. For John the kingdom meant the coming judgment, whereas for Jesus it meant not just that but also Israel's, if not the world's, redemption and the in-breaking of the divine, eschatological banquet. Women were explicitly members of his broader circle of disciples. He claimed to be the "greater one" whom John foresaw coming. He spoke not only prophetically but as a sage and the embodiment of wisdom (though John, no doubt, spoke metaphorically—e.g., Luke 3:7–9). Jesus worked in the villages and eventually also in Jerusalem. He sent out his disciples and charged them with the same ministry he pursued. He challenged the contemporary practice of Torah and interpreted his own death as related to Israel's salvation.[157] Meier's felicitous phrase characterizing Jesus' ministry is apropos here: "It was this exuberant and perhaps shocking newness that was at the center of Jesus' message, action, and attractiveness."[158] A less certain difference is that Jesus taught extensively in parables that graphically portrayed his concept of the kingdom and its presence.[159]

These differences point to Jesus' own baptism as a profound experience that led him not to become a disciple of John but to begin a ministry that portrayed, proleptically established, and embodied the reality of the kingdom. Jesus may have had one aim in mind when he decided to set out and be baptized by John in the wilderness, but he was profoundly changed by the experience itself. There is no question about the possibility of development of his thought, but in this instance, it cannot be known since we are not privy to that information.[160]

These differences, however, reveal how Jesus interpreted his baptism—that is, his behavior clearly reveals what Jesus encountered about himself and his relationship to God in his baptism. He was bound up with his people and their sins, while at that same time he was the son of Israel's Father-God and as his son embodied the coming kingdom that was proclaimed by John. His baptism was a call to a ministry that made the kingdom present in common meals, in forgiveness, in inclusion of sinners, and in his teaching and parables, which graphically portrayed the contours of this kingdom. It was a call to save Israel from the doom that hung over its head because of its rebellious attitude toward Rome and its failure to be a "light to the Gentiles" (Isa 42:6, 49:6). So his baptism involved a break with his former life.[161] Above all, it meant that God would not spare him but would demand the offering up of his life in sacrifice. He would henceforth be fully consecrated to Israel's heritage and destiny.

Although it is not mentioned in the synoptic gospels and never again after John 4:1, we may conclude Jesus continued to baptize; after all, the practice was adopted by the church. Jesus certainly did not reject John but coordinated himself with him (Matt 11:2-3). Yet he was different. There was no greater prophet than John, yet to be in the kingdom is to surpass him (Matt 11:11).[162] John's severe, ascetic lifestyle and his message of judgment contrast with Jesus' own of joyful understanding of the kingdom and his celebrative "eating and drinking."[163] So it will not do to suppose that he began his ministry baptizing and then stopped. His baptizing of those who accepted his message could have meant their entrance into the kingdom and acceptance of the way of being that Jesus proclaimed. It appears then that it was just not the center of his ministry.[164]

The controversy in Mark 11:27-33 demonstrates that Jesus saw no competition between himself and John. The implication of Jesus' counter question to his interlocutors is that he understood John baptized by divine authority and that Jesus' ministry too rested on that same authority. Jesus further implies that he stood in continuity with John, and so we can conclude that he understood himself as the "greater one" of whom John had spoken. That Jesus' counter question focuses on John's baptizing activity suggests that Jesus was baptizing so that it would deprive Jesus' interlocutors, the Temple authorities, of any right to deny the authority of Jesus who stands in continuity with John.[165]

There are two "stray" traditions in Matt 21:31-32 and Luke 7:29-30 that mention John.[166] They apparently do not come from a common tradition, but their meaning converges: marginal people responded to John's preaching and baptism with repentance, which parallels the reports of the kind of people who came out to John in his wilderness harbor (Luke 3:10-14). In these passages John stands alone without any reference to Jesus, which indicates again the esteem in which Jesus held him.

Finally, John 5:33-36 and 10:40-42 make reference to the Baptist. In the former he is described as a "burning and shining light"—that is, not the source of the light but a lamp lighted by the light (Jesus).[167] However, the reference also once again points to the respect in which Jesus held John while at the same time, in the language of the Fourth Gospel, underscoring Jesus' own claim as the "mightier one" whose coming John had foretold. In the latter, the people declare that John performed "no signs" (miracles), which marks again his inferiority to Jesus,[168] although Mark 6:14 seems to allude to the fact that he did. So this verse may be a piece of the church's anti-John polemic.

John and Jesus

In Luke 7:18-23 (and Matt 11:2-19), John while in prison sends two of his disciples to ask Jesus if he truly is the "coming one" whom he had said would follow him.[169] This pericope falls into three easily discernable units: (1) Jesus' reply to the disciples of John (Luke 7:18-23, Matt 11:2-6); (2) Jesus' lauding John before his audience (Luke 7:24-28, Matt 11:7-11); and (3) the parable of the children in the market (Luke 7:31-35, Matt 11:16-19).[170]

The Reply of Jesus to John's Disciples (Matt 11:2–6, Luke 7:18–23)

The first of these is an apothegm or pronouncement story.[171] This unit is provided with a time frame. It occurs after John has been imprisoned and before his brutal execution. Matthew, as is his wont, has attenuated the story, whereas Luke has the fuller account. His disciples had access to him in prison as was the practice of relatives of imprisoned people having leave to bring food and other necessities that the authorities would not provide to the imprisoned (cf., Acts 23:16).

When the Baptist asks if Jesus is the "coming one" (Matt 11:3, Luke 7:19), he's repeating his own prophecy (Matt 3:11, Luke 3:16) that there would be "the mightier one" who was to follow him. The phrase "coming one" is not a mere generalized epithet with no fixed referent.[172] Ps 118 points to a specific understanding of the phrase. The psalm refers to the messianic king, the overthrow of the oppressor, and the establishment of the messianic kingdom.[173]

The psalm was closely related to the celebration of Sukkoth, and this feast was redolent with eschatological ideas that celebrated the ultimate victory of God and the accession to the throne of a Davidic messiah who, as God's vice-regent, would exercise cosmic authority. Sukkoth was perhaps the most popular of all the feasts because it celebrated not only these notions but also egalitarianism when the people during the festival were given extraordinary privileges.[174] So the phrase "the coming one" was a well-known appellation due to the popularity of the feast of Succoth, which celebrated the coming Messiah and establishment of the kingdom of God.

Even a cursory reading of John's preaching (Matt 3:7–10, Luke 3:7–14) reveals he did not speak in vague and fuzzy generalities. He did not mince words or beat around the bush: he spoke plainly, bluntly, and without obfuscation. We would expect that when he spoke of a "coming one," he was using clear and precise terminology. It communicated an unambiguous expectation that would have been understood by every Jew in the Roman Empire. So when John used the phrase, everyone knew that it referred to the coming Davidic messiah and the establishment of the kingdom completing the eschatological work John had begun in restoring Israel. That restoration as he saw it, however, also involved fiery judgment and the condemnation of those who had not repented.

But Jesus did not appear to be bringing the kind of restoration and judgment that John anticipated. He also consorted with outcasts and sinners rather than pronouncing judgment on them as John would have anticipated. So John's expectations had not been met. Now he sat in prison facing death with no sign of any vindication of his ministry, which he had perceived as his call: to usher in the coming salvation of the kingdom and prepare the way for "the coming one." How could he not ask given the clear expectations associated with the "coming one"? Here was no eschatological "cleansing out of the chaff" by the destruction of the unrepentant and the final ingathering and restoration of the "grain" of Israel's faithful into the kingdom (Luke 3:17). Jesus' fame (Mark 1:28) spreading like wildfire would have gotten John's hopes up that the "coming one" had appeared who would initiate God's kingdom saving Israel and annihilating the wicked. But it wasn't happening. John does not want to give up his faith and expectations. Can Jesus somehow vindicate those hopes, or should John simply forget about Jesus as the fulfiller of his prophecy and wait for them to be fulfilled in some other messiah sent by God?[175]

Jesus' answer does not proclaim his unique status by the use of exalted messianic titles or illustrious claims.[176] He tells John's messengers to report what they had "seen and heard" themselves of Jesus' ministry: people are healed of their infirmities, and the good news of the kingdom is proclaimed. Jesus describes what they have "heard and seen" in words that echo prophecies from Isaiah:

> In that day the deaf shall hear the words of a book, and out of their gloom and darkness the eyes of the blind shall see. The meek shall obtain fresh joy in the Lord, and the poor among men shall exult in the Holy One of Israel. For the ruthless shall come to nought and the scoffer cease, and all who watch to do evil shall be cut off (Isa 29:18–20).

> Then the eyes of the blind shall be opened, and the ears of the deaf unstopped; then shall the lame man leap like a hart, and the tongue of the dumb sing for joy (Isa 35:5–6).[177]

> The Spirit of the Lord GOD is upon me, because the Lord has anointed me to bring good tidings to the afflicted; he has sent me to bind up the brokenhearted, to proclaim liberty to the captives, and the opening of the prison to those who are bound; to proclaim the year of the Lord's favor, and the day of vengeance of our God; to comfort all who mourn (Isa 61:1–2).

These references all occur in a context announcing the restoration of Israel right in the midst of her own failures and in the context of the late exile when the captives have been informed of Cyrus's edict to let exiles return to their homelands. Jesus in this way interprets his ministry of healing and raising the dead. John predicted that the "mightier one" would bring the fire of judgment (Luke 3:9, 16–17). Jesus confirms that prediction. He includes both the proleptic inauguration of the kingdom of God and the judgment of fire in his discourse.[178] In this regard, Luke 12:49-51 is particularly significant:

> I came to cast fire upon the earth; and would that it were already kindled! I have a baptism to be baptized with; and how I am constrained until it is accomplished! Do you think that I have come to give peace on earth? No, I tell you, but rather division.[179]

So Jesus thought of himself as going through the eschatological baptism of the sacrifice of his life and being "salted with fire."[180] However, Jesus in this Lucan passage claims to be the dispenser of that eschatological fire— that is, he claims to be that coming "mightier one" prophesied by John. The coming one has arrived. Jesus also claims to be the "stronger one" in his little parable of the binding of the "strong man" in Mark 3:27. Jesus is obviously referring to himself as the one who binds Satan and "plunders his goods." That plundering takes place as he exorcises demons.

Jesus makes an allusive claim to be the coming one by identifying himself as the one who has come to cast fire, by fulfilling eschatological prophecy (Isa 7:18-23), and as the stronger one. John was the "greatest born of woman," but the "mightier one" has come, and now John is the least in the new order (Luke 7:28).

The reign of God is at the door, and Jesus' activity is a vivid enactment of his invitation to enter the kingdom as well as the actual presence of the kingdom itself fulfilling the promises of Isaiah. Healings were conceived as part of eschatological salvation in the Jewish apocalyptic writings of the time.[181] Jesus both announces the kingdom and makes it already present if only the people will hear and see and rise from a death like preoccupation with rebellion against the Roman occupation, intolerable as it is.

In this way, Jesus redefined the activity and ministry of "the coming one." Jesus' messiahship certainly consisted of "a winnowing fork in his hand to clear his threshing floor, and to gather the wheat into his granary" and to consign "the chaff to . . . unquenchable fire" (Luke 3:15). However, this was not some apocalyptic scenario but a historical one. The kingdom was already present in Jesus and his ministry and fully at work in his healings and table fellowship, which included sinners and tax collectors. As people accepted the kingdom, they were like wheat gathered into the eschatological granary of the kingdom of God.[182] Jesus doesn't give up on the consummation preached by John, but the accent now is on what the merciful God of Israel is doing through Jesus to save and redeem his people. In his reply to John, Jesus doesn't allude to the vengeance that would be meted out. He concludes his list of salvific activities with the proclamation of "good news to the poor."

When the kingdom comes in its fullness (it was already at the door, Mark 1:15), those who had not accepted the call, the "chaff," would be consigned to fire (Matt 3:10, 7:19, 18:9, Mark 9:48). In a sense the ax already lay at the root of the trees (Luke 3:9). But it was not quite what John expected. He didn't expect a "miracle worker" who sat with sinners at table but a glorious messiah who would finally end the wrongs under which the nation had to live and establish the kingdom of God by ridding the world of sinners. Jesus did not give up John's message of the consummation to come. He stresses, however, the compassion and joyfulness of the kingdom of God into which he invites everyone including, and perhaps especially, sinners while simultaneously threatening judgment on those who with hardened hearts reject him and the kingdom.[183] However, here Jesus stresses only the salvation aspect of his message and ministry. Jesus, in effect, is saying the promise of restoration by Isaiah is already present and active in this world, and he, "the anointed one" (Isa 61:1, i.e., the servant Messiah), is the means by which the restoration takes place.

His emphasis exclusively on the salvific aspects of his kingdom proclamation and its realization recalls Isaiah's description of the servant as tender, gentle, and kindhearted:

> Behold my servant, whom I uphold, my chosen, in whom my soul delights; I have put my Spirit upon him, he will bring forth justice to the nations. He will not cry or lift up his voice, or make it heard in the street; a bruised reed he will not break, and a dimly burning wick he will not quench; he will faithfully bring forth justice (Isa 42:1–3).

Jesus expressed this character of his ministry in his own words:

> Come to me, all who labor and are heavy laden, and I will give you rest. Take my yoke upon you, and learn from me; for I am gentle and lowly in heart, and you will find rest for your souls. For my yoke is easy, and my burden is light (Matt 11:28–30).

John was the prophet of threatening judgment and disaster if we can judge the main lines of his proclamation by the little evidence we have of his life and preaching. Jesus, while not eschewing that aspect of the impending kingdom, stressed its redemptive and rescuing dimensions. In effect, Jesus says, the end-time prophesized by Isaiah is now here in, with, and under what I'm doing. Come and rejoice with me in this good news of God's saving presence.

Jesus ends the enumeration of his activities with a blessing of those who don't take offense at him (Matt 11:6, Luke 7:23). Jesus could well be referencing Isaiah here again (8:14) where the Lord himself is a "stumbling stone" (NJB, KJV) or "a stone one strikes against" (NRSV). Isaiah's context is the threat of the flood waters of Assyria overwhelming Judah. The prophet was warned by God that the values of the people are skewed, so God in his holiness becomes a trap and a stumbling block to the people. His word was meant to save them, but because they are disobedient, it becomes a word of death.[184] Jesus may have had John specifically in mind in his beatitude and calling him to recognize that the kingdom had indeed arrived. But it was not the denouement to the eschatological drama John expected. John was surely in danger of being "scandalized," having a hard heart, and not accepting Jesus and the "easy yoke" he offered. John could well have been shocked at how he saw Jesus portraying God's kingdom as including corruption while fulfilling the prophecies of the end-time.[185]

But Jesus also had the nation in mind. There were many who rejected him as a "perverter of Israel" (Luke 23:2).[186] Jesus saw clearly the flood that awaited the people in the form of the Roman military machine that would sweep over them if they continued their obstinate delusion of thinking they could drive the Romans away. The nation needed a revolution of the mind and heart. Those who accept the kingdom enter it and find the blessing of comfort, mercy, joy, satisfaction, and fulfillment (Matt 5:3–10).

This whole little scene then has to do with faith or offense, blessing or judgment. Jesus divides believers and unbelievers, those who can hear from those who are deaf, the blind from those who can see, disciples from "this generation."[187] So Jesus says of himself, "Do not think that I have come to bring peace on earth; I have not come to bring peace, but a sword" (Matt 10:34).

The whole scene ends, however, without a disclosure of John's reply. The narrative lacks a proper denouement reminiscent of the parable of the prodigal son, in which the father entreats the elder son to join the celebration of the younger son who has returned to the bosom of his father. We never hear the elder son's response. The narrative closes in silence. Did Jesus have in mind the Baptist in this parable as a representative of all those who question Jesus and remain unsure whether to respond to him in faith and acceptance? The story understood in this way contrasts with Luke portraying the Baptist's "leaping in his mother's womb" (Luke 1:41–44), Matthew having the Baptist say, "should be baptized by you" (Matt 3:14), and John proclaiming Jesus as the "Lamb of God" in the Fourth Gospel (John 1:29, 36). Shocking is the implicit threat for anyone who does not accept Jesus in faith as the "one who has come" (i.e., the promised Messiah) because of the unexpected nature of his ministry. They will have no share in the kingdom. All of this points decidedly to the narrative's historicity as it stands in such a stark contrast with these other portrayals of John as having an unquestioning, solid faith in Jesus. The Gospel portrayals elsewhere praise John, and he is brought onboard in support of Christian faith.[188]

In this whole conversation, there is a hint of a split between Jesus and John in contrast to the high regard in which Jesus held him.[189] John's execution may have been the turning point that led Jesus to see in this crisis that the kingdom was nearer than up to now was thought and a present reality. The kingdom's presence led Jesus further to understand and develop a decisive difference between himself and John that could be traced back to his experience of his call at his baptism. He saw himself as the promised "coming [mightier] one" from whom John explicitly differentiated himself. So Jesus does not simply take up the ministry of John but moves beyond it: the kingdom lies not just in the future but is present in him (the "mightier one"), and this future but present kingdom includes the margins of Jewish society. The message now must break beyond the confines of the Jordan's banks and be taken to the whole nation. The kingdom is not just judgment, but the people can enter it and enjoy even now God's salvation and the proleptic end of exile.[190] God's gracious kingdom is mightily present. If the nation would enter it, the judgment that hung over its head, embodied by the threatening Roman destruction, could be avoided.

Jesus' Address to the Crowd Regarding John
(Matt 11:7–11, Luke 7:24–28)

Jesus asks three rhetorical questions about John's identity and presents three answers, only one of which is correct.

> As they went away, Jesus began to speak to the crowds concerning John: "What did you go out into the wilderness to behold? A reed shaken by the wind? Why then did you go out? To see a man clothed in soft raiment? Behold, those who wear soft raiment are in kings' houses. Why then did you go out? To see a prophet? Yes, I tell you, and more than a prophet. This is he of whom it is written, Behold, I send my messenger before thy face, who shall prepare thy way before thee."

That these verses do not reference Jesus at all nor John's relationship to him speaks for their authenticity in the mouth of Jesus.[191] These questions are attached to the previous unit by a so-called genitive absolute, indicating a close connection to what precedes it.¹⁹² The implication is that Matt 11:2–14 and Luke 7:18–28 each form an original unit.

A "reed shaken by the wind" refers to a person who is helpless or even under the judgment of God.¹⁹³ John was rejected by the Jerusalem authorities (Mark 11:31–32), and so many people might have avoided him for that reason thinking that if the authorities rejected him, he would be like Jeroboam¹⁹⁴ under God's judgment. But as one who risked the wrath of Herod Antipas because of the judgment he rendered on him as an adulterer for marrying his brother's wife (Mark 6:17), John could hardly be thought of in those terms. Antipas also had the symbol of a reed on his coins, and Jesus may be taking up that symbolism. Herod was like a reed in the wind in terms of his vacillating policies.¹⁹⁵ John certainly didn't wear "the soft raiment" of a courtier putting himself forward as an aristocratic person of status and wealth.¹⁹⁶ Here again is a sneering allusion to Herod Antipas and his sumptuous court in Sepphoris in contrast to the lives of Jesus' peasant audience.¹⁹⁷ The reality was that John wore rough clothes and lived on an austere diet (Mark 1:6). Jesus may even be gently mocking his audience who went out merely to "see" John—that is, out of curiosity without a serious intent to take his message to heart and repent.

Jesus ends with his familiar ringing and authoritative, "Yes, I say to you," which points to the authenticity of this address to the crowd. John was indeed a "prophet." That word would conjure up for his Galilean audience their passion for freedom, their ardent loyalty to the God of Israel in the face of paganism, and the fiery Elijah and Elisha, who had confronted the powers of their day and been hunted down like wild animals.¹⁹⁸ They would identify Antipas and his illegal wife Herodias with evil Ahab and his wife Jezebel. He needed to say no more.

But that John is "more than a prophet" is puzzling. What is it to be such a figure? Verse 10 apparently defines what he means. A closer look at this verse reveals that 10a repeats verbally the Septuagint of Exod 23:20a and 10b reproduces Mal 3:1b, except that it substitutes "prepare" (Gk., κατασκευάσει, *kataskeuasei*) for the Septuagint's "look with favor on" (Gk., ἐπιβλέψεται, *epiblepsetai*). Qumran shows us how in first-century Judaism, various Old Testament texts could be woven together in this fashion. Jesus himself could well have done so. Furthermore, the little introduction to this "merged quotation" finds no similar formula in the Gospels other than Matt 3:3. A merged quotation also occurs in Mark 1:2b–3. Do these occurrences of this phenomenon imply Christological reflection and the work of Christian scribes?¹⁹⁹

A closer examination of Matt 11:10 suggests otherwise. The first part of the merged quotation promises that God's angel (or messenger) will go before him. It is God's own emissary, which means the Lord's authority resides in him. So Israel is exhorted to obey his voice as the voice of God himself. This "angel" will fight for them against their enemies in the land.

"Before your face" is a biblical phrase used in contexts that promise God will bring Israel to the promised land—that is, establish his kingdom.[200] So the merged quotation asserts that John is both this fearsome (divine) angel and the promised Elijah who was to come at the end of the ages preparing the way of the kingdom. This synthesis suggests the creative mind of Jesus himself.[201] Jesus is asserting that he is so much greater than all the prophets because something of the divine is in him as well as the prophetic spirit of Elijah. This is hardly the description of a "decreasing John" and an "increasing Jesus" (John 3:30).

Another detail that confirms the saying originated with Jesus himself is the change that he makes in quoting Mal 3:1, which reads "before me" not "before you" (singular). That singular pronoun has the whole people in mind. Israel is thought of as a totality.[202] It also corresponds to John's conception of himself as the forerunner of "the mightier one" (Matt 3:11, Mark 1:7, John 1:15, 27, 30, Act 13:25). Jesus directs the activity of John to the people who prepared the way for them. Jesus may also have had himself in mind as representative of Israel and identifying himself as the "mightier one."

I find this merged quotation to be not a "confirmatory" assertion but rather a challenge to his hearers.[203] Behind Jesus' assertion, you can almost hear the criticism directed against this John who called a supposedly Torah-true nation to repentance: another maniacal preacher[204] leading people astray and subverting the Temple service by claiming to offer the forgiveness of sins! But Jesus places him above all the other prophets.

Following this assertion by Jesus comes a surprising counter assertion in Matt 11:11, in the form of typical Hebraic antithetic parallelism[205] reflecting a Semitic form of expression and thinking that supports its authenticity. Strictly speaking the two halves of the saying contradict one another in this typically Semitic form of expression, and so they have to be taken together as different sides of the same truth: John has a matchless distinction in the old age, but even the least person[206] in the new age of the kingdom of God enjoys a greater distinction. Jesus is obviously not explicitly referring to himself—that is, it is not on the surface a Christological statement—but anyone, "the least of these my brothers," is in view here. For Jesus the kingdom is the great reality, and its magnificence and worth far surpass all other so-called treasures.[207] Jesus' focus here is, as in the parables, on the kingdom of God.

However, the phrase does contain a subtle Christological undertone: if the least in the kingdom is greater than John, what of Jesus himself with and in whom the kingdom is proclaimed as present? He is that "mightier one" whom John promised as the coming one, the thongs of whose sandals "he was not worthy to untie" (Mark 1:7).[208]

Jesus has differentiated himself and his proclamation of the kingdom from John and his proclamation. The kingdom in Jesus has proleptically arrived, and it is not just the "ax laid at the root" and the fire of judgment. It is a joyful time of salvation. The people are invited to proleptically enter the kingdom now and enjoy already its fruits. In Jesus a decisive turn has occurred in the eschatological schedule.

Jesus Sees John as the Turning of the Age (Matt 11:12–13, Luke 16:16)

Verses 11:12–13 are an obvious insertion by Matthew since they occur in a somewhat different form and in an entirely different context in Luke 16:16.

> From the days of John the Baptist until now the kingdom of heaven has suffered violence, and men of violence take it by force. For all the prophets and the law prophesied until John (Matt 11:12–13).

> The law and the prophets were until John; since then the good news of the kingdom of God is preached, and every one enters it violently (Luke 16:16).

The saying probably comes from Q, and Luke appears to be the more original. Matthew uses his famous circumlocution for God in substituting "heaven." It would appear that Luke preserves the original context in Q since it is unlikely he would have torn it from the context of his long discussion about John and inserted it in its present position in his Gospel. The Lucan version would be better translated, "*force their way into it.*"[209] It also looks as if Matthew has expanded the initial phrase in Luke and then repeated it in another form in verse 13. The original saying probably read something like, "The law and the prophets until John. From then on, the kingdom of heaven suffers violence and the violent take it by force."[210]

Jesus, with these words, divides the history of Israel into two periods. He is reflecting his contemporary understanding that prophecy had come to an end. The ancient rabbis insisted prophecy had ended with Haggai, Zechariah, and Malachi. However, Zech 13:3–6 indicates nonliterary prophecy persisted, and, in fact, it vigorously reasserted itself in the first century.[211] He places all of Israel's history up until John under the rubric of the written sacred Scriptures.[212] John was a turning point or fulcrum of history. However, John began the proclamation of the kingdom, and for him it meant fiery judgment. In that sense he ends the old period. Now, a new period emerges. Jesus' proclamation of the kingdom of God breaking into history meant salvation, forgiveness, entering into the joy of the Father, ending exile, feasting, generous hospitality, a jubilee, homecoming, the binding up of wounds, the inclusion of outcasts. In Jesus the kingdom is now both present and yet a future reality when it will break in with all its fullness. In him the end of the ages dawns (1 Cor 10:11). The kingdom is God's presence to save and judge his people at the end of history, but it is also universal and encompasses the Gentile world.[213] That kingdom is now already tangible in Jesus' healings and exorcisms, in his open commensality, in his power to forgive, in his message that reveals the joyful new life in the kingdom.[214] This kingdom, however, is also judgment against those who will not accept it and the new life it brings. So the saying is about the kingdom, not specifically about John.

By referring to those who are "forcing their way" into the kingdom or "taking it by violence," Jesus has in mind all the various revolutionary movements that peppered his time and against whom he directed many of his parables. There were myriads of bandits, prophets, and messianic movements of the first century all focused on the kingdom, many of them by violence seeking to establish the kingdom. The Essenes, though living a tranquil life, envisioned a final eschatological battle that would establish the kingdom.[215] Jesus and his proclamation of the kingdom were set profoundly against these movements, for he saw clearly, as did many another person such as Josephus, where it would end. They would not bring in the kingdom by force, and the only other way was by entering the kingdom already at hand in Jesus' ministry. The kingdom could not be ushered in by violence but by sitting at table with Jesus.

Members of such movements could well have criticized Jesus, but there is no such direct evidence in the precipitate of the tradition that we have in the Gospels. We can assume there was such criticism because Jesus by word and parable taught, counseled, and warned against violence. The kingdom meant passive resistance, praying for the enemy, turning the other cheek, and going the extra mile. One could well imagine what the "political realists" and the militant believers who were convinced that God would once again defeat Israel's enemies as he did in the days of Joshua and the Maccabees had to say about him.[216]

John Identified as the Coming Elijah (Matt 11:14)

This declaration is not included by Luke in his version of this long scenario, and so it can be concluded that it was added by Matthew perhaps on the basis of Mark 9:11-13, which Matthew includes in his Gospel following the Marcan order in 17:10-13.[217] However, in John 1:21 the Baptist denies that he is Elijah.

Identifying John with Elijah was his dress (Mark 1:6), which resembled that of Elijah (2 Kgs 1:8) and the camelhair that of the typical prophet (Zech 13:4). This identification is strengthened by John's attack on Herod Antipas and his wife Herodias, which mirrors Elijah's own struggles with Ahab and Jezebel. Jesus himself was identified by some as the returned Elijah who is coordinated with the Baptist (Mark 6:14-16, 8:28). Suggested is the widespread expectation that "Elijah" would return at the end of the ages. Mal 3:24 describes the work of this returning Elijah: he will establish peace on earth and restore the disorder of the world. The Rabbis reflect the continuation of this expectation. The Mishnah describes Elijah's work:

> To remove afar those that were brought nigh by violence and to bring nigh those that were removed by violence . . . Rabbi Judah says, "To bring nigh but not to remove afar." Rabbi Simeon says, "To bring agreement where there is matter for dispute." And the Sages say, "Neither to remove afar nor to bring nigh, but to make peace in the world."[218]

Or he will reawaken the dead.[219] Because Mal 3:23-24 declares that Elijah will have a role in the future victory of God and as a harbinger of the day of the Lord, the Rabbis understood that he comes to resolve legal disputes and be the means of establishing the peace of the coming kingdom of God. He is often identified as the precursor of the Messiah[220] or will even anoint the Messiah and reveal him to the world.[221]

Luke 1:16-17 presents a summary of the function of the coming Elijah who will appear in the person of John:

> And he will turn many of the sons of Israel to the Lord their God, and he will go before him in the spirit and power of Elijah, to turn the hearts of the fathers to the children, and the disobedient to the wisdom of the just, to make ready for the Lord a people prepared.

The task of "turning hearts" quotes Mal 4:6 in reference to the work of the returning Elijah. However, Luke does not follow Malachi exactly but substitutes Malachi's "[turn] the heart of the children to the fathers" with "[turn] the disobedient to the wisdom of the just." This parallelism suggests that the "unjust fathers" (i.e., Israel) were disobedient, while the unexpected true children of Abraham (the Gentiles) were justified.[222] His emendation reflects the time of the church when it was becoming predominantly Gentile.

This overview suggests that the expectation of the returning Elijah was part of the Jewish culture in Jesus' time. On the basis of verses 11–13, it is not impossible that Jesus understood him to have been the returning "Elijah." After all, "Elijah" was expected to return as the eschaton approached, and Jesus saw him as the final prophet who was to return at the turn of the ages. In this way Jesus also differentiated himself from John. He himself was not the expected "Elijah." If the "least in the kingdom" was greater than John, then Jesus, who is the proclaimer of the kingdom and who proleptically makes it present, must be indeed an exalted figure. So Matthew's inclusion of verse 14 in this context, taking it over from 17:10–13, which he has adapted from Mark 9:11–13, is not without justification.

Jesus' Parable of Children at Play in the Marketplace (Matt 11:16–19, Luke 7:31–35)

I have dealt with this parable in detail in the former volume of my series. Here I provide a summary of that exposition.

The parable is connected intimately with the context of verses 16 and 18–19. Boys and girls reproach other children because they won't play the way they want. So John and Jesus are looked on as betrayers and outside the norms of what is to be considered those who "delight in the law of the Lord" (Ps 1). Both are unmarried. John is an ascetic who lives in the wilderness calling the nation to repentance. "This generation" might respond, "We are Torah true and need no repentance!" This man must have a demon. Jesus participates in normal human activities like eating and drinking but with outcasts and sinners and so is called a glutton and drunkard who apparently is dishonoring his parents (Prov 28:7) if not the Torah norms that call upon the faithful Israelite "not to sit in the seat of the scornful" (Ps 1:1). Jesus further identifies himself with wisdom. Wisdom has a unique relationship with God (Prov 8:22–31, Sir 1:6–8). She reveals the divine will and saving activity (Wis 7:22—8:18). Jesus accesses creation theology in Matt 6:25–34. He held children in high regard, enjoyed feasting, and eschewed fasting, which are also aspects of the wisdom tradition. The universalism of creation theology also appears in many a parable. But Jesus' version of the wisdom tradition propounds a counter order: the last are first, the lost are saved, the least are greatest, the leaders are servants, the outcasts are in and those who are "in" are rejected, and the kingdom will bring a great reversal.

This little parable also draws a definitive difference between John and Jesus, which reflects their quite different views of the kingdom: John fasts, and Jesus feasts (Mark 2:18–20). John lives in asceticism, while Jesus lives in celebratory exuberance.

THE TEMPTATION OF JESUS (MARK 1:12–13, MATT 4:1–11, LUKE 4:1–13)

Matthew and Luke share the same story of the temptation, but Luke reverses Matthew's second and third temptation, while Mark presents us with a very brief account in two verses.[223] Matthew apparently says that the temptation only began at the end of forty days, while Luke states that the temptation continued throughout the forty days. Mark's story, like Luke's, also portrays the temptation as being extended over the forty days. However, Mark does not mention fasting but that the angels ministered to him. The word used there, διακονέω (*diakoneō*), means "to wait at table," which implies that the angels fed him as Israel was fed with the food of angels (Ps 78:25, 2 Esd 1:19). In spite of the differences between Matthew and Luke, the underlying similarity implies that the narrative was part of the Q document that they both used in the construction of their respective Gospels. Luke usually follows the order of his sources, so we might suspect Matthew has altered the order of the temptations. But Matthew's sequence follows the most logical order: from rocks on earth, to the height of the Temple's pinnacle, then to a vista that includes the whole world.

Mark usually has a very fulsome account of the traditions that he has included in his Gospel, so we might intuit that the Q account was a development of the old tradition that Mark has employed. On the other hand, Q was written perhaps twenty years before Mark. Therefore, we must be faced with two separate traditions of Jesus' temptation in the wilderness. That the story appeared in Q, which originated around AD 50, means we are dealing with very old tradition indeed that is closer to the realities it narrates.

The temptation stories must be seen in relationship to other biblical references. In Dan 11 and Ps 2 an eschatological assault by the Gentile powers would take place against the messiah, but these destructive powers would be vanquished.[224] Other references include 2 Bar 40:1–4, where the messiah annihilates the remaining world ruler, and 2 Bar 72:1–6, where he is depicted as destroying all the nations but sparing "every nation that has not trodden down the seed of Jacob."

The temptation stories also has resonances with the Joseph story. Originally Joseph flaunts his dreams of his family's obeisance to himself (Gen 37:4–11) and his status as the beloved son of Jacob by means of his special garment (Gen 37:3). Both his dreams and his chosenness were a challenge to accepting his role of "beloved son" with grace.[225] Instead he uses them as a means to dominate. Jesus reverses this dominating stance. He refuses dominion. He is the one who came to serve (Mark 10:45). That service aligns with the ultimate reversal of the stance by Joseph himself. Though he becomes politically powerful as second only to Pharaoh, he feeds his brothers and father. Jesus too feeds his brothers with healings, exorcisms, and words (Matt 5:18–44, 7:24, Luke 4:22). So Jesus would bid his "brothers" (i.e., Israel) to become "weak" by loving the enemy, practicing forgiveness, going the extra mile, and living by the favor of their little brother.[226] As in the story of Joseph and his family, it would be a long and torturous journey toward reconciliation and peace, but to submit to their contemporary Joseph in the person of Jesus, Jacob (i.e., Israel) would achieve an amazing, divine transformation. But like Jacob of old who sent his beloved Joseph into the hands of his murderous brothers—though, as it turns out, he was actually sending him into God's hands (Gen 45:4–5)—both he and Joseph are transformed when God reunites them.[227] Contemporary Jacob would do the same with the new beloved son, Jesus. He is delivered over to death and actually dies but then is raised and given back to Israel for the transformation of the whole world.

Of course, as the Gospels make clear, the temptation is not the final struggle with Satan. The battle continues as Jesus encounters the demon possessed, his human opponents, the diseased who are under the spell of demonic forces (e.g., Mark 9:14–27)—even in the person of his own disciples (Mark 8:33) and finally in facing his own passion (Mark 14:32–9). The narrative contains two quotations from Deuteronomy. The first follows the LXX, which in this case is a literal translation of the original Hebrew of Deut 6:13. The second quotation substitutes "worship" (προσκενέω, *proskyneō*, literally "bend the knee, do obeisance to") for the LXX's "you shall fear" (*phobēthēsē*, an indicative future passive). The second quotation also follows the LXX of Ps 91:11–12. None of the forms of these quotations suggest that because they conform to the LXX, they are a Matthean or Lucan composition (in the third case it doesn't conform). When the passage was translated into Greek, it would only have been natural to use the LXX in quoting the Old Testament.[228] Meier peculiarly asserts that the temptation story is not mentioned elsewhere, apparently unaware that the writer of Hebrews does so twice (2:18 and 4:15).[229]

What of its historicity? Both Mark and Q agree that Jesus was in the wilderness for a period of forty days,[230] that he was tempted by Satan (Mark) or the Devil (Matt, Luke), and that he was in the end served by angels (Mark and Matt). All three evangelists agree that the temptation followed Jesus' baptism (although Luke interpolates the genealogy between the two events). So these three features of the story are the bedrock of the tradition and form a historical report.[231] In addition, the first two temptations by the Devil (in Luke the first and third) are prefaced with "If you are the Son of God," which connects the Q version with Jesus' baptism where he is declared to be "the son of God," and point to the literary, if not historical and temporal, connection between the two. This is very strong evidence that the baptismal and temptation stories were originally conceived as a unit.

That unity suggests also the historicity of the events involved because there is no doubt that Jesus was baptized. The intimate connection between the baptismal narrative and the temptation means that both are conceived of as historical events. It might be asked, since the temptation was a private event with only Jesus present and no other witnesses, how does it become known and even textualized in Q? The simple answer is that Jesus related the experience to his disciples. The text as it appears in Matthew and Luke reveals that it could have originally been a first-person account with slight alterations of the verbs involved—e.g., the opening phrase "Jesus was led" could originally have been "I was led by the Spirit into the wilderness to be tempted by the Devil." In this way the verbs were altered to the third person when they became textualized.[232]

And what of the figure of the "Devil"? Is it to be considered mythological, unreal, a superstitious remnant from a primitive phase of human development?[233] To our day and age it would appear so. Part of our age's judgment in the matter is the pervasive materialist conviction that there is no such thing as the world of the spirit. So not only devils and angels are nonexistent but God himself. Most of the historical Jesus questers operate within a materialist mode of modern historiography. They consciously bracket out the world of the spirit in their investigations.[234] There seems to be an inherent difficulty with such a stance when the object of their investigation is so thoroughly embedded in a world that understood the material world as only part of a much larger, spiritual reality. But what then are they left with? They can only end up with a rather distorted, diluted, and pretty bland view of the reality they purport to illuminate.

There is growing material evidence for the reality of this world of the spirit, this world beyond us. One such body of evidence is the encounters of those who have undergone near death experiences.[235] Another is the result of the discoveries by physics of the constants that describe the universe and how it functions. These constants all have one thing in common: they are exactly the values that are capable of producing life.[236] The earlier physics made the universe into a mechanical, clock-like thing, and totally random. Life was but a chance phenomenon coming about by crude, irrational, material forces randomly interacting over billions of years. After Copernicus and especially Darwin, the universe was no longer regarded as created by a loving God for humanity. It became a "disenchanted world." Humanity was but a sideshow, a peculiar accident, in the boondocks of the universe. But modern physics has discovered that the universe is not random. The universe, over billions of years, seemed to be directed toward the goal of producing human life.[237] Furthermore, our own planet earth exhibits many unique characteristics that cannot be attributed to chance since they are so numerous.[238] Our universe and our world manifest a design, ergo there must be a Designer, and if there is a Designer, there is a world of the spirit quite beyond the material universe.

Freud was the other great enemy of religion and faith. He designed psychoanalysis to replace religion and worked at producing a complete scientific account of mental life.[239] He insisted religion and faith were mental disorders. The latter half of the twentieth century has totally disproven his, what we now can call, unscientific prejudice. Those who are most mentally healthy are people of faith.[240] This paragraph from Patrick Glynn summarizes the present state of the relationship between faith and reason:

> The very logic of human inquiry is compelling a rediscovery of the realm of the spirit, of God and the soul. This process has both a positive and a negative thrust. In the first place, we see the mounting evidence for the existence of a spiritual dimension or reality. Along with this new evidence has come a growing recognition of the severe limitations of science and reason as tools for understanding the ultimate truths. This recognition has been central to the experience of twentieth-century philosophy, politics, and science itself. A generation and more ago, secular thinkers were filled with faith in reason and convinced that the scientific worldview was destined to replace the religious one. Modern thinkers predicted the "disenchantment of the world"—the disappearance of God from the human horizon. What our century has experienced instead is a disenchantment with reason, the collapse of the Enlightenment's secular and rational faith. Perhaps not entirely coincidentally, God is reemerging in Western intellectual life at the very moment when reason appears to have hit the end of the road.[241]

So what of the appearance of the Devil in the temptation story as a realizable entity? The word for "Devil" appears only in the New Testament, whereas "Satan" appears in the books of 1 Chronicles, Job, and Zechariah—that is, in post-exilic writings and throughout the New Testament. The story emphasizes that evil has a personal dimension. There are devils and evil spirits that can possess a person. I'm reminded of a sermon I heard when I was studying in Germany in the early 1960s. The preacher was a professor of the theological faculty where I was studying. He described his experience during the Third Reich, how the sense of evil was palpable as he walked the streets.[242] Evil is not just a description of some behavior. It has a personal quality that can possess a person and even a society and government. We need only think of the horrors of Nazism and Communism. And these possessions by evil arise out of a denial of God, a rebellion against God, a repudiation of God. The Devil (personal evil) is present where God is driven away.

The story of the temptation has its parallel in the wilderness wanderings of Israel. As Israel was forty years in the wilderness being tested by God (Deut 8:2), so Jesus is there for forty days being tested—however, not by God but by the devil (Matt 4:1). The same word, πειράζω (*peiradzō*), is used in both passages. Jesus here then is recapitulating Israel's story and implies that a new exodus is enacted in his life and ministry. This is the dawn of the new age, the entry into the new promised land, for which Jesus is preparing the way.[243]

The wilderness was thought to be the dwelling place of demons, so Jesus is led right into the heart of Satan's domain. Both Matthew and Luke emphasize that he fasted, so the first temptation has to do with satisfying hunger. In quoting Deut 8:1 against the Devil, Jesus recalls that God fed the Israelites with the miraculous manna, which underscores the point that the faithful are called to trust in God who provides for his people's need and to realize that humans are not just physical matter but spiritual beings whose existence consists of a relationship with their creator. But the Israelites did not pass the test. They gave into their anxieties and fears, which led them obliquely to accuse God by audaciously accusing Moses of bringing them into the wilderness to kill them (Exod 17:3, Num 16:13). They, in effect, indirectly accuse God of deviltry!

In his hunger Jesus directly identifies with the people of Israel in his day as he did in his baptism. He shares their experience of hunger and their hand-to-mouth existence. With full integrity he can exhort his contemporaries not to be anxious (Matt 6:25–34, Luke 12:22–29).[244] The hand-to-mouth existence and threat of starvation under which the average peasant had to live created the anxiety about hunger holding the people in thrall.

This thralldom was coupled with the sense that, though living in the land, they were still in exile, in the desert as it were, living under the thumb of the Roman occupation, its taxes, and its frequent denigration of Israel's faith and culture.[245] Shouldn't the Messiah give bread to the people as Moses seemed to have done in the wilderness? The great picture of the messianic age was that of a banquet (Isa 25:6–8, Matt 8:11). Trusting fully in God as a Father who cares for his people, Jesus refuses to reject standing with the people but simultaneously rebuffs the lure to be a "Bread King" (John 6:15)—that is, allow the good to commandeer the place of the best.[246]

The real issue for his contemporaries was a spiritual one. Physical needs were not the first priority, which if they were would divest his people of their dignity.[247] There is lack of "bread" because in a society where the social idea of "limited good"[248] reigned, everyone sought to guard and protect what he or she had. So Jesus called on his people to "give, and it will be given to you; good measure, pressed down, shaken together, running over, will be put into your lap. For the measure you give will be the measure you get back" (Luke 6:38). His parables of the rich fool and the rich man and Lazarus vividly portrayed the value of sharing and in this way transgressed the socially constructed conviction of limited good. The elimination of anxiety lay in the power and hands of the people. Jesus, by standing with the people and being dependent on their hospitality, embodied the liberation of the people by setting them free from the prison of crippling social mores. Jesus did not want the people to be dependent on him but to become conscious of the power residing in themselves that would be liberated by entering the kingdom and trusting in God.

So his was not just some kind of social justice movement. The basis for the transformation of the people lay in a transcendent reality, the gracious God to whom they boasted allegiance. He was not a far-off God, but his compassion embraced them. Throughout the Old Testament the writers proclaim the depth of God's mercy and compassion for his people.[249] Jesus then carries that forth in his ministry, not by becoming their "Bread King" but by calling people together to table where food was shared and sinners embraced, by healing, and by liberating the demon-possessed.

The second temptation occurs in the "Holy City," Jerusalem. It arises out of Jesus' answer to the first temptation. The Devil now argues, well, if that's the case and your trust in God is so complete, throw yourself off the pinnacle of the Temple[250] because, as the Scripture itself says, his angels will save you. What a spectacular show of faith and trust it would be to the crowds that constantly flocked in and around the Temple. Jesus could obviously then win thousands over to his cause in one fell swoop! He cleverly elides the charge that the angels are there to "keep you in all your ways"—that is, to walk faithfully with God by obedience to Torah. Jesus answers with the words of Deut 6:16, "You shall not put the Lord your God to the test, as you tested him at Massah." ("*Massah*" means testing.) The incident referred to is recounted in Exod 17:1–7. The words that follow in verse 17 coordinate with the words the Devil has left out from his quotation of Ps 91, "You shall diligently keep the commandments of the Lord your God, and his testimonies, and his statutes, which he has commanded you." Jesus directed his life toward doing God's will, not following his own whims.[251] God does not call upon a person to test him but to trust in him. Jesus himself is represented as constantly being tested (Matt 16:1, 22:18, Mark 8:11, 10:2, 12:15, Luke 10:25, 11:16, John 8:6). Jesus will not "force God's hand by taking short cuts to success."[252] But he refuses to give a sign (Matt 12:39, 16:4), except for the "sign of Jonah."

In the third temptation, the Devil presents himself as the ruler of this world (John 12:31, 16:11, 2 Cor 4:4, 1 John 5:19).[253] In his ministry and especially his exorcisms, Jesus understands himself as "binding the strong man" (as Matt 12:29 called Satan in this context) so that he may be plundered of his rule. Satan or the Devil as ruler of this world is an apocalyptic conception. It does not mean that God is not in control—he remains sovereign—but he allows the Devil to have dominion for a time.[254] The temptation is to acknowledge the Devil's rule and dominion in this world and by doing so serve his purposes, which is to keep the world bound in his reign and authority and totally undermine the reign of God and his purpose to free people from the power of this evil one.[255] This is basically a political notion: to simply have power over people and treat them as you will. God's kingdom could not be established by placing it under the ultimate aegis of the Devil, which is what he is suggesting. To make God, his kingdom, and his purposes subject to the evil one would be the ultimate victory of sin, death, and hell. But God must reign.[256] Jesus will not seek God's ends by means alien to God's nature.[257] God's people were in thrall to the Roman Empire. So there is the suggestion here that Rome is equated with the Devil's dominion.[258] The temptation then involves the political defeat of Rome and assuming its authority as a quick fix to the people's oppression. The people had been progressively succumbing to this temptation, which resulted in the tragic war with Rome.[259] The worship of political power and revolutionary force is the real idolatry, regardless of how "realistic and practical" the policies might seem.[260]

Jesus rejects that way altogether. He clearly sees that revolution would lead to utter destruction. There was another way to go forward. God must reign individually in the lives of his people. The people had to see that the kingdom was much broader than they ever expected. If they could understand that, they could more easily give up on rebellious ideologies and find it a divine pleasure to "go the extra mile" (Matt 5:41).[261] Jesus' ministry was the defeat of Satan one person at a time, thereby changing the heart of the nation. To throw off the Roman yoke could seem an achievable goal. The Maccabees had accomplished it against what seemed to have been overwhelming odds.[262] Jesus here chooses the way of the kingdom and subsequently proclaims that the reality of God's kingdom is now among the people and true victory lay in accepting it. By accepting it, Israel would be opting for mercy and kindness and extending that grace to sinners and even to the hated Romans. In this way he would wrest worldly dominion from the Devil's power.[263]

Again, Jesus quotes Scripture from Deuteronomy (6:13). The context of this passage is the warning not to serve other gods and so invite God's wrath, which would destroy them. Israel had already done so in the creating and worshipping of the molten calf (Exod 32:10). God would have destroyed them had it not been for Moses's mediation and intercession. Jesus remains faithful to God and his will that he go the way of the cross as his beloved son (Mark 14:34, Matt 26:29, Luke 22:42). He is like a new Moses who becomes the mediator interposing himself between the world and the wrath of God.

In the context of the political realities of the first century, the only way forward was to eschew political or military means. The path of violence would lead not to God's kingdom but rather to destruction. To choose that path would be worshipping what was not God.[264] To worship God meant now to enter the womb of his mercy, and by that means God would establish his kingdom. John's portrayal of Jesus at his trial is an exact commentary on this scene: "My kingdom is not of this world" (John 18:36).

The three temptations attack Jesus at his greatest strengths: his compassion for his people, his faith in God as his Father, and his commitment to spread the kingdom. In each case he turns back the temptation not with some superhuman strength or ability but with a word of Scripture—something anyone could do. In each case he asserts his humanity, though the Devil questions his filial relationship with God. He is the new Adam who overcomes the diabolical temptation and sets the path forward on the foundation of God's word. He reveals that his consciousness is embedded in Israel's Scriptures, particularly their teaching about the nature of Israel's God. Each quotation reveals too that he understood himself as recapitulating Israel's own history and thereby stood in Israel's stead before God. He places himself under the authority of God's will as it was revealed in Scriptures. Yes, he is Son of God but also a son of Israel. His role is to worship and serve God alone. He is the Servant of the Lord.[265]

Mark's account is extremely brief, one could almost say a notation on the temptation. The testing is represented as lasting the forty days, and there is no reference to fasting or hunger. The angels are represented as providing continuous support to him throughout the whole time, much as they supported Elijah.[266] So the ministry of Jesus is to be understood as carrying on the decisive struggle with the powers of evil. The temptation is the opening fray.

In his brief account Mark adds that Jesus was "with the wild beasts" (1:13). In the Old Testament "beasts" are frequently a metaphor for the Gentile nations (Ezek 17:23, Dan 7, Isa 5:24–30). In Ezek 17:23 the nations, represented as all kinds of animals, will find shelter in the restored royal Davidic messianic kingdom, represented as a flourishing branch (see Jer 23:5–6, Zech 3:8) set out on a lofty mountain (i.e., Mount Zion, Mic 4:1). The messianic age is envisioned as a time of harmony in the creation when animals will be tame (Isa 11:6–8, Hos 2:18). Ps 91:11–13 is particularly suggestive here. The reference to angels is also present in the Matthean and Lucan versions of the narrative coupling the dominion over beasts with the service of angels. Jesus has reversed Adam's defeat by Satan and begun the restoration of paradisial conditions.[267]

SUMMARY AND ANALYSIS

The Birth of Jesus

The commonalities of the birth narratives point to an underlying historical substrate: Jesus' conception was outside of marriage to a virgin named Mary. Joseph, though not the father, accepted him as his own. The birth occurs before Mary and Joseph are married, and it occurs in Bethlehem. The couple finally settles in Nazareth with their child.

Assertions to the contrary, Jesus was never regarded as illegitimate, and the criticisms and epithets hurled at him by his provocateurs only point to his equal social status with them and that they thought he was acting contrary to it by consorting with social inferiors.

He was, however, known as a Davidic descendant, which would ostensibly contradict the assertion of a virgin birth by asserting Joseph was his biological father. Both of these designations, virgin born and of Davidic descent, go back to very early traditions. But they need not be understood as contradictory. The one asserts that Jesus cannot be understood apart from God and the other that he fulfills the divine promise of God's teleological intention for Israel's restoration by a scion of David who is God's adopted son.²⁶⁸ So divine sonship and virgin birth coalesce in the concept of the incarnation of the logos in John 1:14 by which the pre-existent Son takes upon himself human nature.

However, the incarnation did not work itself out purely on a theological, mental, or cerebral level. It worked itself out from the reality of the life, teaching, and ministry of Jesus himself and was clinched by his bodily resurrection. It is clear that he saw the kingdom of God, a transcendent reality, as present in his activity. In the very earthly events of eating and drinking, casting out demons, restoring health to suffering people, enjoying the hospitality of poor peasants, putting people before legal requirements, and meeting the often sneering and sniping carping of his critics with equanimity, the mighty, divine kingdom was active and present. Through the works of this Galilean itinerant preacher from a nowhere town, divinity was present, sealed by the reality of his resurrection. In him heaven and earth met.

In this way the reality of his life, the peculiar events of his birth, and his noble ancestry fused and made possible an answer to the question "Who is this?" (Mark 4:41, John 8:25). God has incarnated himself in our human world. Jesus is the Son of the Father in the deepest sense of that word. In the same way he is only man but the true man because he makes no claim to divinity and being above others, lives in acceptance of being only a human, and is as a servant who is utterly dependent on his Father-God.

In surveying in some detail Robinson's daring question about Jesus' self-understanding, I find a convergence between his investigation and my basing that self-understanding on the Christ Hymn of Philippians 2. He is, as Robinson says, totally one with the Father as he was with humanity. No mere man and no heavenly visitant. His life as "Son" is devoid of anything that could be called divinity. He is as totally only human as any other person with no extraordinary "divine" powers. What he achieves is based only on his total faith—dependence on the Father who has called him "Son" (Mark 1:11) and whom he now can call his "Abba."

Jesus' Baptism

The report of Jesus' baptism has the character of a theophany: it is a manifestation of the divinity. The dove imagery evokes the spirit hovering over the chaos waters at the creation, which suggests that here God is initiating a new creation in the one whom he names as his "beloved son." Imagery at the time of theophanies is recorded frequently in the Scriptures: Micaiah ben Imlah's vision of YHWH enthroned (1 Kgs 22:1–23), Isaiah's vision of the hem of YHWH's robe filling the Temple (Isa 6:1–3), Elijah's fiery chariot and its horses (2 Kgs 2:11), Ezekiel's living creatures and the wheels moving under the spirit's direction (Ezk 1:4–28), John's vision of the resurrected Lord with a face shining like the sun, eyes of flame with a two-edged sword emanating from his mouth standing among lampstands (Rev 1:13–16). These may all be subjective descriptions, but the objectivity of the experiences is not to be gainsaid.

Jesus, like these biblical prophets, would have described his call experience, which was a profound reordering of his existence. He no longer was a *tektōn*[269] but now stood in a filial relationship with God and spoke as no other, not as God's intermediary like a prophet but with a direct "I say to you . . ."[270]

Secondarily, Jesus' baptism meant his identification with sinful Israel, and so it was the sinful and marginalized in Israel (as opposed to the "righteous," Mark 2:17) with whom Jesus consorted and included in the kingdom of God. His baptism was therefore not a personal confession of sin. He probably continued to baptize those whom he had invited into and who had accepted the kingdom. But it is difficult to imagine how that took place given that he was not always near water. However, the Gospels do place Jesus often in watery contexts (e.g., Mark 4:1 and frequently in Capernaum, which was a coastal village on the Sea of Galilee).

Finally, that Jesus is called "beloved son" foreshadows his ultimate humiliation as a sacrifice of his Father. Jesus' consciousness of that fate is evident in his awareness that he has a "cup" to drink, a metaphor made explicit in the predictions of his passion (Mark 8:31, 9:31, 10:33–34).

Jesus and John

It appears that Jesus continued as a disciple of John until he launched out on his own, perhaps when John was arrested. The commonalities between their two ministries suggest a close relationship between the two and Jesus remaining with him for a time. It was during this time with John that the ultimate implication of his baptismal experience would have fully developed and matured in his mind (especially under the pressure of the "mightier one" predicted by John): his self-understanding as "son" and the contours of the kingdom of God. The two are interrelated: the total gratuitousness of God in accepting him as his "beloved" and the gratuitous opening up of the kingdom to all who would accept his loving reign and rule. So God's kingdom was present in his beloved one who would now reach out to the nation to bring the people by his word and deed into the presence of the kingdom.

That understanding of the kingdom then contributed to the form of his ministry: God's gratuitous favor meant to bring the kingdom to the nation, in word and deed, without cost by his beloved son. The people would then also reciprocate and extend hospitality without cost.[271] But the beloved son's service would not end there. He would pay the ultimate cost of service by laying down his life for the sins of the people. The future aspect of the kingdom was also already present in the formation of his inner circle of twelve disciples who would sit on twelve thrones (Matt 19:28) in the judgment to come. This kingdom was universal, which Jesus emphasized by including Gentiles in his kingdom movement, although he seemed to have been forced to that stance by the impressive faith of Gentiles.

It appears that Jesus continued to baptize, and it is not unthinkable that baptism confirmed and constituted the fullness of entry into the kingdom, but it may not have had the central aspect that it had in John's practice. That it had secondary importance may be reflected in Jesus declaring that none was greater than John but the least in the kingdom was greater than him.

The question of John asking if Jesus were the "coming" one (Matt 11:3, Luke 7:19) confirms that John, at least initially, understood Jesus as fulfilling that role. The appellation resonates with Ps 118, which celebrates the Davidic messiah and the eschatological victory of God and Israel's restoration. That Jesus didn't seem to be fulfilling the expectations related to the "coming one" elicited John's query. Jesus answers in terms of the Isaianic prophecies of restoration that he was pursuing in his ministry of healing. This answer then asserted the proleptic presence of the kingdom. His proclamation of the kingdom also was not a mere promise of restoration, but like the ancient prophets, he pronounced judgment. So Jesus announced the coming of the kingdom, its presence already in his activity, and judgment of those who rejected it. The day of salvation was a "now," for the crisis of the kingdom was at the door.[272] One had better accept entry into the kingdom, for it will soon be too late. The perilousness of the time had not only an eschatological aspect but also a historical one: the pursuance of revolution and violence would lead to destruction of the nation. Jesus' proclamation in word and deed was a "winnowing" of the nation with a historical as well as an eschatological reference. As the people accepted or rejected the kingdom, the chaff was divided from the wheat.

The overwhelming characteristic, however, of Jesus' ministry in contrast to John's was the joy of entering the kingdom since he stressed the redemptive and rescuing dimensions of the kingdom. But to reject the saving word turns it into a word of death.[273] The nation stood at a juncture: change mind and heart or be swept away. Jesus' answer to John's statement "And blessed is he who takes no offense at me" (Matt 11:6) almost makes of him an example of those who do not accept Jesus as the "coming one" (i.e., the promised Messiah) and will have no share in the kingdom. Jesus as "the mightier and greater one" is also subtly hiding behind the parallelism of Matt 11:11.

John is identified as the returning Elijah. Jesus further understood John as the turning of the age: he ends the first period of Israel's history and the time of the revelation found in the Scriptures. Jesus, however, also finds a coordination between himself and John in the little parable he tells of the children in the marketplace. Both he and John are outliers: John is criticized as having a demon because he does not conform to social norms, and Jesus in his association with sinners also dishonors normal society. John proclaimed the fiery judgment, and now with the proclamation of Jesus the new age begins: the exile is ending, and the nation is welcomed in a joyous homecoming as guests to sit with Jesus in the intimacy of common meals. The kingdom is ushered in not by violence but by open, accepting, and unbrokered commensality. Jesus further identifies himself with wisdom in whose presence the counter order of the kingdom is established, requiring that one acquires a child-like stance.

The Temptation

The connection between the baptismal narrative and the temptation narrative points to the historicity of the latter. The fact that the narrative is easily converted from the third to the first person shows that Jesus could well have told the story to his disciples and others, no doubt as a lesson in how to overcome temptations as well as to underscore his role as the one who is binding "the strong man" (Mark 3:27). The disciples then continue this work of Jesus by their exorcisms (Mark 6:12). Satan's realm is under siege and is in the process of being conquered.

Commentators like to think of the encounter as an inner, spiritual struggle of Jesus or that the question of internal/external experience is simply unimportant.[274] Is evil real and personal or not? Can it take over persons, or is it just some psychological phenomenon arising from a person's inner struggle? The answer I have come to is that evil is an objective reality that encounters our world and leads it astray. It must be subdued, subjected, and bound. With that subjection Jesus is inaugurating the dawning of a new age, and we are on the verge of entering that new, promised land, where God is "all in all" (1 Cor 15:28).

Jesus is reversing the failures of Israel's previous story. He overcomes temptation in the wilderness to which ancient Israel had succumbed. His hunger is satisfied there, but not as a result of complaint but as faithfulness to, and trusting of, his Father-God. He is enacting a new exodus and preparing its way.

His hunger is an identification with his anxiety-ridden people, who fret over their hand-to-mouth existence. The first priority of Israel is to trust in their Father-God. Israel is not to emulate the nations, for she is a spiritual entity whose God "fashions the hearts of [the nations]" (Ps 33:15) and guides history. Israel's Scriptures emphasize over and over again their God's faithfulness. So trusting God's faithfulness is the chief challenge for contemporary Israel. When that is in place, all else will be in its proper order. The perception of limited good will be overcome, and people will joyfully share with their neighbors. Transformation of the heart is required and to see herself as a transcendent reality borne on the hands of a gracious God (Isa 49:16). So not testing God but trusting him is Jesus' call to Israel, a call that he embodies in overcoming the temptation to make bread of stones. The way forward was not world dominion promised by apocalyptic revolutionaries but entering the kingdom—that is, submitting rather to God's dominion, a dominion already among them in the words, deeds, and fellowship of Jesus. The temptation narrative reveals that the fantasy of driving Rome out was a satanic enticement.

Jesus, in each stage of his temptation, counteracts them with references to the Torah. If the nation would be true to its Torah, then life would ensue (Deut 30:19). So Jesus can, with comprehensive integrity, pronounce that "not one iota or stroke would pass from the law" (Matt 5:18).

In the temptation, the character of Jesus is revealed: he places himself under the will of God as revealed in Torah, so he shows himself to be a faithful "son of Israel" and the true "beloved son" who will take upon himself the sins of the nation, which will be restored through him. Mark's little narrative of the temptation rounds out its meaning by emphasizing Jesus as reversing Adam's defeat and restoring the order of paradise.

2

The Tantalizing Teacher

Biographical Pronouncement Stories

"When the day-spring on high shall dawn upon
us to guide our feet in the way of peace."

Rudolf Bultmann divides the sayings of Jesus into five categories, which seems like a convenient way to classify them: pronouncement stories/apothegms, wisdom, prophetic and apocalyptic sayings, legal sayings, and "I" sayings.[275] I will follow his list of pronouncement stories and his taxonomy of these categories and designations in the following analysis.[276]

DEFINITION: PRONOUNCEMENT STORIES/APOTHEGMS

An "apothegm" or pronouncement story is a saying enclosed in a brief narrative or description of the situation in which it was uttered.[277] Some were occasioned by a controversy with Jesus' detractors or by questions put to Jesus. However, it is not impossible that the primitive church or evangelists could create sayings of Jesus, especially if emitted by an inspired preacher.

But I shall make that determination in each individual case. Overall, Jesus' life and ministry were of a controversial sort, which you have experienced in the second volume of my series, concentrating on the parables. One would therefore expect his sayings to be remembered fairly accurately because of the pointedness of their content and their sharp edginess.

Contra the form critics that credit their existence to their utility in the life of the earliest church, I suggest that their utility consisted of the deep impression they made on the hearts of these early believers, which elicited their faith and then showed the way of being faithful to the trust they placed in Jesus as Lord and Savior.[278]

PHARISEES IN THE GALILEE

In many of the controversies that are part of the setting of many an apothegm, the Pharisees are represented as Jesus' challengers and provocateurs. However, there is strong evidence that there were practically no Pharisees in the Galilee during Jesus' lifetime. A generation later, when the great Pharisaic master Yohanan ben Zakkai lived there for eighteen years, only two cases were brought to him for decision; he reportedly cursed the country for hating the Law. "Galilee, Galilee, thou hatest the Torah; hence wilt thou fall into the hands of robbers!"[279] The story may be a legend since the curse looks like a prophesy *ex eventu* made after the destruction of the war. However, the legend shows that the Pharisees remembered Galilee before AD 70 as a land where they had few followers. More important is the evidence of Josephus. It is clear from his *War* II (569–646) and even more from his *Life* (38–39) that as late as AD 66 the Pharisees might have been respected in Galilee for their legal knowledge, but the implication is that they were a rare presence there since they had to be sent from Jerusalem to the Galilee.[280] Thus the synoptic picture of a Galilee with Pharisees ever present and challenging Jesus is an anachronism. In John's Gospel the Pharisees are present only in Jerusalem, and Jesus goes to Galilee to get out of their reach (4:1–3).[281]

So I must conclude that the Pharisees are in many cases retrojected by the evangelists into the stories about Jesus and represent the evangelists' time and place in their controversies with the Judaism of their day, when the successors of the Pharisees were in the process of seizing leadership within the postwar Jewish communities. However, it is not impossible that some Pharisees made their way to the Galilee and encountered Jesus.

In this chapter I will analyze the so-called biographical pronouncement stories, those sayings of Jesus set in a brief narrative framework that describe a setting in his life and ministry. Two of the narratives described in chapter 3 can also fit under this category: the rival exorcist (Mark 9:38–40) and the inhospitable Samaritans (Luke 9:51–56).

THE BIOGRAPHICAL PRONOUNCEMENT STORIES

The Calling of Disciples (Mark 1:16–20, 2:14, Matt 4:18–22, 9:9, Luke 5:1–11, 27–28)

Bultmann characterizes these stories along with the call of Levi in Mark 2:14 as "ideal scenes" and not historical reports because the emphasis is on the absolute surrender to the call of Jesus, which reveals a fundamental trait of discipleship.[282] He even suggests that the stories characterizing these early disciples as fishermen grew out of the metaphor of depicting them as "fishers of men." This is highly unlikely. They were fishermen (Mark 3:7, Luke 5:1–11, John 21:1–14). These stories of the call of the first four disciples are simply highly contracted, deemphasizing any psychological motivations to stress Jesus' exalted status and the consequent immediate response (cf., Isa 6:1–10). There is no explanation of why these particular men were called or any previous knowledge they had of Jesus. They simply responded with unconditional obedience, left the ties that bound them to family, and abandoned their means of livelihood (cf., Mark 10:28).

So the core of the report is historical. Jesus is depicted as frequently present along the shores of the Sea of Galilee,[283] and he made Capernaum, a lively fishing village on the northwest corner of the Sea of Galilee, a base of his activity (Matt 4:13).[284] The more involved and detailed story in Luke 5:1–11 may represent the actual details of the historical call. The story in this form gives some psychological reasoning for the evangelists' response to Jesus and why he had so impressed them. It also indicates that Peter had known Jesus for some time.

Peter's reaction to the great shoal of fish is a result of the fact that Jesus, this uninitiated, nonfisherman perceived fish in such quantity and at such an unlikely hour that it must have meant he was, minimally, a prophet who was in intimate contact with the divine. For Peter this is a numinous experience like that of Isaiah of old when heaven opened to him and he beheld the King of the Universe. Isaiah's immediate sense was a recognition of his sinfulness before the Holy One of Israel.[285] So Peter's reaction here has to do with being confronted with the impingement of the divine into his everyday life, which is made clear by the fact that he and all those with him were amazed by the great catch of fish (vs 9).[286] He has experienced God's undeserved favor, which leads to his confession and repentance, like the Prodigal

Son whose repentance proceeded after his conversion to his father's love. He can only then address Jesus as "Lord" (vs 8)—that is, he is the one who has mediated this divine acceptance and favor.[287] This may well have been the experience of all the little people who responded to the call of Jesus to enter the kingdom, particularly those who were healed or encountered in him forgiveness and acceptance by the God of Israel.[288]

James and John the sons of Zebedee according to vs 10 shared Peter's experience and are called his partners, although Mark 1:19 might imply they had their own fishing business and were partners with their father. Luke's tradition may have been better informed. Mark's version then looks like a summary of the more detailed Lucan version.

The captivating and provocative mandate that Jesus would make them "fishers of men"[289] calls them, extending his own metaphor, to join him in catching others out of the sea of the present tangle of conflicting factions and rebellious hostilities in which the nation was swimming and into the lifeboat of the eschatological life of the age to come. The metaphor is so provocative because it was normally used in a very pejorative sense.[290] Implied in the phrase is also the insinuation that those not caught by the kingdom would be subject to judgment. The metaphor seems like a reversal of Jer 16:16, where God uses the nations to capture his people and repay them for their idolatrous iniquity. At any rate, Peter, James, and John will now enter a new vocation with Jesus. The roles are reversed: the nonprofessional fisherman Jesus becomes the teacher, and the former fishing experts become disciples.

The story of the call of Levi is compellingly anchored in history. Just northeast of Capernaum there would have been a tollbooth between the Galilean tetrarchy of Herod Antipas and Gaulanitis, the tetrarchy of his brother Phillip. Just beyond this frontier lay Bethsaida, which Phillip wanted to develop into a Hellenistic city. He had renamed it Bethsaida Julias in honor of Augustus's daughter Julia.[291] However, Emil Scheurer avers it remained little more than a large village.[292] No doubt Phillip would have used the tolls collected at this border crossing to achieve his ambitions for enhancing Bethsaida Julias. Levi's call follows the pattern of Mark in his call narratives (1:16–20, 2:14): Levi responds immediately without any of the psychological preparation that Luke provided in the story of the call of Peter. We can well imagine, however, because Jesus was constantly on the move visiting several villages a day, that he crossed this border many times, particularly because Antipas was after him (Luke 13:31). He would have been beyond Antipas's reach in Phillip's territory. So Jesus would have become acquainted with Levi over time and would have had extended conversations with him.[293]

But Levi was not included in the twelve (Mark 3:16–19), although a "James the son of Alphaeus" is mentioned in the list. Is this the same Alphaeus who is said to be the father of Levi (Mark 2:14)? In that case James and Levi were brothers. But why would Mark refer to Levi's call even though he was not included in the twelve? Some manuscript authorities read "James" in Mark 2:14, which would solve the apparent discrepancy.[294] The tradition handed down to Mark could well have been the whole of 2:14–17, which then would naturally make the antecedent of "his house" (vs 15) Levi himself.

This pericope was important to Mark because it contained the pronouncement of Jesus that he had come to call not the righteous but sinners. Levi obviously was a "sinner" in the sight of the people because of his vocation. The tax collectors of all sorts had a bad reputation as a result of their known dishonesty and shaking down of the population in the process of collecting taxes. Although Levi in his collection of the toll as people crossed the border into Phillip's realm was serving not a heathen master, he still would have been lumped together with such folk. Of course, they also consorted with all kinds of people including Gentiles, which rendered them unclean. Levi, and especially his, no doubt, unkosher house, was a perfect example of one of those sinners whom Jesus had come to call.[295]

It is plain to see that not everyone whom Jesus "called" was made the member of the inner circle of the twelve. Luke 10:1 mentions seventy others who were sent out in pairs to go ahead of him into the villages and towns. This reference is part of the Lucan special material and so cannot claim multiple attestation. But it is not inconceivable that Jesus had various circles of followers.[296] Levi may have been included in the seventy. Matthew solves this conundrum by changing Levi's name to "Matthew" in his version of the call (Matt 9:9), which name appears in the list of the twelve (Matt 10:3).

Excursus: The Meaning of the Expression "Son of Man" in the Synoptic Gospels[297]

Jesus' use of "the son of man" appears in a variety of contexts in the Gospels and plays a conspicuous role in the mouth of Jesus. The peculiarity of this nomenclature, however, is its total absence in Christian writing and thinking outside of the gospels. In the following I will spend some time investigating the history and nature of this figure to discern what Jesus meant by bringing the term into play in his ministry. My methodology is to discern its meaning from the contexts in which it appears, rather than trying to determine beforehand its precise meaning.

The usage of Jesus arranges itself into three classes:[298] (1) texts where the "son of man" is depicted as coming, that is, the "parousia sayings";[299] (2) texts where the "son of man" is depicted as having to suffer and subsequently to be raised, that is, the "suffering and resurrection sayings"; and (3) texts where the term is construed with the earthly activity of Jesus, that is, the "present activity" sayings.[300] The table in note 300 indicates that the locution, "son of man," occurs across all of the Gospel sources—Mark, the Matthean and Lucan special material,[301] and Q[302]—and includes all three classes (except class 2 in Q, which is to be expected since Q does not contain a passion narrative). Matthew and Luke have utilized all of the Marcan references. This all strongly suggests that the phrase was used by Jesus in the three ways outlined here.[303]

The pressing question is, however, what did he mean by it? Frequently the phrase is but a paraphrastic form of "I."[304] So one could ask when "son of man" occurs whether it might have replaced an earlier "I" or even vice versa. Furthermore, there is no evidence that the messiah and son of man were equated in contemporary Judaism, which equation the early church evidently made (John 12:31–35).[305] The conclusion presses itself on us: the "son of man" was a distinctive usage of Jesus that he employed as a self-designation. The claim that here we meet the authentic voice of Jesus is remarkably strong.

The figure of the "son of man" occurs in Dan 7 (as part of a series of visions, chapters 7–12), a text that arose during the persecutions of Israel under the Syrian king Antiochus IV Epiphanes.[306] In this vision there is a conflict between chaotic forces, portrayed as terrifying beasts that emerge from the "deep," and God, the King. These beasts represent kingdoms that seek hegemony over all the earth. The fourth beast and its eleventh horn "speaking great things" (meaning Antiochus Epiphanes, by which name he claimed to be the manifestation of Zeus, i.e., a "god") are conquered by the "Ancient of Days." The scene concludes with one like a "son of man" who is given "dominion and glory and kingdom, that all peoples, nations, and languages should serve him." His dominion is declared to be an "everlasting dominion, which shall not pass away, and one that shall not be destroyed" (Dan 7:14). In the explanation that follows the vision, the "son of man" is identified with the "saints of the Most High" (Dan 7:27, i.e., Israel) to whom the "everlasting" kingdom of God is given (see Dan 2:44, 3:29, 4:1–3). They are the ones who remained faithful to the Torah in time of persecution.[307] Since the identification is not explicit, it may be better to say rather that the "son of man" represents these "saints." So here the "son of man" appears to have a transcendent quality while at the same time being associated with the people of God—that is, the figure has both divine and human characteristics. Correspondingly, Jesus never associated his disciples with a corporate idea of the son of man, even though they were decisively attached to him (e.g., Luke 22:28–30).[308]

The "son of man" figure is further developed in Enoch 37–71,[309] where, in a series of visions, a transcendent figure called "the righteous one," "the chosen one," "the anointed one," and the "son of man" works on behalf of "the chosen" and as a judge of those who antagonize them. The "Similitudes" (i.e., parables), as these chapters are called, draw on the imagery and language of Dan 7, Isa 11, 42, 49, 52–53, and Ps 2.[310] The writer has created a fusion of the figures of the "son of man," a Davidic, royal messiah, and Isaiah's "servant of the Lord." With that fusion the various characteristics of these figures are also combined: the royal figure who wreaks judgment on the rebellious hegemons of the world; the one who works justice for the lowly; and the one who is the exalted servant of God. The figure of wisdom also plays a part in the writer's understanding of his nature: he has a hidden preexistence (Prov 8) but is revealed to God's people (the writer of the Similitudes, however, never explicitly identifies the "son of man" with the figure of wisdom). This "mighty one" ultimately vindicates the people of God when he subdues and condemns the oppressors of the people.

The writer has consequently combined the heavenly enthronement of Dan 7 with the royal traditions of 2 Isaiah and their Davidic precursors in Isa 11 and Ps 2.[311] In this way the author of the Similitudes reveals to his audience that, though the son of man is hidden, they have a transcendent champion who prepares their vindication and salvation. Essential to their belief in him is that he will reveal himself and judge the mighty of the earth who have oppressed them.[312] Finally they will inherit eternal life in the presence of the son of man.

Near the end of the Similitudes Enoch is translated to heaven and welcomed as "the Son of Man born for righteousness" (71:14). Though the son of man is hidden from eternity, he takes historical form on earth in various times such as in Enoch, an exceptionally righteous man.[313]

There is a verbal link in Q[314] with the Similitudes that describes the final day of judgment when the son of man is seen "sitting on his throne of glory." In Matt 19:28 (parallel in Luke 22:39) Jesus speaks of the twelve sitting on thrones judging the twelve tribes in Israel. In the trial scene Jesus refers to the son of man sitting on "his throne of glory" (Matt 25:31).

The reflection in 2 Esd[315] on a salvific figure, "resembling a son of man," parallels the Similitudes. He is described as "the one whom the Most High has kept for many ages" (13:26). This writing uses the same language for the Messiah (7:28–29). In one scene, this figure executes divine judgment and destroys all those who oppose him. He finally gathers "the remnant," the righteous ones of Israel.

Second Baruch is another writer more or less contemporary with 2 Esd, in which the emperor of the fourth kingdom is judged and slain by "my anointed one" (i.e., Messiah), who is described as a transcendental figure.[316]

In summary, it can be concluded "son of man" was not everywhere understood as a contemporary title for the Messiah in the world of Jesus. Jesus could choose this rather neutral expression without fear that it would be open to misunderstanding. He could then fill it with whatever content he chose. The Similitudes show that the figure could be combined with other figures such as the suffering servant and even the Davidic messiah. So I conclude that Jesus could speak of a suffering son of man and that this suffering was written of him (Mark 9:12–13). To that he could even add messianic features such as being anointed to bring God's saving actions to the nation (Luke 4:17–20). In this way Jesus, as the son of man, could be his people's deliverer and advocate.[317] What Jesus understood himself to be by using this term can be ascertained from his words and practice as we investigate them in the Gospels.[318]

It is clear then how, in the passage under investigation, Jesus could identify with the coming end-time son of man and also apply the term to his earthly ministry and his suffering. He was taking up an easily malleable concept already used in some early Jewish eschatological understandings of the son of man such as we find in the Similitudes of Enoch, which included the suffering servant of Isa 53.

But was Jesus referring to another figure other than himself in the sayings where the son of man is depicted as the future coming one? In a saying such as Mark 8:38, "For if anyone in this sinful and adulterous generation is ashamed of me and of my words, the Son of man will also be ashamed of him when he comes in the glory of his Father with the holy angels," it can easily be asserted that here Jesus is thinking of another figure separate from himself who will judge people on the basis of how they have related to Jesus. Thus it can be said that minimally Jesus understood that there was a close connection between himself and the son of man. However, given his usage elsewhere, it is clear that this is an example of illeism.[319]

In Mark 14:61–62 "the Christ, the son of the Blessed" appears together with the "son of man." It looks like the Hebrew *paralellismus membrorum*— that is, the two elements are coordinated and parallel to one another.[320]

Jesus identified himself with the eschatological son of man because he understood that in him and in his activity the kingdom of God was already present, but its fullness would arrive imminently. This double aspect of the kingdom, both present and future, also determined this double aspect of the son of man, presently active in Jesus, who would return as the eschatological son of man.[321] The difficulty with ascribing the term to the church is explaining why the church would have used it and applied it to Jesus but then just as quickly dropped its use altogether. The simplest solution seems to be that the church never used the appellation "son of man," and it therefore originated with Jesus, who identified himself as the son of man.[322]

That the two concepts "son of man" and "kingdom of God" never occur simultaneously in the words of Jesus cannot be used against the authenticity of the "son of man" saying since Jesus' ethics and the kingdom of God never occur simultaneously either.

Modern ideas of a sharp distinction between the individual and the collective are irrelevant in ancient Judaism. So Jesus used the term "son of man" to mean both himself and the community of the new age that he led.[323] Jesus called on his generation to enter the kingdom of God, which meant to have a personal relationship with God as king. The kingdom then appears in the world as a people of God who are his agents. The consummation of the kingdom is, however, future. The Old Testament remnant in Isaiah became an eschatological concept: they were the nucleus of God's future people. The concept was further developed in Deutero-Isaiah in terms of the servant. This community was to be the divine agent for bringing about the final consummation of the kingdom.

This kingdom is also the community of obedience. Jesus' ethical call was another aspect of the kingdom and delineated how those in the kingdom were to guide their lives. His ethics were certainly a call to the whole nation, and those who would take up this "yoke of the kingdom" (Matt 11:29–30) would have then entered the kingdom in this way.[324] So eschatology, kingdom, community, son of man, and ethics are all woven together and of a piece.

Jesus avoided applying the title "messiah" to himself probably because he wanted to avoid the nationalistic and militaristic connotations attached to it. "Son of man" lay to hand, and he used it as a simple self-designation (as in Mark 14:60), as the final assurance of messiahship and vindication by God, but infused it also with the ideas of Isa 53 in expressing his approach to his own death (Mark 8:31).[325]

In his freedom to fill the concept of "son of man" with his own content, Jesus did not adopt any apocalyptic scenarios. His proclamation was that the kingdom was at the door and could appear at any time (Mark 13:33–37).[326]

The crux of how the "son of man" tradition is to be interpreted in relationship to Jesus centers on the passage Luke 12:8–9,[327] where the relationship between Jesus and the "son of man" surfaces immediately. The Matthean parallel reveals his understanding of the "son of man" as identical with Jesus, who simply understands it as a circumlocution for "I." The Marcan form is the original because it is the most difficult. At first blush it appears that Jesus and the "son of man" are two different figures. But Jesus says that when the son of man appears, it will be "in the glory of his Father." Paul's exhortation in 1 Thess 3:13 parallels the language of Mark here, "so that he may establish your hearts unblamable in holiness before our God and Father, at the coming of our Lord Jesus with all his saints," where Jesus and Father are coordinated.

But why would the church not have taken up the term in its own confession? It could have seemed unsuitable to express the church's complete understanding about Jesus, and the Gentile church may have found it a peculiar expression in Greek and also not befitting Jesus' dignity as Son of God.

In conclusion, Jesus used the term "son of man" sometimes to mean man in general but more commonly as a circumlocution for himself to express his understanding that he was in an intimate relationship with God.[328] The term coordinated with his understanding of the kingdom: that he was the "suffering servant" already present and active who embodied the nation and who would return when the kingdom broke in and achieve the ultimate salvation of Israel and the world.

The Cost of Discipleship (Luke 9:57–62, Matt 8:19–22, Q)

Matthew includes only the first two encounters with persons who want to follow Jesus and makes of Luke's indefinite "someone" a scribe and the second a disciple, whereas Luke refers only to "another." Luke obviously has maintained the original Q version referring to unspecified individuals.[329]

Jesus here underscores the reality of his itinerant ministry. Filial piety and loyalty to family were foundational to Jewish society. Indeed, the fourth commandment required absolute fidelity to one's household and to father and mother. But Jesus relativized the family and created a new family. In Mark 10:28–30 Jesus alludes to this new family that is created among those who have left family and livelihood and followed him. However, in vs 10 leaving a wife is not included in Jesus' enumeration. Evidently wives accompanied those who joined his itinerant ministry (cf., 1 Cor 9:5).[330]

The use of "son of man" could easily be taken as a circumlocution for "I" in this passage. However, Jesus is contrasting himself with the animals, and if he meant merely "I," why wouldn't he say that? The phrase is intentional. In Dan 7:3 and 13 there is a contrast between the "son of man" and the beasts. So Jesus chose the "son of man" locution quite deliberately to imply that he was that son of man who would come in the future and to contrast his present lowliness with his future glory. Ps 8 is even more pointed. In this psalm the "son of man" has been given glory and honor along with dominion over the beasts and the birds, but Jesus here asserts he does not have the shelter that the animals possess. (Itinerants in Jewish society were evidently suspect, Sir 36:26.)[331] Implied again is present lowliness as compared with future glory.[332] Also implied is that Jesus, as "son of man," possesses the highest of authority so that his call supersedes all other obligations.

In the second encounter Jesus calls upon a person to follow him, but the person asks for a delay so that he might bury his father. The burying of family members was an absolute obligation.[333] Jesus asserts that the kingdom admits of no delays, not even to fulfill one of the most sacred of familial obligations. Jesus perceived that the kingdom was "at the door" ready to break in at any moment, so to join in the proclamation of the kingdom was absolutely urgent. Not to respond now to the kingdom places one in jeopardy because once it has arrived, it will then be too late, and entrance to it will be denied (Luke 13:25). "The dead" who are to bury the dead are those who have no interests beyond daily life and its obligations.[334] They are, in effect, "dead" to the kingdom.

That same urgency is intensified in a call to a third person. The kingdom's call will not wait even to let someone return to take leave of those in his household. The demand of an immediate response to the kingdom is more rigorous than even Elijah's call of Elisha, who allowed the latter to return to kiss his mother and father goodbye. The saying about the plowman may have been suggested by this same story where Elisha was plowing when Elijah encountered him. The plowman cannot make a straight furrow if he's looking behind at what he has already done (cf., Phil 3:13). If daily cares and concerns occupy a person, there is no room for being concerned with the kingdom, which is of far greater value, indeed the highest value (Luke 8:14, 12:21, 34, 18:22, cf., 1 Cor 7:33). It is, in effect, rejecting the kingdom and so becoming "unworthy of it."

Are these all idealized little scenes to illustrate the seriousness of the kingdom and of following Jesus in his ministry of the kingdom? Could the first saying have just been a free-floating proverb that expressed man's homelessness in the world as contrasted with a wild beast?[335] Similar judgments are made of the following two pronouncement stories. If they are free-floating traditions then Q placed them in the mouth of Jesus and provided the context.[336]

However, these sayings need to be placed into a wider context within the ministry of Jesus. The three vignettes in which they are set are part of a type of call narrative belonging to a "logia source type."³³⁷ These sayings all reflect the nature of Jesus' ministry: it was itinerant, and his disciples were called to a permanent relationship with him. These characteristics are in contrast to the Pharisees who established a "house of study" and whose disciples were not permanently attached to them.³³⁸ Furthermore, Deut 20:5–8 lists those who are exempted from going into battle to prosecute holy war against Israel's enemies: one who has built a house, one who has planted a vineyard, one who has just become betrothed and not yet married, and one who is fainthearted.³³⁹ So Jesus conceived of his ministry and that of his disciples as involved in a sort of military campaign against the forces of evil and human perfidy, and as such it had to be unencumbered by other worldly concerns (cf., 1 Cor 7:33).³⁴⁰ The kingdom of God stood in opposition to all merely worldly concerns and the power of the evil one.

The form of discipleship with Jesus still entailed, in spite of the precedents of exceptions to social norms, that his movement would be stigmatized by the way of life reflected in these three pronouncement stories, which call three prospective disciples to itinerancy, dispensing with familial obligations, and abandoning social connections.³⁴¹ These features—including the conformity of these sayings with what we know of Jesus' form of discipleship and the fact that this passage occurs in Q, written not long after the events it portrays—lead to the conclusion that the three vignettes represent occurrences in the life of Jesus and his ministry. They are truly biographical.

It is not inconceivable to think that these three little vignettes were brought together by the editors of Q since they all involve the theme of call and discipleship. The various subthemes of each cohere with one another and with Jesus' self-designation as "son of man." The functioning of the designation "son of man" may be more complex than the three neat categories that I've charted above since in the first pronouncement story in this little collection of three, "son of man," as we have seen in our analysis, alludes to both Jesus' future coming and his present ministry (which made the future coming of the kingdom already present). Therefore, the kingdom is the operative dynamic behind the whole passage: the call of the kingdom requires a total surrender and an unreserved trust that in following Jesus a disciple is freed from every duty and past obligation.³⁴²

True Kinsmen (Mark 3:20–21, 31–35, Matt 12:46–50, Luke 8:19–21)

Mark has interpolated the accusation of being in league with the devil (vs 22), Jesus' refutation of this accusation (vss 23–26), the saying about the function of his exorcisms (vs 27), and the saying about the unforgivable sin (vss 28–30) between the reference to his family coming out (vs 21) and their arrival at the house in which he was teaching (vs 31).[343] So 3:20-21 and 31–35 formed the original tradition received by Mark. Jesus here gives expression to the family of the kingdom, which was not fashioned by blood ties but by entering the kingdom. It shows too that the kingdom did not consist of only disciples who followed him but also those who remained tied to local communities. Neither Matthew nor Luke include the reference to Jesus' family as "coming out to seize him" because they considered him to be "out of his mind."[344] That attitude of his family perhaps seemed to them too harsh a judgment and as reflecting badly on Jesus himself. Matthew makes of the crowd about Jesus in Mark "his disciples" (Matt 13:48), which broadens Jesus' concept of who was included in the kingdom.

Vs 35 is often questioned as a redactional addition to the passage, but it is so closely tied to the verse preceding it that the two verses form a unity. In addition, the progression implied is in keeping with Jesus' practice: one enters the kingdom, and repentance and "doing the will of God" follow. "Doing the will of God," in Jesus' ministry, included entering the kingdom as well as the actions that proceeded from repentance.

The estrangement of Jesus' family from his kingdom work reflects the authenticity of this tradition since his family played a role later in the postresurrection community, as Luke in his book of Acts records.[345] Why would his family have made such a pejorative judgment about Jesus' sanity? He appeared as a charismatic prophet.[346] He did not wear the peculiar clothing of John the Baptist, but he had left his home and family and relied on the hospitality of others for lodging and food. These behaviors were outside the norms of society, and the abandonment of family was seen as particularly egregious. Moreover, his prophetic functioning would have been seen as hubristic coming from a man with the lowly occupation of a woodworker. Mark 6:2–3 expresses the offense he gave to his own townsfolk because he seemed to claim a greater status above these lowly villagers.

So the family remained outside the kingdom. As in the preceding passage, blood relationships mean nothing in the kingdom, as John the Baptist too had proclaimed (Luke 3:8). This fellowship with Jesus within the kingdom had the ethical quality of a family demanding that the Jewish values of loyalty, concern, care, and love be transferred to it.[347] For Jesus the kingdom was not some kind of abstract concept but a personal fellowship with God and the brothers and sisters of this community of the new age.[348] Noticeable also is the absence of a reference to "fathers." That omission resonates with Mark 10:28–30 (see above). It is not only that Joseph was not present among the family members who sought Jesus but that the father of the community of the new age was God (Matt 23:9).[349] Implied is a rejection of social patriarchy in favor of the reign of God, the only real Father of the community of the kingdom. The comprehensiveness of the grace of the kingdom is Jesus' sweeping statement (one could imagine Jesus sweeping his hand toward the crowd around him) that those who sit and listen to his teaching and accept it are incorporated in this new family of God. "Where Jesus is there is salvation."[350]

The physical depiction of the family as outside the house and the true "mother and brothers" as within reflects who is inside the kingdom and who remains as an outsider. This family renunciation shatters the very underpinnings of Jewish and, one could say, the whole of Graeco-Roman society.[351] This practice very well could have led to the accusation that Jesus perverted Israel (Luke 22:2, 14).

The Blessing of Mary (Luke 11:27–28)

Bultmann cites a series of parallels to this blessing so he can justifiably assert that such blessings were a widespread feature in Judaism.[352] The criticism in vs 28 of the blessing in vs 27 is in keeping with the previous passage where Jesus declares that it is not human descent and achievement that ensure the divine blessing but the personal relationship with God in his kingdom. Jesus' vociferous emphasis contrasts with the Jewish penchant to emphasize one's inclusion in the elect people of Israel by blood relationship. Rather, it is a personal dynamic of acceptance of the invitation to enter the kingdom and then, as one who listens to God's word, carry it out in one's life. As Paul puts it, these are people who have "no confidence in the flesh" and count all human achievement as "refuse."[353] Even motherhood along with patriarchy is subject to the kingdom's critique. In a certain way Jesus is the "mother" (Luke 13:34) as God is the "Father."

Rejection in the Hometown (Mark 6:1–6a, Matt 13:53–58, Luke 4:16–30, John 1:11)

All four Gospels agree that Jesus' home was Nazareth in the Galilee.[354] It appears that both Mark's and Luke's versions of the story quote a different part of a broader aphorism that is found in the Gospel of Thomas:

> A prophet is not acceptable in his own country
> Neither does a physician heal those who know him.[355]

That Jesus could not work many healings in his home country would seem to authenticate the tradition.[356] Matthew follows Mark's account. However, Matthew calls Jesus "the son of a woodworker"[357] rather than a "woodworker" himself as in Mark. He also repeats the people's question (vss 54 and 56). Matthew summarizes, as is his wont, Mark's exception to Jesus' limited power in the brief statement "he was not able to do many mighty works there because of their unbelief" by eliding Mark 6:5a and 6, which places the reason for Jesus' not having done any mighty works squarely on the people and their lack of faith. It is probable also that Mark added the phrase in vs 5b as a way to soften the same failure of Jesus to do any mighty works.

Jesus' hometown folks do not deny that he performed "mighty works" nor the wisdom of his teaching (Mark 6:2) but rather affirm it. They are offended by him because he is a former member of their little village who had been a lowly, ordinary artisan and born of a humble family known intimately by them. How could he be a prophet sent by God? Envy and jealousy hide behind their reaction. "We could not perform such deeds as is rumored of him nor speak with such eloquence as he seems to. Just who does he think he is?" Behind their questions about his deeds and words is the conviction that they do not come from God (vs 2). That they also refer to Jesus as a "son of Mary" and do not designate him as a son of his father perhaps expresses their intention to insult him.[358] They see him as a self-promoting pretender who sets himself above them (see John 6:41–42). They had forgotten the stories of the past: a slave people chosen by God to be his people; a Gideon, a meager son of a farmer, visited by the angel of the Lord to become a great leader in Israel (Jud 6–8); or an Amos called by God though he was a mere shepherd and dresser of sycamore trees (Amos 7:14). Such stories of the rejection of God-sent messengers were so well known that Jesus can quote a proverb circulating in his culture that a "prophet is not without honor except in his own country." Mark has probably added "among his kin and in his own house" since he has already recorded his family's negative reaction to him and his activities (see above).[359]

That Jesus could not perform many works of power in Nazareth because of the lack of faith of his hometown's folks is not a psychological observation but emphasizes that Jesus underscores the faith of the individual in his healings (Mark 2:5, Luke 7:50, 8:12). In this way he does not demand dependence on him but preserves the person's autonomy and personal responsibility. Instead of being a strategy of a supposed "messianic secret" theory, demanding that people not spread the story of his healings, it is rather a natural part of this understanding of his therapeutic activity (see, e.g., Mark 1:44). He is not just some miraculous healer, but the healings are to be the sign of the in-breaking of God's kingdom.

Luke has a much more detailed description of this visit of Jesus to his hometown. Luke specifies "Nazareth" in the place of the more generalized "home country" of Mark and Matthew. He lays out the pattern of the whole of Jesus' ministry: early acceptance, then opposition, and finally the threat to his life. Having reported Jesus' birth at Bethlehem, Luke calls Nazareth merely the place where he "grew up" (4:16). He includes both parts of the proverb cited above.

In Luke's rendition of the story, Jesus is in the synagogue and reads from Isaiah.[360] This reading, which Jesus says is now fulfilled, declares that the time for pardon, healing, and liberation has dawned—that is, the messianic age has now begun. Jesus sees his ministry to proclaim the "acceptable year of the Lord"—the year of Jubilee (Lev 25:10) when debts were cancelled. This was the way of salvation for the Israel of his day: to be concerned for the poor, to relieve debts (even the Gentiles inadvertently do that; see the parable of the unjust steward[361]), and to forgive even the enemy. When Jesus says, "Today this word is fulfilled in your hearing" (vs 21), he is stressing his own concept of the kingdom as already being proleptically present rather than in some kind of apocalyptic future.[362] He calls on his hearers for an immediate response (cf., 2 Cor 6:2). This is not the time for debating the finer points of Torah and how to fulfill them.[363] His words are described as "gracious," which implies they are the words of a sage, a wise man (Sir 20:13, cf., Mark 6:2). Jesus follows this up with a word of indictment of his hometown folk. His mighty works will not be performed in Nazareth but among the poor, the sinners, and even the Gentiles.

In addition, Jesus' limited power in this hometown seems to be a decision on his part, and so Jesus himself voices the implied criticism that he elicited on the part of his hometown people:

> And he said to them, "Doubtless you will quote to me this proverb, 'Physician, heal yourself; what we have heard you did at Capernaum, do here also in your own country.'" And he said, "Truly, I say to you, no prophet is acceptable in his own country" (4:23–24).

The first proverb indicates that the people thought "charity should begin at home"—that is, the residents of Nazareth felt that they should have been the first beneficiaries of his activities.[364]

The people also become so enraged at his allusion to the two Old Testament stories that seem to portray God as more graciously disposed toward Gentiles than his own people Israel that they try to throw him off a cliff. Jesus asserts that there is no privilege when it comes to the pure grace of his gospel. God's grace abounds wherever sin abounds. Surely then Gentile "sinners" could claim to be first in line to receive it! Luke seems to be drawing on his own special source here, or he has radically altered the tradition handed down in Mark.

Each evangelist has interpreted the story to fit his general narrative, but all agree that Jesus visited his hometown (country), was rejected there, and could perform no works of power. The absence of works of power and the people's rejection speak for the authenticity of the core of this narrative. However, Luke only obliquely refers to the lack of doing deeds of power. Frederick Danker understands the Lucan version of the story as a fulfillment of Simeon's prophecy that Jesus "is set for the fall and rising of many in Israel, and for a sign that is spoken against" (2:34). Like Elijah, Jesus will fall under the disfavor of official Israel.[365] The people see him as a false prophet and therefore seek to carry out his execution (Deut 13:1–5).

So how are we to understand the differences between the Mark/Matthew version of the story and Luke's and the implication of the historicity of each narrative? The scholarship is divided on the issue.[366] However, that there are two different and not incompatible sources to the passage speaks for its authenticity. One real problem is the lack of archaeological evidence for a synagogue in Nazareth. Perhaps "synagogue" is used loosely since the people would come together on the Sabbath and might have met in the domicile of one of the residents, considering that place as their "synagogue." Some commentators understand that Luke has used the Marcan narrative and added to it on the basis of tradition that was at his disposal. That may be the best explanation of the relationship between these texts. As I've pointed out previously, Luke was after "writing an orderly account, having followed all things closely for some time past" (Luke 1:3). Based on his own intention, it seems unlikely that Luke would have been inventing imaginary scenes. The fact that his passage reflects a "programmatic" prologue to the rest of his story of Jesus in his Gospel does not vitiate its historicity. The programmatic character of the tradition may have been observed by Luke before he even brought these several traditions together. The explicit quoting of an amalgamation of texts from Isaiah may have been based on Jesus' own words in characterizing his ministry to John's disciples (7:22).

I conclude that Mark reproduces the tradition available to him and that Luke took it up and amalgamated other traditions with it to produce his more detailed account. One need not assert that the Isaiah texts represent exactly what Jesus read, but rather it is a summary of texts from Isaiah that reflected Jesus' own understanding of his ministry.

In summary, Jesus visited his hometown and was rejected there, was left undefended even by his family, who participated in the rejection, performed no works of power, and had his life threatened because he was seen as a false prophet (John 1:11).

Jesus Blesses the Children (Mark 10:13–16, Matt 19:13–15, (Luke 18:15–17)

Has Mark 10:15 been inserted in the story because its point is quite different from vs 14?[367] Vs 14 asserts that children are part of the kingdom, while vs 15 declares that their reception of the kingdom is the model of how the kingdom is to be received. That difference in function is, however, not a reason to question whether vs 15 was originally part of the pronouncement story. The latter builds on the former and is like the *parallelismus membrorum* of Jewish poetry and thinking.[368]

> Let the children come to me . . . of such is the kingdom of God. Whoever does not receive the kingdom of God as a child cannot enter it. (Mark 10:14–5)

This is an example of the antithetical parallelism of Hebrew poetry. There is a contrast of opposing ideas: those who come to the kingdom and those who do not. Those who do not are not like the children who do come. But the second line of the parallelism is supplementary, adding the idea that because children come to the kingdom and receive it, one must emulate them.

Children, along with the poor, hungry, and persecuted, are among those who have physical or moral defects.[369] But the kingdom of God revalues these stigmatized groups and blesses them. Because of their humility, they are brought into the kingdom.[370] The "poor" are poor both in an economic sense and in the sense that they are humble of heart and oppressed by the powerful and therefore fully place their trust in God. Consequently, they come under his protection. So "the poor" are those who lack power.[371] Children are quintessentially powerless and lack even the power to resist, so the kingdom belongs especially to them. To become as little children means to fully place one's trust in God and "wait for the Lord" (Ps 27:14). This message was particularly poignant in the Israel of Jesus' day, where armed insurrection and violent dreams of driving the Romans out were so popular.

It is understandable why the disciples wanted to forbid the coming of the children: they had not the power of personal responsibility to make a decision about following Jesus; or, perhaps the parents also were not followers of Jesus. How could they then expect a blessing? Why would parents bring their children to Jesus for a blessing anyway? Blessing in Israel (Heb., ברך," *Barak*, Gk., εὐλογέω, *eulogeō*) is a statement of a positive and favorable relationship between the giver of the blessing and those who receive it. It conveys good will and benefaction (Num 6:24–26). It is also a way of thanking a person. When God is blessed, it is a form of praising and thanking him.

In the world of Jesus, the flow of human events and history was not conceived as accidental or directed by human beings but depended on the will of God.[372] Blessing a person is seen as an effective utterance that brings about weal for the person so blessed, which averts and counteracts evil. In Israel this was not a magical notion but rather religious: it was more like a prayer invoking the action of God.

Blessing was also involved in the biblical conception of the power of the spoken word. Once a word is spoken, it has a life of its own and continues in effect regardless of whether circumstances change or the speaker has a change of mind (Isa 55:11). This effect, however, depends on the authority of the person who has spoken, such as a king, priest, or prophet at an appropriate time or place (cf., John 11:51).[373] A blessing's effectiveness ultimately depends on God's will and purpose (Job 12:13–25), and he can reverse promises that had borne a blessing (Jer 1:10).

Blessings may be accompanied by gestures, as in our passage where Jesus enfolds the children in his arms. The effect of receiving a blessing is happiness (Ps 144:15) and the experience of peace (Ps 29:11).[374]

There were certain situations, such as crises, a time of decision, the coming of a struggle, or a turning of the times, in which God's blessing was needed or expected.[375] The imminent in-breaking of the kingdom in Jesus' proclamation and ministry meant that Israel and the world were facing a crisis. So this is a time that calls forth God's blessings and curses (Luke 6:20–26, cf., Matt 5:3–11, 23:13–33). At Jesus' hand, people receive the blessings of the coming kingdom in healings and exorcisms.

Those who bring[376] their children are responding to Jesus' proclamation of the nearness of the kingdom. They want these children to be included in its blessings.[377] Nowhere else is Jesus portrayed as being "angry, incensed."[378] It is a strong word indeed, and it is so offensive when describing Jesus that Matt and Luke omitted it. It implies that Jesus was indignant at how the disciples could so misunderstand him when his whole ministry was directed toward the marginalized and sinners.

The meaning of the phrase "of such is the kingdom of God" may relate to passages like Matt 21:15–16, which quotes Ps 8:3, and the Q passage in Luke 10:21. It is God's immutable will that the truth be hidden from "the wise" and "revealed to babes." The language is metaphorical and refers to the little people of the world who have nothing to boast of:

> For consider your call, brethren; not many of you were wise according to worldly standards, not many were powerful, not many were of noble birth; but God chose what is foolish in the world to shame the wise, God chose what is weak in the world to shame the strong, God chose what is low and despised in the world, even things that are not, to bring to nothing things that are, so that no human being might boast in the presence of God (1 Cor 1:26–29).

Children, who are at the bottom of the social pyramid, have the least to boast of in terms of property, honor, and social position. They are the quintessential members of the kingdom because they simply trust. So Jesus means both children and those who share their characteristic of simple acceptance, trust, and reliance on God fully in heart, mind, and spirit.[379] That attitude is in line with the will of God. The word for "receiving" (vs 15, Gk., δέχομαι, dechomai) also means "accept" and in its biblical usage implies that one's behavior accords with the will of God.[380] The kingdom is pure gift and not dependent on human action or any human claims. One can only trust and rely on God's gracious will. It must be simply accepted. All the wisdom, knowledge, and learning of the world will not suffice.[381]

The final verse contrasts in the strongest degree with the attitude of the disciples in vs 13. The disciples chided (rebuked, scolded) those who brought the children to Jesus. Jesus embraces them. He does more than what was requested of him.[382] They are symbolically surrounded by the kingdom, resting, as they do, within his encircling arms and being blessed. Here is a graphic portrayal of the kingdom and what is asserted in the previous two verses.[383] Because children in their simple trust embody the ground of inclusion in the kingdom, blessing must ensue. Jesus' blessing validates and verifies that these children are in a right relationship with God. Jesus himself is the kingdom. Inclusion in the kingdom is pure weal.

The Widow's Mite (Mark 12:41–44, Luke 21:1–4)

Stories of the sacrifices of the poor, whose narrative lines refer to a seemingly small gift that is nevertheless more pleasing than the extravagant gifts of the rich, were current in Greek literature from the sixth century BC to the first century AD, in the rabbinic literature, and in Buddhist tradition.[384] Because of these parallels outside of Judaism and the purity of the Greek of this passage, it must be concluded that the story took shape outside the land of Israel.[385] However, it could have originated with Jesus as a parable, and the Marcan community turned it into an incident in the life of Jesus.[386] The κατέναντι (*ketenanti*, "opposite") of vs 41 is Marcan redaction and indicates that what takes place or is said in the passage is to be understood as opposed to the treasury (cf., Mark 13:3). The "treasury" referred to must be the one in the Jerusalem Temple. There was no other place for the people to deposit offerings.

There are, however, difficulties in the passage. How could Jesus know the amounts, sitting as he and his disciples were at some distance from the containers in which people deposited their offerings? This feature points to the parabolic nature of the passage.[387] In a parable the storyteller can act as an omniscient observer and know any detail that he wishes to use in telling the story. The parabolic nature of the story is strengthened by the similarity with the Buddhist version. Luke does not include the rather general description that Jesus "observed how the crowd deposited bronze [coin] into the treasury,"[388] which implies that we have Mark's hand at work here giving a greater verisimilitude to the scene. Luke's version gives the impression of an ideal scene.

The commentators find only the pronouncement of Jesus traditional.[389] It seems unlikely that Mark knew only the pronouncement, and it would be peculiar to find it without a narrative setting. All of this points to Mark retelling a traditional story in his own particular way since it had no fixed form in the tradition. But there were fixed elements in the tradition. Luke shares the "two lepta," that the widow was "poor," the reference to the "treasury," and the word of Jesus. Obvious Marcan brushstrokes are his numismatic translation ("which is a *quadrans*"),[390] his notice that Jesus "called his disciples to him," and perhaps the redundant "those who deposited into the treasury" (vs 43b). All of these phrases are absent from Luke. The story, however, is also loaded with traditional vocabulary.[391] So the tradition as Mark knew it may have read something like the following:

> Jesus saw how they deposited bronze [coins] into the treasury. And when one poor widow came she put in two lepta. And he said, "Truly I say to you, this poor widow deposited more than all, for all of them deposited from their abundance but she from her poverty deposited all she had (her whole life)."

The story is therefore portrayed as an incident in the life of Jesus that took place on the Temple mount. An analysis of its structure determines its function in the life of Jesus and its meaning (following the Greek word order):

> Jesus saw how they deposited bronze into the treasury.
> And when one poor widow came she put in two lepta.

I say to you that

> A. This poor widow more than all deposited
> B. For all of them from there abundance deposited
> B'. but she from the poverty of her
> A'. all she had, the whole life of her

The repetitive use of "deposited" is striking, as is the parallelism of the members. A and A' are comparable, while B and B' are contrasting statements, as indicated by the "but" in B'. Each of the two pairs of lines ends with the same words. The parallelism underscores comparison and contrast, which is what the content itself conveys. The woman has given more because of her poverty. In fact, she has given her whole life. The statement is positive, with no hint of criticism or accusation being leveled at any person or groups of persons. The contrast is stressed between the widow and her poverty and the others in their abundance.

A widow was thought of as a barren person (2 Kgs 4:1–7) whose condition was lamentable (Exod 22:4). She could be a sign of divine punishment (Exod 2:22–4, Jer 18:21) as well as low esteem and shame (Isa 5:4). The Bible demands benevolence toward them, that justice be done to them, and that they be aided.[392] These injunctions serve to illuminate the social ostracism and economic hardship that the widow had to endure and show that the figure was a symbol and a sign of God's displeasure (Isa 9:16).

In the tradition behind our passage, the widow is made a symbol of something entirely different: the widow and her mites portray two spiritual realities that are congruent with the teaching of Jesus elsewhere:[393] (1) the true measure of what is given is not the absolute amount but must be compared to what is left; (2) the gift made by the widow, because there is nothing left, indicates the total commitment of oneself to God's mercy in unsullied trust. The giving goes beyond all legalities, obligation, and sensibilities. One could even say the story bursts the bounds of morality in that the widow has divested herself of the last leg of support and is now totally bereft.[394]

We seem to meet here the world of Jesus' parables, which so often turn commonsense reality on its head to make a point and bring the hearer to a decision.[395] The widow who symbolized being bereft of God's blessing now becomes the symbol of fecund faith, precisely because of her widowhood.[396] All of the others admired for their generous donations pale into insignificance. Jesus' solemn asseveration (vs 43) fits what is said about the widow. It usually prefaces an eschatological threat or promise that applies directly to those who are being addressed.[397] Implied is the nearness of the kingdom in and through the one who speaks these words. The story calls the hearer to the realization that one would do well to emulate the widow in the face of eschatological realities. The story in this way challenges the hearer to evaluate one's position on wealth in the light of the kingdom.

As a parable the story could have had the following form:

> Jesus told them this parable: "A rich man and a poor widow went up into the Temple to deposit gifts into the treasury. And the rich man deposited much. And the widow deposited two lepta." And Jesus said, "Truly I say to you, the poor widow deposited more than he for he from his abundance deposited it but she from her lack, all as much as she had, her whole life."[398]

A close parallel is the story of the rich man (Mark 10:17–22). Paradoxically, the man's "lack" in this story (vs 21, ὑστερέω, *hystereō*) is that he does not lack wealth as the widow lacks wealth. He has not given to the poor like the "poor widow" who has given her whole life, and therefore he does not have "treasure in heaven," which, by implication, the widow does have because of her total reliance on God. Paul too emphasizes these spiritually paradoxical realities.[399]

Another close parallel to the story is Mark 10:23–31, which is presented as a commentary on the story of the rich man. This saying of Jesus concerns the difficulty of the rich entering the kingdom. Peter asserts that he and the disciples have left "everything and followed" Jesus, to which the answer is given that he will receive all that he has left and "eternal life in the age to come." Expressed in this long section (10:17–31) is an ethic of divestiture that willingly gives up everything for the sake of something of far greater worth. The parables of treasure in a field and the pearl of great price (Matt 13:44–46) vividly illustrate the same idea. This paradoxical quality is expressed most pointedly in Mark 8:35, where losing to gain finds explicit expression:

> Whoever wishes to save his life shall lose it.
> Whoever loses his life for my sake and the Gospel shall save it.

However, the story of the widow's mite, in contradistinction to the parallels, lacks a reference to either a spiritual or worldly gain. The rich man misses discipleship and consequently eternal life, something that Peter gains. The Corinthians gain spiritual gifts and Paul the transcendent power of God.[400]

The real parallel to the story occurs in LevR 3,107a, where a woman brings a handful of flour to the priest who has despised it but who was told in a dream she has "offered her life" (*Nepheshah*).[401] Again, the value of the gift in relationship to the giver is stressed and the total commitment to God implied. Our story, like the rabbinic parallel, implies that the widow gains a spiritual gift.

Finally, it must be noted that there is nothing critical of the Temple in the story; rather, one's offering in the Temple is equated with devotion to God. It is only in the Marcan redaction that the story is made to express Mark's anti-Temple theology and critique.[402]

Mary and Martha (Luke 10:38–42)[403]

In this pronouncement story, scene and word are so inextricably connected so that it can only be concluded that its conception forms a unit. The one cannot be conceived without the other.

It appears that Luke did not know that the village where Mary and Martha lived was Bethany since he does not mention them in that connection in 19:29 and 24:50, which again reference Bethany. None of his sources, Mark and his special material, provided him with that information.

Mary, by sitting at Jesus' feet, assumes the posture of a disciple (cf., Acts 22:3). Martha is eager to please Jesus and bustles about preparing a meal for him. However, by complaining about the lack of help from her sister, she reveals that her busyness is not a freely offered action but is done with something of a grudge. Her complaint includes Jesus since she blames him for not encouraging the help of Mary. By doubling her name in response, Jesus is quietly reprimanding her and reminding her that she should know better. After all she was a faithful Jew who would have repeated the Shema every day: "Hear, O Israel, the Lord your God, the Lord is one" (Deut 6:4). Hearing was a fundamental aspect of Judaism. It was a hearing and listening culture.

The listening posture of Mary also relates to the repose and rest of the Sabbath, when no activity related to work is to be done. The Sabbath rest, of course, is related to the divine rest of the Creator on the seventh day and so to the ultimate, eschatological "rest" (Heb 4:1–11). Here the kingdom is reenacted and present. The scene with Mary evokes the whole of Jesus' ministry, his table fellowship, his healings, the gathering of people to hear him teaching, all of which evoke repose and run counter to the calls for active resistance to the Roman occupation. Jesus' movement was not an Essene withdrawal, for the kingdom was in their midst. It was not a preoccupation with holiness, for Jesus conveyed holiness to the people.

Jesus had put eating in its proper place in his temptation when, instead of miraculously creating loaves of bread out of stone, he asserted that "man does not live by bread alone but by every word that proceeds from the mouth of God"—that is, listening to the word of God takes priority over even bodily nourishment (Luke 4:4, quoting Deut 8:3). This is why Jesus warns that one should "not fear those who kill the body but cannot kill the soul; rather fear him who can destroy both soul and body in hell" (Matt 10:28). To die because of lack of bodily nourishment is preferable to the death of the spirit by the neglect of hearing the word of God. The "good part" that Mary chooses is the kingdom itself. It is the "one thing" that is truly needful.

Similarly, in Luke 22:31 Jesus addresses Peter with a double "Simon, Simon" and declares that Satan is scrutinizing[404] him so that he might "sift him as wheat." "Sift" here means to destroy (Isa 30:28).[405] This is a scene of great pathos. Jesus, in the night of his betrayal and abandonment by his disciples, facing his passion and death, addresses the first among the disciples with sadness and sorrow as he sees Peter falling into the hands of Satan. As Jesus addresses Mary's sister with the repetition of her name, he sees her accusing question as part of, and on the continuum with, his own ultimate rejection, abandonment, and passion.

Jesus does not disparage action in this story. He stresses action elsewhere in such terms as being of service, turning the other cheek, or going the extra mile. But all of those actions are based not on mere unreflective activity but on "doing the will of the Father." To do his will, one must hear and listen. Jesus' ministry was not just a matter of deeds, although they were powerfully present in his ministry, but he was also a proclaimer of the word and constantly called on people to listen.[406] That was crucial in Jesus' context. Just what were the people listening to? The revolutionaries, the militants calling people to arms? Those wanting the people to rise up in revolt? The saving of the nation depended on hearing the genuine word of God and then living with mercy as their Father in heaven was merciful (Luke 6:36).

Healing of the Ten Lepers (Luke 17:11–19)

It was common for lepers to live in groups (2 Kgs 7:3). They congregated near, but outside of, populated towns and villages to receive sustenance from sympathetic passersby. It can be asked why a Samaritan[407] would be sent off to a Jewish priest to be declared clean. First, no one could discern the difference between a leprous Jew and a Samaritan since lepers had to wear torn clothes and cover their beard (probably to avoid infection of others even with their breath) while they warned others of their condition (Lev 13:45, 14:2–10). In addition, the Samaritan would have gone to a Samaritan priest anyway (notice that Jesus says "priests," not "priest"). The priest had to give judgment as to whether a person was cured and freed of the disease, and then the person could reenter society. Even if one could recognize a Samaritan in the group of ten, that Jesus cures them all is only recognition of his proclamation of the kingdom, which invited all and included all. His inclusion of all outsiders is clear especially in this case from his telling of the parable of the good Samaritan. The kingdom's in-breaking included an invasion of the realm of disease and sin.

Leprosy was interpreted as a punishment of God, and so the presence of a leprous person was a threat not only to the community's physical health but to its status as a holy people. The disease was connected with death since the skin gave the appearance of a corpse (Lev 22:4, Num 5:2).

Only the Samaritan turns back and "falls on his face" before Jesus giving thanks. "Falling on one's face" is an act of worship (Gen 17:3, Num 22:31) but also an act of submission and showing respect to a person (2 Sam 14:22). It is not anomalous that Jesus wonders why only one returned to give thanks when he had told them all to leave and show themselves to the priests. It was only while they were "on the way" that they all were cleansed. All had the opportunity to return and give thanks. That the Samaritan's faith "had saved" him (i.e., "healed him") was also true for the others.

In a certain respect this pronouncement story is a commentary on Jesus' parable of treasure in a field. The parable does not tell us what the man who found the treasure did with it. This story illustrates two possible ways of dealing with the overwhelming joy one stumbles upon when encountering the kingdom. The nine, out of their joy, run off to the priests to be reintegrated into society, family, and friends. The Samaritan's joyful reception of the treasure of healing is not left without result for him. He uses his treasure. He turns back in his joy and gives thanks. "Giving thanks" in the psalms reflects an intimate relationship with God.[408] There is consequently a special nuance to Jesus' declaration that the Samaritan "has been saved."[409] He is not only healed but is enfolded in God's everlasting kingdom.

Zaccheus the Toll Collector (Luke 19:1–10)

Zaccheus is a "chief tax collector"—that is, a "toll collector" overseeing those who physically collect the taxes from the people. That he is described as "rich" only emphasizes his conversion since Jesus has declared the difficulty of the rich entering the kingdom (Luke 18:24–27).

A structural analysis of the story reveals its meaning:

A. Zaccheus is identified as a rich toll collector who sought to see Jesus but could not because of the crowd and because he was so short. He climbs a tree to get a better view of Jesus.
B. Jesus has sought him, calls him by name, and tells him to come down for he must stay at his house.
C. Zaccheus climbs down and receives Jesus into his house with joy.
C'. Some mummer against Jesus for lodging in the house of a sinner.
B'. Zaccheus announces he will restore anything he has gotten by fraud.
A'. Jesus identifies Zaccheus as a son of Abraham and pronounces that salvation had come to his house.

The story exhibits a ring construction. A and A' emphasize a contrast. Though he is small of stature, he finds real stature by the salvation that he encounters in Jesus. He cannot add to his own stature (Luke 12:25), but Jesus brings the kingdom, and Zaccheus enters it. His identity switches from "toll collector" to "son of Abraham." B and B' are a call and response and demonstrate that, in the presence of Jesus and entering into the kingdom, repentance follows. So Zaccheus makes restitution for his sinful life. C and C' contrast the joy of the sinner Zaccheus and the hostility of the crowd to the grace and open commensality of the kingdom.

The structure also reveals in both sections a tension that is resolved. In the first, Zaccheus seeks to see Jesus and finally receives Jesus into his house. In the second, the crowd discontentedly grumbles that Jesus enters the house of a sinner, but salvation comes to his house, and Zaccheus is reintegrated into the "house" of Abraham.

In vs 3, Zaccheus seeks Jesus, but in vs 5, it is Jesus who has been seeking him and in whose house he must stay. This "must" usually indicates the divine will and something that has already been ordained by that will.[410] Jesus has perceived that Zaccheus is like the finder in the parable of treasure in a field" who will receive the kingdom with joy and consequent repentance. (Could Jesus have conceived of the parable on the basis of this encounter?) Or he is like the lost sheep in the parable of that name whom Jesus must search for and find and bring back into the fold of Israel. After all, he too is a "son of Abraham" and so is not excluded, no more than any others who were part of the lost sheep "without a shepherd" (Matt 9:36) because they were rejected by the righteous.

The story also indicates the presence of the kingdom already among the people: Jesus must stay "today" in Zaccheus's house (vs 5), and "today" salvation has come to him and his house (vs 9, cf., 2 Cor 6:2). Zaccheus stands in marked contrast to the rich man who was offered the kingdom but could not give up his many possessions (Mark 10:17–22, Luke 18:18–23).

That latter's grief and sorrow in leaving Jesus only enhance the contrast with Zaccheus's joy.

The depth of Zaccheus's repentance is underscored by his resolve to give half of his fortune away to the poor. In the case of extortion, only 20 percent was required above the restitution (Lev 5:16), but Zaccheus binds himself to the law imposed on rustlers who were liable to a fourfold restoration.[411] The story also relates to Jesus' parable of the Pharisee and toll collector: in the parable, the toll collector confesses his sin and relies on God's mercy. Here Zaccheus finds forgiveness and responds with great mercy by promising to restore what he has swindled out of Israel's taxpayers.

The Disciples' Praises (Luke 19:39–40, Matt 21:15–16)

Matthew has placed this incident in the Temple court, while Luke refers the incident to the praise that accompanied Jesus' entrance into Jerusalem. The former has "children" in the place of Luke's "whole multitude of disciples." Matthew interprets the behavior of the "children" like a good rabbi by substituting a quotation from Scripture, "by the mouth of babes and infants, thou hast founded a bulwark because of thy foes, to still the enemy and the avenger" (Ps 8:2, although he has substituted for the second phrase in the quotation "thou has brought perfect praise"), for Luke's "I tell you, if these were silent, the very stones would cry out." Matthew has coordinated his "children" with the Psalm quotation and the addition of the healings that were performed, to both of which his antagonists react.[412] Matthew's rendition looks like he has totally reshaped the tradition.

Furthermore, Luke is usually more faithful to the Q tradition. Because of this and because it appears the Matthean hand has intervened so aggressively in this Q tradition, it would appear that Luke has the original reading. In that case would Jesus be thinking of the stones of the Temple crying out as a "recompense against his enemies" (Isa 66:6)? That interpretation is strengthened by Luke's reference to the stones of the Temple in vs 44.[413]

Luke's "Pharisees" reprove the noisy reaction of the disciples, apparently concerned about a ruckus that could invite Pilate's violent response in putting down demonstrations, a not unreasonable concern.[414] (Matthew substitutes high priests and scribes who "are angry and incensed.") The Pharisees here appear not as opponents but as concerned friends, much as they appear in Luke 13:31, where they warn Jesus to get away from the Galilee because Herod wants to kill him.[415] Luke 17:20 also falls into this category: Pharisees ask him a neutral question concerning the coming of the kingdom. That the Pharisees appear not as opponents but even as friends kindly disposed toward Jesus distinguishes their depiction from the usual negative portrayal elsewhere in Luke's Gospel, which speaks for the authenticity of this report.[416] The presence of the Pharisees also places the story more firmly in a Judean and Jerusalemite context and so most probably as Jesus entered the city before his passion.

What is the point of this pronouncement story? Luke 19:37 indicates that those who are joining in the celebrating of Jesus because of his "mighty works" are "his disciples," which implies that it does not include the general crowd that was flocking into Jerusalem. Jesus' popularity in the Galilee was not matched in Jerusalem or Judea, or by pilgrims from elsewhere. Hab 2:11 declares, "For the stone will cry out from the wall, and the beam from the woodwork responds." The phrase is part of a taunt against Babylon for its extortion, which was so grievous that even the stones cried out in protest against the crimes of this illegitimate "master of the house."

Jesus is saying that his works are so monumental in their significance that inert stones would witness to them if human beings didn't. His works are so significant because they witness to and have brought the kingdom of God near.[417] The God who could raise up stones to be children of Abraham could make men from stones who would sing the praises of Jesus' mighty works.[418]

This pronouncement by Jesus is also a witness to his understanding of himself. He is the Son of the Father, the stone rejected by the "builders," whose actions are God's own works pointing to the imminent in-breaking of the kingdom.

Paying the Temple Tax (Matt 17:24–27)

This narrative consists of two parts: the question about paying taxes and the apparently legendary motif of finding a coin in the mouth of a fish.[419] The first part is old tradition and concerns paying the half-sheqel tax that every Jew in the empire had to pay annually to the Temple.[420] Why would the collectors of this tax approach Peter and not Jesus himself? When the disciples are approached rather than Jesus directly, it is thought that the tradition originated in the church, for which Peter or the disciples stand in (vs 24). The "What do you think?" of vs 25 is Matthean phraseology, as is the wording of the whole passage. Matthew may be using strictly oral tradition here. Vs 25 is intimately connected with the previous verse because it says Jesus "anticipated" (προέφθασεν, *proephthasen*) a question from Peter. Thus, vss 24–26 form a unity. However, Peter had answered "yes" to the question of whether Jesus paid this tax, so what question was Peter ready to ask of him, having already been given an answer? Since Matthew has shaped the telling of this narrative, it seems that originally Peter would have responded to the half-sheqel tax collectors that he would ask Jesus whether they should pay. As it stands, Matthew shaped the entire narrative but without major alterations, and vss 25–27 are less edited than the preceding verses.[421] The heart of the tradition seems to be 25b–26.[422]

Jesus' answer is clear: since the sons of the earth's kings do not pay their father's levies on the people, neither should the free sons of the kingdom of God. Jesus here is critical and relativizing of the Temple as an economic institution making the payment of the tax a voluntary affair. Jesus in this passage also removes private piety from public control.[423] He is declaring that his disciples, sons of the kingdom, need not pay the tax; they are "free" and have a direct relationship with God.[424]

But then he announces a principle that has shaped Christian practice ever since. In order not to give offense, he pays the tax. Jesus will not use his freedom to offend Jewish law and practice. Paul says he has every right to demand payment from his churches for his work in the Gospel. "The Lord has commanded that they who preach the gospel should live from the gospel" (1 Cor 9:14). But he has not made use of this right: "we endure anything rather than put an obstacle in the way of the gospel of Christ" (1 Cor 9:12).[425] Paul's application of the principle to himself witnesses to the authenticity of Jesus' words in this passage.

Herod Antipas Threatens Jesus (Luke 13:31–33)

The Pharisees here appear to be friendly to Jesus and concerned for his welfare. Given what I've said above about such an anomalous portrayal, that attitude speaks for the authenticity of the narrative.[426] This attitude is not to be taken as subterfuge as if Herod were using the Pharisees to drive Jesus from his land, not yet daring to take any action against him, particularly because of the execution of the very popular John the Baptist. Rather their solicitude speaks for the true relationship between Jesus and this group of scholars and against the overwhelming negative portrayal in the Gospels, which for the most part stemmed from a later time and is more a description of the relationship between them and the church. The appearance of the Pharisees indicates that Jesus was not in the Galilee but in Perea, part of Herod's territory, across the Jordan and opposite Jerusalem.

Jesus was noted for teaching "not as the scribes" (Mark 1:22). This meant more than not quoting learned scholars and not passing on a tradition. Rather it was a matter of speaking in a way that indicated he had a whole new way of interpreting the Torah.[427] He was announcing the coming of the kingdom of God, which was the font of how the law and the prophets were to be understood. Fundamental to that understanding was the mercy and compassion of the God of Israel. He was provocative, turning Israel's world upside down: God's kingdom was already present and showed itself under the guise of unexpected events, people, and circumstances calling the people to turn a favorable eye to the world and eschew the demonic dreams of political independence, violence, and destructive rivalry and animosity toward their compatriots.

His was not some kind of timeless message such as a call to decision (a word never used in the tradition)[428] but a subpoena served on both individual and nation from the King, the Lord YHWH, to enter the kingdom and change the heart and the direction of life to prepare for the imminent catastrophe of the in-breaking of the kingdom.[429] For those who refused to respond, judgment awaited. The exile was about to end; God would vindicate his people and establish the longed-for justice. The people could abandon their anxieties, share their goods, break down the interparty hostilities, and join as one people in the joyful expectation of the long-awaited time when God would visit his people and save them from their enemies and from the hand of all those who hated them so they could serve him without fear in holiness and righteousness before him (Luke 1:71–75). The covenant would be renewed and creation restored.

Jesus certainly respected the law (Matt 5:17–18). But that did not mean just repeating the words of Israel's legal tradition. He had an urgent message that required an immediate response. Biblical images of him would be like David the freebooter, who was derided with the questions "Who is [this] David? Who is [this] son of Jesse? [This slave] . . . breaking away from [his] masters" even though he acted with kindness and forbearance (1 Sam 25:10); or an Isaiah wandering around Jerusalem naked, trying to provoke repentance and reliance on their God (Isa 20:3); or a Jeremiah, for whom they dug a pit (Jer 18:22) because his message was so opposed to the soothing and palliating platitudes of the leadership; or a Hosea, who not only consorted with prostitutes but married one to limn YHWH's faithfulness and Israel's idolatrous whoredom.

Jesus was constantly in danger of being arrested. Over and above Jesus' provocative message, Herod identified him with the Baptist redivivus, that man who had dared to confront him with his lewd lawlessness (Mark 6:17). He would have to be eliminated. But Jesus kept moving around, concentrating on the villages and avoiding the urban centers of Sepphoris and Tiberias. (That is why neither of these cities are mentioned in the synoptic gospels.)

Jesus calls Herod "that fox." Neh 4:3 uses the fox metaphor to ascribe totally fragility to Jerusalem's wall that Nehemiah was successful in restoring. "Tobiah the Ammonite was by [Sanballat the governor of Samaria], and he said, 'Yes, what they are building—if a fox goes up on it he will break down their stone wall!'" The fox was considered the weakest of all animals, and the wall was so insignificant that even the fox could break it down. So Jesus is saying that Herod Agrippa is no one to be feared because of his inherent weakness. He's "a misdirected man who lacks real power"[430]

Jesus said, "Look, I cast out demons and accomplish healings today and tomorrow and on the third day I am brought to my goal" (vs 32, my translation).[431] The passive is important in that it points to God as the one who is directing Jesus and whose will he accomplishes in his ministry and toward whose ultimate goal he is heading. Herod is totally insignificant. God is in control and directing him toward the aim and purpose of his life. Here Jesus again shows he does not just call others to faith in the gracious God of Israel, but he himself acts by this faith in him and through him.

Jesus then expands on what he sees as God's goal for him: that he, his prophet, should end up in Jerusalem, where his life will be taken from him (vs 33). His parable of the wicked tenants makes clear that Jesus understood that death awaited him, as do the three passion predictions (Mark 8:31, 9:31, 10:33).[432] How did he then conceive of his death? Why would that be God's purpose for him? His life is a "ransom" (Mark 10:45),[433] and he, the rejected stone (Mark 12:10), would be vindicated by God and become the "corner stone" of a new temple "not built with (human) hands" (Mark 14:58, cf., John 2:19). The authentic word of Jesus is as the evangelist John reports: "Jesus answered them, 'Destroy this temple, and in three days I will raise it up.'" He was talking about himself as Temple, so Mark can report that the witnesses were false when they accused him of saying he would destroy the physical Temple (14:57–59).

Furthermore, John's placing of the "Temple cleansing" early in Jesus' ministry probably is more accurate historically since it was an act of preparing the Temple for the eschatological feast of tabernacles (Zech 14), when God would establish his kingdom and all the nations would join in worship with Israel. Whereas, when Jesus enters Jerusalem for the last time, he predicts its demise since Israel had not responded to his call to enter the kingdom and repent. His attitude toward the Temple has changed.[434] So now his death would bring in the kingdom. He, the son of man, the representative of the people of God, would indeed be vindicated and establish the reign of God.

N. T. Wright cogently points out that the mind-set of Jesus' contemporaries was the hope of a true and final Passover, an "exodus" when Israel would be free of foreign control (i.e., the exile would in reality be ended) and their sins finally forgiven (the cause of the exile). That would come about by going through the "messianic woes," the sufferings of the eschaton (Mark 13:8, "birth pangs"). In this regard Jesus understood himself as Israel's representative who would, by his suffering and dying in her place, rescue Israel from the "present evil age" and restore her in the "age to come."[435]

The Cleansing of the Temple (Mark 11:15–17, Matt 21:12–13, Luke 19:45)

For this passage I am going into some detail because, if it is an authentic reproduction of Jesus' action and words, it could provide clarification of how Jesus thought about and understood the kingdom and the details of its contours. In other words, this passage could provide us with the contents of Jesus' eschatological expectations and clarify exactly how he understood the coming of the kingdom and of what that kingdom consisted.

First, I will provide an overview of the various positions and viewpoints that early Judaism cultivated regarding the Temple. Then, I will provide a detailed analysis of the passage itself and determine its authenticity and how it resonated with or differed from the various stances extant in the world of Jesus.

Excursus: Attitudes toward the Temple in Late Antiquity

In this investigation I discover two basic attitudes toward the Temple: one views it negatively, as an institution that must either be rejected altogether or be replaced by a heavenly temple. In terms of this view the empirical Temple is dispensable. A second attitude views the Temple positively, even if its contemporary administration is rejected. This latter point of view conceives the Temple as essential to the world's and Israel's existence before God and looks forward to its eventual and eschatological renewal.

VIEWPOINT A: THE TEMPLE IS CRITICIZED AND REJECTED

Trito-Isaiah contains a complex of materials stemming from various times. In general, these writings universalize and democratize.[436] The prophetic writer sees the Temple as corrupt, so Israel is no longer conceived as a unity but divided between the righteous and the wicked.[437] The text transforms the hope of restoration from the present world order to a supernatural one.

The harshest condemnation of the Temple found in either testament occurs in chapter 66. However, the closing verses of this chapter envision the nations being drawn to an idealized day when the Temple worship is restored and becomes the center around which the nations gather. It is the divine will to even draw Temple functionaries from the latter (cf., 56:1–8). God alone is seen as the one who can bring about the proper conditions for an acceptable cult. *In nuce* here we find the idea of the old era as beyond restoration. The basic prophetic hope of the renewal of Israel remains the same, but the context of fulfillment shifts from the real historical events of the nation to a context detached from the political order.

We find this outlook of antipathy toward the Temple and the transferring of hope to a new age continuing down through the first century AD. In the "Dream Visions" of Enoch (1 Enoch 83–90), 87:73 asserts that the showbread placed before the Temple was "polluted," which implies that the Temple had a defect.[438] In 90:29–33, an eschatological Temple is anticipated that will be built by God, into which Israel and all the nations will be gathered.

The author of The Martyrdom of Isaiah lived in a time that he regarded as wicked, especially in Jerusalem, where, for him, the Temple cult had become satanic worship (4:8). During the first century AD the author of the Apocalypse of Abraham also had a negative regard for the cult. This author understood the destruction of Jerusalem in AD 70 as punishment for wrong cultic activity that he considered to be idolatrous.[439] However, he foresaw the Temple restoration taking place in the eschaton.

The Greek Apocalypse of Baruch offered a similar explanation for the Temple's destruction and interpreted it as being due to the people's sin. There is silence about any future age, however, of a glorified Jerusalem. God is enthroned in his heavenly temple, and future hope for the nation is replaced by an individualized salvation in heaven.[440]

The Syriac Apocalypse of Baruch also presents a similar construct. God himself is understood as the one who had destroyed the city (chapter 4) and abandoned the Temple before it was captured. Hope is placed in a heavenly Jerusalem that God holds in reserve for the faithful (4:2–7). Jubilees 1:28–29 also envisions the building of an eternal temple in the final messianic epoch.

For Qumran God's presence was no longer bound to the Temple but to the true and pure Israel represented by the community. The Temple had been defiled by the "wicked priest" and his people (cf., 20:22–23).[441] Qumran made serious accusations against those who served in the Temple because they failed to obey the law according to how the community thought it should be observed. So the community itself took the place of the Temple even though it looked forward to a new temple of the last days when the cultus would be restored and the life of Israel perfected. So Qumran criticized the Temple as institution yet retained a positive attitude toward the sacrificial offices and the Temple cultus. This double attitude is related to Qumran's zeal for Torah.[442]

Beginning with Trito-Isaiah I have followed a line that has led us down to the sectaries of Qumran and revealed a fairly consistent critical attitude toward the empirical Temple while simultaneously waiting for the eschatological temple that God would erect. Sometimes the Temple is the locus for all people and at other times only for a perfected Israel. At other times, the notion of a Temple building is abandoned, and salvation is seen in terms of the individual who participates in the worship of God's supernatural, heavenly temple. In all of this, the Temple, whether earthly or heavenly, figures as the place, or symbol, of God's presence where true worship is to be restored. The empirical Temple is always the object of criticism due to some lack or defilement. At other times, it is rejected altogether as beyond restoration, in which case the heavenly temple or just heaven is awaited as its fulfillment.

Viewpoint B: The Temple Is Renewed

There is another, more positive trajectory of the Temple tradition that traces a view of the Temple as essential in God's eschatological plan of renewal.[443] This trajectory begins with the prophecies of Ezekiel, which promise that God will bring back the exiles, set up his dwelling place in Jerusalem, and reestablish his presence there (37:26–28). The prophet introduces a new theme, the belief in a future divine presence. He transforms the promises of the festivals into an eschatology. The old order has collapsed, and the new will be a fulfillment of ancient hopes.[444] Ezek 40–48 detail how YHWH's return is possible without profaning his holiness. His Temple theology is firmly grounded, however, in mundane realities establishing the conditions necessary for YHWH's dwelling among his people through concrete sacral ordinances. So he presents a program for the restored community.

Ezekiel images a stream flowing from the Temple in consequence of the divine presence (47:9), which produces a paradisial prodigality employing imagery connected with the festival of Sukkoth. Though the details of his vision seem otherworldly, they are related to mundane occurrences and the renewal of the community within the exigencies of the world.

The Priestly Writing[445] develops a tradition found in Ezekiel, namely, that of YHWH coming from heaven on a cloud. According to this priestly perspective, for God to be God of Israel, he had to dwell with the community. Israel's existence was possible only when God dwelt in it, which required the possession of the tabernacle.[446] The actual conception of the divine presence is ambiguous perhaps because of the ambiguity of the priests themselves.[447] But they also critique the ancient Near Eastern pattern, which would make of a God's presence an assured fact regardless of the moral behavior of the people. In addition, they theologize various features of the cult so that they become symbolic of theological truths.[448] The Temple is first "restored theologically" by the Priestly Writers before its actual reconstruction in 515 BC.[449] Combined with this concern is the command for Israel to be "holy because God is holy" (Lev 26:3, 11–12).

Both Haggai and Zechariah follow 2 Isaiah in promising a golden age under the aegis of the Davidic and priestly messiahs of Zerubbabel and Joshua. The rebuilding of the Temple would bring honor to Israel, and the treasures of the nations would flow into it. But Israel's response and the quality of her life are also required (Hag 2:14, Zech 1:3–6). Temple and cult and holy people would bring about the restoration of the community.[450]

Malachi, the name given to an unknown prophet of the fifth century BC, carries on the tradition of Ezekiel, the Priestly Writers, Haggai, and Zechariah with his concern for the failure of the priesthood. He complains that the Temple should be the place where God is honored, but instead it is where he is insulted (1:6—2:19). He finds the Temple to be somehow incomplete. So he looks to God to do something greater than has yet been seen, when the cult will be transformed and made acceptable (3:4). However, the fullness of the divine presence will not be a day of blessing but a purging of the people from sin (3:1–4). Israel's sin delayed YHWH's return, and the community was not transformed. So the prophet eschatologizes the hoped-for presence of God.

In Deutero-Zechariah, mythic elements from Israel's liturgical tradition come to the fore as postexilic prophecy seeks to confront the issues of the restored community. Chapter 9 begins with an optimistic assessment of historical events and envisions God taking up his abode in the Temple to be a guardian of his people. In the chapters immediately following, however, optimism vanishes. For example, in chapter 11 the wages paid to the prophet are cast into the Temple treasury, a gesture that coordinates with the breaking of the staffs, "Grace" (11:10) and "Union" (11:14). In this way the covenants are annulled and the sanctuary rejected for being the source of corruption and exploitation.[451] At first blush it seems that the writer has given up on the empirical Temple. But in chapter 13 the Temple as a source of cleansing reappears (cf., 14:8 and Ezek 47:1).

In chapter 14 we meet a full-scale eschatological drama with roots in the Divine Warrior hymn,[452] in which the restored empirical Temple figures prominently. A life-giving stream issues from the Temple inaugurating the fulfillment of the promises of Sukkoth: YHWH's universal reign is established, and Jerusalem and the Temple become the axis of the world (14:1–12), the wicked of the whole world, including those within Israel, are destroyed (vss 12–14), YHWH's universal reign is acclaimed, and the nations come to Jerusalem to participate in a perpetual feast of Sukkoth. All distinctions between sacred and profane, priest and laity, are eliminated. The activity of the "traders"[453] is ended, and all vessels are declared holy to the Lord. We meet here a thoroughgoing democratizing and universalizing tendency that emphasizes discontinuity with the past and the sovereign action of YHWH. All of these actions are conceived as an explication of the hopes connected with the feast of Sukkoth. In spite of the exotic quality of the occurrences described, they remain in the realm of the mundane.

The Chronicler's work, dating from c. 300 BC, represents something of a "realized eschatology."[454] He finds the realization of the promises in the theocracy established by David. Eschatological expectation almost disappears. The focal point of his historical presentation is Israel, to the exclusion of the nations. The Temple forms the connecting link between the pre- and postexilic community. The Chronicler sees the prophets purely historically as guardians until the community based on the law of Moses takes its final shape. The kings, priests, and prophets who erected the Temple, whose plans were received directly by David from God and passed on to his son Solomon, maintained the true cult and contributed to the constitution of the new community. The theocracy as idealized in the Davidic kingdom is the paradigm for the new postexilic community. Past history is not used to point beyond the present to the future fulfillment, but the present is seen as the fulfillment toward which the past has been moving. The ideal kingdom had been realized once and now needs only to be implemented again. The history finds its fulfillment in what has been and in the new Temple that is built after the exile under Zerubbabel and Joshua.

Ben Sirach represents a quieter and more settled outlook where the conduct of daily life appears at the focal point and where the various themes of wisdom, particularly of the biblical book of Proverbs, are further developed. Sirach conceives of the Temple as the place where wisdom takes up her abode in Israel and where she ministers before God (24:10). Here Israel's three great traditions of Torah, *Chokmah* ("wisdom"), and cult are joined.[455] Wisdom has been received by Israel alone, and only Israel is open to her and rightly serves her.[456] Sirach could give no greater approbation to the second Temple than he does.

Tobit 14:5, on the other hand, resonates with the theme of incompleteness of the second Temple in comparison to the first. But the writer does not reject the empirical Temple, because he envisions the Temple's perfectibility in the eschaton when it will be rebuilt an eternal edifice and the Gentiles will be converted, who will then "show mercy" to the Jews.

The Sibylline Oracles also regard the Temple positively as the center of Jewish life (II, 702–31) and the locus of God's protecting presence. In a similar vein the Letter of Aristeas[457] and all of the Maccabean literature[458] hold the Temple in highest regard.

In this excursus I have traced the Temple tradition complex from the time of the exile through the first century AD and discovered that the Temple is positively evaluated. It is the central element in the conception of the Jewish community as the locus of God's presence, a wellspring from which the blessings of God's presence are ensured for the people and land (Ezek 47:9, Hag 2:19, Zech 1:17), a place that requires ethical conduct of those who worship there (Lev 26:3, Hag 2:14, Zech 1:3–6), and the focus of God's eschatological purposes.

The Temple, however, is not above criticism even if it is never looked upon as an institution that is inherently corrupt and must be done away with (Mal 1:6–2:9, Zech 9–14, Tob 14:4). These somewhat disparate elements converge in Zech 9–14, which may be taken as a redactional whole, although its component parts may originally individually have had a different orientation to the Temple. These chapters portray a cosmic drama in which God chooses the Temple but rejects it when its leaders apostatize and then ultimately reestablishes his presence there in an eschatological drama wherein Jerusalem and Temple become the nucleus of the world. It is then that the world becomes converted to YHWH and dedicated to his worship.

The Chronicler is the most radical in his glorification of the empirical Temple. He severely limits eschatology and sees the fulfillment of the Davidic ideal kingdom in the postexilic community by means of his theologized history. Ben Sirach affirms the Temple as the dwelling place of Wisdom, a kind of sagacious version of the Deuteronomic name-dwelling conception. Herod's massive reconstruction of the Temple and its courts and Josephus's description (*War* 5,5) point to the Temple's importance both theologically and in the popular mind and heart.[459]

The "Temple Cleansing"

Having reviewed the various attitudes toward the Temple, we are now in a position to understand the so-called Temple cleansing episode as it is recorded in the four Gospels. Mark introduces the action in the Temple with the words "he began," unusual in good Greek but corresponding to

Semitic usage.[460] The vocabulary of the passage is intensely traditional without a trace of Marcan influence.[461] The language is violent and elemental and appears very primitive. Matthew follows Mark except that he deletes the phrase "all the nations" (vs 17). Luke goes even further and attenuates the whole passage: he allows only three things to stand, that Jesus "cast out," the Isaianic citation, and the reference to "den of bandits." In comparison to Mark, Luke makes of it a rather innocuous occurrence. Only Mark refers to Jesus not allowing anyone to carry any "vessels" through the Temple (courts). The phrase "and he taught and was saying to them" occurs nowhere else in Mark. The phrase "it is written" is often used redactionally by Mark as in 1:1 and 9:12.[462] So Mark is apparently responsible for the introductions to the Old Testament citations.

Several considerations make the controlling interest of the passage ambiguous: the action of "cleansing" can be interpreted either as the suspension of the economic function of the Temple[463] or historically as a desire of Jesus to establish the precise conditions in which the messianic deliverance was to be achieved,[464] or the quotation from Isaiah can be understood as providing the interpretive framework explaining the action. The analysis above suggests that Mark provided the introduction to the quotation, which in turn suggests that the quotation also goes back to him. To ascertain the original extent of the passage and the relationship between vss 15–16 and 17, we must make the core of the story the focus of the initial investigation.

I begin with that core and place it within the tradition history of the Temple as I have outlined it above. That core reveals not a shred of opposition to the Temple as such, but on the contrary, it evinces a concern for the Temple's proper use and a fitting regard for it. Opposition is expressed against those whose behavior does not align with the Temple's sacred purpose and function according to the expectations related to Sukkoth, namely, to be free of traders and buyers. The cultic functions are neither mentioned much less attacked. The Temple is held with a positive regard, and the narrative aligns itself with the tradition that views it as central for the life of the community and as the locus of God' eschatological activity.

Tracing the trajectories of attitudes taken toward the Temple reveals a plethora of connections associated with Temple cleansing, the restoration of the nation, and the new messianic age that would be attendant on those actions.[465] Jesus' behavior in the traditional shape of the narrative (i.e., without the Jeremiah quotation) is congruent with the concepts as we found them expressed in the second trajectory, which viewed the Temple in positive terms. This trajectory converges with Zech 9–14. Those who "bought and sold" are related to the "traders" of Zech 14:21, a connection that is made explicit in John 2:16.[466] The evidence shows the extensiveness of the economic activity in the Temple and how a Temple official could perform purely commercial functions there.[467] However, it must be said that these commercial transactions were well regulated and neither interfered with, nor corrupted, the sacred functions carried on in the Temple proper (confined as they were to the huge court expanse on the Temple platform).[468]

There were certainly various abuses and problems connected with the sale of sacrifices, the exchange of coinage, and the regulation of those by the priestly families.[469] The text itself, however, refers to no particular abuses as, for example, the practice of charging for changing Tyrian for Roman coinage,[470] or taking a shortcut across the Temple mount,[471] or that Jesus may have been enforcing precautions that prohibited a person from wearing "a sleeved cloak or shoes or sandals or phylacteries or an amulet" when entering the Shekel Chamber to take up the heave offering.[472] Nor is there any evidence that he interrupted the sacrificial services supposedly administered by a corrupt priesthood. The emphasis is on the cessation of commercial transactions. That brings the text into the provenance of Zech 14, which prohibits traders on the Temple mount on eschatological grounds because the eschaton has arrived, and everything and everybody is considered "holy to the Lord."[473]

The language of vs 15—namely, τράπεζα, (*trapedza*, "table") and κολλυβιστής, (*kollybistēs*, "money-changer")—is unique and does not occur in the LXX. With no particular Old Testament counterparts, the narrative must be a result of the storyteller's art, which evoked actual circumstances as he knew them. Furthermore, the narrative interprets the (*KeNa'ANY*) of Zech 14:21 as those who "bought" and "sold" and "exchanged coin." That interpretation finds widespread support in subsequent tradition of the text of Zechariah. The Targum renders the Zechariah passage with "itinerant trader" and Acquila with "*mercator*" ("merchant, trader, dealer"). However, 4Q174Florilegium excludes all but Jews from the Temple.[474] This is not surprising since the Essenes included only their community in the "Sons of Light." But bPesahim 50a repudiates the literal rendering of the Zechariah text and supports the Targum and Aquila.[475] By adopting the sense of "traders," that is, "those who bought and sold," Mark 11:15 also resonates with the broader context in which Zech 14:21 occurs—namely, the gathering of the nations at the Temple on the day of the Lord.

If Zech 14 is the interpretive nexus in which the cleansing story functioned, then the story was seen as the enacted fulfillment of the prophecy that prepared for the day of the Lord and the end-times. The goal of the story would not be the cessation of the Temple's functions but rather its preparation for the establishment of God's universal reign and the end-time when the nations would flow to Jerusalem and to the Temple.

Now the function of vs 16 becomes clear. As already noted, Jesus was not interrupting the Temple sacrificial service but rather preparing the Temple for God's eschatological act. The connective "and" (καί, *kai*) introduces the verse coordinating it with the preceding list of Jesus' actions in vs 15. In each of these cases, the καί (kai, "and") introduces a separate action of Jesus: he "*enters into* the Temple" and "*overturns*" the tables and seats. So the καί of vs 16 appears to introduce a final action in a series of actions, which indicates an original relationship between the verses. If Mark had added vs 15, we would expect the construction found in 1:34c: "and not he allowed the demons to speak," an infinitive followed by the subject, rather than the subordinated subjunctive phrase found here.

Furthermore, vs 16 fits the same purpose that vs 15 does, and the action recorded in vs 16 is congruent with the eschatological description found in Zech 14, where all the vessels are declared holy so that there may be enough for all the nations that will be gathered at the Temple to make their sacrifices in the new age now being inaugurated.[476] The Isaiah quotation from 56:7 occurs in a context where eunuchs and foreigners are included within the covenant people whose sacrifices will be acceptable to the Lord. The whole economic function of the Temple is suspended so that all may freely join in the worship of Israel's God.[477]

These actions were not then conceived as revolutionary measures, though they were a challenge to the Temple authorities and a possible threat to the Roman procurator. They look like pure prophetic actions, like any of those of the classical prophets.

These actions would bring Jesus into collision with the Sadducees and be perceived by them as part of all the revolutionary movements percolating at the time.[478] And who but a king could determine what is allowed to take place on the Temple mount?[479] Jesus bears the same name as the high priest in Zech 3 of whom it is declared that he will "rule my house and have charge of my courts." When Jesus is portrayed as not allowing vessels to be carried through the Temple, one who has "charge of God's courts" is implied. Jesus in his action appears as an anointed king and messiah[480] preparing Jerusalem and the Temple for the in-breaking of the kingdom of God, when the nations will stream to the Temple, participate in its sacrifices, celebrate with Israel the eschatological feast of tabernacles, and live under the rule of the one, true God.[481] He prepares for the inauguration of "that day," the messianic age as Zech 14 prophesied.[482] He has no external authorization, and so, like the prophets, he performs a prophetic act. He acts here as a messiah with prophetic gifts.

Jesus took nothing from the Temple, destroyed nothing such as records of debt (which the revolt did later), nor led armed forces to carry out his purposes as he confronted the traders on the Temple mount.

Mark's redaction completely alters the meaning of the "cleansing" narrative. First, he embeds it within the story of the cursing of the fig tree (Mark 11:12–14, 210–21). The tree is "withered from the roots." "Withering" of the root precludes any future continuation of either the people or the messianic kingdom. The election of Israel is proclaimed to be dead with all its messianic hopes.[483] The Temple is doomed. But not only the Temple as a building is threatened but the removal of the salvific significance of the totality of Temple/Israel/eschatological hopes connected with Davidic messianism in general and the feast of Sukkoth in particular.

Second, Mark adds the saying from Jer 7:11 in vs 17, which underscores the message of the cursing and stands as a direct contradiction of the Isaiah quotation. The Jeremiah quotation occurs in the context of announcing the doom of the Temple by threatening it will become "like Shiloh." It is a "den of bandits" being prepared now for destruction. Mark 13:1–2 makes explicit what is here only limned.

The Healing of an Official's Household Member (Matt 8:5–13, Luke 7:1–10, John 4:46–53)

Both Matt and Luke report Jesus entering Capernaum and refer to a centurion, but John says Jesus is in Cana and that a "royal official"[484] came to him from Capernaum. Matthew refers to a paralyzed, tormented child, Luke to a valuable slave who is doing badly and near death, and John to a son who is ill with a fever. Luke goes on to say that the centurion is not present but sent elders of the Jews who ask Jesus to come and heal his slave, which emphasizes that the centurion is worthy of Jesus' attention because he loves the Jewish people and had built their synagogue. Jesus accompanies them, but not far from the centurion's house, they are met by friends of the centurion. Then follows the centurion's message, which Matt recounts as being delivered by the centurion himself: the message declares that as his underlings obey his orders, so Jesus can command the healing of the one who is ill. It expresses the conviction that disease and illnesses are subject to Jesus. In both Luke and Matt, Jesus declares he has not found such faith even in Israel. At this point Matthew appends the pronouncement of Jesus that the Gentile world will recline at the feast of the kingdom with Abraham, Isaac, and Jacob, while Luke includes that saying in another context (13:28–29). Matthew concludes the story with Jesus declaring the healing accomplished on the basis of the man's faith, while Luke reports that when the man had returned, he found his slave healed. In all three versions the miracle seems to be accomplished at a distance.

Contrariwise, in John, Jesus rebukes the official, accusing him of not having faith but seeking signs. A belief that cannot exist except for signs is deficient. The man responds by begging Jesus to come and heal his son before he dies. Jesus then tells him to leave because his son lives. John reports that the man "believed the word that Jesus spoke to him" (vs 50). The man now has the fullness of faith. He relies on the truth of what Jesus has promised. He returns and is met by his slaves, who report that the son is alive. He concludes the story by recounting that he and his whole house now believed. John emphasizes the healing as the "second sign" that Jesus performed, that is, as one of Jesus' seven signs in the Gospel (4:54). These seven signs, which include Jesus' own resurrection, suggest that they are the complete and perfect witness to the reality of Jesus' existence: the one sent by God, indeed God himself in the flesh, who has come to redeem the world. The miracles are "signs" of his true identity.

In the rendition of the story as told by Matthew and Luke, the centurion's faith precedes the healing, whereas in John it follows. Matthew emphasizes the story as the beginning of the inclusion of the Gentile world into the kingdom, while the "sons of the kingdom" (i.e., Israel) are cast out into "the outer darkness." So for Matthew there is a discontinuity. The church is God's new creation.

Luke emphasizes the kindness and benevolence of the centurion toward Israel and his impressive faith. For Luke it is like a presentiment of the conversion of the centurion Cornelius in Acts 10, who also was positively disposed toward Israel in that he had adopted her faith. Both stories witness of turning to the Gentiles and bestowing the Gospel on the whole world. So Luke's version of the story fits into his overall scheme of the continuity between Israel and Christianity. Christianity is part of the holy history begun in God's choice of Israel as his people. The church is included in chosenness.

The story functions in a different way for each evangelist. But the underlying elements of the story stand out: the encounter is connected with Capernaum, and a man comes to Jesus asking to have someone in his household healed.[485] The faith of the man (or its initial inadequacy as in John) is emphasized. A healing seems to take place at a distance. However, there is no explicit word of Jesus that is reported to have effected the healing. In Matthew Jesus says, "Be it done for you as you have believed"; in Luke there is no word at all; and in John Jesus says, "Go, your son will live." The three evangelists no doubt understood that Jesus effected a healing from a distance, but only Matthew could be interpreted as suggesting that in an explicit way. The underlying substrate of the story seems to suggest that Jesus only pronounced the healing that had already taken place, much as is intimated in the other example of this type of story, that of the Syrophoenician woman (Mark 7:24–30).[486] Minimally it could be said that a healing took place because of the suppliant's faith in Jesus' power to heal.

This experience of Jesus, if indeed the suppliant was a Gentile, could have been, along with his experience with the Syrophoenician woman as I suggested in my previous book, the wellspring of both Jesus' conviction that the kingdom was meant to include Gentiles as well as of the parables that emphasized the often strange and unexpected circumstances in which the kingdom of God could express itself. Although the faith of the woman is not explicitly mentioned in that story as it is in this case, her indomitable faith conquers Jesus' own initial unwillingness to fulfill her appeal for the healing of her daughter. In both cases it is Gentiles who are pushing their way into the kingdom. They are also ones who have faith that in Jesus the kingdom of God was powerfully present and active.

The multiple attestation of the event speaks for its basic authenticity even as it appears in somewhat different dress in each iteration.[487] The authenticity of the story is also supported by the criteria of discontinuity and embarrassment. Jesus is described as being "amazed" (Matt 8:10, Luke 7:9). The only other occasion on which Jesus is said to be "amazed" is in Mark 6:6. This reaction emphasizes Jesus' humanity, and so it is not surprising that John does not include this detail. The story is anchored in Capernaum, where an "official" or centurion is located who asks for healing for his "boy," which accords with the reality of the times and supports the authenticity of the story.

The Woman Taken in Adultery (John 7:53—8:11)

This story has been inserted in John secondarily. The evidence is overwhelming. It is absent in a diverse number of manuscripts including the two great fourth-century uncials Vaticanus and Sinaiticus and the oldest form of the Syriac version. In the West it is absent in the Gothic version and from several old Latin manuscripts. No Greek church father prior to the twelfth century comments on the passage.[488] However, not unsurprisingly, the fifth-century Codex Bezae includes it. This codex is notorious for its expanded text, particularly in the book of Acts. Some manuscripts insert it after 7:36 or after 21:25. One family of manuscripts inserts it after Luke 21:38. Textually the language of the passage is not Johannine, and it interrupts the sequence of the Gospel between 7:52 and 8:12. For example, the particle *de* (δε, meaning "and" or "but") occurs ten times in the passage but only 202 times in the rest of the Gospel. John usually uses the word for the "crowd," whereas this passage uses λαός (the "[elect] people"). The "scribes" are also mentioned in this passage but occur nowhere else in John's Gospel.

This evidence leads to the conclusion that the passage was a free-floating piece of the oral tradition that never found a home in any of the Gospels. Yet it has all the earmarks of a genuine historical report of an incident in the life of Jesus. It can be compared to the story of the forgiveness of the sinful woman (Luke 7:36–50) and how Jesus remonstrates with those who would not believe John's call to repentance while the prostitutes did respond (Matt 21:31–32).

The sixth commandment forbids adultery, and the Torah demands the execution of those who commit it (Lev 20:10). Idolatry is also interpreted as adultery (Jer 3:9, Ezek 23:37, Hos 4:13, Rev 2:22) because such activity entails unfaithfulness to the God of Israel, her husband and lover. Jesus himself intensifies and interiorizes its meaning by saying that "every one who looks at a woman lustfully has already committed adultery with her in his heart" (Matt 5:28), whereby he puts the focus on men who were prone to only hold women accountable to the prohibition. In the same way he makes marriage to a divorced person adultery (Mark 10:11–12).

If the incident took place in Jerusalem, however, it would imply that it was Sadducees challenging him, those who held to a strict interpretation of the Torah. His presence in the Holy City also implies that Jesus replaces the Temple, from where forgiveness emanated. Forgiveness comes from him who sat at table with sinners and conveyed to them his purity by bringing them into fellowship with God. However, that Jesus was not on the Temple platform is shown by vss 6 and 8: Jesus is described as bending and "writing with his finger on the ground." The Temple mount was paved with stones, which would have rendered that action impossible. The tradent who entered the incident into this context in John placed Jesus on the Temple mount to connect it to the Gospel context. The story itself visualizes Jesus on some street or perhaps square where it would be easy to write with one's finger in the dust. Such a location makes more sense than dragging a woman from the city all the way up onto the Temple mount. Furthermore, no one would do such a thing as take an abject sinner and unclean woman onto the holy site. It would hardly have occurred that an adulterous woman would have been dragged up to the Temple mount, the Holy Place, where only the purified were allowed entrance (cf., Ps 15).

The Pharisees generally tended to mitigate the harshness of the law. However, their Shammaite branch tended toward strictness. So quite possibly they were the ones who were not involved in this discussion.[489] It is

Shammaites who are obviously challenging and tempting Jesus with this incident of a woman caught in "the very act" (αὐτόφωρος, *autophōros*) of adultery.

The Sadducees obviously would not have regarded Jesus as competent to render a judicial decision, which points to Shammaites. They would also have been more likely to ask him for a formal verdict.[490] They are setting a snare for Jesus: he must answer that either she should be stoned to death in obedience to the Torah or she should be acquitted, in which case he could be accused of being a false teacher (cf., the verbal trap set for Jesus in Mark 12:14–17). In other words, Jesus' reputation was well known: he consorted with law-breakers and sinners, so he is to be caught in his own practice of leniency and become liable to death himself supporting what the Torah condemns. They could denounce him as a blasphemer who contradicted the law of Moses.

It is, of course, impossible to know what Jesus wrote when he bent down and wrote in the sand. One commentator, however, makes an intriguing suggestion:[491] the word for "write" here (καταγράφω, *katagraphō*, lit., "write down") is used in the LXX with the sense of "to register." By writing in the sand, Jesus was making no permanent record. It connects with Jesus' final sentence, "Neither do I condemn you . . ." (vs 11), and means that even the sin of adultery can be forgiven and wiped away as the wind shifts the sand. This gesture could also mean that Jesus did not stare at the woman as the rest of the crowd obviously did with looks of contempt and judgment. To them she was not a person but an "adulteress" stripped of her dignity and worth.[492] This very gesture suggests his respect for her as a person in spite of her sin.

Jesus' "verdict" to those who pressed him for an answer is: "let the one who is without sin cast the first stone at her." "Without sin" or "innocent" (ἀναμάρτητος, *anamartētos*) occurs only three times in the LXX, two of which are in the apocrypha. It is used nowhere else in the New Testament.[493] So the usage points to the time of the Hellenistic milieu of early Judaism. Generally the word means "free from sin." However, here it has perhaps the more specific connotation of sexual sin, and Jesus implies not one of them has been free of "looking at a woman with lust" (Matt 5:28). The only one who is justified in condemning is God in his perfection. Here Jesus identifies himself with the God of Israel and declares the woman forgiven.

Jesus and the woman are left alone after all the accusers have left "one by one" (vs 9). Jesus stands up from his writing on the ground and like a judge is ready to render a verdict. However, he asks first where her condemners are. He establishes that there is no human authority who has claimed the right to render a judgment on her. They've resigned their right and competency to act as judge. Noteworthy is that the woman expresses no repentance. Jesus simply declares that she is free of condemnation. It is clear that being free of condemnation means that the door is open to restore a right relationship between herself and God. Jesus exhorts her to "Go and from now on sin no longer." The story illustrates what John 8:15–16 proclaims, "You judge according to the flesh, I judge no one. Yet even if I do judge, my judgment is true, for it is not I alone that judge, but I and he who sent me."[494]

Jesus met the woman exactly where she was but treated her as a forgiven daughter of Israel, one with him under the Fatherhood of God.

Foretelling the Destruction of the Temple (Mark 13:1–2, Matt 24:1–2, Luke 21:5–6)

Scholars have judged the description of Jerusalem's fall here as a *vaticinium ex eventu*, composed on the basis of known facts after the event it describes.[495] The conjecture is that it is based on Josephus's description of Jerusalem's destruction. But as Wright points out[496] there are some features of Josephus that do not appear in the Gospels' descriptions and some features of the Gospels that do not appear in Josephus such as "dashing children to the ground" (vs 44). Nor were all the stones of the Temple thrown down so that there was not "one stone left on another" (another example of Jesus' use of hyperbole). Rather the evangelical descriptions are based on Old Testament biblical prophecy (e.g., Mic 3:12, Isa 29:3, Ps 137:9).

That this saying stands in contradiction to Jesus' action and pronouncement in the cleansing narrative speaks for the authenticity of both.[497] But how can both be authentic? I think the solution lies in the history and development of Jesus' ministry. John's chronology of the cleansing, which he places at the beginnings of Jesus' ministry, appears to be more accurate. In this way it would have set the rest of his ministry within a context of how Jesus understood it. He was carrying forth the promises of the eschatological Sukkoth as it appears in Zech 14. His ministry would be the "living waters" flowing out from Jerusalem and the Temple that he had prepared for the influx of the nations. His subsequent ministry brought healing and forgiveness to the people (Zech 13:1, 14:8) in preparation for the great day when YHWH would become king over all the earth (Zech 14:9)—that is, the kingdom of God would have arrived.

However, it became clear to Jesus that this expectation was not met. The nation did not respond to his proclamation of the kingdom. It did not give up its anti-Roman sentiments and actions but pursued its own way of militant nationalism to drive this "evil empire" out. The "holy war" ideology gripped great segments of the population, which Jesus saw as the way to national devastation.[498] The nation did not enter the kingdom of God that

Jesus proleptically inaugurated.[499] There were the many sinners and even the well-to-do who sat at table with Jesus to share the blessings of the kingdom already present. But as a whole the nation did not respond (Matt 21:31, Luke 13:28–29, 19:41). So, having chosen that path, it would only end in "not one stone being left another." The destruction was in the wings and would come to Jerusalem. It would be the divine judgment on YHWH's rebellious people through Rome's terror directed against their mutinous subjects. At the same time the destruction would be a vindication of Jesus' own proclamation and ministry.[500]

Jesus Weeps over Jerusalem (Luke 19:41–44)

Jesus' weeping could be compared to his tears at Lazarus's grave site facing the death of his friend (John 11:35). Jesus sees his beloved people and the Holy City through the eyes of a prophet foreseeing its demise. He does not delight in that because they are his people, the city his delight (Pss 122:3–6, 128:5, 137:5–6). He weeps for what he sees coming upon his beloved. He is facing a death.

Similarly, some 40 years later when the sacrifices had been discontinued and as Titus and the Roman army were about ready to raze the foundation of the Fortress Antonia, which would then lead directly to the destruction of the Temple and Jerusalem, Josephus, under Titus's orders, addressed John of Gishala, who at the time held the Temple mount, to come out of the city and do battle and thereby prevent the threatened destruction. But John cursed Josephus. Josephus began his message with biting irony:

> Certainly you have kept [the city] pure for God, and the holy place too remains unpolluted! You have never dishonored your hoped-for ally and He still receives the customary sacrifices![501]

At the end of his peroration Josephus reports he had spoken with groans and tears and finally had broken down with sobs.[502] His bitter weeping was exacerbated because he was a priest and so had a deep connection with the Temple and its liturgies. And what faithful Jew could not but shed tears at the disaster that was about to befall city and people right before one's very eyes?

Jesus had called the nation to the way of peace: to give up anger, pray for the enemy and respect their humanity, practice hospitality, forgive the sins of others, to see that God's reign could appear in the most peculiar of circumstances and places, and to exorcise the demons of enmity and antagonism that now possessed the nation.[503] The nation had not grasped what would make for peace and was enamored with and plagued by animosity and rivalry, revolution and war. Not that there wasn't a war to be fought: that war was with the demonic powers that had captured Israel and worked toward its doom. The Jews both inland and outland were an island in a sea of paganism. But Jesus did not see that sea as the real enemy. God's kingdom could also reveal itself there.[504] The struggle was with a cosmic enemy, and that involved not just the Jew but also the whole pagan world. Jesus makes that clear in his exorcisms, which were the preliminary way of "binding the strong man" that Satan's household might be plundered, that is, devastated, and Satan shorn of his power.[505]

It is within such a context that Jesus declares that Jerusalem (i.e., the people) does not know in what peace consists (vs 42).[506] Its peace was not in violently establishing the independence of the Jewish state and freedom from Rome. That would only lead to the sorrow of devastation. Rather it was in the exorcism of the "seven demons" from the body politic (the parable of returning demons). That peace was embodied in Jesus himself, in his message, in his healings and exorcisms, and in him now as he stood right before their eyes. The nation's inability to accept the kingdom as Jesus brought it darkens Israel's eyes, and so peace remains "hidden." Jesus asserted that the nation with its vaunted wisdom and understanding did not grasp the kingdom and living by its way of life, while "children" did (Luke10:21). Jesus meant perhaps both literal children and the simple (cf., 1 Cor 1:26–28). Whoever will not see cannot see (Isa 29:10).

Jesus and his proclamation of the kingdom with its open commensality, healings, and exorcisms was God "visiting" his people (vs 44). God "visiting" his people meant a time of restoration (Gen 50:24, Jer 29:10) but judgment for the iniquitous (2 Esd 6:18–19, 9:2–12). Jesus' weeping is in the face of the judgment that now will befall the people.[507]

The Anointing of Jesus at Bethany
(Mark 14:3–9, Matt 26:6–13, John 12:1–8)

Both Mark and Matt relate that the incident of his anointing took place in the house of "Simon the Leper," while John places it in the house of Lazarus and his two sisters Mary and Martha.[508] Matthew substitutes "very expensive vial of myrrh" for Mark's "very costly alabaster vial of ointment of pure nard." John identifies the ointment as "a pound of very costly ointment, pure nard." In Mark and Matthew the woman anoints the head of Jesus and remains unnamed, while John identifies her as Mary, who anoints his feet. John adds the detail that Mary, after anointing his feet, "wiped them with her hair (a detail also found in Luke's story). Matthew, whose wont it is to abbreviate Mark, writes that the "disciples" ask "why this waste for it could be sold for much and given to the poor" in place of Mark's "But there were some who said to themselves indignantly, 'Why was the ointment thus wasted? For this ointment might have been sold for more than three hundred denarii, and given to the poor.' And they reproached her." John identifies the complainer with Judas Iscariot. Again, Matthew shortens Jesus' defense of the woman in Mark by eliminating "whenever you wish you can do good to them [the poor]." John eliminates the interpretation of Jesus that explains the anointing as preparation for his burial (which never took place because of the Sabbath laws) and that the deed of the woman would be proclaimed along with the Gospel "in memory of her." However, Jesus says that she should be left alone so that she can "keep the [ointment] for the day of his burial." So these three versions of the anointing of Jesus before his passion are all based on the same tradition despite differences in detail. Finally, the multiple attestation suggests its authenticity.

Mark's identifying the house as that of "Simon the Leper" suggests he was referring to someone known to his community since he makes no attempt to identify him with further details (the same may be said of Simon of Cyrene, whom he names in 15:21). John, who depicts in detail the little family of Mary, Martha, and Lazarus in chapter 11, places the incident in their house in Bethany apparently because he knew nothing of a "Simon the Leper." He apparently assumed, since Jesus was so intimately related to the family and because he was in Bethany, that he surely would have taken a meal there. In such stories as this, the word of Jesus is most important, not so much the staging.[509] That Mark's version is much older than John's and the mention of an otherwise unidentified "Simon the Leper" suggest that his account represents more nearly the historical circumstances.

The action on the part of the woman stems from her respect and devotion to him (not thankfulness as in Luke's story). The ointment was indeed costly, especially among the peasant folk of the villages, and elicited therefore criticism for what seemed to be an extravagant waste, especially on just one person. But the person of Jesus occupies the center of the story, and he is revealed as one who incited the devotion of others, as the Gospels attest, and as the gracious defender of those unjustly criticized. He enhances his defense with a forceful justification by interpreting the anointing as preparing for his burial.[510] Is this a possible word in the mouth of Jesus? He may not have had his actual burial in mind, because he foresaw the actual circumstances but knew his death was coming and used these words as a compelling vindication of the woman's action.

Vs 9 is another matter. We encounter here the vocabulary of the church in its universal proclamation of the Gospel. The saying could have been built on the actual proclamation of the church as the Gospel was brought to the world. That in itself would be a witness for the authenticity of the story and the word of Jesus that the woman's action was a witness to his burial. However, the reference to the telling of the story as a "memorial to her" could have been part of a prophecy of Jesus. But then why would her name have been forgotten?[511]

That Mark (and Matthew following him) has the woman anoint Jesus' head is also telling. Kings (the "anointed of the Lord," i.e., "Messiah") were anointed with oil on the head (Exod 29:7, 2 Kgs 9:3–7, Ps 141:5). By placing the story just before Jesus' suffering, these two evangelists proclaim that it is the Messiah who receives his kingship by going through the coming passion (cf., the *titulus* placed on the cross, Mark 15:26, "The King of the Jews").

On the Way to the Cross: Simon of Cyrene (Mark 15:21, Matt 27:32, Luke 23:26) and the Lamenting Women (Luke 23:27–31)

Technically, of course, the impressment of Simon to bear Jesus' cross is not a pronouncement story. However, the story implies Jesus' silent appeal for help. Again, Mark mentions a person without explaining any other connection with Jesus. Simon of Cyrene's[512] sons, Alexander and Rufus, were probably contemporary members of Mark's community and well known to his readers.[513] He is described as coming "from the field," which suggests he had been working. Work was forbidden during the feast (Exod 12:16). He had to have been Jewish, bearing the name that he does.[514] The phrase "from the field" means having worked there.[515] Translating it as "coming from the country"[516] has no justification in biblical usage, and Mark just might be emphasizing that Simon was a lawbreaker. Like one of the sinners with whom Jesus ate and drank, a sinner ends up bearing his cross.

The present tenses of this report lend a vividness to the account and serve as a witness to the veracity of the crucifixion. Simon is commandeered (ἀγγαρεύω, *angareuō*, a Persian loan word, "to impress into service") to bear the cross[517] evidently because Jesus, so weakened by his flagellation (Luke 23:16, John 19:1, Matt 27:26), could no longer do so. Why did the soldiers grab him as opposed to other bystanders? Perhaps it is because he was not part of the crowd and for that reason stood out. The "cross" that he bore was the *patibulum*, that is, the "cross-beam." The upright parts of crosses were left standing in the places of crucifixion with a tenon (projection) at the top that fitted into the mortise (opening) on the cross beam.

Then this woeful entourage meets the wailing women who raise a funeral dirge in anticipation of the coming death on the cross. The words of Jesus are primitive, rest on an Aramaic original, and have parallels in Jewish tradition,[518] which speak for their authenticity. The women stand in contrast to the crowd that called for Jesus' crucifixion (Mark 15:13–14, Luke 23:21–23, Matt 27:22–23). His answer turns the tables on a normal curse: a barren woman who never gave birth was considered cursed (not fulfilling the original blessing of God to be fruitful and multiply, Gen 1:28). Here Jesus says the day will come when the barren woman is blessed for not having to see the terrible suffering of her children brought about by the horrors inflicted on the nation in the coming catastrophe.

Jesus then quotes Hos 10:8, which was part of an imprecation against Israel threatening disaster for the nation because of her idolatry, when they will lose their king, their children, the Temple, and the whole land. To be buried under mountains and hills will seem a better consequence than facing the terrors that will be visited upon them. Now too, the nation was choosing hostility and armed revolution rather than entering the kingdom of peace where forgiveness, mutual love, and sharing the goods of the earth prevailed. The quotation dovetails perfectly into the mission and ministry of Jesus: the judgment on trusting military power, the ominous warning to mothers and their children, and the death of the king. "Jerusalem" (i.e., the nation) had rejected Jesus as their true king and his invitation into the kingdom of God. His death at the hands of the Romans will now be the pellucid sign of the fate of the nation.

The final discomfiting statement of Jesus is clear in its meaning (vs 31).[519] It echoes passages like Isa 10:16–19:[520]

> Therefore the Lord, the Lord of hosts, will send wasting sickness among his stout warriors, and under his glory a burning will be kindled, like the burning of fire. The light of Israel will become a fire, and his Holy One a flame; and it will burn and devour his thorns and briers in one day. The glory of his forest and of his fruitful land the Lord will destroy, both soul and body, and it will be as when a sick man wastes away. The remnant of the trees of his forest will be so few that a child can write them down.

Israel is compared to a forest that is consumed by the fire of the Lord's judgment. So what can the guilty expect from Rome, whose fire destroys the one who had been declared innocent, but the arm of divine judgment expressed in the coming of the Roman fire that will incinerate Israel because of its failure to repent and its hostile militarism. Jesus was the green tree and impenitent Israel the dry. "Simon may carry the patibulum; but Jesus is already carrying on his heart the cross of Israel's condemnation."[521]

3

The Tantalizing Teacher

Controversy and Scholastic Dialogues

"I will utter what has been hidden
since the foundation of the world."

In this chapter I will again follow the catalogue of Bultmann for what he names the controversy and scholastic dialogues. In the analysis I will follow the themes that characterize Jesus' pithy comments as he encounters various interlocutors who challenge or question him about his practices or the behavior of his disciples as well as questions put to him by his disciples and others.

THE PRONOUNCEMENT STORIES: CONTROVERSY AND SCHOLASTIC DIALOGUES

Healing of the Man with a Withered Hand (Mark 3:1–6, Luke 13:10–17, 14:1–6, Matt 12:9–13)

The controversy is occasioned by a healing: should one heal on the Sabbath or not. Healing would be considered work, and keeping the Sabbath holy by refraining from work was enshrined in the second of the ten commandments. However, even Pharisees would say the Sabbath law could be broken when it comes to the saving of life, including that of an animal (Matt 12:11–12, Luke 13:15). Of course, in this case the man's life was not at stake, and one could say with the synagogue president in Luke 13:14 "There are six days on which work ought to be done; come on those days and be healed, and not on the Sabbath day." Jesus asserts here all kinds of saving work are to be allowed on the Sabbath. This insistence reflects his kingdom proclamation: the kingdom will not wait; it is present in the here and now in this healing as he engages in the battle against Satan. He binds the "strong man" (Mark 3:27). The time is urgent, and the kingdom is at the door, so Jesus urges watchfulness in the parable of the door (Mark 13:33), readiness in the parable of the thief, and the compelling of people to come to the great supper in the parable of the great feast (Luke 14:23). The warfare against Satan cannot take a break.[522]

Matthew's version is clearly parallel to Mark, but he introduces the saying of the legality of rescuing animals on the Sabbath (Matt 12:11) as a counterargument to his unnamed interlocutors who ask an apparently accusatory question of whether it is lawful to heal on the Sabbath.

The Man with Dropsy (Luke 14:1–6)

The story is not a variant of the man with a withered hand. The man's hand is not withered, but he is described as "dropsical" (i.e., he has edema, the swelling of his body with water). The location is not a synagogue but a house, and the argument is not a matter of saving someone on the Sabbath but the lawfulness of doing work on the Sabbath, which is allowed in the case of rescuing an animal,[523] an argument from the lesser to the greater (a fortiori) or, as the Rabbis called it, *Qal VaChomer*. Jesus speaks here using the argumentative rhetoric of a Pharisee.

Jesus was not abrogating the Sabbath nor opposing its observance. He is pictured as entering the synagogues on the Sabbath to teach (Mark 6:2, Luke 6:6, 13:10), and Luke 4:16 states that it was "his custom" to do so. What he does do is observe that there are exceptions to the Sabbath laws prohibiting work as when a baby is circumcised on the Sabbath (John 7:23). Jesus was not being frivolous and flouting the law as some kind of modern-day counterculturalist. He understood himself as a servant (Mark 10:41–45). In Luke 4:18–21 he identifies himself with Second Isaiah's Servant of the Lord (Isa 42:1–7), which alludes to the Jubilee, God's plan for the restoration of his people.[524] With that identification he aimed his ministry particularly at the weak and the oppressed. In Isa 35 the Jubilee has an eschatological association, when nature itself will be transformed.[525] In this way the Jubilee's imagery is used to depict God's final plan for the world that will bring about the restoration of creation. Combined with that is the restoration of people: sight to the blind, hearing to the deaf, healing to the lame, and speech to the dumb.

All of this accords with how Jesus conducted his ministry of proclaiming the presence of the kingdom and its immanence: healing, restoring sinners to communion with the God of Israel, freeing the possessed from demons, and calling the nation to eschew violence and restore brotherhood.[526] Because of his proclamation (see the parables) that the kingdom was at hand, Jesus conceived of an eschatological Jubilee that stood "at the door." He was calling the people to live here and now the ethics and ideals of the Jubilee. He sets forth these ethics and ideals in the parables of the rich fool, the unforgiving servant, seats at a feast, a neighbor comes at midnight, the good Samaritan, and the two debtors.

Healing of the Crippled Woman (Luke 13:10–17)

Bultmann understands the story as a variant of the healing of the man with a withered hand (Mark 3:1–6) apparently because it takes place on the Sabbath. However, the details of each story deviate from one another to such an extent that it would be difficult to explain a man getting transformed into a woman or a withered hand into a cripple, the description of how long the woman had suffered with her infirmity, and the specification that it was the ruler of the synagogue (not the usual "Pharisees" or "scribes") who criticized Jesus but then not with the usual ad hominem argument we find in the tradition.[527] Jesus' argument in the apothegm employs a typical rabbinic argument from the lesser to the greater, as in the passage above: if animals are rescued on the Sabbath, why not a human being, an argument that would be entirely acceptable to a Pharisee, who would agree with him. That his opponent would not have anticipated this argument supports the fact that he is not well versed in legal reasoning like a Pharisee or a scribe.

The crippled woman is described as having a "spirit of weakness," which implies that her condition is the result of the work of demons. The number "eighteen" appears frequently in the Bible and might mean simply "for a long time."[528] Jesus calls her to himself and touches her. A woman is generally considered unclean; men were advised not to keep their company both for that reason and to avoid any hint of immorality. The woman's condition also renders her unclean and suspect of being sinful since she had suffered as a cripple for so long. His touch achieves her thorough restoration. Her healing leads her to glorify God, a witness to Jesus' divine authority.

The president of the synagogue addresses the congregation gathered there. He uses Jesus' action as a teaching moment for the people about the law and the need to take it seriously. He knows well the command to honor the Sabbath (Exod 20:9-10, Deut 5:13-15). These were sweeping laws that were applicable to everyone including Gentiles connected with Israelite households and their animals.[529] He appears to be vaunting himself as a knowledgeable teacher of the Torah, but Jesus reveals his amateur status: the Pharisaic master held that human life came before the requirement of Torah, and even the strict Essenes allowed a man to be pulled from a cistern.[530] Judaism recognized the higher worth of human life. Jesus reflected that same concern when he reminded his hearers that they were worth much more than sparrows (Luke 12:6).[531] Jesus plays on the words "loosing" an animal and the woman who is to be "loosed" from being "bound by Satan" (vss 15-16). In the latter case the verb is in the passive ("to have been loosed"), which implies the hand of God is at work in her healing. His action is another assault on the kingdom of Satan and his house. It verges on an apocalyptic victory by God over Satan. The woman certainly could have waited to be healed on the following day and avoided trespassing the Sabbath prohibition of work. But the kingdom of God is present and active here. Victory over Satan will not wait another day![532] Jesus says it is a "must" (Gk., ἔδει, *edei*, imperfect tense, i.e., it is an ongoing necessity) for her to be loosed from her bond—that is, it is a divine eschatological demand.[533] The liberation from Satan's bonds must go on seven days a week. The Sabbath was actually the preeminent day for the work of liberation. After all, the Sabbath was given to have a weekly loosing of Israel from the bondage of labor and a foretaste of the rest to come with the in-breaking of the kingdom, which would be the release from all bondages. To liberate the woman from her crippling bonds was therefore a fulfillment of the purpose of the Sabbath, not its profanation![534]

The Dispute about Exorcism (Mark 3:22-30, Matt 12:22-37, Luke 11:14-23)

Jesus' double image of a divided kingdom and a divided house is in a form typical of Jewish debates.[535] Matthew's and Luke's versions seem to have come from Q, although each has reproduced the story in his own style. Mark's version does not follow Q, which has Jesus defending his exorcistic activity by asking if he works with the power of Satan by whom do their "sons" cast out demons.[536] He neither includes the remark that follows, "But if it is by the finger [Luke 11:20, Matt 12:28, "Spirit"] of God that I cast out demons, then the kingdom of God has come upon you," nor the declaration "He who is not with me is against me, and he who does not gather with me scatters" (Luke 11:23, Matt 12:30). Matthew follows Mark in the saying about binding the strong man, and Luke adds a longer version (10:21–22). Matthew also reproduces Mark's saying about the sin against the Holy Spirit, which Luke eliminates but includes in another context in 12:10. Q looks like the more original version of the apothegm.

The name Baalzebub ("lord of the flies") occurs in 2 Kings 1:2 as a derisive reference to the god of Ekron, Baalzebul ("lord of the house"). The name evokes the imagery of flies gathered on a carcass. Judaism identified the gods of the pagans with evil spirits (1 Cor 10:20–21).

The charge against Jesus that he performs his exorcisms by the power of Satan does recognize that a supernatural power is at work in him.[537] Jesus answers the charges of being in league with Satan with three arguments: Satan wouldn't be so foolish as to allow civil war among his minions. Possession by his demons and striking people with illness are his stock in trade for afflicting people and getting them to "curse God and die" (Job 2:9) and so place themselves eternally within his clutches. There is an implied accusation here of the foolishness of his own society, which is presently divided and at war with itself and so if it continues on this path it will not stand.

His second argument refers to other exorcists who free people from demon possession. Finally, his detractors should know that it is only by God's power that the grip of Satan can be broken by the "finger of God" (Exod 8:19).[538] That God can do that with merely his "finger" confesses God's infinite power over the puny devil (1 Kgs 12:10). This should lead them to conclude that Jesus is the strong man who is binding Satan and plundering his house. Jesus' metaphor here limns the name of the "demon-god" who is "lord of the house." Jesus plunders his house by liberating those possessed by his demons having made of them his chattel. But Jesus is the stronger one binding the "strong man" first by facing Satan in his temptation and now by his exorcisms,[539] which presages some final "plundering" of his house (i.e., his dominion). Perhaps Jesus saw that denouement in the final in-breaking of the kingdom of God whose way he pioneered by his words and deeds (Heb 2:10, 12:2).

Jesus places his exorcistic activity in the framework of the kingdom of God, which, though it lies in the future, is present already in his driving demons out of people. Jesus sees the world as enemy occupied territory—which it was politically. But that political occupation was nothing compared to its tyrannical occupation by Satan, who keeps it in the power of his clutches that no human can shatter. In Jesus the kingdom of God invades this enemy-occupied territory. So Jesus' final statement about it and against it is a judgment: if you don't stand with him, you are siding with the evil one (Luke 11:23). So quite appropriately Luke follows up this apothegm with the parable of the returning demons (11:24–26).

Q, Mark, and John all make clear that Jesus was indeed accused by his opponents of being in league with the Devil. The study of the parables made clear that Jesus' concept of the kingdom included corruption in the sense that sinners, outliers, and Gentiles were included in it and that even repentance beforehand was not required. Implied here is that Jesus seemed to question the law as divinely given, which he did not do (Matt 5:18). That and his healings could well have aligned him, at least in the eyes of some Pharisees who may have been present in the Galilee, with those excluded from the world to come and so a heretic.[540]

The Healing of a Paralytic (Mark 2:1–12, Matt 9:1–8, Luke 5:17–26)

Many interpreters find Mark 2:5b–10 as in interpolation into the story.[541] The only other story about Jesus himself forgiving sins is the story of the sinful woman (Luke 7:36–50, in which the parable of the two debtors is included) and the story of the woman taken in adultery (John 7:53—8:11).[542] The fact that the faith of those who brought the paralytic to Jesus does not appear outside these verses does not tell against the inclusion of these verses in the original pericope. To excise these verses makes the story look truncated since in that case the pallet is let down in front of Jesus through the roof, and he immediately says to the paralytic, "I say to you, take up your pallet and go to your house." Compare that to the stories in Mark 5:21–43, the healing of the blind man in 8:22–26, the epileptic boy in 9:14–29, and blind Bartimaeus in 10:46–52 and the conversations that take place there. To excise these verses would make the remainder look like a fragment of a story. So on its form alone, compared to other healing narratives the story as it appears in Mark has to be judged a unity.[543]

But does Jesus heal, as the story seems to imply, only to prove that he can forgive sins? Elsewhere he eschews the "giving of signs" (Mark 8:11–12). It need not be understood in that way. Rather, Jesus is saying forgiveness and healing are all a part of the restoration that the kingdom represents. In addition, the story seems to imply that illness and sin are coordinated, which Jesus elsewhere denies (Luke 13:1–5, John 9:2–3). However, their coordination is within the kingdom, which is the restoration of the whole person and the whole society. The coordination of sin and disease, since it occurs only here in the Gospels, may point to the fact that it applies only to this paralyzed man. Finally, the scribal reaction is not reported but rather only the usual reaction of the crowd (vs 12). The implication is that these scribes simply remained silent, perhaps quietly seething in their offense at Jesus' words or simply struck with amazement as in Mark 11:17.[544]

The reference to "son of man" in the original Aramaic (Heb., *Bar Nash*) could simply mean "man" or "human being" as it does in Mark 2:28. In which case Jesus is not claiming any special powers to forgive sins but rather that it is a prerogative of human beings, which is how Matt 9:8 understood it.[545] That people in general have that right seems odd at first and has no parallel in Jewish teaching.[546] However, such authority is underscored in Matt 18:18 and John 20:23. Where the kingdom is, there forgiveness reigns. His contemporaries could well take offense at this aspect of the kingdom.

Forgiveness lies at the heart of Jesus' ministry and concerns. It is part of the prayer that he teaches his disciples (Matt 6:12, Luke 11:4). He declares that without forgiveness of others one cannot expect divine forgiveness (Matt 6:14-15, Luke 6:37, Mark 11:25, the parable of the unforgiving servant) and that forgiveness is to know no boundaries (Matt 18:21, Luke 17:3-4). Jesus founds his sacramental meal on forgiveness (Matt 26:28). He himself pronounces forgiveness (see above) and finally asks for forgiveness for those who have crucified him (Luke 23:34). Without forgiveness, Jesus declares, the nation cannot survive because the divisions and animosities of his day will lead to destruction. Such is the kingdom that he proclaimed. He establishes the peaceable kingdom where "the wolf dwells with the lamb." Such is the true knowledge of the Lord (Isa 11:6-9).

Plucking Grain on the Sabbath (Mark 2:23-28, Matt 12:1-8, Luke 6:1-5)

This story asserts that the breaking of the Sabbath can be defended on the basis of Scripture. It looks like an idealized scene that was composed by the church in its controversies. How are we to imagine the presence of the Pharisees? Were they walking with Jesus and the disciples through the fields? If the story actually took place, it could have been any Jew who happened to observe the activity of the disciples. But then another question raises its head. Why were they walking through a field on the Sabbath anyway since one was only allowed to go a certain distance on the Sabbath?[547] It looks like the scene was invented for the words of vss 27-28.

That vss 27 and 28 are introduced with the attachment formula "and he was saying to them" also suggests that they were added to the story by Mark. However, vs 27 presupposes the walk through the grain field that introduces the apothegm. At any rate, here "son of man" is coordinated with "man" (Gk., ἄνθρωπος, *anthrōpos*, human being, person) and therefore clearly means that all human beings are "lords of the Sabbath."[548]

The Sabbath was the sine qua non of Jewish life and existence and important for the survival of Judaism, surrounded as it was by a Gentile world.[549] By observing it, a Jew made a public profession of faith. The Rabbis enumerated thirty-nine activities that were not allowed to be performed on the Sabbath. To question the sacredness of this day was more or less a direct attack on Jewish faith and existence, so any violation of Sabbath observance would elicit vigorous opposition.

The hungry traveler was allowed to feed himself in this way (Deut 23:25, but Mark's story does not say that the disciples were "eating"; Matt 12:1 and Luke 6:1 add that detail). Reaping, however, was forbidden on the Sabbath (Exod 34:21). Without the reference to David, Jesus is portrayed as using an argument employed by the Pharisees. The words "have need" (vs 25), a Marcan phrase (see 11:3, 14:63), and the reference to "Abiathar" (vs 26), neither of which are included by Matthew and Luke, suggest the hand of Mark is at work interpolating the reference to David into the original story.[550] In addition, Jesus is portrayed as passive while the disciples make their way through the fields plucking the grain, so the reference to David's action, leading those "with him," does not fit the situation. The point of the story is the apothegm in vs 27–28. Without the reference to David, the pericope is a unitary construction and is conceived in terms of a thoroughly Jewish milieu and its argument in a thoroughly Jewish and Pharisaic manner that would be accepted by anyone who was concerned with keeping the law: the Sabbath laws were expendable in the case of human requirement. The higher law allows the breaking of the lower law.

So in vs 27 Jesus seems to reiterate the rabbinical principle "the Sabbath is delivered unto you and you are not delivered to the Sabbath" (Mekilta on Exod 31:13).[551] If vs 28 was original to the story, then it could be that Jesus is using Hebrew parallelism, and the two verses are to be coordinated. Jesus' conclusion is that a human being stands above the requirements of the law, which is precisely the stance he takes in his healing activities: the present needs of people take precedence over the law's prescriptions.[552] Since these words, understood in this sense, differentiate themselves from Jewish ideas, we can assume they were spoken by Jesus, but their context was lost, and the present story was composed to supply them with a context.

The Dispute about Clean and Unclean
(Mark 7:1–23, Matt 15:1–20)

At first, this long pericope looks like the amalgam of various pieces of traditional material.[553] The story begins with a question of hand washing as a way of ritually purifying the hands, which then evolves into a discussion of why the disciples do not conform altogether with Pharisaic prescriptions. The Pharisees had not only studied the written Torah but also developed what they called the oral law, traditions of the people handed down from time immemorial.[554]

Vss 3–4 are one of those famous asides of Mark that he addresses directly to the reader and which he has obviously interpolated into the story.[555] Another occurs in vs 19, where Mark interprets the words of Jesus as declaring that "all foods are pure."

There are two parts to Jesus' reply. Jesus is represented as opposed to the oral tradition (the "tradition" mentioned in Mark 7:3, 5, 8, and 13) in both of these parts. In the first he quotes Isaiah 29:13 as a rebuke against making human traditions divine law and even using the tradition to disobey the written law, which is truly divine having been given to Moses by God. However, the quotation is from the LXX. Jesus would hardly have quoted the Greek translation of the Scriptures. The original Hebrew was a judgment against perfunctory worship. However, the Targum, the Aramaic paraphrases of Scripture, which is highly likely what Jesus would have quoted, reads:

> Wherefore the Lord has said, because I am magnified by the mouth of this people and with their lips they do honor me, but their heart is far from my fear and their fear toward me is as the commandment of men teaching (them).[556]

Jesus could well have quoted this Aramaic paraphrase. In other words, Jesus, by reference to this passage, accuses the Pharisees of not really honoring God by their insistence on the oral law and characterizes this "new teaching" as nothing but human commandments.[557]

Second, Jesus gives a concrete example of how this oral law and its observance conflicts with the written Torah. The "Korban" (vs 11) was an offering dedicated to the Temple. Philo had a strict view of this vow. "If a man had devoted his wife's substance to a sacred purpose he must refrain from giving her that substance."[558] The schools of Hillel and Shammai also differed in their interpretation of these vows. The Shammaites were generally more strict and conservative in their interpretation.[559] In Mishnah Nedarim ("Vows") 3,2 it reads:

> If a man saw others eating [his] figs and said, "May they be Korban to you!" and they were found to be his father and brothers and others with them, the School of Shammai say: For them the vow is not binding, but for the others with them it is binding. And the School of Hillel say: The vow is binding for neither of them.

The intent of the man who declared his figs Korban was to prevent others from eating his figs, and they were to be treated as if dedicated to the Temple and therefore could not be eaten. In this case the two houses thought that at most it was only partially valid (Shammai) perhaps because of its frivolousness. Vows were taken seriously, as the Torah demanded (Deut 23:21–23, Num 30:2).[560] The Mishnah seems to say that if a vow prevented someone from supporting his parents, he had the right to break the vow.[561]

In the example that Jesus gives, a person could declare by a vow certain property dedicated to the Temple, that is, owned by the Temple, so no one could make use of it. Such a declaration could have been made out of a malicious intent to deprive parents of the use of such goods. So Jesus rules that the vow is invalid because of the written law that demands honoring of parents as opposed to the Pharisees as they are represented here, who declare such a vow as valid. However, the Torah has strict provisions regarding both vows and honoring of parents, so it is not a matter of oral law versus written. (But we must notice here that Jesus hardly criticizes, much less attacks, the written Torah but upholds it.) On the other hand, it is doubtful that the Pharisees held to such a position as is ascribed to them here, given the discussion quoted above from the Mishnah. It might be so that the Shammaites took the position that Jesus is attacking and would have declared such a vow valid even though it contradicted the written Torah.[562] Supporting this is Philo's strict interpretation indicating that other Jewish teachers could have held the same view as the Shammaites.[563]

To render the hands clean, the Mishnah required the use of a quarter log (equal to the amount of liquid of an egg and a half) of water poured over the hands. That amount would suffice for one or two persons. It was also the custom to give the hands a double rinsing, and the water had to reach the wrist. But if there was not enough water to reach the wrist with the second, a fresh quarter log had to be used.[564] The heave offering required ritually cleansed hands.[565] However, to offer "hallowed things" (those offerings to be in whole or in part offered on the altar) and the sin offering,[566] the hands had to be immersed.[567] In addition, utensils that were considered ritually clean required immersion for the hallowed things but not for heave offerings. A distinction was made between the parts of utensils: the outer, the inner, and the holding part. If the utensil was held by the holding part and the outer part was unclean, clean hands were not made unclean. Nor did the liquid within become unclean if the outer part was unclean.[568] In cases of doubt as to whether the hands were clean or unclean, they were considered clean.[569]

This practice of hand washing may indeed represent a later development within rabbinic Judaism (the Mishnah was finally written down c. AD 200), but it may have been practiced by the Pharisees in the time before the destruction of the Temple and so may not be an entirely theoretical discussion. In any case, there is no mention of hand washing before a common meal. Mark may be referring here to certain Jewish Christians in the Hellenistic milieu who were demanding the practice based on the practice they had adopted from the Gentile world.

The Pharisees, at least in the land, did not wash their hands before eating common meals but only in connection with priests' food and sacrifices. Edward Parish Sanders speculates it may therefore have been a practice in the diaspora imitating pagan practice (that is implied by Mark in 7:3 when he says "all the Jews" practice this hand washing). Hand washing then was not a particular trait of Pharisaism (which Mark recognizes in vs 7:3). At any rate, Sanders says even if some Pharisaic groups practiced hand washing before meals, there were many more serious breaches of the law for which they could have criticized Jesus and his disciples.[570] He further notes that if Jesus had really wanted to challenge the purity laws, he would have visited Tiberias, which had been built on a graveyard, rendering every inhabitant there tainted with corpse impurity.[571] That coupled with the fact that hand washing was an unimportant matter can only lead one to conclude that Jesus was not engaged in a dispute with his contemporaries over purity laws. Furthermore, Jesus accepts the laws of purity when he tells the leprous man to "show himself to the priest and offer the sacrifice commanded by Moses" (Mark 1:44).

A clear break occurs at vs 14 as Jesus "calls together the crowd." Vss 14–15 are only tangentially related to what has preceded them, which suggests that Mark appended it to this previous discussion. There was no legislation that said unwashed hands imparted impurity to food that was eaten; rather they could only impart impurity to sacrifices. But there were laws in the Torah that forbade the eating of certain foods (Exod 23:19, Lev 11, Deut 14:3–21, cf., Acts 10:14). These dietary regulations set the people of Israel apart from the nations, identifying them as God's own peculiar people (Exod 19:6). They declare that ritual purity is demanded of the people to build, as it were, a fence between them and the rest of the world's people, providing a daily means of reminding them not to be defiled by pagan beliefs and practices. But Jesus' declaration here seems to radically dissolve all of this legislation on ritual purity: only right behavior counts, "what comes out of a person."

I have suggested this was an independent saying that Mark interpolated into the present chapter. If that is so, we have lost the original context into which it was spoken. Taking into consideration what we have discovered about Jesus' message in the parables, it could well be he was answering criticism regarding his consorting and eating with sinners and other marginalized Jews. He would be saying something like this: "Yes indeed, these are people who appear outside the law and looked upon as law breakers. But they are the ones who have entered the kingdom, and what is important now is their inner attitude and not external ritual purity. They have, with open hearts, received the treasure of the gifts of the kingdom. This kingdom of God is not only for the ritually pure but for all who have been found by it, even Gentiles. It is for those who have accepted the invitation, accepted God's incredible treasure of mercy and forgiveness, and so are themselves imbued with mercy and love." Jesus' focus here is exclusively on the inner disposition of a person. That alone is what matters to him.

The words are repeated and expanded in vss 18–19 and then in vss 20–23, which appear to be attached to the preceding by the formula "and he was saying that," he enumerates the evils that can issue from the human heart and cause the real defilement of a person. But how is this to be reconciled to his apparent acceptance of the authority of the Torah? These words apparently undercut all of the Mosaic legislation dealing with pure and impure foods and this after he has just criticized the Pharisees for nullifying the Torah. The answer lies in its original context, which I have suggested occurred when Jesus was criticized for his practice of an expansive commensality. In that case he need not be understood here as uttering a rejection of Judaism's dietary laws.

The list of sins is much like that found in Galatians 5:19–21 (and in fact share four of the sins in that catalogue). Suggested is that we have here a list widespread in Hellenistic Judaism, where such catalogues were a common feature of the world.

In conclusion, this whole section appears to be a Marcan construction in which he has taken a controversy from his own milieu in its interaction with Judaism (or perhaps even Jewish Christians, vss 1–2), appended his explanation of Jewish practice in that milieu (vss 3–4), attached a controversy with some Shammaite Pharisees, which could well present an actual interaction between them and Jesus (vss 5–13, which deals with the use of Korban and not hand washing), added a word of Jesus (vss 14–15), and then constructed a conversation with the disciples built on that saying that included a catalogue of sins in common use among the Christians of Mark's community. So Mark constructed this narrative to meet a critical situation in his own community.

Eating with Tax Collectors and Sinners (Mark 2:15–17, Matt 9:10–13, Luke 5:27–32)[572]

Here Jesus' opponents are described by the unique expression "the scribes of the Pharisees," a phrase occurring nowhere else in the New Testament.[573] The hand of Mark is at work, adding the phrase "of the Pharisees" to the tradition as he received it. The Pharisees were a group with whom Mark's community was in conflict, and he imports them into his Gospel as a way of meeting the needs of his community in dealing with them. The tradition would have mentioned only scribes. Scribes in the Galilee would have been a ubiquitous group not only because of the court of Antipas in Sepphoris but because the towns circling the Sea of Galilee were teeming with a fishing industry, which would have required the use of scribes to keep the books of these businessmen and -women and help them to ensure that their wares were in keeping with kashrut and thus capable of being sold to the Jewish public.[574] So, of course, they would have been well versed in the Torah. In the case of Antipas's court, they would have served him as advisors, counseling him on policies that would have kept him within the bounds of Torah.[575]

The meal is pictured as taking place in Levi the toll collector's house (vs 15, "his house").[576] Vs 15b, "for there were many who followed him," is a Marcan insertion underscoring Jesus' outreach. The pericope describes a thoroughly possible scenario. Jesus is in Capernaum (Mark 2:1), which he had made a sort of base camp (Matt 4:13).[577] It was a busy fishing town, and scribes would have been expected to mix with the townsfolk. Nearby was the frontier between Herod Antipas's tetrarchy and Philip his brother's, where Levi's tollbooth would have been located. What we have here is a historical description of the actual physical situation on the ground. In fact, the whole of Mark 1:21—2:17 looks like an eyewitness report of a day in the life of Jesus.

Given their ubiquitous presence, it is not difficult to imagine how scribes could suddenly appear on the scene, unlike the presence of Pharisees in the story of plucking grain on the Sabbath. Since Levi would have been quite wealthy, his house would have been spacious and able to accommodate a number of people. Being wealthy would have made him well known and the goings-on in his household a source of gossip. So these scribes, steeped in the prescriptions of Torah regarding tithing, ritual cleanliness, and the preparation of kosher food, would not have been at Levi's table, where all those things would have been in question, to say nothing of eschewing any association with his despised vocation.[578] They would have avoided such an intimate contact with a sinner.

The scribes would not have entered the house, which would have rendered them unclean by association with a public sinner (Ps 1:1, Acts 10:28). Table fellowship expressed intimacy. In Levi's house they could well have encountered food not properly tithed and therefore not kosher as well as contact with furniture and utensils that were unclean, to say nothing of the host who was engaged in a despised vocation. Torah clearly forbids such association. Repentance was always a possibility, and the repentant sinner would always be welcomed back into the faithful of Israel (2 Chr 6:37–38, Ezk 14:6, Sir 17:24). But to contravene the Torah in the process of bringing someone to repentance was unthinkable.

We might imagine then that they accosted Jesus and his disciples as they entered or left the house to ask their provocative question about his table fellowship. That is not improbable, much as the woman in Luke 7:37 appeared on the scene as Jesus reclined at table in a Pharisee's house. Only, in this pericope the disciples are the ones asked about the behavior of their master, which points to the authenticity of the report. The question is only natural from their perspective: how could Jesus, who claimed to be the agent of God's kingdom, keep company with those who, according to the will of God expressed in the Torah, were to be avoided? They did not address Jesus himself, perhaps as a way to slight him by not speaking to him directly. By ignoring him they deprived him of the courtesy of treating him as an equal.

But Jesus steps in and directly engages their implied criticism. He refers perhaps to a common proverb, stating the obvious that the physician is there not for the healthy but the sick. Jesus as the healer has come to bring back those who are sinners. The "righteous" obviously do not need his "cures." The physician had to deal with people who were ritually unclean, and so Jesus has come, as the Lord's agent, to bring healing to the nation and bind up its wounds. So again, Jesus appeals to something above Torah, which demands separation from uncleanness: the behavior of God himself. Jeremiah characterizes Israel with an incurable and grievous wound for which there is no medicine available to heal her, but YHWH will restore her health and heal her (30:12–17).[579] He answers their question: God himself has dealt with and been faithful to unclean Israel in her sins of idolatry. A physician, of necessity, must deal with the unclean and the impure, otherwise he is not fulfilling his purpose. He would indeed be a worthless physician!

This is not just some new and fine moral principle about helping the broken. But Jesus is the embodiment of the divine presence as he brings the kingdom to the world. He who forgives sin does not have to concern himself with the "contagion of human sinfulness."[580] Indeed he seeks out sinners to restore them to the kingdom (rule) of God.[581] The call of Levi the toll collector graphically portrays that Jesus as God's agent does not demand righteousness according to the Torah but invites people who have no uprightness of their own into the kingdom. It's as if he reverses the perspective that uncleanness is contagious but not holiness.[582] Jesus functions as an "inverse" priest. He conveys holiness and removes impurity and uncleanness.

But was Jesus not concerned with the so-called righteous? Did he exclude them from the call to enter the kingdom (vs 17)?[583] Or were they considered to be already in the kingdom? For the Torah and the prophets, righteousness had to do with concern for justice and care for the poor, the widow, the fatherless, and the stranger.[584] Our study of the parables has shown that Jesus is concerned with forgiveness and that it is forgiveness, extending acceptance to the brother and even to the Roman oppressor, that would save Israel from catastrophe. So Jesus would be using the word in that sense. He was referring to people who were already in the kingdom because they were living the ethics of the kingdom. But it could also have the meaning of those who lived the righteousness of the law, and so it was a subtle judgment on those who would not accept the life of the kingdom. Perhaps Jesus meant the term to be ambiguous.

The Question on Fasting (Mark 2:18–22, Matt 9:14–17, Luke 5:33–38)

The situation in which Jesus' saying is located is indefinite. Was it during the time of a fast?[585] The situation as described in vs 18a could mean either the disciples of John and the Pharisees kept the custom of fasting or they just happened to be fasting at the time for some special reason. If Jesus' disciples were not fasting, there is no motive for a controversy. Jesus himself is not questioned about his practice but that of his disciples. These observations suggest that the saying was originally unattached and was taken up by the church in its controversy with the followers of the Baptist or with the Pharisees and provided with the present context.[586]

Whatever the relationship between the introductory sentences, the meaning of Jesus' saying about the impossibility of fasting when the bridegroom is present is clear. One could hardly fast at a wedding celebration. In the Jewish context, wedding celebrations lasted for a week and people were exempt from certain religious requirements.[587] Jesus again expresses the good news of the presence of the kingdom: this is the time for nonpareil jubilation. His presence, the good news that he brings, the joy of healings, and the festival-like rejoicing at his table all suggest the inappropriateness of any kind of fasting exercises. The marriage feast was used as imagery for the time of salvation. How could Jesus and his disciples fast in the time of the wedding feast of the kingdom?[588] Whoever is motivated to ask a question about fasting fails to fathom the identity of Jesus and the eschatological character of his presence.[589]

However, his reference to a bridegroom could be a general reference meaning that the time will come when weddings will not be celebrated because of the doom that has come upon the nation. Jeremiah ends his oracle of doom that will come upon Judah with the threat that "I shall silence the shouts of rejoicing and mirth and the voices of bridegroom and bride, in the towns of Judah and the streets of Jerusalem, for the country will be reduced to desert" (Jer 7:34).[590] Jesus may be saying something similar: now there is rejoicing, but that will come to an end, and it will be a time of lamentation and fasting, and the feasting associated with weddings will be silenced. Jesus would be making a prophetic prediction about the destruction of the war with Rome, which was already being fomented by certain elements in the society. However, vs 20 could also be a saying that arose in the church when it practiced fasting and so could well have been a formulation of the church.[591]

The synoptists, on the other hand, certainly understood it as applying to Jesus. The metaphor of God as bridegroom of his people appears in the Old Testament (Isa 62:5)[592] and also in the New Testament as a relationship between Christ and his church (Eph 5:22–33, 2 Cor 11:2). These predecessor and successor images make a strong case for understanding Jesus' imagery as applying to himself. The identification of Jesus as a bridegroom also appears in John 3:29, which supports this interpretation.

Were vss 21–22 part of Jesus' saying interpreting his presence as a bridegroom? They could have easily been attached to many another saying or activity of Jesus, particularly in the face of being criticized. Joachim Jeremias notes that both the words about the bridegroom and a wedding feast and the references to patches and wineskins deal with the senselessness of the actions involved.[593] He notes further that the cosmos is compared to a garment (Heb 1:10–12, Ps 102:26). Again, in Acts 10:11–13 the image of a cloth lowered from the heavens filled with all kinds of animals limns the reconstituted cosmos, which is now declared to be pure.[594] Similarly, wine is an image for the new age: Noah plants a vine after the deluge (Gen 9:20); it is on a vine that the Redeemer binds his donkey and "washes his garments in wine and his vesture in the blood of grapes" (Gen 49:11); and when it says that Jesus manifested his glory in the changing of water into wine (John 2:11), wine again is a symbol for the time of salvation.[595] The underlying harmony of the three images—bridegroom, patch, and wineskin—speaks for their original unity in the mouth of Jesus. In these images Jesus declares that the new age of the kingdom of God has dawned, and the old has passed away.

In this, Jesus is not expressing a radical attitude toward Judaism and saying it has been superseded. Rather, he is saying that, in and through him and his proclamation of the kingdom, Judaism has reached its goal, and as that goal has now been reached and is standing at the door, there is no reason to try and bring it in and establish it by other means such as rebellion against Rome or perhaps even working to update the Torah or fasting as if in a time of lament during the exile.[596] The kingdom is already at work, so all of these endeavors to try and establish it are like fasting at a wedding, sewing new patches on old garments, or pouring new wine into old, dilapidated skins. Look here, he says, and see the kingdom at work. Enter it and enjoy even now its presence. This is a time of celebration!

The Question on Authority (Mark 11:27–33, Matt 21:23–27, Luke 20:1–8)

This pericope is not strictly an apothegm since the focus is not on a word of Jesus but rather his person as the agent of God's eschatological authority.[597] In other words, Christology forms the controlling interest of this pericope, which proclaimed to the Marcan community the "eschatological victory of Jesus over the power of the old age."[598] Jesus functions as the end-time prophet victorious over his opponents and deposes them from their right to speak with God's authority.

The first question that arises in the reading of this apothegm is what do "these things" (vs 28, Gk., ταῦτα, *tauta*) refer to? At first blush it would seem within the context, they refer back to his cleansing of the Temple (Mark 11:15–17). To answer this question, we have to determine if there was an original relationship between these two pericopae (as well as the "entry narrative" in Mark 11:1–10) in the tradition as Mark received it.[599]

In the entry and temple cleansing stories, which immediately precede this pericope, Jesus is portrayed in a similar manner: he acts authoritatively and with seeming divine approval. This coherence suggests that the three narratives were conceived as a unity within the pre-Marcan oral traditional. In this tripartite complex, we encounter various themes found in the feasts of Sukkoth and Hanukkah, although there are no explicit references to either.[600] But the reference to John's baptism seems to stick out like a sore thumb and seems unrelated to what preceded it. Mark has already narrated John's death. But in the context of the feasts in which water played a prominent role, John's baptism and his authority make sense. A paradisial stream was associated with Jerusalem in the eschaton that would cleanse from sin and fructify the land.[601] John's baptism was also thought of as preparation for the end-time. He was the eschatological messenger of God, and his baptism was an eschatological act anticipatory of the in-breaking of the kingdom. The water rites of Sukkoth anticipated God's blessing in the coming rains but also his coming kingdom when eschatological prosperity and peace would be established. So John's baptism could well have been understood as the fulfillment of the stream that would cleanse the people.

Eschatological hope was also centered in the house of David. When the Messiah appeared, YHWH's decisive intervention was at hand.[602] Sukkoth thus celebrated a number of themes including God's universal reign, the Davidic messiah, the blessings of the eschaton, and a cleansing and fructifying stream associated with Jerusalem. It is clear John's ministry coordinated with the expectations surrounding the feasts of Sukkoth/Hanukkah. The temple cleansing narrative also finds resonances with the prophecies of Zechariah. In Zech 14:21, cleansing the Temple courts of traders is associated with YHWH's universal reign.

In conclusion, in view of the congruence between the entry, cleansing, and question on authority and their resonances with the feasts of Sukkoth/Hanukkah and their Haphtarah (the prophetic reading associated with the feasts), this tripartite complex forms a unity.[603]

In the context of the entry–cleansing narrative (Mark 11:1–11, 11:5–17), the reference to "these things," therefore, is to the "temple cleansing." The reference to John's baptism and his authority to engage in that activity points to God as the source of that authority and specifically an eschatological authority.[604] Jesus understood John to be the prophetic figure of Elijah whose return was promised (Mark 9:12). His baptismal activity was an eschatological rite by which the true people of God were prepared for the coming denouement. So his preaching and call to repentance occur under the pressure of the imminent eschatological event of judgment.[605] His baptism brought together the true people of God in preparation for the denouement. When Jesus references John and his baptism, it is meant as no casual remark. Rather he is asserting that John had a decisive role in salvation history and that his own authority had the same divine source as John's.[606] God's eschatological authority is active in both. Jesus' counterquestion then indicates that just as John's baptism was an eschatological calling to repentance, so Jesus' activity, his entry into Jerusalem accompanied by an acclamation, and his cleansing of the Temple are eschatological signs that bore God's full authorization. Jesus acts as one directly commissioned to carry out the signs that prepare for God's kingdom. The old age is passing away, and the new age is dawning. The victory of Jesus proclaimed in entry and cleansing is shown to be an eschatological one with God's authority and approval behind it.

In this unredacted tradition of entry, cleansing, and question on authority (i.e., the tradition as Mark received it before contextualizing it in his Gospel), Jesus presents himself as the fulfiller of the Zecharian prophecy: the new age is dawning when God will establish his kingdom and the Gentiles will stream into Jerusalem joining in worship with the people of God in a great, egalitarian, and universal feast of tabernacles.[607]

The question put to Jesus, of course, was to call into question his authority. His interrogators may have had in mind human authorization. He replies with a counterquestion, a typical rabbinic way of responding to opponents. The rabbinic counterquestion, however, usually settled the argument.[608] So the story may have ended with vs 30, which would assume then that these Jerusalem authorities accepted John's divine commission—not likely since his baptism circumvented the Temple's sacrificial system for effecting forgiveness. The discussion in vss 31–32 therefore is apropos to Jesus' question: they did not accept John as having divine authority and therefore could indeed fear the people who did.[609] To repeat, Jesus speaks as the end-time prophet victorious over his opponents. Because they do not "believe" him, he deposes them from claiming the right to speak with divine authority.

Wealth and the Kingdom (Mark 10:17–31, Matt 19:16–29, Luke 18:18–30)

The three pericopae in this section are intimately related, and they can scarcely be understood without their connection with one another, although the tradition following Peter's assertion in 10:28 is complex.

The Rich Man and His Question

Vincent Taylor finds the details of the story so vivid (the man running up to him and kneeling, Jesus looking on him with love, he becoming sad and grieved, and the man owning large estates) and woven so intimately into the story that Mark's originality is obvious.[610] Furthermore, these details suggest that it was also not simply an apothegm but a remembered incident in the life of Jesus and could well be designated a "biographical apothegm." It is hardly possible that Jesus' answer in vs 21 was a free-floating word and later was provided with the framework of the story as we have it. It is also closely connected with the sayings that follow regarding the difficulty of the wealthy to enter the kingdom of God. Along with the previously examined pericope, it is a historical report that emphasizes Jesus' authority, in this case, as the one who knows what is demanded of those who wish to enter the kingdom.

Mark has only a very general description of the man as "one who ran up to him," while Matthew designates him as a "young man" (which is contradicted by the man's assertion that he has kept the law "from my youth," Mark 10:20), and Luke calls him a "ruler."

There may be an aspect of flattery with the man's use of "good," which is underscored by his falling on his knees before Jesus. It is difficult to avoid questions about the psychology of the man. He cannot give up his riches and follow Jesus, so the interpreter seems forced to ask the question of his motivation in coming to Jesus in the first place and beginning a conversation with flattery. It looks like he may have been searching for an easy answer that would bolster even more the self-confidence of this man who has "kept all the commandments." Or did he honestly sense a lack in his life, which was led as a faithful Jew? He evidently thinks there are conditions beyond the keeping of the law that "eternal life" demands. Had the following of the commandments become hollow and rote, and he sought a deeper spiritual life? Jesus' affirmation by looking on him with affection would support this latter understanding (vs 21).

The interrogator addressing Jesus as "good teacher" was not contrary to Jewish convention or tantamount to calling him holy or even divine, as D. E. Nineham avers.[611] For example, "goodness" is applied to David (1 Sam 29:6). That Jesus refused to be called "good" was a problem for Matthew (but not for Luke, who follows Mark), who has the young man ask, "what good shall I do in order that I might have eternal life." Jesus' denying the description of himself as "good" has the effect of directing his interlocutor to the transcendent God and that man is not good absolutely as God is.[612] It also emphasizes that Jesus thought of himself only as a human being (empty of all that is divine), and so his own goodness was "subject to growth and trial."[613] Jesus' assertion points to his own filial relationship with God: his whole being and action were directed to doing the Father's will and fulfilling his purpose. Jesus is also implying that the man who stands before him "who has kept [all the commandments] from his youth" is not "good" and so calls him to judge himself against the absolute goodness of God, who alone can be called truly "good." So he calls on his questioner to focus his attention not on himself but on God (and his kingdom) and on doing his will (Matt 7:21, 12:50, Mark 3:35). It is much like Jesus correcting the woman who called his mother blessed because of bearing him and telling her, "Blessed rather are those who hear the word of God and keep it!" (Luke 11:28).

The question about what to do to inherit eternal life was unusual. It is not a question a Jew would normally ask. One was called simply to observe the law and the commandments. The commandments cited by Jesus are all from the second table of the law: one's duty toward one's neighbor. But the man apparently sensed there was more to one's relationship with God than being blameless in the sight of the law. Jesus then gets to the nub of the matter: the man's riches stand between him and a fuller relationship with God. His wealth secured his place economically and socially. He needed to rid himself of earthly treasure and have "treasure in heaven."[614] That "treasure in heaven" was right in front of him by joining Jesus in his ministry. You cannot serve two masters (Matt 6:24). He rejects Jesus' challenge to join him, and so he loses the joy of finding the kingdom, the far greater treasure than all his riches. To give up wealth is indeed a challenge as it provides status, security, and the pleasures of life. To give it up then is to experience the essence of the kingdom: to rely solely on God. The man obviously thought he had to achieve more than being faithful to Torah. The kingdom (i.e., "eternal life"), however, that the man sought was not something that could be earned and achieved but could only be accepted, in this case to "sell all" and follow Jesus.[615]

The Danger of Riches

The following verses (23–27) flow naturally from the story of the rich man, although Mark probably sandwiched vs 24 between 23 and 25, which is indicated by Matthew and Luke eliminating it.[616] Furthermore, vs 24 underscores the universal difficulty of entering the kingdom as compared to vs 23, which mentions only the difficulty of the rich entering the kingdom. Vs 25 with its intensifying hyperbole then flows naturally from vs 23. So the original (historical) sayings consisted of vss 23 and 25–26. Luke strengthens the connection with the preceding story by deleting the rich man's leaving the scene (Mark 10:22, Luke 18:23) and having Jesus direct his comments to the man himself (Luke 18:24) rather than to his disciples. The connection between the rich man narrative and the pronouncements about the rich is so intimate that it most probably represents the historical situation and was a conversation that followed after the departure of the rich man, taking Mark's version as the original. The hyperbole, a camel going through the eye of a needle, is characteristic of Jesus[617] and helps us to see that Jesus was no pedantic, dour prophet but appreciated healthy and hearty humor.[618] His piercing metaphor was meant to prick the conscience of the wealthy and challenge his hearers to reassess their ideas about wealth and poverty. Jesus presents his critical understanding of why the wealthy won't have an easy time of entering the kingdom in the parables of the rich fool and the rich man and Lazarus. These parables pick up on Jesus' challenge to the rich man to sell all he has and give to the poor (vs 21).

In Jewish religion and culture, wealth was a sign of God's special favor, and so the wealthy were thought of as especially pious and as paragons of virtue.[619] The reaction of the disciples is therefore entirely understandable. If the rich, who have been blessed by God because of their piety,[620] cannot enter the kingdom, then it would seem all are excluded. But grace wins out in the end when Jesus emphasizes the mercy of God, who can make a way even for the wealthy. What is impossible for humans to achieve God can make possible. Participation in the kingdom is an impossible human achievement. It is a gift and cannot be earned. Human effort cannot attain the kingdom. It is totally due to God's grace. But human action and striving are also required. That contradiction is resolved by Jesus' word that "all things are possible with God."[621]

The Rewards of Discipleship

Did Mark attach this saying to the preceding, or was it originally part of the tradition? Peter's question in vs 28 connects most easily with vs 21, where the rich man refuses to follow Jesus. In its present position, it looks like Mark's hand at play. Peter appears here as a spokesman for the disciples speaking in the first-person plural. He only rarely is represented in that role. Most often the disciples speak as a group (e.g., "they said," Matt 14:17, Luke 5:33).[622] To say the disciples had "left all" in light of Mark 3:9 and Luke 5:4–5 is somewhat of an exaggeration.

The present gift of the kingdom as community comports with Jesus' understanding of the kingdom as both future and present reality (Luke 17:21) and also as a kind of extended family (Mark 3:35). However, it seems unlikely that vss 29–31 were a free-floating tradition, although it resonated with an early Christian milieu in their estrangement from their environment and manifesting the experience that they found in the fellowship of their community.[623] Peter's question begs for a context.

Matthew has added a further saying (19:28) about the twelve sitting on thrones and judging the tribes of Israel. Luke records the same saying in 22:28–30, which indicates Matthew had interpolated it in his present context. Matthew also substitutes "a hundred times over" for the list of things lost that would be received again, perhaps having found the repetition too prolix. But such repetition is Semitic practice and suggests a Jewish environment.[624]

That "father" is omitted by Jesus in the second enumeration of things that are left behind (vs 30) gives the saying an authentic ring in his mouth because for him God is father in the age to come (cf., Matt 23:9). The "with persecutions" is not necessarily an add-on and is certainly a characteristic attendant on the ministry of the word (Mark 4:17).[625]

Finally, the reference to "eternal life" in vs 30 differs from Jesus' usual expression "life" (Mark 9:43, 45). In addition, the phrase "age to come" is never used by Jesus (except in Matt 12:32, which does not appear in the parallel Mark 3:28). The saying as a whole, however, is authentic, but the language has been adapted by the evangelist or his source.[626]

This analysis has suggested that the three parts represent a historical situation. The whole has the appearance of a historical report, and the interdependence between the three parts suggests that Mark has not conjoined them. Certain, however, is that we have before us here authentic words of Jesus whether the three pericopae were conceived together or separately.[627]

In this vignette we encounter Jesus' teaching and understanding of the relationship between wealth and the kingdom. He challenges his social world's understanding of wealth and poverty. Wealth stands in the way of accepting the kingdom, and self-chosen poverty on behalf of the kingdom is true wealth. The former is subject to decay and corruption (Matt 6:19-20); the latter is what endures. He spells out the great wealth of the kingdom, which is already realized in the community of those who have entered it: they have the riches of one another in this community of the end-time.

The Chief Commandment (Mark 12:28-34, Matt 22:35--40, Luke 10:25-28)

Matthew has shortened Mark by eliminating the repetition of the law's summary by Jesus' interlocutor. He makes Mark's scribe into a lawyer from among the Pharisees. Luke merely refers to a lawyer, and it is not Jesus who gives the summary of the law but the lawyer. He has also reformed the whole as an introduction to the parable of the good Samaritan. Neither Matthew nor Luke records Jesus' final words, "You are not far from the kingdom of God." This concluding verse contains two words used nowhere else in Mark: μακράν (*makran*, "far") and νουνεχῶς (*nounechōs*, "reasonable, sensibly"), which suggests that he is replicating the tradition as he received it. Matthew and Luke seem to witness to a shorter form of the tradition in which only Jesus or his inquirer quotes the relevant Old Testament texts. So the relationship between the three is somewhat obscure.[628]

The passage has a strongly rationalistic cast due to a vocabulary that characterizes the intellect: διάνοια (*dianoia*, "understanding, intellect, mind," vs 30), σύνεσις (*synesis*, "practical discernment, intelligence," vs 33), νουνεχῶς (*nounechōs*, vs 34). The two phrases of the framework, "What is the first commandment of all? (vs 28) and "You speak the truth" (vs. 32), also reflect this rationalistic cast.[629] Rabbinic exegesis was not interested in some principle by which the Torah was to be understood and applied, although it employed varied criteria for making a distinction between greater and lesser commandments.[630] There was no all-encompassing juristic principle, only basic pedagogical rules.

It was Hellenistic Judaism that sought to explicate the law as rational and to measure it by reason. So a Hellenistic environment suggests itself as the provenance of the passage.[631] This impression is strengthened by the way the Shema is quoted in vss 29 and 32. In the Jewish environment it expressed the exclusivity of YHWH's claim, recalled his mighty acts, and obliged those who confessed it to fulfill his commands.[632] In a Hellenistic environment, however, it was an independent confession of faith in opposition to heathen polytheism. The commentators assert that the focus here is on the confession, rather than on the unity of the confession and the obligation to fulfill the Torah.

However, there are factors that stand in opposition to these arguments for the origin of the passage in a later Christian Hellenistic environment. The rabbinic sources are later, and the rabbis from the earliest times were exclusively focused on the Jewish community. Jesus' concerns, however, were more universalistic. Second, in Jesus' day the lands of Israel were surrounded by pagan civilization[633] and many opportunities for contact between Jews and Gentiles. So it could well be that even in Jewish lands there were efforts to rationalize and objectivize the Torah. Third, though there was a widespread critique in Hellenistic Judaism of cultic sacrifice (vs 33), it is a well-known part of the message of the prophets and of the psalms, and it is found in the proclamation of Jesus himself (Matt 9:13, 12:7). The implicit universalism of the love of neighbor fits well into the ministry and teaching of Jesus. His ministry included the call to Israel to love the enemy (Matt 5:44). Jesus universalized the concept of neighbor to include not only one's fellow Jew but all people everywhere. Furthermore, the citations agree with the text of the LXX that is closest to the Hebrew text except for some stylistic changes in the scribe's answer apparently made to avoid an exact repetition of Jesus' words.[634] The quotation, as attributed to Jesus in Mark 12:20, rests on the same Septuagintal text except for the addition of διάνοια (*dianoia*) after ψυχή (*psychē*, "life, soul").

In Luke's text Jesus himself does not provide the answer, but he asks the "lawyer" for the answer to his own question. It appears that Luke has structured his version on the basis of the rich man narrative (Luke 18:18–23) by having him ask about how to inherit eternal life. Jesus' answer consists of the parable of the good Samaritan, which follows. So Luke eliminated having Jesus answer with the summary of the law. Matthew, following Mark, has Jesus answer the "lawyer's" question, but the "lawyer" does not repeat Jesus' answer. In this way he asserts the uniqueness of Jesus and as the originator of the summary.

Marcan redaction is evident in vs 28a, which connects it to the preceding narrative, and vs 34b, which rounds out the series of confrontations that Jesus encounters in 11:27—12:34a. So I conclude the text of Mark is the originating structure of the narrative.

The mutual affirmations in 28a and 34a (and the approval by the scribe of what Jesus has said, 32a) make of the passage less a controversy dialogue and more a "school discussion."[635] The parallelism of these two phrases is striking (following the Greek text's word order):

> seeing that well he answered them
> seeing that sensibly he answered

Mark's hand is at work here. In this way the evangelist has Jesus affirmed on the basis of his objective teaching that he is of God and represents God. Jesus and the scribe also play a variation on the same theme of the double love commandment and commend one another's summation of the law. So the summation is doubly approved, and Jesus receives the approval of an official representative of Judaism.

What remains constitutes the original tradition: the question, Jesus' answer, the repetition of what Jesus has said by the scribe (which doesn't include the reference to one's "whole life"), and Jesus' judgment that the scribe "is not far from the kingdom." Because the scribe has omitted one's "whole life" in his description of the foremost and fundamental commandment, he is not ready to give his entire life and so dispossess himself of his property and follow Jesus. In this way, like the rich man, he is not in the kingdom (cf., Mark 10:21, 8:35) but only on the verge of it. Sifre on Deut 32:29 associates the idea of the kingdom and the double command: "What did [the Law] say to them (Israel)? Take upon you the yoke of the kingdom of Heaven, and excel one another in the fear of Heaven, and conduct yourself one toward another in charity."[636] For Jesus the kingdom was a present as well as a future reality, and people could enter it now by accepting it as Jesus revealed it in his words and deeds. Discipleship means giving up all and even one's life

(Mark 10:39) to follow Jesus (Mark 10:21, 28). Jesus also refers to his way as a "yoke" (Matt 11:29–30).

The Marcan text is without a rhetorical structure. The two halves of the passage do not match since the reply of the scribe extends the affirmation of the one God to the only God, and the double love commandment is exalted above ritual sacrifice.[637] We are left with the impression of a somewhat amorphously structured piece that finds its unity not in its structure but in its contents. This amorphousness implies a lack of being reworked in the oral tradition and therefore suggests the historical authenticity of the passage, although it was handed down rather freely.[638]

In Jesus' Jewish environment, by citing Deut 6:4–5 he could well be including a complete section of the Scriptures by its initial verse and thus affirming all the commandments of the Torah.[639] So Jesus stands in continuity with Israel's God and the revelation of himself in the Torah and congruence with the deepest roots of Jewish teaching.

In this passage Jesus understands love as a matter of the will. Jesus' own actions and ministry embody his understanding of the two commandments: he called sinners into fellowship with God and excluded any kind of legalism that no longer was concerned with the will of God but focused on fulfilling individual laws (cf., Rom 13:8–10).[640] He limned the fulfilling of love of God and neighbor in parables such as the lost sheep and the good Samaritan as well as negatively in the unforgiving servant, the rich man and Lazarus, and the rich fool.

The surprising denouement to the story asserts the scribe is "not far from the kingdom," which implies that the keeping of the double love commandment does not qualify one for inclusion in the kingdom. Suggested is that what he lacks is "denying himself and taking up his cross and following Jesus" (Mark 8:34).

The Dispute Over an Inheritance (Luke 12:13–14)

Jesus' answer to his petitioner is only intelligible in terms of the request that is made to him, so the whole forms a unity and implies that the passage is a historical report.[641] The adjudication of inheritances usually was brought before scribes.[642] So Jesus must have been viewed as a scribe who was well versed in the Torah. Perhaps more likely the petitioner was one of Jesus' own disciples and therefore would have naturally turned to him for the adjudication of his complaint. For the disciples he was a socially prominent person. It is not by chance that in this situation he is addressed as "teacher."

The firstborn would normally receive more than the other sons. The man was perhaps a younger son who felt he had not received his proper due of the father's property. Or perhaps the elder son was delaying the division of the property, and the petitioner was asking Jesus to rule on making a speedier disposition of his father's estate. The possible issues at stake, however, were myriad and often complex, so what the petitioner was asking was probably a multifaceted legal case requiring a wise and astute judgment.[643]

Jesus' answer reflects the hostile protest of the man against Moses when he sought to adjudicate a quarrel between him and a fellow Israelite: "Who made you a prince and a judge over us?" (Exod 2:14). The LXX reads "an official and judge" (ἄρχοντα καί δικαστήν, *archonta kai diskastēn*). With these words Jesus declares that he is not like Moses, and he refuses to take on the role of judge in terms of one of the judges of ancient Israel whose role also included martial aspects. In Jesus' day bandits proliferated and took on the role of Israel's ancient judges.[644] So Jesus was also eschewing their often violent means as well as their politics. He was negatively defining himself.

As is characteristic of Jesus he looks at the inner disposition of people. There would be no dispute if it wasn't for covetousness, which makes a person think that the abundant life consists in one's possessions. In Jesus' culture ownership of goods provided the grounds for acquiring honor by showing beneficence. Wealth and goods were then really a means to an honorable name.[645] The man coveted what he saw as his rightful inheritance so that he could enhance his honor and prestige in the community. Jesus elaborates where one's real treasure should lie (cf., Luke 12:33, Matt 6:21).

The Slaughter of the Galileans and the Tragic Death of Some Jerusalemites (Luke 13:1–5)

Jesus' sayings here cannot be understood apart from the setting in which they appear, so like the previous passage it forms a unit and is a historical report (Luke uses it as an introduction to the parable that follows). There are no other reports of this incident. Pilate's vindictiveness and odious actions against the people are well known.[646] The event reported here is in keeping with his character. Why Pilate moved against some Galilean pilgrims while they presented their sacrifices in the Temple can only be guessed. Some violent action on their part did not necessarily take place. Pilate moved against even innocent and peacefully assembled people. They may therefore have been involved in peaceful demonstration against some provocation by Pilate. Laymen killed the sacrificial animal, while the priest offered it in sacrifice.[647]

The incident of the tower in Siloam is also not known from other sources. We know the existence of the Pool of Siloam (Joh 9:7–11),[648] and a tower may have been built near the pool or that part of the city that took its name from the pool.[649] The eighteen men killed there may have been purifying themselves in the pool or perhaps hoping for a cure in the pool's waters.

The people would have been steeped in the stories of Sodom and Gomorrah and Israel's conquest tradition in which the sinners and idolatrous pagans are slain. That the wicked are punished and that the righteous are saved and rewarded was popular wisdom in Israel (cf., Prov 2:21–23, 10:24–25, Pss 1, 9:5, 34:21). When all went well in one's life, it was easy to conclude that one was blessed by God and so must be righteous. Jesus here goes against popular conceptions (cf., John 9:1–3). Suffering and sin are not to be equated. Rather, Jesus is saying, when untoward things happen such as the incidents recounted, the correct conclusion is that judgment is at the door for all people, and the only proper response is to look at one's self and see where repentance is called for.

There is a subtlety here obscured by the translations. Jesus says in vs 3 that the unrepentant will "likewise" (ὁμοίως, *homoiōs*) be destroyed, whereas in vs., 5 it reads "in the same way" (ὡσαύτως, *ōsautōs*). Jesus addresses the inhabitants of Jerusalem and says Jerusalem will fall in the same way as the tower did (Luke 19:41–44) unless there is repentance. Jesus saw clearly where things were headed in terms of the fate of the nation unless there was a complete turning around from the violence, animosity, and hostility that was invading the mindset of the populace as it was putting its trust in the inviolability of the Temple and the Holy City and apocalyptic dreams of God's miraculous intervention (cf., Jer 7:4).

Jesus is eschewing judgment, especially of Israel's enemies and in particular the Romans (Matt 7:1, John 8:15–16, 12:47), even in the face of Pilate's horrendous provocations and violations. The way forward is through the love of the enemy, forgiveness, and going the extra mile.[650] Rather than being seen as the wrathful avenger of Israel, God is the beneficent one who causes the rain to fall on both the just and the unjust (Matt 5:44–45). Jesus was calling his people to a revolution in thought, word, and deed. This is the way of life in the kingdom that is impending. It demands repentance, for at its appearance God will exercise judgment.

The Question of John the Baptist (Matt 11:2–19, Luke 7:18–35)

Luke has the disciples "sent to the Lord," and in Matthew John has heard about the "deeds of the Christ." Both formulations imply Christian vocabulary and may be from the pen of each evangelist. The actual pronouncement is found in vss 4–6 in Matthew and in vss 22–23 in Luke. Both evangelists are following Q, which also contained vss 7b–11 in Matthew and vss 24b–28 in Luke. Matthew has also added vs 12 (from Q, which occurs in another context in Luke 16:16), to which he has also appended vss 13–15 picking up on the saying of Jesus in 17:12 (which depends on Mark 9:12). Luke for his part has added vs 21, which actualizes Jesus' subsequent answer, and vss 29–30, which depend on his rendition of the Q story of those who came out to John to be baptized (Luke 3:10–13, cf., Matt 21:32).[651] Jesus' reply to the question in Luke 9:22–23 and Matt 9:4–6 is not a saying developed in the church along with the Baptist's question as a way of pressing John into service as a witness to the messiahship and superiority of Jesus.[652] That would require the whole of the pericope to have been a community product. And why would the church invent a rather embarrassing story in light of John's earlier prediction about the coming greater one (Luke 3:16–17, Matt 3:11–12) to make a rather oblique point of Jesus' messiahship?

John's question sent via his disciples from his prison cell[653] may have been motivated by the fact that Jesus did not seem to be fulfilling his prophecy of the "mightier one" who would baptize the people with "the holy spirit and fire" and bring the day of judgment that would purify the people ("fire") and destroy the "chaff" (the unrepentant).[654] John saw a fiery judgment in the offing brought about by the mightier one who would succeed him. No doubt John thought of the fire as brought about by the flame of the spirit of God and not the Holy Spirit of Christian understanding. Joel 2:28–32 may have been in his mind, which saw the day of the Lord as the outpouring of God's spirit as well as the coming of fire that would alter, if not destroy, creation. But a remnant would be saved.[655] However, this apocalyptic scenario had not ensued in Jesus' ministry. In fact, Jesus seemed to be in fellowship with the very sinners John had called "the chaff." Jesus' ministry was no apocalyptic fire but rather a peaceful ingathering of sinners into a conception of the kingdom of God as premonition of the feast to come. That coming of the kingdom would include, however, a judgment of those who had refused the invitation.

Jesus' answer was put in the unmistakable language of Isa 61:1–3, which was part of 2 Isaiah's exuberant understanding of the glory of the restoration after the exile (cf., Isa 29:18–19, 35:5–6). Jesus proclaimed in his answer that in him the restoration was beginning, the exile was over. He was inviting the nation to enter the kingdom and consummate the end of exile. To refuse would only mean disaster. This was a realized and historicized eschatology.

Finally, Jesus pronounces a beatitude, "Blessed are those who take no offence at me." Jesus is sensitive to John's perplexity and apparent disillusionment.[656] John's prophecy about the mightier one was being realized but not in the way he had announced. John was not alone in the implied offense he took at Jesus. Much offense was taken of Jesus generally in the society of his day.[657] Not to take offence meant entrance to the kingdom, the joy of eating together as a foretaste of the coming feast of the kingdom, the delight and pleasure of those who were healed, the good news of the kingdom that rang forth, and the elation of the promise of the fulfillment of the kingdom and the end of exile. In the kingdom, people found true happiness. Think of the joy of the man who found a treasure in a field.[658]

The Question of John and James (Mark 10:35–45, Matt 20:17–19, Luke 18:31–33)

Bultmann understands vss 35–37 and 40 as a unit to which has been added vss 38–39. These latter verses he interprets as a *vaticinium ex eventu*, that is, a "prophecy" constructed by the church and retrojected back into the life of Jesus.[659] Luke 22:24–27 includes vs 41–45 as part of the conversations at the Last Supper, which might indicate it was an independent tradition. Matt 20:24–28 includes it in the same context as Mark does. However, Matthew has the mother of James and John ask the question of Jesus rather than her sons (20:20). He apparently wants to protect the future apostles from the accusation of making a selfish and arrogant request. That Matthew's hand is at work here becomes obvious because he maintains the construction of Jesus' answer as addressed to the two brothers rather than to their mother, who, according to him, had made the request.

Does Jesus provide two answers to the disciples' request, one in vss 38–39 and one in vs 40? Some find the latter answer as the original and the former as an interpolation into the story.[660] But in that case it is difficult to conceive vss 38–39 as some free-floating tradition without a context. As the passage reads, the two flow smoothly together, and it can be claimed the total is a well-remembered word of Jesus directed to his disciples.

Jesus has his own baptism in mind here by which he was anointed for his ministry as the "beloved one" to announce and enact the coming kingdom. That kingdom, when it came in its fullness, would be a fiery ordeal of judgment on the world as John had foretold. The "woes" of the end-time were in the offing. Jesus saw clearly his impending suffering as the pioneer who would endure proleptically these end-time "birth pangs" (Mark 13:8). To cast his sufferings in terms of a baptism finds its parallel in the psalms where disaster is metaphorically represented by a "flood" (Pss 69:2, 15, 88:17, 124:4, cf., Job 22:11, 27:20). He uses the imagery of baptism because his ministry began with his baptism and included his ultimately taking on the end-time woes.

That Jesus thought of his suffering as a baptism is also indicated by Luke 12:50: "I have a baptism to be baptized with; and how I am constrained[661] until it is accomplished." G. B. Caird captures precisely the import of what Jesus is thinking and expressing here:

> This rare glimpse into the inner mind of Jesus reveals an agonizing mixture of impatience and reluctance. Convinced that God's redemptive plan requires him to bring upon the earth the fiery baptism of judgment, not be inflicting it on others but by undergoing it himself, he feels handicapped and thwarted until this mission can be accomplished. But he knows also that his death will be caused not only by "the definite plan and foreknowledge of God" but by the free choice of Israel's leaders, he is loath to force their hands, to bring upon the people the inevitable conflict of loyalties, to compel them to choose once and for all between God's kingdom and their own nationalism; for he knows that, in rejecting him, they will be rejecting their last chance of national safety.[662]

Vss 41–45 strictly speaking are not quite apropos to what precedes them since they deal with priority in the community of Jesus and not with preeminence in the coming kingdom of God. Mark has already included an abbreviated form of vss 43–44 in 9:35, and Matthew includes the saying at 23:11, which suggests that this saying was a free-floating tradition waiting to be inserted where and when the evangelists wished. So the passage is a Marcan construction of words of Jesus appended here as an appropriate commentary on the request of James and John.

The authenticity of vs 45 is highly contested, and it has been interminably debated whether Mark inserted the saying here or it was originally part of the passages found in vss 42 and 44.[663] Commentators have difficulty with Mark's saying since it transitions from service to the idea of ransom, a concept that appears nowhere else in the Gospels (except in Matt 20:28, where he is following Mark).[664] Luke's version reads, "Who is greater, the one who reclines at table or the one who serves? Is it not the one who reclines? But I am in your midst as one who serves" (Luke 22:27, my translation). The artlessness of this latter saying has much to commend itself as the original. At first blush it might seem the theology of the church has worked itself into a saying of Jesus.

However, in our analysis of the reply of Jesus to John's disciples (Matt 11:2–6, Luke 7:18–23), Jesus casts his ministry in terms of reference to Isaiah.[665] In this saying, he is doing the same. For him the kingdom concerned service, so it would not be anomalous that he cast his ultimate service in terms of the "servant" in Isaiah. The language here matches Isa 53:12: "He poured out his soul to death, and was numbered with the transgressors; yet he bore the sins of many." Furthermore, the Judaism of the time considered the martyr's death a ransom for the nation's sins.[666] I conclude that the passage (vss 42–45 minus perhaps vs 42) is an authentic reproduction of the words of Jesus. This final verse clinches Jesus' assertion about the nature of his community. His service extends to giving his life for the nation. He in effect was saying, "The punishment of your iniquity, O daughter of Zion, is accomplished, he will keep you in exile no longer" (Lam 4:22).[667] Israel was still in exile suffering under foreign domination, which meant that her sins had not yet been forgiven. The "age to come" had not yet arisen.[668]

The Rival Exorcist (Mark 9:38–41, Luke 9:49–50)

Jesus' saying can hardly be conceived apart from the situation described, so the passage is a unified construction presenting an incident in the life of Jesus and his disciples. The penultimate vs 40, however, may have been an addition by Mark, perhaps a variant of Matt 12:30: "Whoever is not with me is against me, and whoever does not gather with me scatters."[669]

The story in Acts 19:13–16 shows that early on the church had to confront pagan exorcists who were not Christians but used the name of Jesus in their exorcisms. The story implies that those who used his name used it as a magical incantation. Directly contradicting Jesus' attitude depicted by Mark and Luke is Matt 7:21–23, where Jesus in the words of Ps 6:8 utterly rejects such people. In the psalm those rejected are the ones who harass the psalmist. Suggested then is that the people he refers to are not just using his name but opposing, if not rejecting, him and are really against him (Mark 9:40, Luke 9:50).[670]

Jesus appears here as very tolerant of such activity, which attitude is distinguished from later Christian attitudes, therefore begging for the saying's authenticity. This tolerance and openness to others is also reflected in his parables where the kingdom of God is portrayed as at work in completely unexpected places, circumstances, and people.[671] Vs 39 strengthens the argument for authenticity. It parallels his forbidding the disciples from preventing children to be brought to him (Mark 10:14). Its authenticity is also supported by the use of John's name since it is inexplicable why his name would have come to be attached to this narrative. Here Jesus perceives that using his name means that those who use it have accepted him and that they are furthering the kingdom by extending its onslaught against the rule of Satan and his minions.

Vs 41 could well be a commentary on the parable of the great Assize and indicates perhaps a step toward the construction of that parable by Jesus. Here Jesus is working at softening the often harsh attitudes toward the outsider and the stranger, which he then narrativizes in his parables. He makes the point even more explicit in enjoining love and prayer for the enemy (Matt 5:43–48).[672]

The Presence of the Kingdom (Luke 17:20–21)

Bultmann points out that the introduction to the apothegm is in the Hellenistic form used in Greek philosophical apothegms, which indicates that Luke has received the saying from a Hellenistic milieu. That we are encountering here a saying of Jesus is, however, certain because it differentiates itself from both Jewish and Christians expectations regarding the kingdom. Many of the renewal movements in the Holy Land had the expectation that opposing Rome either passively or actively would bring in the kingdom.[673] Early Christians lived in the glow of anticipating Christ's return and the coming of the kingdom during their lifetimes (cf., 1 Thess 4:13—5:1).

With the words "not by observation or being able to say it is here or there," Jesus is stressing that the kingdom will in a moment manifest itself universally. The word ἐντός (entos) in Greek is rendered variously by the versions: "in the midst" (RSV, NAS), "among" (NJB), "within" (KJV and Luther). The Aramaic New Testament translates the word with *LeGW* (literally "to the interior" or "within"). Jesus obviously did not mean an internal, private, spiritual experience since he warns of the kingdom's impending arrival and its objective, historical existence (e.g., Mark 1:15, Luke 13:29). Taking the message of the kingdom parables as the hermeneutical nexus, it is obvious Jesus means that the kingdom is proleptically present, waiting for people to accept it and enter into it.[674] It is clear Jesus understood the kingdom as present in his proclamation, healing activity, open commensality, and even mere presence.

In other words, Jesus was warning against trying to calculate the arrival of the kingdom, against trying to figure the day of the coming catastrophe. The kingdom was right there in front of their eyes if they had the eyes to see it as people accepted his announcement, sat at table with him, received forgiveness, and were healed of their diseases. The kingdom was, indeed, palpable.

The Cursing of the Fig Tree
(Mark 11:12-14, 20-21, Matt 21:18-19)

Commentators have found this vignette difficult to understand because of its seeming unreasonableness, its irrationality, and the difficulty of relating it to the ministry of Jesus, which emphasized forgiveness and faith.[675] So it is frequently understood as an enacted parable and consequently treated "symbolically."[676] Three commentators seem to have grasped its sense and function adequately by means of a careful form and redactional critical analysis.[677]

Vs 12 is a Marcan formulation fitting the fig tree cursing into the temporal framework by which he has ordered the materials in chapter 11. Why would Jesus alone among his disciples be hungry just coming from Bethany? His hunger must have been part of the tradition as Mark received it and explains why he sought fruit from the tree. The vocabulary of vs 13 has caused no end of problems for the commentators.[678] It seems irrational to look for figs when none are to be expected. However, the rest of the story implies that one could expect to find them. That the tree is still in leaf suggests that at that time of year, late fall, figs might yet be found on trees. Mark then had added the phrase "not the season for figs." The rest of the vocabulary of vs 13 is traditional (particularly the phrase translated "ever"). In addition, the optative mode of "eat" is the only example of such a grammatical usage in Mark. Mark has probably added the involvement of the disciples in 14c. Vs 20 describes the tree as "withered from the root," while in vs 14 the tree is only cursed with the fate of "no one ever eating from it again." This verse is also formulated in terms of Mark's temporal scheme. Vs 21 is linked to 14c. So vss 20-21 come from Mark's hand.

The earliest form of the story consisted then of vss 13ab and 14ab. Matthew's form of the story supports this result. In Matthew the withering occurs immediately and is used directly as an example of a faith that can "move mountains." No day interrupts the results of the curse; the whole action occurs subsequent to the Temple cleansing and has no relationship to it.

Three sets of texts reference Israel in horticultural images: (1) Isa 1:30, Jer 24:1-6, Ezek 17, Joel 1:6-7, Hos 9:10; (2) Num 13:25, 20:5, 1 Kgs 4:25, 2 Kgs 18:31, Ps 104:33, Isa 36:16, Joel 2:22, Zech 3:11, Hab 3:17, Mic 4:4 (these texts make of the vine and fig tree typical images of social and religious weal); and (3) Pss 1:2-3, 90:6, 102:11, 129:6, Job 8:12, Isa 40:6-7, Jer 17:8, Lam 4:8 (these texts refer to withering as imagery for the life of the individual and the people especially in their religious life). These passages lead to the conclusion that a tree can be a symbol and employ as well an action that is executed on it or a word that is spoken over it. Objects of such messages involving plant imagery can be individuals, particularly the powerful, the godless, or the whole people of Israel. Important here is that inanimate objects such as the Temple are never compared to a tree.[679] These sayings appear mostly in prophetic threats and allude to God's action.[680]

Figs are used as a symbol of peace, security, and prosperity and appear prominently in descriptions of the "golden ages" of Israel's history such as the Exodus and the reign of Solomon and Simon Maccabaeus (Jer 8:13, Isa 28:3–4, Hos 9:10, 15, Mic 7:1, Joel 1:7, 12, 1 Macc 14:12). Common also are the motifs of blessing and judgment and YHWH's visitation of his people with fruitfulness or withering. Frequently, YHWH judges because of cultic corruption. Even the land can be subject in this imagery to God's curse, which withers the trees, especially the vine and fig tree. The weal of Temple, land, and people are interconnected.

The rabbinic material furthers the use of the fig imagery.[681] The search for and plucking of figs represent God in his dealing with his people, and the figs themselves are used as symbols for the nation and its representatives. Figs are also associated with eschatology. But it is in the ideation of the stories of the Haggadah (the Passover liturgy) that the Marcan story fits most securely. In these stories the world of plants is anthropomorphized. Blossoming and withering have a moral and symbolic significance. For example, withering occurs when cultic aberrations occur in the Temple, and fruit lost its savor when the Temple was destroyed, which effect would only be reversed in the messianic age. In this narrative world, the "Rabbi's curse has incontrovertible efficacy."[682] A close parallel to Mark's story occurs in bTa'an. A rabbi's son causes figs to grow for workers whom his father could not feed because of another obligation. When the rabbi discovers how they have been fed, he says to his son, "you have troubled your Creator to cause the fig tree to bring forth fruit before its time, may you too be taken hence before your time."[683] So in the original of Mark's story, the cursing of the tree was the central point with its implication of Jesus' prophetic authority to effect such a curse. It fits then the overall picture of Jesus, who taught and acted with authority.

Significant is that Jesus' curse denies future "fruit" to the tree, not "figs." "Fruit" is everywhere used as a symbol of the person in her religious relationships. The parable of the fig tree (Mark 13:28–29) shows that the tree can be a symbol for the in-breaking of the eschaton. Jesus spoke in terms of people bearing fruit (Matt 7:17–19), that is, works befitting repentance. So Jesus' curse is pronounced over the tree either because the people did not repent at his preaching or simply because the tree was in no condition to produce fruit. Jesus' curse is not that the tree continue in unfruitfulness but that "no one will ever eat from it"—that is, it has lost its character as bearer of divine revelation.

Another possibility is a link with "eating" in Jewish eschatological expectation, which is associated with the kingdom of God.[684] Because Jesus does not actually curse the tree to death (that effect only appears in the Marcan addition to the story in 11:20) but to unfruitfulness—"no one will ever eat fruit from it"—it seems that the curse was meant to convey that the tree will have no part in the age to come. Not to produce the fruit of response would mean the tree (Israel) would not enjoy the bliss of the eschaton. But the imagery is elusive, and no detail can be precisely defined as to its meaning. Obviously, if the tree, Israel, has not produced the fruit of faith or an adequate response to the preaching of the kingdom, Jesus cannot be portrayed as condemning it to not producing fruit forever. What he is saying, since there is no fruit now, is that Israel's decision vis-à-vis his kingdom proclamation has been made, and that decision has both temporal and eschatological consequences.

The problem here is that there is no word of explanation offered as to what this prophetic action meant to depict. There may have been such a word in the tradition (such as is found in Jer 1:11–12) to effect that "this is how it will be with Israel because it did not bring forth fruit in the *kairos*" ("opportune time").[685] But Mark is using the story for his purposes, so he may have eliminated the word that explained the action. It follows that Jesus was offering a prophetic threat. An absolute rejection of Israel was not intended.

Jesus' hunger, in this connection, could then be also understood metaphorically.[686] The time is ripe. The time for accepting the active presence of the kingdom has arrived, and so the season for fruit, the new age, is dawning, and the renewal of the people would be the natural response to that fact. But the tree (Israel) withholds the expected fruit, so Jesus excludes the tree from the kingdom. As the Jewish war progressed, the imagery would have taken on increasing poignancy. So Jesus appears here as a prophet who, with authority and power, proleptically announces God's judgment on the nation if it does not turn from the path that it is following—rejection of Jesus' call to enter the kingdom—and eschew the way of violence. He is saying that this is how it will be with Israel if it does not bring forth the fruit of repentance now in this season of opportunity.[687]

The Inhospitable Samaritans (Luke 9:51–56)

Vs 51 is a Lucan addition that fits the passage into his so-called travel narrative (9:1—19:27), which begins with this verse. There is no apothegm present forming the point of the story. The manuscript tradition sensing the lack has, however, provided a response of Jesus in answer to James' and John's request: "You do not know what kind of spirit you are. The Son of Man has not come to destroy the life of people but to save."[688] These copyists obviously felt the lack of a saying of Jesus beyond the report that he merely "reprimanded" James and John.

Jesus' rejection by the inhabitants of the Samaritan village he enters contrasts with the other encounters with Samaritans (Luke 10:33, 17:16).[689] The passage explains the reason for the rejection because Jesus' "face was set toward Jerusalem." The Samaritan's holy place was Mt. Gerizim, a fact that divided them from the Jews, who found that identification as heretical.[690]

James and John want to call down upon these rejecting Samaritans an apocalyptic fire. They share in the hostility of their Jewish compatriots toward Samaritans. Could this be an indication that these two disciples thought of Jesus as an Elijah redivivus who called down fire on the twice-sent fifty messengers of King Ahaziah (2 Kgs 1)?[691] But Jesus rebukes them as he had Peter (Mark 8:33), the storm (Mark 4:39), and unclean spirits (Mark 1:25, 9:25). Jesus "rebukes" what is opposed to his purpose and the way of God. His ministry is the salvation of those who are lost (Luke 19:10).[692] Here is the patient vinedresser (Luke 13:7) who keeps working on the "unfruitful tree" to bring about the readiness to enter the kingdom.

The Question to Jesus Concerning the Census (Mark 12:13-17), Matt 22:15-22, Luke 20:20-26)

The saying of Jesus here about rendering what is appropriate to Caesar and to God could not have been some independent saying. The passage is a unity and represents a historical report. There is little sign of any Marcan redaction, and he has transmitted the tradition intact. Because paying taxes was such a burning issue throughout the whole period of the first century in the Holy Land, the pericope probably retained its relevance and consequently was transmitted intact from its inception to its inclusion in Mark's Gospel.

The question in itself indicates the hostile intent of his questioners: the payment of taxes was a flash point in the land of Jesus' day.[693] To affirm the payment would draw the ire of his compatriots. The tax for his fellow Jews was a sign of their occupation by a pagan foreign power, and to have to pay it with the idolatrous coin that bore the human image of Tiberius offended every Jew who took the prohibition against images in the Torah seriously. To reject payment would be tantamount to treason. So the question was meant to put Jesus between a rock and a hard place.

The pronouncement of vs 17 without a doubt originated with Jesus. The present form of the passage, however, is carefully constructed and suggests the work of scribal elements within Mark's community. The whole passage evinces a ring structure:

> A. Leaders are sent with the intention to ensnare Jesus (vs 13).
> B. Flattery focused on Jesus (vs 14a–c).
> C. The leaders' double question (vs 14d).
> D. Jesus sees their hypocrisy (vs 15a).
> E. Jesus' question: "Why tempt me?" (vs 15b).
> D'. Jesus' command and compliance that exposes their hypocrisy (vss 15c—16a).
> C'. Jesus' double question (vs 16b).
> B'. Opponents' answer: Caesar is the focus (vs 16c).
> A'. Jesus' pronouncement that ensnares his opponents (vs. 17).

In this ring construction ("chiasmus"), the corresponding parts are coordinated: (1) the leaders are sent to ensnare Jesus, but Jesus' pronouncement ensnares them; (2) the flattering adulation focuses on Jesus, whereas the answer to Jesus' question about the coin focuses on Caesar; (3) the leaders ask him a double question, and Jesus asks them a double question about the coin; (4) Jesus sees their hypocrisy, which is overtly expressed in the fact that they produce the coin (they have it in their possession!); (5) the central element, which stands by itself, contains Jesus' question, "Why do you tempt me?"

This analysis verifies that the piece is a carefully wrought linguistic production that more than likely existed prior to Mark and which Mark has faithfully reproduced. Furthermore, the antithesis God/not-God characterizes the whole and its parts.[694] In vss 13 and 15 the contrast is between the guileful questioners and Jesus; in vs 14 between God and man; in vss 16 and 17 between Caesar and God; and in the final phrase of vs 17 again between Jesus' interrogators and himself. Both the central element and the contrasting sides of the chiasmus witness to a theological concern. On the one side Jesus' inquirers are active; on the other side Jesus is active. The passage therefore is not merely concerned with a religio-political question concerning taxes but also with a Christological and theological question.[695]

The contrast, however, can be further defined. In reality it is not so much a matter of God/not-God but God/anti-God. Jesus' inquirers are oppositional and intend to do evil. Caesar is not only merely "not god" but "anti-God" because he sets himself up as a god.[696] So he is in opposition to the one God of Israel. The interchange between Jesus and his opponents is not merely verbal sparring but an engagement of hostile forces that are mutually exclusive. Here we meet not merely what is not of God but what opposes God. The coin, the denarius, was a:

> Symbol of power and of the cult . . . together . . . [and] of the metaphysical glorification of policy which runs through the whole of ancient imperial history, and which also determined the Roman philosophy of domination from the time of Julius Caesar. Though perhaps the most modest sign, this denarius of Tiberius is the most official and universal sign of the apotheosis of power and the world of the *homo imperiosus* in the time of Christ.[697]

Jesus stands here in opposition to Caesar and his denarius. By implication he is the true image of God, represents God, and stands in his stead. The ἐκθαυμάδω (*ekthaumadzō*, "amazed, wonder greatly") of vs 17 has a numinous quality to it. It implies standing before the face of the divine. Caesar's divine claims are dethroned.

Two implications can be drawn from these structural aspects and the consequent contrasts: (1) the dichotomy "render to Caesar . . . and to God" must be understood as opposing orders of reality; Jesus asserts that sovereignty of God over all orders of the world;[698] and (2) Jesus is being addressed as he is in vs 14 to portray him as involved in the contrast God/anti-God. In this way he stands in a unique relationship with God.

That the final reaction of his opponents is described with the verb ἐκθαυμάδω (*ekthaumadzō*) also places the passage in the provenance of the exorcism stories where the cognate word θαυμάδω (*thaumadzō*, "wonder") is employed. In the story of the Gerasene demoniac (5:1–20), the people are amazed. Robinson called attention to the fact that there is a similarity of form between the exorcism stories and the debates.[699] The common features they share are (1) an identifying of Jesus; (2) a contrast between the antagonists; (3) hostility; (4) physical gestures; (5) a silencing; and (6) the reaction to Jesus' action and to his person. The word "test" (vs 15, πειράζω, *peiradzō*) is not the Old Testament idea of God who tests a person; rather it is the diabolical testing found in the traditions such as the temptation narrative (Mark 1:13). This is an apocalyptic perception that sees a diabolical origin in temptation and conflict within the world of the spirit.[700]

The association with the exorcism stories, the dualism of structure and content, but above all the contrast God/anti-God suggest an apocalyptic outlook. The root of the idea finds expression in Ezek 38–39, which rests on an even earlier mythological conception of the conflict between God and the chaos monster Leviathan.[701] The antidivine figure can assume a variety of associations with historical persona such as Antiochus and Nero.[702] The apocalyptic viewpoint perceived the series of crises facing the Jewish people between the time of the Maccabees and the war with Rome not only as a struggle between Israel and a world power but as a struggle between light and darkness, between Satan and God.[703]

As reflected in the exorcism stories, Satan and his minions are God's archenemies bent on destroying man and all of creation. Apocalyptic thought conceived of two armies composed of God and his angels and Satan and his angels arrayed against one another. However, this was not an absolute dualism, for the evil forces only exercised their power by God's sufferance. In this way history was seen to have a supramundane character.

The exegesis above on the question on authority, which understood that this passage included in Mark 11 had a mythological background rooted in the feast of Sukkoth and Zech 14, suggests that the census question may share a similar provenance. Zech 14 is based on a conflict myth.[704] The nations gather against Jerusalem in conflict with the Divine Warrior. Israel itself is understood as divided: there are two Israels. One is cut off by exile, and the other remains united within the city. The Divine Warrior then enters battle against the nations and defeats them (Zech 14:1–3). In vss 4–9 the theophany of the Divine Warrior occurs, nature is reordered, the old creation is supplanted by the new, and God is proclaimed king of this new creation. With this new creation, Jerusalem becomes the axis of the world where heaven and earth meet (vss 10–11). God holds a universal judgment, and the nations are condemned to the curses of the covenant. The survivors of the nations make a pilgrimage to Jerusalem to acclaim YHWH's universal reign by the celebration of Sukkoth (vss 16–19). Finally, the celebration takes place in which all distinctions between priest and people, sacred and profane, Israel and the nations are eliminated. This ultimate restoration, which democratizes and universalizes, is effected by YHWH alone (vss 20–21).

The themes of conflict between God and the wicked both within and outside Israel, the division of Israel, and the opposition but final unification of Jew and Gentile from Zech 14 resonate with our passage. This question about the census presents Jesus and his inquirers not as neutral debaters of an issue to be decided as in a rabbinic debate but as two opposing forces. The one wishes to "ensnare the other." The oppositional elements God/Caesar are particularly noteworthy in view of the divine claims made by the emperors. The division between Jesus and the men with evil intent who are sent to him implies a division within Israel.[705]

The address to Jesus in an ingratiating manner ironically speaks the truth. Jesus presents the way and the truth of God in contrast to his opponents, who indeed have "concerns about others" and "look in the face of men."[706] Not "looking in the face of people" is a divine attribute (1 Sam

16:7). So addressing him in this manner is doubly ironic. They are in reality opposed to him and actually intend his destruction.

The passage portrays Jesus as the decisive vanquisher of his opponents, who are manifestations of hostile demons to be exorcised or appear as hostile persons to be exposed and confronted with the truth. Jesus here functions in the place of and as closely associated with God as the Divine Warrior who overcomes the forces hostile to God. His victory is a proleptic enactment of his ultimate victory. The "render to . . ." statement asserts both the sovereignty of God over all worldly orders and a coordination of two realms, Israel and the Gentile world.

Because of its sophisticated ring structure, carefully arranged form, and subtleties, the passage as we have it cannot claim to be an exact description of Jesus' historical encounter with some questioners about paying taxes.[707] If we take into consideration what Jesus has expressed elsewhere in terms of nonviolence and benevolence toward the Roman occupier, he must have meant what most commentators see implied in Jesus' pronouncement, something like the unification of Jew and Gentile and the reordering of worldly relations with duty to Caesar and duty to God coordinated.[708] On the other hand, in Jesus' context a Roman governor could just as easily see his reply "to render . . ." as not rejecting the "new philosophy's" boycotting taxes but understanding his words in the context of the Jewish attitudes about images, seeing clearly that:

> [t]o want to give the emperor back his coins doesn't go very far. In [the Jewish view] the emperor has transgressed the commands of your God. He has allowed himself to be portrayed on coins. Readiness to give him back his wicked coins doesn't amount to loyalty to the state. One could just as easily see it as contempt. Give this blasphemous emperor back his blasphemous coins. God is more than the emperor![709]

So both conflict between Israel/world, God/Caesar, and God/humanity and the ultimate resolution of these dichotomies seem to be comprehended in Jesus' answer. And that resolution is in the cross, which is intimated in the hostility of Jesus' interrogators.[710]

The Sadducees and the Question of the Resurrection (Mark 12:18-27, Matt 22:23-33, Luke 20:27-38)

This passage exhibits a modified chiastic structure:

    A. The Sadducees identified (18a).

B. The Sadducees question Jesus (18b).
    a. Address to Jesus as "teacher" (19a).
    b. Scripture citation (19b).
    c. The problem posed: focus on death (20–22).
    d. The question asked: "whose wife?" Tacit conclusion: no resurrection (23).
B'. Jesus answers the Sadducees (24a).
    a'. Address to Sadducees: "they err" (24).
    d'. Question answered: "no wife" (25).
    b'. Scripture citation (26).
    c'. The problem removed: focus on life (27a).
A'. Jesus re-identifies the Sadducees (27b).

The subsections do not occur in the right order to create a proper parallelism. Evidently, the logical requirement of the story demanded that the pattern be revised because the problem posed in vs 23 had to be addressed first. However, this makes the correspondence between the various sections all the more remarkable.

The temptation is to excise one of the out-of-sequence members.[711] To eliminate vss 26–27 as foreign to the original tradition, however, destroys the unity of the piece as well as the logic, not to mention the structure. Nineham's observations are exactly to the point: the Sadducees want to demonstrate by rabbinic methods that the Torah has nothing to say about resurrection and that what it does say about levirate marriage is incompatible with such a belief. Their point would be that if Moses commanded levirate marriage, he could not have taught the idea of resurrection.[712] In fact, levirate marriage renders the idea ludicrous. If Jesus' reply consisted only of vs 25, it scarcely would have met the argument. A logical reply demanded an argument from Torah. So vs 25 prepares for vss 26–27, which assert that only a false form of resurrection hope could be reduced to the absurd by the provision for levirate marriage. But merely to assert that the Sadducees need to think differently about the nature of resurrection life would be inconclusive from their point of view. Therefore, vss 26–27 are essential to meeting the question. The structure outlined above reinforces this conclusion. In fact, both assertions are essential to meeting the scriptural question put by Jesus' opponents.

The chiastic structure formed by use of the word πλάνω (planō, "cause to wander, cause to err") in vss 24 and 27 strengthens the impression of the unity of Jesus' answer. This internal chiasmus also helps to explain the deviation from a strict parallelism between the two main sections:

    a. vs 24: Jesus addresses the Sadducees.

    b. vs 25: the manner of the resurrection life.
    c. vs 26: quotation from Torah.
    b'. vs 27a: the fact of the resurrection life.
    a'. vs 27b: the final address to the Sadducees.

The passage reveals a studied balance between the question posed and the answer tendered, between the Sadducees on the one side and Jesus on the other. The various sections stand in antithesis to one another. A whole series of antitheses also emerges from the content: life/death; God's own words/Moses's law; Jesus/Sadducees; truth/error; knowing Scripture/ignorant of Scripture; God's power/human opinion; this age/the age to come. Form and content correspond. Implied again is an apocalyptic outlook that views the world and reality in terms of opposing orders of God and the demonic forces of evil.[713]

The fundamental underlying antithesis involves what is and what is not of God. The word πλάνω and its antithesis "knowing the Scriptures and the power of God" (vs 24 stated positively) provide the fulcrum of the balance. The Sadducees deny the resurrection and use scripture to bolster their position by applying it in a manner that denies God and his fundamental character. Jesus, however, asserts this fundamental character of God by which he freely chooses to relate himself to humanity, that is, life.

The "power of God" is also essential in explicating the meaning of the passage. In the Old Testament God's power is salvific and manifested in saving action in history.[714] God, in the manifestation of his power, is considered personal in his forming and shaping of history. A historical occurrence experienced as God's act is explained in terms of the goal of history, viz., that YHWH is to become known to all nations and Israel is to serve and obey him. Connected to these conceptions is the designation "YHWH Zevaoth." This angelic host surrounds him, represents his power, fights for his victory, and in this way shapes history. After a long development, this historical character of God found expression in belief in him as Creator (Second Isaiah). Finally, this characteristic also finds expression in the relationship between God and the individual (Ps 86:16, Isa 40:29–31).

These three strands of the tradition, God as creator, his angelic host, and his relationship to the nations and the individual, also find their expression in the apocalyptic literature that grapples with the question of how history, the world, and individuals are subject to powers, including death, which are at enmity with God. The hope grew that God in an eschatological battle would reveal his power, destroy his opponents, and save those who belong to him. God's "power" ultimately involves the power to save from death and bring to life.

The writers of apocalyptic literature made the connection between the eschatological victory of God's power over evil and the fate of the individual. To restore Israel meant the restoration of the individual. That God's power to save is linked in our passage with resurrection places it firmly within an apocalyptic-eschatological horizon. So the reference to angels and resurrection is not unexpected. This view contradicts that of the Sadducees who rejected both angels and resurrection.

Divorce and Celibacy (Mark 10:2-12, Matt 19:3-12, Luke 16:18)

This discussion appears in Mark's Gospel at a peculiar point. Chapter 9 closes with a discussion of the character and cost of discipleship, a theme that continues in 10:13-52. This passage looks as if it were sandwiched in between this long section dealing with discipleship.

No Pharisee would ask about the lawfulness of divorce. Matthew, with his scribal learning, being more informed of the Jewish situation,[715] makes the question asked by the Pharisees more plausible by having them ask if one could divorce for "any cause" (vs 3), which they did discuss and on which they had reached no agreement. A Pharisee might well be interested in Jesus' opinion, particular if he were a Shammaite.[716] But it would be a more plausible question in the mouth of an average Jew.[717] The Pharisees were quite well settled on the matter on the basis of Deut 24:1-4. Their only disagreement was on the grounds, not the right, to divorce.[718] So if the Pharisees were not unified on the allowable causes for divorce, it could well be that the average Jewish man would be curious about the question particularly if he were considering such an action. So this vignette presented by Mark has all the characteristics of a report of an actual encounter between Jesus and a man who perhaps was looking for some reason to rid himself of his present wife.

The Torah permitted divorce provided that the wife's interests were taken into consideration. She was given a *Ketubah*, that is, a written document at the time of marriage, which required the husband to assign a certain sum of money to her in the event of death or divorce. Matthew places the discussion in the realm of Jewish discussion: the proper causes for divorce.[719] And he has Jesus say there is only one ground for divorce, viz., *porneia* (vs 9, i.e., literally "consorting with prostitutes, fornication"), compared to Mark, who makes the divorce prohibition absolute, as does Luke. (Luke appends it to the various interpretations of the parable of the unjust steward.) Matthew has added the exception, which Mark certainly would have included if that were the original saying handed down by the tradition. Matthew has Jesus agreeing with the school of Shammai.[720]

So there are four versions of the saying, which can be classified in this way:

1. Mark 10:10–12: a man who divorces and remarries commits adultery (A).
   A woman who divorces and remarries commits adultery (B).
2. Matt 5:32: a man who divorces his wife, except for unchastity, causes her to commit adultery (C).
   A man who marries a divorced woman commits adultery (D).
3. Matt 19:9: a man who divorces his wife, except for unchastity, and marries another commits adultery (A).
4. Luke 16:18: everyone who divorces his wife and marries another commits adultery (A).
   He who marries a woman divorced from her husband commits adultery (D).[721]

In the Jewish milieu, only the man could initiate divorce. And Jesus was speaking to men and to the sin of men. But (B) can be judged to also be a word of Jesus even though a Jewish woman had no right to divorce her husband.[722] However, Luke's version might have been the original form of the saying.[723] No doubt Jesus may have frequently been asked this question and said slightly different things in each situation.

Jesus regards the Mosaic allowance of divorce as a concession to human weakness and not the will of God. He then reaches back into the creation story and quotes Gen 1:27 and 2:24 to assert that God's original intention in creating male and female was to bring them together into an indissoluble union.[724] The order of creation eclipses the law of divorce. He corrects Moses by Moses and asserts that Mosaic law is a second best.[725] Jesus, in this way, declares that the law is not a law at all but a mere dispensation. Jesus' interpretation of the Scriptures and their authority is related to his understanding of the kingdom of God. The kingdom will restore the world and mankind to its original condition. So those who have entered the kingdom through his proclamation are to live in accordance with that kingdom and God's original intention. He is setting forth one aspect of the new existence before God.

Jesus' declaration of the indissolubility of marriage also makes the man and woman equal (cf., Gal 3:28). Their "one flesh" (vs 8) means that their union in marriage is as close as between two blood relatives, a relationship that can hardly be "sundered." God's will is engraved in his very act of creating male and female forming a permanent union between two persons. The verb translated "asunder" (χωριζέτω, *chōridzetō*) is a present third-person imperative that can only be translated in English with "let not." To catch the force of the meaning of the imperative, it could be translated "you are forbidden to separate." The present mode makes the forbidden action successive, continuing indefinitely into the future. With sovereign authority, Jesus declares God's original intention for marriage in an apodictic command.[726] Jesus asserts that God's primordial will, built into the very structure of the creation, makes of marriage a permanent, indissoluble union that no one can undo, not even Moses.[727]

Given the cultural situation, it is no wonder the disciples ask Jesus for further elaboration (Mark 10:10–12). Here Jesus puts the prohibition on divorce into the form of a casuistic law that says divorce and remarriage on the part of either man or wife constitute adultery. This latter declaration follows from the former: if marriage is indissoluble, then leaving it and joining oneself to another is obviously adultery since the original marriage is still in force.

Jesus speaks here with authority, that is, "not like the scribes" (Mark 1:22). As expressed here, that authority is radical because it asserts that the Old Testament is not everywhere the absolute and unqualified word of God. He declares then that he speaks as the one who is greater than Moses as he is greater than Solomon, Jonah, and the Temple (Luke 11:31–32, Matt 12:6). Jesus has qualified the application of Torah and says the primal history supersedes the later law, which was given because of their "hardness of heart."[728] This "hardness of heart" means stubbornness, an unyielding spirit, and obduracy. Jesus characterizes Israel as stubbornly refusing at the core of man's being to hear and obey God's will and live according to his nature. Divorce is pure rebellion against God.[729] Hosea is perhaps the husband after the Lord's heart who remains faithful and true even when his wife was not. So Jesus' understanding of marriage rests ultimately on God's own nature: he remains the faithful husband to Israel even when she has apostatized and committed "adultery" with her idolatry and pagan practices.[730]

It must also be said that there was no total agreement on just how the Torah was to be applied and obeyed in first-century Judaism. Jesus was no outlier in interpreting the Torah in his unique way. However, his declaration would have put him on a path of certain antagonism and hostility from the Pharisaic Hillelites and the Sadducees.

SUMMARY AND ANALYSIS: CONTROVERSY AND SCHOLASTIC DIALOGUES

The Message

Jesus' healings were not just some kind of antinomian protest (healing the man with a withered hand, the man with dropsy, and a paralytic, Mark 3:1–6, Luke 14:1–6, Mark 2–12). Jesus upheld the validity of the Torah. His healings must be seen in the context of his proclamation of the kingdom. The kingdom is present, the time of salvation is here, so healing cannot wait. The kingdom has priority over the Torah. Jesus also asserts (in agreement with the Pharisees!) that human need has precedence over the law (Mark 2:27–28). He does not abrogate the law but fulfills its intent: it was given to keep the faithful close to God and his will. To enter the kingdom means to be in the closest fellowship with God. Community with God has been restored.

His regard for the Torah is emphasized in his debate with some (Shammaite) Pharisees over the use of Korban, which could foster disrespect for parents, something that the Torah prohibited (Mark 7:6–13). Sitting at table with Jesus was a proleptic experience of the feast of the kingdom. The Jubilee had arrived. One now lived with the ethics of the kingdom: forgiveness, hospitality, binding up the wounds of the neighbor, sharing goods. And rather than hostility toward a brother and especially toward Rome, the kingdom meant to be willing to turn the other cheek and go the extra mile. Forgiveness is stressed in the healing of the paralytic. In the kingdom there are no boundaries to forgiveness. This aspect of the kingdom is so important because the nation cannot survive without it. "Son of man" is Jesus' self-designation (Mark 2:10) by which he identifies himself with humanity, with his own people, and with the weak and the humble. In this he was representative of the new Israel, the bearer of God's judgment, the presence of the kingdom, and the embodiment of forgiveness.

Jesus asserts that his exorcistic activity was the binding of Satan (dispute about exorcism, Mark 3:22–30). The plundering of his power would be fully effected with the arrival of the kingdom. The kingdom has invaded enemy territory. Satan's kingdom has begun to fall.

Like John, Jesus works with divine authority (the question on authority, Mark 11:27–33). John prepared the people for the coming kingdom and Jesus prepares for and proclaims God's victory in the entry and cleansing narratives as he fulfills Zechariah's prophecy (Mark 11:1–10, 15–17). The new age is dawning when God will establish his kingdom. The Gentiles will stream into Jerusalem and join in worship with the Jews in a great egalitarian feast of tabernacles. His interrogators in Jerusalem did not accept John's divine authority, nor did they believe that Jesus acted with that same authority. So he rhetorically deposes them from claiming that they function with God's authorization. In this he appears as a prophet who proclaims God's word, which does "not return to me empty, but it shall accomplish that which I purpose, and prosper in the thing for which I sent it" (Isa 55:11).

When Jesus refuses to be called "good" (the rich man and his question, Mark 10:17–31), he witnesses to his divine emptying, which directs attention to God and his kingdom. As in the parables of treasure in a field and the pearl of great price, he demands of the man who is searching for salvation that he sell all and follow him. But the man refuses the invitation because of his wealth. Jesus makes some provocative statements about the difficulty of the rich entering the kingdom. He had illustrated that difficulty in the parable of the rich fool and Lazarus and the rich man. In this he upsets Jewish society's identification of wealth with exceptional piety and God's favor. But God can make a way even for the wealthy. The kingdom is pure gift. The kingdom, the community of the end-time, is true wealth, for it endures while earthly wealth fades. Wealth can stand in the way of accepting the kingdom and its poverty, which paradoxically is true wealth because the entrance into the kingdom provides the wealth of a new family consisting of a plethora of brothers, sisters, and mothers under the one Father-God.

The law as summarized by the double love commandment is universalized, extending it to the world of Gentiles.[731] Jesus vividly portrayed this universalism with the parables of the mustard seed and leaven in a lump. Assenting to this commandment, however, does not gain one's entrance into the kingdom. Jesus tells the scribe that he is "not far" from the kingdom"— that is, he's not yet in. The kingdom is not merely a mental matter of the understanding, the intellect, and reason, or even a matter of the "heart" (i.e., the will). It is a matter of one's "whole life" (the one element not repeated by the scribe in Mark 12:32). The whole person, including one's life in the world, is demanded: "If anyone would come after me, let him deny himself and take up his cross and follow me. For whoever would save his life will lose it; and whoever loses his life for my sake and the gospel's will save it" (Mark 8:34). Only by "losing oneself" will a person enter the kingdom. The scribe's distance from the kingdom comes from not being ready to dispossess himself of his goods and take up his cross and follow Jesus.

At the same time, Jesus affirms the scribe's declaration that the double command is "greater than all holocausts and sacrifices." Implied in this affirmation is that the Temple sacrifices are superfluous and no longer required.[732] The Temple rather is to be a "house of prayer for all nations" (Mark 11:17). The supersession of Temple sacrifices by the love commandment affirmed by Jesus refers also to the ultimate sacrifice of himself on the cross. The scribe is not yet in the kingdom. He lacks one thing: the giving of his whole life, which is precisely what Jesus will do on the cross. Jesus himself is the embodiment of the love commandment, which demands one's whole life. The cross is where Jesus' love for his people finds a climax. In it he achieves victory over evil. His love leads him to give himself, his very life, for others (Mark 10:45, Gal 2:20, Eph 5:2).[733]

Jesus negatively defines himself as not being a "judge," that is, not like a judge in ancient Israel nor the form of the judge taken by contemporary bandits (the dispute over an inheritance, Luke 12:13-14). Both of these forms of judges included martial aspects. His ministry was one of reconciliation, forgiveness, and acquiring "treasure in heaven." The kingdom would be established not by violence but by hospitality; not by seeking honor through wealth and acquisition but by the sharing of goods; not by external security but by service.

The popular wisdom of the day assumed that when untoward events overtook someone, it was a punishment for sin. The great underlying support for this view was Israel's own history. The people were subject to exile for the sin of idolatry and the social sins of not caring for the least. Jesus contradicts this notion (slaughter of the Galileans, Luke 13:1-5). Pilate's slaying of pilgrims and the fall of the tower of Siloam taking the life of eighteen men were not to be thought of as the result of sin on their part. But such incidents were really a divine call to repent. Jesus used these incidents to warn that if there were no turnabout in the attitude of the nation, which was becoming inured to violence, animosity, and hostility and trusting in the inviolability of the Temple and apocalyptic dreams of divine intervention, the nation would be destroyed. Jesus was countering a revanchism against Rome and even Pilate in spite of his sadistic provocations. He was reminding Israel of the steadfast love of their God, his mercy, and his compassion. The people were to emulate him and save the nation by love of the enemy and forgiveness. Judgment would surely come when God's kingdom arrived.

Jesus uses the request of James and John to sit by his side (i.e., share in his glory) in the kingdom as a teaching opportunity (Luke 18:31-33): there is a fiery ordeal awaiting him and his disciples. He and they would go through the "birth pangs" that would precede the coming of the kingdom. Here we can glimpse the inner struggle of Jesus: the judgment is coming, and he faces death, taking upon himself the end-time pangs. By rejecting him the nation will reject their last chance to escape the national disaster that will ensue. He gives his life for his people, takes their sin upon himself to preserve them.

Of the separation of "insiders" and "outsiders," Jesus will hear nothing, for even if there are those who do not follow him yet exorcise by his name, they are expanding the invasion against Satan and his rule, and they will hardly "curse" him (the rival exorcist, Mark 9:38–41, cf., Prov 20:9, Exod 21:16). His attitude here is in keeping with his perspective in the parables that perceives the kingdom appearing in unexpected and surprising places and persons.[734] He softens the hard attitude toward outsiders especially in his command to love the enemy. This attitude on his part points clearly to his understanding of the kingdom, which is present in the here and now through his proclamation, healings, table fellowship, and even mere presence. In this way the kingdom is not brought in by force nor is one to try and calculate the time of its arrival. Jesus' call remains dynamic: enter the kingdom now and live now in its powerful presence by practicing its ethics. His message is both personal and social, temporal and with eternal ramifications. Even if you don't follow him directly, use his name to further expand the kingdom and rid people of the rule of Satan and his minions.

The kingdom was not some neat colloquy of like-minded people. It was messy, filled with down-and-outers, sinners, people who grasped the power of even the name of Jesus, women high and low, the sick and scorned who clutched the hem of his garment, military officials who understood his power to heal. Jesus opened doors, and out of joy the world in all its motley colors pressed into this kingdom. It was palpable, and it was present and active among those who accepted his invitation and lived with the ethic of forgiveness, love for enemies, and expansive hospitality. The kingdom's expansive love, which includes even the enemy, Jesus expresses in his rebuke to James and John, who want to call down fire on the Samaritans who would not accept Jesus and his entourage.

In the story of the cursing of the fig tree (Mark 11:12–14), Jesus prophetically announces that if Israel refuses the invitation, to bring forth the fruit of repentance God's judgment will come upon the nation, and it will be reduced to fruitlessness—that is, it will not enjoy the bliss of the eschaton.

The rejection Jesus experiences comes to a head in his interchange with those who want to catch him in the question of whether to pay the poll tax with Tiberias's idolatrous coin, which claims his divine sonship (Mark 12:13–17). This story has apocalyptic overtones that pit Jesus against his antagonists, who are manifestations of Satan—that is, it is a conflict between God and anti-God, between God and Caesar. Jesus vanquishes his opponents by a word. He is intimately associated with the Divine Warrior who overcomes the hostile forces of evil. He proleptically enacts God's ultimate victory. Jesus' "render to God" asserts the sovereignty of God over all worldly orders. Jesus' cross is intimated in the hostile intent of his interrogators. But it is in the cross that is imposed by Rome through Pilate that Caesar submits to God's will and by which God exercises his sovereignty over the world.

These antitheses reappear again in one of Jesus' debates with the Sadducees (Mark 12:18–27). In this case the antithesis is between God and not-God. The Sadducees' denial of resurrection denies God's fundamental character as the life-giver. The apocalyptists struggled with how God and the powers that subject history, the world, and the individual to death and corruption can coexist. So they asserted God would ultimately be victorious because he is a saving God, and life would be finally restored to the individual.

In the question on divorce (Mark 10:2–12), Jesus explicates yet another aspect of the kingdom: the kingdom restores the world to its original condition. Those who enter it are to live in accordance with its primordial order established by God, which has been built into the very structure of creation. Jesus speaks as the one greater than Moses and with sovereign authority. Marriage rests on God's own character. He is the faithful husband of his "wife" Israel and will never abandon her.

Jesus did not run some kind of protest movement, political program, or social movement, though what he said and did had an impact on politics and social life. He was calling Israel back to life with God and his purposes for the nation. Everything he said and did centered in and was comprehended in the reality of God's kingdom, his royal rule.

In the apothegms under discussion in this chapter, Jesus does not abrogate the Torah—it remains in force until the kingdom is fully established (Matt 5:17–20). However, because the kingdom is already present in his words and deeds and in the community it has established through him, the Torah must submit to its sway and sovereignty. Under its gravity, people are healed on the Sabbath, sinners enjoy fellowship with God, and the Mosaic legislation on marriage and divorce must give way to the primordial state intended by God at the creation. The inclusion of women in Jesus' community of the end-time and their equality also come under the same rubric.

The Messenger and His Hearers

Jesus is totally embedded in the kingdom that he proclaims. Or to put it differently, he is utterly subject to God and his rule (i.e., his will and purposes). However, he does not quite speak as one of the classical prophets. His embeddedness in the kingdom makes him speak in a sovereign way: the Sabbath is subject to him, as are the demons. Obedience to the law does not qualify for existence in the kingdom. The scribe who affirms the double love command is "not far from the kingdom." Israel's leaders must also submit to his authority and the power of his pungent arguments. Because he cannot be trapped and meets the arguments of his opponents head-on, they are deprived of their authority and are reduced to attacking him with ad hominem arguments: he is demon possessed, he is a blasphemer, and he is obliquely judged as unclean and a sinner because he consorts with such people.

His speech and language are forthright. He doesn't mince words, and yet his words are not caustic or biting. He refuses to act as a judge and arbiter over the legalities connected with an inheritance (perhaps he wants to avoid the militant characteristics associated with a judge).[735] Although he rejects the popular equation of wealth and piety, he receives a rich man with "love." His capacious attitude is evident in his refusal to equate sin and untoward events: he observes that God's goodness is showered on both good and evil persons (Matt 5:45); he accepts those who do not follow him yet use his name to exorcise; he refuses to let his disciples call down judgment on those who refuse to accept him. That same commodiousness appears in his prohibition of divorce because it implies man and woman are equal in the kingdom (cf., Gal 3:28).

Because the kingdom is already present in Jesus' activities and his followers live in this new reality, fasting is inappropriate like pouring new wine into old, dilapidated skins or mourning at a wedding feast. Healing cannot wait until the morrow. This is the day of salvation (2 Cor 6:2). Jesus is living out his baptismal call as the "Son of God" and the divine call to the nation to "listen to him."[736]

Though present already, the kingdom will come in its fullness in the future, but it will be preceded by the woes of the end-time, its "birth pangs" (Mark 13:8, ὠδίνων, ōdinōn). Jesus understood himself, though he didn't use the terms of the suffering servant of Isaiah, as the one who takes upon himself the end-time woes. He speaks of his own "baptism" (suffering) as the "beloved son." In the Old Testament, God's love is connected with the covenant.[737] The covenant has to do with exodus and God's election of Israel as his own people. God's love is selective, voluntary, spontaneous, and related to his righteousness, judgment, and forgiveness.[738] There is no explicit statement that the divine love extends to the nations.[739] However, Jesus does so perhaps most poignantly in the parable of the prodigal son. "Beloved" is used of Israel (Pss 60:5, 108:6, Isa 5:1–2, Jer 12:7), which suggests that the application of Isa 42:1–4 to Jesus[740] and the use of the word in the baptismal scene and transfiguration story imply he is representative of the nation.[741] In this way he would have understood himself as recapitulating the people, their history, and their relationship to God.[742] This representational role is further suggested by the connection made between God's love and election (Col 3:12, Rom 1:7, 9:11–13, 11:28, Eph 1:4–5) and by the fact that he demands allegiance to himself (Matt 10:37–38) and to God (Matt 6:24, Mark

12:29–30). That allegiance is what the scribe in his affirmation of the double love command lacks.

Jesus sees himself, though he doesn't use the word, as a pioneer (Heb 2:10, 12:2) who is invading the kingdom of Satan, the "strong man," and plundering his house (Mark 3:27) by his exorcisms and ransoming "the many"[743] from satanic power. In a parallel way Jesus invades the world of sinners and sin and rescues the sinner from the threatening peril of sin when God comes in judgment. This consorting with sinners, whom Jesus has come to call (Mark 2:17), puts him in the place of the Lord who "instructs sinners" (Ps 25:8) and in the messianic role of returning sinners to the Lord's way (Ps 51:13).

4

Summary and Analysis

The Beloved Son as Tantalizing Teacher

SURVEY OF JESUS' SETTING IN THE HOLY LAND OF THE FIRST CENTURY

In this chapter I want to present a brief overview of the historical realities in which Jesus was active as a more detailed reminder of the context in which Jesus' words and activities functioned among his contemporaries.[744]

The near history that perhaps had the greatest impact on the thought world of the Jews of Jesus' time in their relationship to their oppressors was the great successes of the Maccabean revolt. The Maccabean brothers, Judah, Jonathan, and Simon, against all odds and expectations were able to achieve victories over the Syrian empire, cleanse the Temple, wrest Jewish freedom from this Hellenistic state, and restore the independence of the government and priesthood within twenty-four short years of the beginning of the revolt (166–142 BC). Their achievement was confirmation of the Old Testament stories and ideology of the holy war[745] that assured, no matter the size of Israel's armies, God would fight on their behalf and win for them victory. That the Maccabeans thought and acted in terms of this ideology is clear from their practice of carrying out the *Herem*, that is, "the ban," the extirpation of everything connected with idolatry including pagan peoples themselves.⁷⁴⁶ This led, of course, to the smoldering animosity that developed between Jews and Gentiles. The Maccabees understood themselves as God's instruments in the image of the ancient judges and also in terms of the royal, messianic figure of David.⁷⁴⁷

However, the nation was divided. There were those elements that supported greater openness to the world and sympathy for the Hellenistic spirit of the age. In the time of Jesus, the priestly caste especially was quite content to live as subjects under the aegis of Rome's foreign rule. After all, that arrangement, which I call the "dependent hieratic state," had proved very viable and comfortable under the liberal Persian Empire for over two hundred years.⁷⁴⁸ The priestly leadership had learned very well the art of accommodation to a foreign overlord. Of course, the Persians made that very easy. There was no interference on the part of the empire in Jewish matters as long as the taxes were paid. Those years were evidently so peaceful and devoid of controversy that we have no sources that give us any information about them.

The situation under Rome was poles apart from the Persian experience. Rome indeed made certain accommodations with Jewish law. Jews were not required to serve in the army. They could collect the Temple tax. Pagan symbols were to be kept out of the Holy City. And Gentiles who violated the Temple could be punished. But Herod and his successors filled the land with pagan temples, and the procurators often seemed to delight in transgressing Jewish sensibilities and provoking the people. The elites and their retainers, the Sadducees, the kings and tetrarchs, and the procurators had the power of taxation and followed Roman ideals of land ownership by acquiring large plantations. They had little concern for the masses and above all were interested in preserving the status quo. Their concerns were geopolitical, maintaining power and pacifying the unruly masses.

The renewal movements could not reconcile Roman hegemony. All of them burned with the desire to bring about the conditions under which God would act and intervene and rescue the nation from the Roman occupation. There were three such movements that called upon patterns of leadership from Israel's ancient past that thrived in the first century: prophets, judges, and royal messianic claimants.⁷⁴⁹ All of them found the Roman occupation as intolerable and usurping the divine prerogative to be the nation's king and to live under him and his gift of liberty.⁷⁵⁰

The first of these movements was largely pacifistic and fell into the pattern of what might be described as an active quietism. These prophets rose up from the people as a response to the crisis of the times, following the accepted pattern of leadership of the nation that had developed historically.⁷⁵¹

The prophets who emerged in the first century followed the pattern of Moses, Elijah, Elisha, and the later prophets who proclaimed both God's judgment and promises for a future peaceable kingdom. They performed prophetic actions that undergirded their message. The New Testament witnesses to a strong expectation and longing for the rise of a prophet who would apparently usher in the action of God, who would establish his kingdom and root out both apostasy within the nation and oppression from without.[752] As Moses had performed signs and wonders at the birth of the nation, so now these first-century prophets would perform signs and wonders that would liberate the nation in its present circumstances.

There were also more or less quietistic elements who placed their trust in God to work things out for his people and so were quite ready to accept whatever historical conditions they had to live under and depended on God to alter them. This did not necessarily mean total inaction. For there were hundreds who followed, for example, the Samaritan prophet who, during Pilate's term of office, gathered a throng at Mount Gerizim, promising to go up the mountain to retrieve the Temple vessels that had, according to tradition, been buried there. The Samaritans believed in a Taheb, "the Restorer," through whom God would act and bring about the restoration of the people. Pilate viciously put the movement down ostensibly because they bore arms, implicitly threatening violence against the Roman occupation.[753]

The rise of these movements reveals that the people interpreted their occupation under Rome as still languishing in exile and longing for the freedom that was to accompany their entrance into the promised land. In their sights was a new exodus and a new conquest that would be accomplished by divine intervention by either the actions or the words of these prophets. All of these movements were harshly eradicated by the Romans no matter how peaceful they were. John the Baptist was more in the mold of the classical prophets of the word who pronounced judgment on the nation and urged repentance on the people.

A second movement was that of judges (who are called "bandits" in the sources). They were militaristic like the messianic movements and used explicit martial means to further the cause of Israel's independence. Since messianic leadership and prophetic activity were functions combined in and exercised by Moses but became divided with the rise of the monarchy under Saul and David, it is not surprising that messiahs also emerged alongside prophetic activity in the first century.[754] David became the model of a royal messiah (i.e., "the one anointed [with oil]"). Josephus describes two such movements during and shortly after the reign of Herod the Great and two during the years of the revolution. However, he also indicates that some of the bandits/judges made such assertions, so the existence of messianic claimants appeared throughout the period.[755] The expectations of royal messiahs received a clear description in Psalm 17 of the so-called Psalms of Solomon[756] and above all in the accession narrative of David.[757] These sources celebrated the exploits of the messiah who would, by God's support, rid the land of foreign oppressors by "destroying the unlawful nations,"[758] establish God's kingdom, and drive out the (Gentile) sinners from the Holy Land and the nation.

During the 50s an urban terrorist group arose called the Sicarii.[759] They mingled in the crowds in Jerusalem especially during the festivals with concealed daggers and killed their opponents by stabbing and then melted back into the crowds.[760] This violence, turned in on itself, came to a head in the final years of the war when the three groups that held Jerusalem fought with one another rather than present a unified front against the Roman war machine. They thoughtlessly destroyed the food caches to deprive their competitors of sustenance.[761]

Other movements included the Essenes (Qumran), and the Pharisees fell in between the extremes of quietism and activism.[762] The Essenes were ready to wait until the (divine) conditions arose and then enter the fray to conquer Israel's enemies. When the revolt began in AD 64 and the Jews were able to enjoy an initial victory over the Roman military, they joined in as the right time to strike. They were apocalyptic revolutionaries. Their leadership was assigned to priests, and their way of life was the way of purity and submission to their understanding of Torah. They were a true sect because they conceived of the true Israel as confined to their own members, the "sons of light." Their answer to the crisis was rejection of the present religious and political leadership and withdrawal to the wilderness to live in priestly purity and prepare for the apocalyptic moment when the war with the "sons of darkness" would begin and ultimately be won by the "sons of light."

The Pharisees could be involved in revolutionary activity too. For example, they were behind the development of a new "Fourth Philosophy" (so named by Josephus) that equated the payment of taxes to Rome with idolatry. They were also involved with tearing down the eagle over the Temple, which was tantamount to declaring war against the occupier.[763] However, for the most part they worked for an egalitarianism claiming equality for every Israelite before God and worked to interpret Torah so that all of its commands could be obeyed in whatever circumstances. They put a "fence" around the law—that is, they expanded its application to avoid any infringement of the law. Their focus was on Israel and being faithful to God and the covenant he made with them. (They pursued what has been called a "covenantal nomism."[764]) They worked at interpreting the law in lenient, humane directions placing human requirements above the law. They also adopted the practices and mores of the people (the "oral tradition") as an equally divine revelation of Torah, which made them immensely popular with the Judean people. They were highly regarded as faithful Jews. They pursued their own trades and earned nothing by the teaching of Torah. Their answer to the crisis was the renewal of the individual and the nation by being concerned for following the Torah in all of life's situations. However, they seemed to have little success in the Galilee in gaining adherents.

All of these groups were possessed with what the Bible calls "zeal," that is, passion to establish righteousness and the will of the Lord.[765] The concept stretches from Phinehas punishing idolatrous violations of the law (Num 25:1–15) to the revolutionary actions of the Maccabees fighting to cleanse the land of the Syrian oppressors and beyond into the first century, where every group could be described as "zealous." This "zealousness" meant a person was willing to give up one's life in defense and preservation of the people in fidelity to the Torah and was willing to take action by word or deed to achieve those ends.[766] All of these movements sought:

> to bring about conditions whereby Israel could live in a land not polluted by foreign cults and idolatry, not imposed upon by Roman-Hellenistic culture, not driven to despair by an economic system imposed from above, especially by a foreign ruler, and where God's exclusive right to reign as king was not flaunted by the arrogance of a Gentile power or Jewish elites.[767]

The peasants, who represented more than 95 percent of the population, lived with their "backs against the wall."[768] I have described their hapless situation in my previous book as rural residents farming small plots of land. They led a more or less hand-to-mouth existence, paying perhaps as much as 40 percent of the produce of their small farms in taxes, leaving what was left over for food, seed for the next harvest, and purchasing or bartering for other needs.[769]

In contrast to them, the upper 2 percent of the wealthy enjoyed living off the production of others; their indolent lives depended on and exploited the work of others. Work to them was considered beneath their station (cf., the parable of the rich man and Lazarus[770]). Included in this class of people were the high priests and their elite and wealthy lay associates who, when taken together, were known as the Sadducees.[771] Although the high priests were accepted as legitimate and as the leaders of the people because they filled divinely appointed offices, they were generally despised as individuals. We get an indication of that antipathy by the people who, during the last two years of the revolt, anointed a nonaristocratic priest to serve as the high priest. Of course, there were exceptions to this general antipathy because some of them were magnanimous, and not all grasped for power, wealth, and status. They could be called "secularists" who had no spiritual sensitivities but applied the law literally and woodenly, never accepting what they would have regarded as the new-fangled idea of resurrection. That means they had not moved along with how Judaism had developed.

From AD 6 to 37 and again from 41 to 64, Roman procurators governed Judea. Generally speaking, they were hated and despised. They understood their appointment as sanction to enrich themselves. They had little understanding of Jewish sensitivities and little or no respect for those they governed. Pilate, who governed from AD 26 to 36, that is, during the time that Jesus was active, was a particularly egregious example of a despotic, cruel, and high-handed authoritarian whose behavior can justifiably be called anti-Semitic.[772] So there is little wonder why the people finally rose up in revolt. Rome's vacillating policy of how the land was to be governed was no small factor: now it was a procurator, then a Jewish prince. It never allowed the development of a strong center of authority that could demand the people's allegiance. The contempt of most of the procurators for their Jewish subjects only exacerbated the hatred for Rome. Nor did the Sadducean leadership actively work to ameliorate the conditions of oppression.

During Jesus' lifetime, Herod Antipas[773] was the Roman appointed tetrarch (i.e., "the ruler of a fourth") of the Galilee and Perea. He was popularly known as "king" (Mark 6:14–27), although he never received that title from the Roman overlord. He pursued building projects much like his father, Herod the Great. His first capital, Sepphoris, just a few miles from Nazareth, was abuilding during the time Jesus was growing up. He later founded Tiberias along the western shore of the Sea of Galilee, named after the emperor. It became his new capital city. During its construction graveyards were found there, rendering it ritually unclean. But he forced some Galilean Jews to live there along with a large number of Gentiles. He adorned the city with magnificent structures. He made himself an enemy of Pilate by bringing a complaint against him for profaning Jerusalem with votive shields. Only the trial of Jesus finally eased the animosity between them (Luke 23:12).

On a visit to Rome he fell in love with Herodias, the wife of his halfbrother Herod Phillip. She divorced and married Antipas, an unlawful marriage according to the Torah for which he was denounced by John the Baptist, leading to his arrest and execution. Though Antipas protected Jewish sensitivities, he acted pretty much like any Hellenistic potentate. He saw in John the potential for an uprising given the tinderbox conditions in the land, where smoldering resentment against Rome and its client kings could have, with the slightest provocation, easily burst into the flame of revolution.

He saw Jesus as a possible provocateur and so sought to take his life too.[774] He finally had the opportunity to see Jesus when he was in Jerusalem for Passover. Pilate, wishing to spare himself passing judgment on Jesus, sent him to Antipas to render judgment. Antipas wanted some kind of demonstration from Jesus. But he refused to satisfy Antipas's self-indulgent curiosity and remained silent. Frustrated, Antipas sent him back to Pilate.

In the first volume of this series, I analyzed the dynamics of Jewish society in the first century from six perspectives, characterizing each factor on the basis of the reality of the times. It is clear from this overview that the society suffered under economic inequality, social tensions, political injustice, religious competition, ecological divisions, and the hopes for a renewal that would restore the historical society of old.[775]

The vast difference between the economic situation of the peasant and the elites under whom they were exploited fed animosity and revolt. Drought and famine were a constant threat to the life of a peasant. This often led to borrowing to make ends meet and further added to the stress of producing enough to make a livelihood. In such situations the peasant often would sell his land to a large, elite landholder and then live in serf-like conditions, working the land for the new owner that once had been his own. I have already referred to the taxes that had to be paid.[776] Loss of land also contributed to men becoming the day laborers who tried to find work each day to support their family (see the parable of the workers in the vineyard, Matt 20:1–16[777]). In addition, it fueled the ranks of the revolutionary groups.

Many a son, deprived of any thought of inheriting land, became a landless day laborer or ran off and joined the revolutionaries, particularly the bandits.[778] Josephus indicates how extensive these groups were when he says they were "overrunning much of the countryside."[779] He also describes them as burning with a desire for liberty. They were not merely "bandits" who robbed the rich and gave to the poor, although they did that too (so they received support from the people). They were taking on the role of "judges" as we find them described in the Old Testament book of that name. That is, they thought of themselves as national leaders, appointed by God to save the nation from the oppressor. They were struggling to bring in the day of salvation, the kingdom of God. During the last years of the war, they elected a commoner to the high priesthood, asserting this was the practice in ancient times. They were clearly thinking of the old theocratic, egalitarian ideal of the time of the tribal confederation and recapitulating the Mosaic ideal of being led by a divinely chosen leader into the promised land.[780]

Social tensions infected the whole society: hatred between Jews and Gentiles[781] as well as the exploitation of the peasants by the government, by elites, and by the urban areas that more or less advanced and promoted their own interests at the expense of the rural population. Added to these tensions was the press of population density. In such circumstances it is to be expected that movements would arise that longed for the return of the time when justice and righteousness prevailed and "every man sat under his own vine and his own fig tree" (1 Kgs 4:25).

Political injustice further exacerbated the festering condition of the people. Roman rule vacillated between direct rule and the rule of client kings or tetrarchs, which did not allow the establishment of a Jewish government that could win the support and affection of the people. Agrippa I's rule came close to approximating such acceptable conditions, but he died after four short years of rule over the entire nation.[782] Client kings such as Herod the Great and his sons Archaelaus[783] and Herod Antipas were known more for their Hellenistic proclivities than their zeal for the integrity of the Jewish nation. The Jewish leadership was regarded largely as simply illegitimate.

As becomes clear from this discussion, religious competition plagued the nation. There was no agreement on exactly how Torah was to be observed. Sadducees, Pharisees, and Essenes all had their own notion of how Torah should function. The people themselves probably had a more relaxed attitude than any of those groups, but they also followed certain traditions in their daily life that had not been codified in the Torah. Apocalyptic ideas also thrived providing a literature of consolation for the people but also heating up the already fervent longings for revolutionary change.[784]

Ecological divisions added to this volatile mix. For Rome the Holy Land was but a buffer state between it and the Parthians in the east. They had only one policy: keep the peace at all costs. But their procurators, with their own narrow and destructive policy of self-aggrandizement, only exacerbated the stresses and strains on the body politic. As Josephus reports, the countryside was overrun with revolutionaries, while the urban areas tried to maintain a delicate balancing act with the Roman government. The conservative rural population with its fervent connection with Scripture and the egalitarian divine institutional ideals of the past stood in stark contrast with the urbanites who were much more at home with and positively disposed toward the Hellenistic-Roman world.

These factors all contributed to an almost inevitable clash with Rome and sparked the revolution. It would have taken some mighty intervention indeed to avoid an open and fiery conflict.

THE PEOPLE'S ENCOUNTER WITH THE ROMAN OCCUPATION

It is clear the Jewish people in the Holy Land lived under Roman oppression. Of course, most of the Roman Empire lived with those circumstances. But the Jews were distinctive. They would not be integrated into the imperial union of politics and Roman religion and its pagan gods that every other people of the empire were without compunction. For all the other peoples of the imperium, Roman gods could easily be identified with their own. The Jews stood out like a sore thumb with their insistence on their imageless one God and denying the existence of all other gods, with their faithfulness to Torah, and with their love for the divine gift of their land. Any thinking person of that day would recognize the inherent rebellion against worldly powers that was inherent in Jewish faith and belief.

So they were a marginalized people, a people whose "backs were against the wall."[785] Memories of Israel's past played a lively role especially among the peasants. Roman domination and its debasing of Jewish institutions were an ever-present reality in the minds of the people. They felt like they were living in exile even while living in their own land. The egalitarian ideals of the ancient theocratic tribal confederation expressed by the contemporary prophets and the bandits/judges were largely supported by the peasant population. They were pursuing a thorough revolution of present circumstance that would replace foreign domination with the establishment of the kingdom of God, God's reign and rule, a theocracy. The messianic movements drew not only on the Davidic ideals for Israel's existence but also on the Maccabean successes against the Syrian overlord. They dreamed of the united kingdom of old and the subjection of Israel's enemies to the new messianic king.[786]

It is clear from the historical overview outlined above of the political, religious, economic, and social situation in the land of Israel of the first century that the peasant class especially was wrestling with survival not only economically but religiously in the face of external pagan pressure on their society. They were a small island in the great sea of the Roman-Hellenistic world. Even the institutions and leaders of the nation that were supposed to be their protectors seemed arrayed against them. In such a world the peasants felt themselves understandably to be living in exile. The world seemed opposed to the great Jewish troika of God, land, and people: their faith, their status as the people of God, their right to the land. These countervailing forces were disintegrating and dehumanizing assaults on life as it was supposed to be. They were cornered. They had little room to maneuver. The consequences of such alienation had toxic psychological effects, trapped as they were by poverty and alienation from the ideals of Jewish society.[787] So they were affected not merely in a social way. The psychological, spiritual, and ethical dimensions of human life were profoundly in danger of collapse. They were, in effect, disinherited. How could God's promises be reconciled to the fact of exile and Roman occupation?

Howard Thurman's analysis of hate and anger provides a deeper and more personalized insight into its functions and effects in the individual Jew in the land of Israel in the first century and his relationship with the Roman occupation.[788] I draw extensively on this study in the reflection that follows.

It is a psychologically shattering experience to live in an atmosphere that conveys the message that a person and his or her life are of no account and that one's livelihood and family are unprotected. The Jewish peasants knew themselves to be the people of God, but Roman hegemony exercised either indirectly through client kings or directly through procurators belied that reality and could rob people of a sense of self-esteem and self-worth, effecting a devastating assault on a person's well-being.[789] The power wielded by the procurators demonstrates the peasant could not rely on any protection of the occupying power. Even peaceful demonstrations were put down with violence.[790] The individual in general and the peasant in particular simply did not count in the Roman imperium. The struggle for the Jews in the Holy Land was how to survive as a minoritized group living in the Graeco-Roman world under foreign occupation.[791]

However, obviously the Jewish peasant had a hidden strength. They knew themselves to be embedded in an imposing history of triumph, divine guidance, and favor: the Exodus and the nearly contemporary deliverance of the nation achieved under the Maccabees. They knew themselves as the chosen people of the one, true, and only God of the universe. So the picture that emerges is, yes, that of an oppressed people but also a people who had a robust sense of their identity, and consequently many of them could aggressively pursue mutiny against their hated overlord.[792] Banditry (or as I call them "judges" in the biblical sense) erupted like geysers giving vent to pent up frustration and resentment with the affront of the economic and religious assaults against their existence. Peasants do not typically take such drastic measures unless conditions have so deteriorated to the point their traditional lifestyle is severely interrupted.[793]

The historical overview above shows the several ways peasants related to the powers that controlled political, social, economic, and religious life: active, violent resistance leading to revolutionary activity, nonviolent passive resistance with contempt, but also the quietism of a comforting trust that God, in an apocalyptic intervention and turn of history, would set things right. This latter stance required great patience, total leaning on God's faithfulness to act according to his promises (Ps 71:6), and an almost superhuman faith.[794]

But, as the Gospel tradition makes clear, there was also the quiet desperation of victimhood and accommodation that could lead to repressing a seething hatred, an overwhelming fear, living in deceit, and an enervating hopelessness. This reaction opened the way to a debilitating self-loathing and consequent depression and possession by satanic powers. The demonic possession so prominent in the Gospels was a phenomenon that appeared only during this time as the people were subject to foreign domination.[795] The psychological aspect of demon possession was the internalizing of anger toward the Roman occupier and the turning inward against oneself that produced depression and mental illness.

Hatred of the Roman overlord was rampant, and that hatred could spread even to one's fellow Jew who would not join in one's particular view in opposing the Roman occupation.[796] Hatred is one of the "hounds of hell."[797] It becomes particularly respectable during times of war. In the case of first-century Jews under the heel of the Roman occupation, hatred grew out of bitterness and an unrelenting resentment restrained until the pressure reached the point where it burst forth now unable to resist any containment. The power of this hatred was aggravated by the knowledge of their identity as God's people who had been liberated from slavery to serve him and him alone. Hatred became a way to self-realization and protecting oneself from moral disintegration by becoming a screen through which one interprets circumstances validating bringing death upon others while at the same time preserving ethical values. Hatred becomes a moral justification.

> The oppressed can give themselves over with utter enthusiasm to life-affirming attitudes toward their fellow sufferers, and this becomes a compensation for their life-negating attitude toward the strong.[798]

Behind hatred is the conviction that there is a rule of justice upon which one can rely on pursuing, out of hatred, the destruction of the enemy. So hatred is creative. It is a matter of survival.[799] Hatred, burning in the heart of a freedom fighter, seems positive and dynamic. But ultimately it blinds to all worthy standards. It cannot be confined to offenders, as the rise of the Sicarii illustrates, but erupts and gets directed against one's own people.[800] It kills the spirit and wrecks ethics and morals, dries up creative impulses, and spells death to fellowship with God.

Fear was a constant companion of the struggling peasant. The threat of going under was a constant in their lives. It was not just the external threat of bodily harm but also the menace of losing even their subsistent production of the land that loomed pervasively on the horizon. In a society that was permeated by a sense of limited good, others' success was an intimidation. The threatening cloud of isolation and helplessness continually sat at the door. However, it must be said that though isolated from the fears of these little people, even a Herod the Great could step in when starvation threatened the people. In 25 BC a grave drought occurred in Judea, and he used all the artifacts of precious metals in the palace to purchase food from Egypt to feed the populace.[801]

Violence was endemic to this period, as the history of the procurators makes plain. Peasants joining the various revolutionary bands were put down violently by these Roman officials. Entire villages were often attacked in retaliation for support of these groups. Examples are portrayed in the pronouncement stories of the slaughter of the Galileans (Luke 13:1–3) and Herod Antipas's threat against Jesus' life (Luke 13:31–33), not to mention Herod Antipas's execution of John. The threat of violence and contemptuous disregard for the life and personhood of the peasant by the governing authorities always hung over the heads of the people and had a degrading and humiliating effect.[802] The fear reaction is rooted in experience whether actual or reported.[803] Burned into the psyche is the effect of the contempt in which the people were ensnared: you simply do not count and you are totally expendable.

Fear is a protection for the psyche against a total nervous breakdown.[804] Imprinted in the mind and body are behaviors that avoid the possibility of gratuitous violence. Fear also has somatic effects.[805] The most prominent way these somatic effects expressed themselves among the Jewish peasantry was demon possession (see below). One of the preferred antidotes to fear for the first-century Jewish peasant was banditry. It accomplished two goals: finding an outlet to attack the system and simultaneously supporting villagers by attacking the rich and giving to the poor. Of course, the procurators expended great efforts eliminating banditry with devastating violence. The options for the peasant were few, and life was a matter of either quiet desperation or the risk of direct conflict with Rome. Life was restricted, inhibiting the enjoyment of the freedom of the elect people of God. They were not exactly "disinherited," but they did not have the full enjoyment of Israel's sacred theocratic heritage.[806]

Deception is an old skill developed by oppressed people of every time and place to deal with the overlord.[807] One cannot meet the opponent on equal terms, so winning on any level is an acceptable solution. Deception no doubt was practiced by the Jewish peasantry against the rich, the powerful, and the Romans. That it was also part of the culture predating the first century is evident from its proscription everywhere in the Bible.[808] The deception of the Gibeonites in Josh 9 illustrates the strategy demonstrating its survival value. No moral appeal or preaching can change such conduct. Only in an environment where individuals are not required to put forth the most extreme effort just to stay alive can they begin to think about and pursue ends besides those of physical existence.[809] In such circumstances the preservation of life is the moral center, and until that center is altered there can be no change of behavior. Revolution then becomes a real option.

Beyond deception, a hyper-patriotism takes over, and the destruction of the oppressor becomes the great moral value. Life and the life of others are cheapened. This led to the chaos that finally descended on the various factions that defended Jerusalem in the waning days of the war. Even the life of one's fellow Jew had lost its value as faction fought faction for the upper hand rather than forming a united front against the Roman war machine.[810] Buried in the background was the conviction of Judaism that one's life was lived *coram Deo*, before God, and that there is "no really significant living for a man, whatever may be his status, until he has turned and faced the divine scrutiny."[811]

On the other hand, the rise of these various movements and the number of people who followed them shows that some of the peasantry did not accept a passive victimhood. They perceived these movements as options for rebelling against the powers that opposed their heritage as the free people of God and the divine institutions of Israel. However, it was probably more the sons of peasant fathers, the "young Turks" (such as the younger brother in the parable of the prodigal son[812]), who joined the revolutionary movements (although it is not inconceivable that perhaps the fathers themselves, dispossessed of their property, along with all of their sons could have run off to become members of these movements). But a majority of the peasants remained tied to their land and worked at making the best living they could from their ancestral property.

Also obvious from this overview is how Israel's tradition, history, and Scriptures were very much alive and active in the minds and hearts of the people: the grand story of exodus, conquest, and settlement; the prophets who cried out for justice and righteousness and the abandonment of pagan practices; the Temple, its worship, and the priesthood providing a visible link between heaven and earth and its assurance and effecting of the divine blessing on the land and people; messianic kings and judges who embodied the rule of God and through whom God conquered Israel's enemies; the guidance of Torah showing the path of life with God; the promise of the land where Israel could live free from her enemies and serve God in holiness and righteousness; the divine pledges that God cared for his people and would come to establish his kingdom that was especially and powerfully enunciated in apocalyptic literature and ideas.[813] These numerous factors all contributed to an almost inevitable clash with Rome and sparked the revolution. It would have taken some mighty intervention indeed to avoid an open and fiery conflict.

JESUS' ENCOUNTER WITH HIS PEOPLE

The pronouncement stories reveal how Jesus functioned within this historical, social, religious, ecological, economic, and political complex. He was no otherworldly figure speaking only of divine and heavenly realities. Nor was he a secularist working like a modern social activist to overturn the injustices of his society and establish a new political order. He was emphatically not a little bit of both. His parables explicated in the second volume of this series and the pronouncement stories examined in this volume clarify the matter.

Jesus absolutely was part of the peasantry, but he also grew up as an artisan[814] and therefore, by the standards of the day, was not "poor." Nor was he homeless. He intentionally chose an itinerant ministry that eschewed working and consequently earning a livelihood and depended on the support of settled followers (Luke 8:3) and the hospitality of the villagers for his lodging and sustenance.[815] In other words, he chose to live more abjectly poor than even the peasants, renouncing work, earning a livelihood, and having a fixed dwelling and therefore having no ongoing personal relationship or dependence on any one of his fellow villagers. His "homelessness" was a chosen vocation to support his proclamation of total dependence on Israel's Father-God and his providence. He embodied his preaching of not being anxious and by doing so bolstered and authenticated his message, which he proclaimed to both the peasantry and the well-to-do.

His message and lifestyle eschewed hostility and violent revolution and labored in favor of an interdependence and mutual support where all were givers and all receivers. In this way he intimately identified with the peasantry by living in solidarity with them and the oppression they experienced. He took upon himself their poverty, their struggles, and their longing for justice. At the same time he embodied the kingdom of God. The kingdom proclaimed in his message and present in his table fellowship was the alternative to both a victimhood mentality and violent aggression toward the Roman overlord.[816]

The following summary of the preceding chapters will add the details of Jesus' self-understanding and his relationship with his environment.

Birth, Baptism, and Temptation

The commonalities of the birth narratives point clearly to anomalies surrounding his conception and birth. Nowhere was Jesus accused of being a *mamzer* (i.e., a bastard, although the Gospels are filled with the invectives of his opponents). That can be explained only by the fact that Joseph and Mary were married and being so recognized (John 6:42) vitiated any grounds for questioning Jesus' legitimacy. No one was scandalized by socializing with him. The narratives make clear, however, Jesus was not Joseph's son and therefore underscore that there was a transcendent aspect to Jesus' existence (see the calling of the disciples, Luke 5:1–11, 27–28). He was known to be of Davidic descent, which does not contradict the affirmation of his virgin birth. Both go back to early traditions. The one asserts that Jesus cannot be understood apart from God and the other that he is to fulfill the divine intention for Israel's restoration. Although Jesus possessed no divine power (the *kenosis*), he had a consciousness of a unique relationship with the God of Israel that was expressed in his magisterial teaching without reference to previous authorities; his forgiving sin; his power over unclean spirits; and his claiming exclusive knowledge of God (Matt 11:27).

Jesus understood himself as at one with God and at one with his people—indeed, all of humanity. He was so totally human that he subjected himself to both God and man. He saw himself as nothing but human. His self-understanding did not include a consciousness that he was God incarnate but rather that he had a unique filial relationship with God. That understanding developed from his peculiar conception and baptismal experience. The former led him to the latter. He had to grow up knowing there were unusual circumstances surrounding his birth, and, though Joseph was the mundane protector of the family, he had an inchoate realization that he had a distinctive relationship with God. He had to know too that his name was not given by chance but was divinely revealed.

Then John appears on the scene, a priest standing in the River Jordan, proclaiming the necessity of repentance for the kingdom of God was at hand. That way of preparation meant being washed in the Jordan. That washing, appearing now as Israel was in a crisis of faith with disparate answers as to how faithfully to meet the crisis that created the experience of exile, meant that those submitting to John's baptism recognized from the prophetic witness that the eschatological time of cleansing had arrived and

God was about to act. "[God's] winnowing fork is in his hand, to clear his threshing floor, and to gather the wheat into his granary, but the chaff he will burn with unquenchable fire" (Luke 3:17). John in this way proclaimed that the end of exile was imminent. But now the new Joshua must come (the "mightier one," Mark 1:7) and lead the people out of exile into the new promised land of the kingdom of God.

Jesus went to the Jordan recognizing that he too must submit to the coming kingdom. What happened at the Jordan, however, confirmed his incipient self-consciousness of a filial connection with his Father-God. The voice confirmed his sonship with the Father and that he was the "beloved son"—that he, in a priestly fashion, represented all Israel. The panegyric to truth in 1 Esd 4:38–41 may suggest that Jesus was approved as embodying fidelity to God.[817] The descent of the Spirit was a sign of his call as a prophet to lead Israel out of exile into the new creation of the kingdom of God. So all of Israel's holy offices coalesce in Jesus at his baptism, where he is named the "beloved son."

The "beloved son" designation bore, however, the whole weight of biblical associations: he was the "first-born" son who belongs to God by sacrifice (Exod 13:2). Isaac was beloved of his father, Abraham (Gen 22:2), Jacob was the divinely chosen favorite (Gen 25:23), and Joseph was beloved of God (Gen 39:21). Each had to go through humiliation (a sort of death) before being exalted. And Jacob had to send his beloved son Benjamin into a death-threatening experience so that the family might be saved from starvation (Gen 43:1–11). The "beloved son" is marked for death and as the one who must be sacrificed. The Judaism of Jesus' day understood Isaac's "binding" (the Aqedah) as a sacrificial death that atones for sin and by whose merit God will resurrect the dead. It even became the foundation of the Passover and the liberation of Israel.[818] Jesus understood this and called it his "cup" and his "baptism" (Mark 10:39, 14:36). Furthermore, he associated his death with the Passover and initiated a new Passover covenant (Mark 14:22–23).

Closely associated with Jesus' baptism is the story of his temptation.[819] His forty days in the wilderness recapitulate Israel's forty years of wandering in the Sinai desert. But he reverses Israel's faithlessness. Jesus enacts a new exodus corresponding to the turn taken in the eschatological schedule between him and John. The new age of the kingdom is dawning for which Jesus, the new Joshua, is preparing the way. But he shows the way of faithfulness. He enters Satan's domain and, in contradistinction to Israel, does not perversely accuse God of deviltry by bringing Israel into the wilderness to kill them but relies solely on God's word. In this way he identifies with the peasant of his time who lives a hungering, hand-to-mouth existence. In this Jesus emphasizes that the real issue for his society is a spiritual one. Their philosophy of limited good lay within their power to expel by a fulsome trust in God the giver: "give and it will be given to you!" (Luke 6:38). As in his healings, when he pronounces that one's faith has made a person well, Jesus is not about creating dependence even on himself, so he refuses to be a "bread king" (John 6:15). He relies on God and his word to conquer temptations, which any person is capable of doing.

In the second temptation, to test his total trust in God, Satan tells Jesus to throw himself off the pinnacle of the Temple. Jesus replies that the one who commits himself to God does not test God but merely trusts him. In addition, Jesus eschews the very temptation that was cloaking his people: world dominion. The nation was in danger of making a Faustian agreement under the guise of liberating Israel from the clutches of Rome. To adopt Satan's ways is to keep the world in his thrall and undermine God's reign and purpose to liberate his people. Jesus had not come to be served but to serve. His messiahship imaged David when he left Jerusalem in weakness and sorrow and later was restored to his kingship by allowing the Lord to steer events.[820] The way forward was not the way of idolatrous worship of power and rebellious ideologies but rather the way of "weakness."[821] Victory lay with the kingdom, and personal victory lay in accepting it. The way of revolution would lead to destruction.

His hunger is also an identification with his anxiety-ridden people who fret over their hand-to-mouth existence. The first priority of Israel is to trust in their Father-God. Israel is not to emulate the nations, for she is a spiritual entity whose God "fashions the hearts of [the nations]" (Ps 33:15) and guides history. Israel's Scriptures emphasize over and over again their God's faithfulness. Trusting God's faithfulness is the chief challenge for the people. When that is in place, all else will be in its proper place. Limited good will be overcome, and people will joyfully share with their neighbor. Transformation of the heart was required and to see oneself as a transcendent reality borne on the hands of a gracious God (Isa 49:16). So not testing God but trusting him was Jesus' call to Israel. The way forward was not world domination promised by the apocalyptic revolutionaries but entering the kingdom, that is, submitting rather to God's dominion, which was already among them in Jesus' words and deeds, and in fellowship with him. The temptation narrative reveals that the fantasies of driving Rome out was a satanic enticement. Jesus reverses Adam's defeat by Satan and now begins his ministry of binding the strong man, ending the exile, and restoring Israel.

His self-consciousness was also expressed in his use of the "son of man" title. His usage was distinctive. No other figure in early Judaism used it as a self-designation. The "son of man" in Daniel and in the Similitudes of Enoch has a transcendent quality and represents both the faithful of Israel and their defender. In this latter writing the son of man is also fused with a royal messiah and Isaiah's servant figure. As messiah the figure exercises judgment on the world and works justice and vindication of Israel's oppressed. The Enochian author also connects the figure with wisdom and a hidden preexistence (2 Esd also understands him in this way). In his presence Israel's oppressed will also inherit eternal life.

He used the appellation in three distinctive contexts: as the coming one, as the presently acting one, and as the one who would suffer and be raised. Sometimes he simply meant "I." Other times the collective view of Dan 7 is reflected where the "son of man" both has a transcendent quality and is identified with Israel. His reference to the "son of man" in Daniel is clear when he contrasts himself with animals (Luke 9:58), which implies a contrast between his present lowliness and future glory as the coming "son of man."

When Jesus employed the phrase in the parousia sayings, he identified himself with the eschatological "son of man." This is clear because he understood that in his activity the kingdom of God was already present. The double aspect of the kingdom as both present and future is reflected in the double aspect of the "son of man" who is present and would return. In this way Jesus avoids the messianic ascription that contemporaneously designated an earthly figure of limited authority and with military and nationalistic connotations.

But "son of man" also included a collective sense. Jesus' call to enter the kingdom meant that those who enter the kingdom appear in the world as God's agents for bringing about the final consummation of the kingdom. Those in the kingdom are also called to obedience. In this way, Jesus' ethics were another aspect of the kingdom. Eschatology, kingdom, community, son of man, and ethics are all essential facets of the "pearl of great price" that constitute the kingdom.

The phrase was not always used as a title for the Messiah in early Judaism. It was a rather neutral term not open to misinterpretation. Jesus could then fill it with whatever content he chose. In this way he could speak of the suffering son of man and the one who was anointed of God (i.e., "messiah," Luke 4:17–20) to bring God's salvation to Israel and be her advocate. Jesus could use the title, with its fluid characteristics, to refer to himself as the future judge of the nations (Matt 25:31) and sit on a throne of glory (Matt 19:28).

Jesus as the son of man embodies the kingdom. It is in and through him that the kingdom is present. When he returned as son of man, the kingdom of God arrived in its fullness. He also used the title in a collective sense. It included the community of the new age that he led. This community was the divine agent for bringing about the final consummation of the kingdom.

Being this divine agent involved obedience. So Jesus' invitation to enter the kingdom was also an ethical call. The kingdom had a "yoke" that one was required to take up (Matt 11:29–30).

Jesus' use of the title "son of man" expresses his intimate relationship with God, his function as suffering servant, that he embodies the presence of transcendent wisdom,[822] and will be the future judge who also embodies the kingdom and Israel. John's Gospel then makes explicit what is only implicit in the synoptics: he is the preexistent Son of God, the Word of God who is God and who was incarnated as a human being whose actual Father is God himself. So when Jesus uses the pronoun "I," that does not mean his ego but his being as "one with the Father" in the sense that his whole being is determined by his relationship to his Father-God. He "speaks only what he has heard" (John 8:26). This understanding of the historical Jesus is congruent with the Christ Hymn of Phil 2. He was both human and divine but had emptied himself of all divinity so that he was totally human, subject to all the exigencies of human life including human development. He never presented himself as anything other than a human being. In fact, he subjected himself to God, his will, and the historical realities of life under the Roman fist. He differentiated himself from others who claimed a more exalted status by trying to put themselves forward as God's chosen to lead Israel in resistance against the occupier.

Why would Jesus choose most often to refer to himself as "son of man" rather than using the absolute term of "son" as in Mark 13:32 and Luke 10:22? It could be due to a certain diffidence and reserve and, as John's Gospel shows, to avoid abject rejection by and the animosity of his Jewish contemporaries (e.g., 8:59, 10:31). But, as I have already pointed out, Jesus filled his use of "son of man" with his own content, which included transcendence and the associations of the absolute use of "son."

All four Gospels seek an answer to Jesus' identity: the synoptics illusively and John explicitly. His relationship with John the Baptist continues to be an element of debate. Jesus probably remained a disciple of John for a period of time (John 3:23) that may have ended with John's arrest and execution. He shared aspects of John's ministry and preaching: repentance and baptism, the call to "bear fruit" and judgment of "fruitlessness," the fire of judgment, and the working of miracles. But there were conspicuous differences. Jesus was itinerant, he ate and drank with sinners, the kingdom was related to himself and his practices and was already present, he sent his disciples out as envoys, and, in contrast to John's asceticism, the life of the kingdom was characterized by joy, merriment, eating and drinking, and exuberance.

Jesus negatively defines himself as not being a "judge," that is, not like a judge in ancient Israel nor the form of the judge taken by contemporary bandits (the dispute over an inheritance, Luke 12:13–14). Both of these forms of judge include martial aspects. His ministry was one of reconciliation, forgiveness, and acquiring "treasure in heaven." The kingdom would be established not by violence but by hospitality; not by seeking honor through wealth and acquisition but by the sharing of goods; not by external security but by service.

Jesus witnesses to his divine emptying when he refuses the epithet "good" (the rich man and his question, Mark 10:17–31) It is God and his kingdom that stand at the center of his proclamation. As in his parables[823] he demands that his interlocutor sell all and follow him. But the man's wealth inhibits his following Jesus into the kingdom. So Jesus provocatively announces the difficulty of the rich entering the kingdom. Perhaps such experiences led him to propound parables such as the rich fool and Lazarus and the rich man.[824] He profoundly turns Jewish society on its head which identified wealth with outstanding piety and God's consequent favor. But even then God can make a way for the wealthy. The kingdom is, after all, pure gift which is already realized within the new community of the end-time which will endure in contrast to fading wealth.

It seems that Jesus ultimately realized that the nation as a whole would not accept his proclamation of the kingdom, so he, by drinking the "cup" of his death, would take upon himself the end-time "messianic woes" and suffer in Israel's stead, thereby ransoming the nation from the threatened judgment of the coming kingdom.[825] That would mean the ultimate salvation of the nation and the world, fulfilling the divinely appointed plan for terminating the exile and accomplishing Israel's redemption.

Jesus did not proclaim any apocalyptic scenarios. He merely proclaimed that the kingdom was at the door, and one had only to prepare for it and live in its light, that is, in fellowship with him.[826] As the suffering servant who embodied the nation, he would return when the kingdom arrived to judge the nations.

Jesus claims by word and deed that the kingdom, though in a proleptic way, is already present in and through him; he proclaims, as divine Wisdom, God's invitation and sends forth envoys; he asserts that he is lord of the Sabbath; he announces the forgiveness of sin; he binds Satan; and he will hold the final judgment. So in him there is something greater than Solomon, Moses, and Abraham. Speaking and acting as a human being, he does not lift himself out of the ranks of humanity but rather in his baptism identifies with his people and their sins. But he does assert precedence. His sonship is not an ego statement but relational: God is at work through him who lives in a loving bond of a son with his Father. That bond defines the human person of Jesus. His whole person, thought, word, and deed were simply defined by his relationship with God. At the same time, he was yoked with Israel's heritage and vocation.

It is precisely that relationship to which he calls individuals and the nation. Israel is God's son (Exod 4:23–24, Hos 11:1), so Jesus, as his son, embodies Israel and explicates what that relationship means in its historical context. Jesus didn't quite meet John the Baptist's expectations. John didn't expect one who would sit at table with sinners, rather one who would end injustices, inaugurate the kingdom, and purge the world of sinners. Jesus didn't give up on the consummation to come, but he stressed God's compassion and love and the joyfulness of the kingdom. Jesus understood his ministry in terms of Isaiah's gentle Servant of the Lord (42:1–3, cf., Matt 11:28–30) who restores wholeness and liberates (Isa 29:18–20, 61:1–2). But Jesus and John are inextricably bound together, and Jesus held him in the highest regard as "more than a prophet."

Jesus, however, distinguishes himself from John as the coming "mightier one" whom John foretold,[827] that is, the messianic king who, according to Ps 118, would overthrow the oppressor and establish the messianic kingdom. John's question arose from the fact that Jesus did not appear in a militaristic guise. Rather he was establishing a peaceable kingdom that overthrows the oppressor by an inward revolution of the people's heart and mind issuing in the practice of radical love, forgiveness, servanthood, and the sharing of the goods of this life. He reversed the social norms of limited good and the strict accounting of the give-and-take of the patron-client relationship. He included sinners and Gentiles in this kingdom of nobodies rather than thundering on about the eschatological cleansing away of the "chaff." So for Jesus the kingdom was not exclusively future but present and meant to include sinners. The kingdom was no longer confined to the banks of the Jordan and the associated holy history conjuring up the entry and conquest of the land that John transmuted into the entry into the coming kingdom and preparation for its judgment. It moved out into the quotidian world seeking the lost.

Between John and Jesus a decisive turn had taken place in the eschatological schedule: the joyful time of salvation and the end of exile have arrived as Jesus proclaims that the kingdom has proleptically arrived in himself and the people can already enjoy its fruits. So Jesus partitions the history of Israel into two periods. John is the ending of the first period and so its greatest representative.[828] However, Jesus initiates the new period, and the joyful time of salvation and those who enter it are "greater" than even John because they enjoy its reality. Jesus makes the difference between himself and John explicit in his parable of children at play (Matt 11:16–19, Luke 7:31–35).[829]

The kingdom indeed comes but not in a show of political power. Jesus brings healing to the people and binds Satan with his exorcisms. The eschatological time of salvation has dawned. The restoration of Israel and the end of exile are happening in the here and now as people respond to Jesus' proclamation. The separation of the wheat from the chaff occurs as people respond to the invitation to enter the kingdom. Jesus recognizes that he is a stumbling block bringing the kingdom, which includes corruption. So Jesus also brings division (Matt 10:34–36). But then he is no different than God himself (Isa 8:14). There certainly was a judgment, but that lay in the impending future when God would establish the kingdom in the fullness of his power.

The Pronouncement Stories

The biographical pronouncement stories further elucidate Jesus' personal experiences, his interaction with individuals, how people responded to him, his understanding of himself and the current events of the day, and some of the activities of his ministry. More importantly they reveal how he met the circumstances of his people in their encounter with the oppression under which they lived.

The call of his twelve disciples must have occurred early in his ministry after he left his experience in the wilderness and went back to the Galilee and used Capernaum as a home base for his ministry (Matt 4:13). Jesus established an inner circle of twelve disciples, a number fraught with associations, least of which is not the number of the tribes of Israel.[830] They were constituting the leadership of the new age and the restoration of Israel. He was thinking of a reconstituted Israel in contradistinction to empirical Israel, which was not fulfilling its divine mission to be a light to the world. His call of "twelve" must be seen in connection and correlated with his action in the Temple. Within this setting the Temple action was a preparation for the reconstituting of Israel. The twelve with Jesus as their head no longer confined that reconstitution to a given time and place; it could be encountered in the existence of the kingdom's representatives right there among the people. When the kingdom arrived in its fullness, Israel would be reconstituted. That new people of God was already now in formation as Jesus established the reign of God by his healings and table fellowship. The kingdom was not confined to the realm of ideas but had a corporeal reality.

The consciousness of the disciples of their sinfulness in the presence of Jesus at the time of their call (Luke 5:1–11) illustrates one aspect of those calls: they recognized a numinous aspect to this figure who bid them to follow and reverse the directions of their lives.[831] They responded positively like the prophets of old when they encountered the powerful presence of the divine. He would make of them "fishers of people," catching them and incorporating them into the kingdom of God. The call of the toll collector Levi (Mark 2:14) is a concrete example of Jesus' call to and inclusion of sinners in the kingdom.

To answer that call meant to join Jesus in his itinerant ministry, which relied solely on the hospitality of villagers so that this entourage of the kingdom didn't always know where the next meal would come from or where one would lay his head when night fell. Following him and joining his new family configuration took precedence over all other social obligations, even that of burying a dead relative (Luke 9:59–60). These stringent requirements, however, applied only to those who joined Jesus in his itinerancy.

I've suggested that John's chronology of placing the "temple cleansing" early in Jesus' ministry is probably closer to the historical truth. It would seem, however, that he was active for a time in the north before this occurrence.[832] The faith of the official (Luke 7:1–10) along with that of the Syrophoenician woman (Mark 7:24–30) had a profound effect on Jesus and his outlook. He came to see that the kingdom included Gentiles, which led to his propounding of many a parable that insisted that the kingdom could appear under peculiar circumstances and among unexpected people and their actions. It must also have ultimately precipitated his going to Jerusalem to prepare it for the in-breaking of the kingdom, which would include the Gentiles attaching themselves to Israel. Jesus' eschatological expectations were tied to the Temple on the basis of the end-time scenario outlined by Zech 14.[833] The original tradition exhibits no opposition to the Temple but rather opposition to those whose conduct does not align with the Temple's sacred purpose. Jesus ends the commercial transactions there. All the financial dealings are suspended so that all may freely join in the worship of Israel's God. Jesus was preparing the Temple for the day of the Lord and the instituting of God's universal reign when the Gentiles would be included in his kingdom.

Since Jerusalem was the ultimate goal of Jesus' ministry, the Temple also functioned within his conception of the kingdom. My analysis of attitudes toward the Temple in early Judaism revealed that there were some quarters within Judaism that criticized and rejected the Temple. However, there was also another, more positive arc that viewed it as essential to God's eschatological plan of renewal. Jesus' "cleansing" (Mark 11:15–17) falls into this latter category. The original tradition behind Mark 11:15–17 reveals no criticism of the Temple, but rather the emphasis is on the cessation of commercial transactions, orienting the story to Zech 14, which prohibits traders in the Temple. That prohibition heralded the arrival of the eschaton when God's universal reign would be established, and all the nations would participate with Israel in the Temple worship. These actions coordinate with the Isaiah quotation that the Temple should be a "house of prayer for all nations." So Jesus' actions are purely prophetic like any of those of the classical prophets.

To suspend the economic functions of the Temple would bring Jesus directly into conflict with the Sadducees, whose livelihood was derived from those functions.[834] Pilate, the procurator, would also likely interpret it as a provocation.[835] Jesus' actions also resonate with Zech 3, where the high priest Joshua is named as the one who will "rule my house and have charge of my courts." So Jesus' actions are more priestly than prophetic, and he is preparing the Temple and Jerusalem for the in-breaking of God's kingdom when the nations will flow to the Temple, participate in its sacrifices, celebrate with Israel the eschatological feast of tabernacles, and live under the rule of God.

Jesus, by this action, would also be claiming royal prerogatives as one who has "charge of God's courts." Jesus appears as an anointed king and a messiah with prophetic and priestly gifts preparing city and Temple for the coming kingdom of God when the nations will stream to Jerusalem and all, Jew and Gentile, will live under the rule of the one, true God of Israel. Important in Jesus' action is that it was not a revolutionary action. Neither he nor any of his followers were armed. He was preparing the Temple and Jerusalem for the coming kingdom.

His action was also a protest against the festering anger and hostility toward Rome. That seething resentment was easily justified: Rome, especially in the emperor's claim to divinity, was an affront to Jewish sensibilities as her life was to be lived under the canopy of God, her only true king. The frequent egregious actions of the procurators more than anything else flamed the fan of hatred and discontent.[836] In this action Jesus aligns himself with the so-called action prophets of the era who undertook performances that ostensibly would bring about the longed-for deliverance and restoration and fulfill his eschatological plan of redemption.[837]

Sometime during Pilate's tenure, one of these action prophets, a Samaritan, gathered a following and promised to ascend Mount Gerizim to uncover the holy vessels of the Temple that Moses had, according to the belief of the time, buried there. This man understood himself as the longed-for Samaritan restorer, or Taheb, Moses's eschatological complement. However, there were two striking differences between Jesus and this "restorer." The latter had a large mass of followers who were armed. They evidently were anticipating a holy war against Rome in which God would participate and achieve the longed-for deliverance. But Jesus' action called out to the people to eschew violence and hatred. His action proclaimed that God was about to act and turn even Israel's enemies into fellow devotees of the God of Israel.

Of the separation of "insiders" and "outsiders" among his followers, Jesus will hear nothing, for even if there are those who do not explicitly join the fellowship of disciples yet exorcise by his name, Jesus includes them as those who are expanding the invasion against Satan and his rule, and they will hardly "curse" him (the rival exorcist, Mark 9:38–41, cf., Prov 20:9, Exod 21:16). His attitude here is in keeping with his perspective in the parables, which perceive the kingdom appearing in unexpected and surprising places and persons.[838] He softens the hard attitude toward outsiders especially in his command to love the enemy. This attitude on his part points clearly to his understanding of the kingdom, which is present in the here and now through his proclamation, healings, table fellowship, and even mere presence. In this way the kingdom is not brought in by force, nor is one to try and calculate the time of its arrival. Jesus' call remains dynamic: enter the kingdom now and live now in its powerful presence by practicing its ethics. His message is both personal and social, with temporal and eternal ramifications. Even if you don't follow him directly but use his name to further expand the kingdom and rid people of the rule of Satan and his minions, you are one with him.

The kingdom was not some neat colloquy of like-minded people. It was messy, filled with down and outers, sinners, people who grasped the power of even the name of Jesus, women high and low, the sick and scorned who clutched the hem of his garment, military officials who understood his power to heal. Jesus opened doors, and, out of joy, the world in all its motley colors pressed into this kingdom. It was palpable, and it was present and active among those who accepted his invitation and lived with the ethic of forgiveness, love for enemies, and expansive hospitality. Jesus expressed the kingdom's expansive love, which included even the enemy, in his rebuke to James and John, who wanted to call down fire on the Samaritans who would not accept Jesus and his entourage. This community of the new age, resting on the spiritual experience of Jesus himself, believed that access to God did not require some mediation but was direct, not requiring formal structures like the temple, a holy text, or purity regulations.[839]

In his love ethic Jesus was merely calling on the fundamental and foundational confession of Israel that every Jew recited each day: "Hear, O Israel: The Lord our God is one Lord; and you shall love the Lord your God with all your heart, and with all your soul, and with all your might" (Deut 6:4–5). Jesus coordinated this confession with the command to love one's neighbor as oneself (Mark 12:31).[840] He expanded and included as one's neighbor the other, those outside Israel (the parable of the good Samaritan[841]). But that was always implicit in the concept. The Torah commanded the inclusion in the Sabbath rest of everyone in one's household (Exod 20:10). That is, the blessings of the Sabbath rest were meant for all. He stressed neighborliness as qualitative and not spatial. This nonspatial love encompassed not just the friend (Luke 14:12–13) but the enemy in Israel and beyond Israel, even the Romans (Luke 6:29, Matt 5:41). In this he was courting treason and the accusation that he was a traitor. To urge love of Rome was somehow to approve of her idolatry and so by extension participate in that idolatry.

So the enemy included the personal, a friend with whom one had a falling out. To love this intimate enemy required reconciliation (Matt 5:25). It meant confession of a wrong done. This is the easiest enemy with whom to deal, those who have a natural claim on you. The term "neighbor" would have been restricted to them.

A second group would include those who are offensive to the nation such as tax gatherers, who embody the presence of the oppressor extorting the little wealth the peasant had to feed the iron hand of the oppressor.[842] They were regarded as the betrayers of Israel, the collaborators with a hated regime. They caused shame and humiliation. They were utterly despised and the epitome of an outcast. Because they knew the people so well, they could function with a psychological ruthlessness and exploit them.[843] On top of all that, they were wealthy, while the peasant lived a hand-to-mouth existence. To love such people would be making an insane demand. To even be associated with such people would place one at odds with the people and bring shame upon oneself engendering the contempt of others and radically lowering one's status in the eyes of the community.

Jesus by including even tax collectors in the kingdom was again calling on the deepest of Israel's convictions that their God was one who was "merciful and gracious, slow to anger, and abounding in steadfast love and faithfulness" (Exod 34:6).[844] Jesus emphasized in the case of the tax collector Zacchaeus that he was included in God's mercy toward his people because he too was a "son of Abraham." He was counted as part of the elect people. He was not merely a tax collector but also a son of God. God's unity and uniqueness applied also to his people Israel. They were to be one as he was one. To love such betrayers of the nation required the uprooting of the poison of bitterness that issues from a sense of betrayal.[845] Understanding must be sought as to why people would take up such an occupation. Given the poverty of the times, it is easy to understand that people would grasp at anything to secure themselves in life. Love means a deep respect for people but does not demand condoning their actions. Love demands separating actions from the person.

A third group of enemies was political: in the case of Israel of the first century, it meant Rome and its occupation. In that day, there was no distinction between "religion" and "politics." To be Roman meant the worship of the pantheon of gods and also the emperor himself, who was considered divine. So Rome was a "double enemy," both politically as the occupier and religiously as a center and promotor of idolatry. The love of the enemy in this instance meant that Rome had to surface as individual, concrete persons, those with whom one could have personal contact and a face-to-face relationship as between two human beings, such as the procurator, his bureaucrats, and the Syrians who made up the Roman cohort in the land.[846]

The Roman, seen against the background of his empire and its power, would be endowed by the Jew with arrogance and the power of coercion. The Roman could not disentangle himself from these associations no matter how much he might want to make common cause with the Jewish individual or community.

From the Roman standpoint, the Jew was in the same position and could not be encountered as an individual person: he was different and one who despised quite off the bat the presence of these "invaders." Of course, if the Jewish person made overtures toward a personal relationship, his own compatriots could well regard him as a traitor or, worse, a denier of the faith. To be separated means to be at the mercy of suspicions, stereotypes, and prejudices.

On the other hand, what happens if one dares to turn to the other in love and is met with only more contempt and condescension? Has the love ethic failed? There must be a radical assault on the idea of "enemy."[847] There must be a multiplicity of contacts that are not of the nature of formal, socially defined contacts.[848] They together have to work on the social milieu and develop a sense of mutual worth and value. Rome, in her way, had provided a basis for this: Jews did not have to serve in the military, the sanctity of the Temple was ensured and protected, and they were allowed to faithfully follow the Torah. On the Jewish side, however, there was a prohibition against entering Gentile houses, to say nothing of partaking of nonkosher food.[849]

Of course, a Gentile would have no scruples about being in a Jewish house or eating with a Jew. So the initiative would have had to have been on the Jewish side. How can this separateness be overcome and some kind of equanimity be created in such a situation? It is clear Jesus is speaking to his own people and his nation when he says "love your enemy" and "go the extra mile," when he eats with tax collectors, those collaborators with the hated Romans, and when he rebukes his disciples who want to call down punishment on Samaritans who reject him. If Jesus can eat with tax collectors, why not show the gracious hospitality that is exercised by God's people even to Roman soldiers or Gentiles in general? Dare to reach out and find a way to experience a common sharing of mutual worth and value.[850] Dare to see the Roman in the context of a shared humanity; after all both Jew and Gentile have a common Father in Adam and Noah. Be the light to the nations that you already are (Matt 5:14–16).

Love demands a respect and even reverence for persons. One way out of such general respect is to regard a certain individual or groups of people as "exceptional" and therefore worthy of one's respect, while excluding the majority from that same respect.[851] Love cannot be choosey. It is either there for all or there for none. Respect for persons issuing from love presupposes that all involved are within the same "ethical field."[852]

In the story of the healing of an official's household member, the Roman centurion put aside his status as a representative of the occupying power. His respect for Jesus and his Jewish sensibilities is emphasized by his not even asking Jesus to enter his house. The man exhibits true humility, which the kingdom requires.[853] He, in effect, tears down the barrier between ruler and ruled. In his desperate need, all class differences and distinctions become inconsequential and even trifling. Remarkable here is that the centurion has acquired the attitude of the kingdom quite apart from fellowship with Jesus and his proclamation. So Jesus in his parables tells stories in which the kingdom appears in unexpected and surprising circumstances and places.

The kingdom is not some theoretical preaching of love for one's enemies. The kingdom demands a discipline, discipleship. For Jesus that meant overcoming hate, fear, and deception with love. That love was not some general good disposition toward others and the stranger but the concrete acting out of that love by being in relationship to one's compatriots and the representatives of the occupying power.

But love is possible only between two mutually free people. So Jesus evokes in his eschatological message the imagery of the Jubilee and the liberty that it proclaims. To offer a better grasp of this imagery, the following excursus develops the meaning and function of the Jubilee. Following this explication, I will clarify how the Jubilee resonates in Jesus' words and practices as they appear in the pronouncement stories that have been investigated in this volume. We shall see that Jesus does not promulgate some wishful thinking or some theoretical desire but rather a discipline, a concrete method, actions and attitudes that lay the groundwork for the love that will require the transformation of Israel to save her from the chaos that will surely come at the end of her present path. That transformation will even have the potential of being realized in the world beyond Israel.

Excursus: The Jubilee

In the early history of Israel the Canaanite kings owned the land, and their populations worked the land as serfs, whereas in Israel the land was distributed to the clans and households according to their size and need (Num 26:52–56, Josh 13–21).[854] In the Jubilee, the year after seven Sabbaths of years (i.e., the fiftieth year), the soil was to lie fallow, debts were to be remitted, bonded servants were to be set free, and property that had been remanded to others was to be restored.[855] The emancipation of indentured servants stands in contrast to earlier legislation that provided for such release at the end of six years (Exod 21:2–6, Deut 15:12–18). There was no other legislation that provided for the return of property to its original owner as we find in the Jubilee legislation. There is also no evidence the Jubilee was ever actually practiced (cf., Neh 5:1–13), or if it was, it fell into desuetude. Apparently, the idea of the Jubilee was an entirely theoretical construct.[856]

The Jubilee understands the land distributed to the family and clans of Israel as inalienable. The land had ultimately to remain within the family or clan. The economic viability of the family is the concern here (in today's terms, economic justice).[857] The ultimate ownership of the land rested in God (Lev 25:23), so he stood behind the inalienable right of family and clan to their property. This theological understanding of the land and the status of Israel as God's people undergirds the meaning of the Jubilee. The land was Israel's "inheritance" (Deut 4:21, 15:4). Election of the people and their inheritance of the land were closely bound together, and the goal of the Exodus was entering and taking possession of the land that God gave to Israel as her heritage.

Conversely, God's judgment meant exile from the land, and the restoration of that relationship meant return to the land. Possession of the land was a witness to the Israelite's membership in God's people, his family. In response to this grace of God, a tithe of the land's produce was given back to him by offering it at the Temple (Lev 27:30–32, Deut 14:22–28). At the same time this offering was a recognition and confession that the land ultimately was YHWH's.

Israel herself was a slave of God who had been brought out of slavery. So the Exodus was a divine act of redemption. Israel was a people whom God had bought for himself. The Exodus was in this way the model of the Jubilee and its redemption theology. His people whom he has freed are not to make slaves of one another.

The resident aliens in the land, that is, those who were not Israelites, were also objects of concern for justice (e.g., Lev 19:10, 25:40, 35:15, Deut

10:18). They were to have a relationship of safeguarded dependency in Israel.[858]

The fundamental meaning of the Jubilee, theoretical as it is, had to do with liberty and restoration: freedom from the burden of debt and its attendant bondage and the restoration of ancestral property.[859] It would prevent the accumulation of land by the wealthy that could eventually turn into a system akin to the Canaanite land structure that Israel had abolished. It preserved the equality and independence of the individual Israelite family. In this way it also preserved Israel's relationship with her God: YHWH had brought them out of slavery to give them the land, so no one could lose the land apportioned to him (Lev 25:38); no Israelite was ever to be enslaved because YHWH had liberated Israel from slavery (Lev 25:32); but every Israelite was God's servant and belonged to him, so one could not belong to another (Lev 25:55). Put succinctly, the Jubilee conserved or restored the socioeconomic foundation of the nation's covenant relationship with God, the unity of God, land, and people.[860]

However, the two senses of the Jubilee, liberty and restoration, metamorphosed into prophetic eschatological thinking. Isa 35 envisions a future redemption and return when nature itself will be transformed while simultaneously maintaining an ethical application to the present. Deutero-Isaiah in 41:1–7 depicts the servant of God who will establish justice, restore liberty and wholeness, and make of Israel a light to the Gentiles. Again, in chapter 58 he calls for social justice and liberty and a proper observance of the Sabbath (which summons every living thing within Israel to a time of rest). Most pointedly, in chapter 61 the prophet uses Jubilee imagery: the Servant of the Lord is to proclaim liberty and announce the year of God's favor (the Jubilee!). So the people of God and indeed the whole world have to be set at liberty. The Jubilee must dawn (Lev 25:8–17).

Jesus and the Jubilee

Luke's version of the visit to Nazareth presents a clear programmatic statement of inaugurating the Jubilee (4:16–30, 7:22). Jesus explicitly interpreted his ministry in terms of the Jubilee by proclaiming the acceptable year of the Lord, heralding the good news, healing people, and liberating from oppression. It is important to observe here that to proclaim release and liberty was a royal prerogative.

However, there are no indications that Jesus spoke directly of leaving the soil fallow. This is not surprising since the Sabbath year prescription for leaving the soil fallow was common practice. The practice, of course, took great courage, especially among the peasantry who lived a hand-to-mouth existence and demanded faith that God would provide, as the Torah promised (Lev 25:20–21), what was needed.[861]

Jesus calls for the Jubilee remission of debts in his prayer (Matt 6:12). The word used there, ὀφείλημα (*opheilēma*), means primarily "debt" and only secondarily "wrong, sin, guilt."[862] The corresponding verb ἀφίημι (*aphiēmi*) means "to release, let go, remit, forgive." Jesus makes clear that he has in mind both the forgiveness of monetary debt and by extension the forgiveness of offenses (Matt 6: 14–15, cf., Luke 11:4). In Luke's version of the prayer, both "sin" and "debts" are coordinated. In the parable of the unforgiving servant,[863] Jesus portrays the forgiveness of monetary debts and obviously by extension the offenses perpetrated by another. This latter aspect is vividly portrayed in his answer to Peter's question of how often one should forgive such offenses (Matt 18:21–22). What Jesus bids us to pray for in his prayer is to practice the release of both monetary debts and the offenses of others just as God has released us from the debts we owe him and our sins against him.

Jesus calls on Israel to practice even now the Jubilee. Jesus' prayer is a "jubilary" prayer. His prayer means the time is here to abolish all debts that hold the poor captive and to live in forgiveness with others. His proclamation of the kingdom and its presence declares that God in his grace has wiped away all debts. Jesus makes that clear in his pronouncing forgiveness (Mark 2:10, John 8:11) and his open commensality with outcasts, sinners, and tax collectors who are received into the kingdom.

In his call to forgive debts, Jesus had in mind the wealthy who lent to the peasant (see the parable of the unjust steward[864]) when circumstances forced borrowing, such as during a poor crop season, to tide them over to a year with a better yield. Progressive indebtedness frequently led to losing one's property, being forced to be a sharecropper for the usurer or being forced into the day laborer market. As I described above, such men were also recruits for the various revolutionary groups. In the worst-case scenario, the man and his family could have been imprisoned until the debt was paid (Matt 18:30). A Jubilee of debt forgiveness would have solved much of the social crisis into which Israel had fallen; it would have deprived revolutionary groups of recruits and the very reason for revolutionary activity, prompted prosperity, engendered joy and relief, and fostered harmony and mutuality among all the people and factions. In the parable of the unforgiving servant, Jesus alludes, however, to the incongruous response to his declaration of the presence of the kingdom and the inauguration of the Jubilee by the nation: the servant whose gigantic debt had been forgiven turns around and throws his fellow servant and family into prison because he could not immediately repay what was a trifling debt in comparison to his own. In this way Jesus portrays the response to his proclamation.[865] Sadly, the nation refuses to celebrate the Jubilee of the kingdom. The divine judgment will thus ensue (Matt 18:34-35, cf., Luke 19: 41-44).

Jesus' call to inaugurate the Jubilee could be seen as totally impractical and not meeting the daily needs of the little landowner. The great Pharisaic master Hillel (an older contemporary of Jesus who died c. AD 20) enacted a method to circumvent the devastating economic effect of the release from debts in the Sabbatical year.[866] However, Jesus' answer to these economic hardships was simply to stop charging interest, in fact, simply not expecting repayment of a debt at all. The wealthy, and especially the rulers and Sadducees, could afford to do so. So he calls for the absolute forgiveness of debt and to give without expecting a return:

> Give to him who begs from you, and do not refuse him who would borrow from you (Matt 5:42).

> If you would be perfect, go, sell what you possess and give to the poor, and you will have treasure in heaven; and come, follow me (Matt 19:21).

> Give, and it will be given to you; good measure, pressed down, shaken together, running over, will be put into your lap. For the measure you give will be the measure you get back (Luke 6:38).

> Sell your possessions, and give alms; provide yourselves with purses that do not grow old, with a treasure in the heavens that does not fail, where no thief approaches and no moth destroys (Luke 12:33).

> But when you give a feast, invite the poor, the maimed, the lame, the blind, and you will be blessed, because they cannot repay you. You will be repaid at the resurrection of the just (Luke 14:13).

> And if you lend to those from whom you hope to receive, what credit is that to you? Even sinners [i.e., Gentiles] lend to sinners, to receive as much again. But love your enemies, and do good, and lend, expecting nothing in return; and your reward will be great, and you will be sons of the Most High; for he is kind to the ungrateful and the selfish. Be merciful, even as your Father is merciful (Luke 6:34-36).

This willingness to give is based on unsullied trust in God and his desire to do good for his people. "If you then, who are evil, know how to give good gifts to your children, how much more will your Father who is in heaven give good things to those who ask him!" (Matt 7:11). As an example of putting one's total trust in God rather than in wealth, he tells the parable of the widow's mite. Zacchaeus the tax collector is a living model that demonstrates that trust as he vows to return fourfold whatever he had gotten by fraud. Jesus emphasizes in the strongest possible terms this trust when he says to "render to Caesar what is Caesar's and to God what is God's." Jesus' clever response to the payment of taxes could be interpreted to say, "Give this blasphemous emperor back his blasphemous coins! God is more than the emperor!"[867] God is more important than your wealth and your ease. And you will be repaid with the life of the kingdom.

> There is no one who has left house or brothers or sisters or mother or father or children or lands, for my sake and for the gospel, who will not receive a hundredfold now in this time, houses and brothers and sisters and mothers and children and lands, with persecutions, and in the age to come eternal life (Mark 10:28–30).)

The parable of the unjust steward illustrates this "leaving." The steward, by lowering the debt owed to his master, creates a Jubilee, and he has been reduced to poverty, thrown out of his position, and downgraded to total dependence on the poor villagers. But he has gained their approbation and will enjoy their hospitality, a sign of the kingdom.[868]

Jesus' proclamation of relieving debts and eschewing wealth as security in this life is to be seen under the pressure of the impending kingdom and the inauguration of the eternal, joyous Jubilee. The Torah assures that God will be faithful to all who trust in him because he is the "God of the living" (Exod 3:6, 15, Mark 12:27). But Jesus also calls on the peasant to be honest and repay his debt. John Howard Yoder interestingly interprets the sayings about going to court (Matt 5:25–26, 40, Luke 12:57–59) as Jesus' way of responding to Hillel's *prosbul* when the creditor takes the debtor to the council that holds the debt to sue for repayment.[869]

The exorcisms must be seen under this rubric of the Jubilee's liberation. For example, the story of the Gerasene demoniac depicts a person who has internalized somatically the political environment.[870] When Jesus drives out the "legion" of demons, he metaphorically drives out the Romans' occupation of the land and at the same time drives out the animosity toward the Romans, preparing for the end of hostilities. Jesus is literally enacting the Jubilee.[871] So here again, he acts as a royal figure as he encounters metaphorically a foreign power and drives it out. His healings must be seen in the context of the dawning Jubilee.

In this, Jesus was not standing outside Israel or opposed to Judaism. Rather he was plumbing the depths of Israel's faith and her God of love (Num 14:18) and his will to liberate. Jesus would resolve the social problems of his day by abolishing debts and setting debtors free and relieving them of the anxiety of a hand-to-mouth existence.

The Jubilee kingdom was made most tangible and conspicuous in Jesus' table practice as he ate in intimate fellowship with the outliers and sinners. These people knew exactly where they stood with the rest of society. They were cognizant of being rejected by the faithful and, by implication, even by God, even though they would have still considered themselves as children of Abraham. When Jesus dined with them, it had to have been like a liberation from their despised status and an assurance they were not excluded from claiming God as their own. They had found their way home, or rather, the kingdom of God had found them. It might well have been in such circumstances that Jesus declared that the "kingdom of God was among" the people as it was made manifest in the joy of sharing table fellowship (Luke 17:20–21). His open commensality was also meant as a sign to the whole people of God's forgiveness and liberation from exile.

This proleptic kingdom of God stood in contrast to present Israel, whose world mission to be a light to the world and gather in the Gentiles to join in the eschatological worship of God in the Temple was obscured by her internal divisions, antagonisms, revolutionary enthusiasm, and hostility toward Rome in particular and the Gentile world generally. She was oriented inward and focused exclusively on obedience to Torah and, in the case of many a prophetic, messianic, and bandit leader and their followings, on the forcible establishment of an Israel freed from Roman occupation.

The kingdom demanded an alteration of one's loyalty. To enter the kingdom meant even the family had to take second place, while the kingdom created a new family and kinship (Luke 9:60–62, Mark 3:31–35). However, a man's relationship with his wife remained inviolate.[872] Jesus' altering of one of Israel's most essential understandings of her society illuminates his understanding of himself as possessing the highest authority so that his call supersedes all other obligations. To be discipled to the person of Jesus and the kingdom freed a person from every social obligation and required total self-surrender.

Jesus did call disciples to follow him and share in his voluntary self-denial and divesting of all goods for the sake of the kingdom (e.g., Luke 12:30–33). By giving away, all the disciple-followers accepted destitution and dependence on others for hospitality and in this way practiced the

Jubilee that relieved the poverty of others. However, not all were called to this dependence on others and Jesus' itinerant ministry. There were those who remained in settled communities and continued to pursue normal lives. A superlative example would be Johanna, the wife of Chuza, Herod Antipas's steward (Luke 8:3). This did not mean that either form of discipleship was superior to the other. Each was given a different gift and call (1 Cor 7:7).

For Jesus the tithe was not sufficient (Luke 11:42). The tithe went to the Temple and the priests anyway, that is, to those who hardly participated in the hard-scrabble existence of the peasant. The tithe certainly was demanded by the Torah.[873] Jesus' underlying criticism of the Pharisees was not their concern for a faithful observance of Torah and their strict observance of the tithe but rather that such a tendency focused intensely on the external observance and seemed to exclude the inner disposition (Luke 11:40). Interiority and the purity of intention played a large role in Jesus' thought due to his stress on eschatology and focus on the individual. He accentuates the primary causes and the ultimate aims of the religious act. Anger leads to murder and the lustful gaze to adultery (Matt 5:21-22, 28).[874] So Jesus exhorts the Pharisees to "give alms" (Luke 11:41), which is the practical manifestation of mercy.[875] The Jubilee requires mercy, and to extend it one needs not to be so concerned about ritual purity and contracting the contagion of impurity from external things. Mercy is divine and imparts a purity that mere avoidance of external impurity cannot impart.

Jesus wasn't abolishing tithes (after all, that would lead to the destitution of the priests). He went beyond the easy achievement and consequent easy moral contentment coming from obedience to the law of tithes.[876] One's righteousness had to "go beyond that of the scribes and Pharisees" (Matt 5:20) and, in effect, extend the tithe by showing the mercy of the Jubilee in giving alms to the poor and forgiving debts. Jesus was not looking to found a utopian state but a way of bringing in the Jubilee and saving Israel from utter destruction. He was calling Israel back to her deepest roots to be children of their merciful and compassionate God. In this way he was making the Jubilee a permanent state of affairs, ushering in the new age of the kingdom of God.

It is like the exemptions of those who were called to holy war and acquired a holiness as they were set apart for a divine and priestly action (Deut 20:5-8). Jesus evidently thought of his ministry and that of his disciples as involved in a countermilitary campaign, not against a tangible foe but against satanic forces both supramundane and as they had become embodied in the nation. That struggle required being unencumbered by worldly concerns. So Jesus drew on Israel's history and Scripture to characterize his ministry. It was not merely a flaunting of social norms. Even so, Jesus and his disciples were stigmatized: they were itinerant, left off familial obligations and social connection, and made themselves dependent on village hospitality.

Jesus reconfigures the family and breaks the bonds of the blood ties of the extended family. True kinsmen consist of those who have entered the kingdom. He extends the ties spiritually to include all those who have submitted to the kingdom and are bound together in mutual love, both settled followers and itinerant companions and disciples. In this family, God is Father, which means one "hears the word of God and keeps it." They are all brothers and sisters, together with mothers and children. Evidently whole families that remained settled in the villages joined the kingdom movement of Jesus. No doubt, they were the majority of those who extended hospitality to Jesus and his disciples. This new family configuration stands in glaring contrast with the understanding of Judaism that equates blood descent from Abraham as constituting inclusion in the people of God. Jesus was gathering and constituting the new Israel at whose head were the inner core of twelve disciples. Over them all was their Father-God (Matt 23:9).

The community of the kingdom had the ethical quality of a family that transferred the Jewish values of loyalty, care, and love to it. It was a personal fellowship with God as their Father and with one another, as they were to regard themselves, as brothers and sisters (Mark 10:29-30). In this pattern social patriarchy is eschewed, and God becomes the real Father in this community of the new age. Blood relationships do not count in the kingdom, and even motherhood is relativized (Luke 11:27-28). Because the family was the bedrock of Jewish society, Jesus was accused of "perverting" Israel (Luke 22:2).

In this somewhat ragtag kingdom, children become a model for how the kingdom is to be received, upending the priority and honor with which elder men were held in the society and undermining again the society's patriarchy. Children along with the physically and morally defective are the powerless and enter the kingdom because of their humility. They have the least to boast of in terms of property, honor, and social position. To become as one of these is to accept the kingdom as pure gift fully, which means trusting God and relying on him in heart, mind, and spirit, a quality of the Jubilee. With that comes God's blessing, which is actualized in Jesus' healings and exorcisms. The purest portrayal of the kingdom is Jesus embracing the children.[877]

In this way he again reverses the pyramidal social order, turning it upside down and placing the humblest and meekest at the top of the topsy-turvy kingdom of God. The children in their quintessential powerlessness and without standing in the world have nothing but pure trust in God. How poles apart they are from those who by force of arms would bring in the kingdom. Jesus' blessing of children (Mark 10:13–16) is related to the proclamation of the kingdom, which means it is a time of crisis that will bring God's blessing and curse, weal and woe (Luke 6:20–26). The presence of the kingdom in Jesus' activity makes it a time of Jubilee blessing: he brings healing and liberation from the bonds of Satan. Like a child, one can only accept the kingdom. The kingdom is pure gift, independent of human action or claims.

That does not mean Jesus was forming a sect, for his ministry was to all Israel. He healed all indiscriminately who came to him and indiscriminately appealed to all with his message. The call to enter the kingdom into his fellowship was, like the message of the prophets before him, an appeal to all Israel that comprised both a promise and a threat of judgment (Matt 7:13, Luke 13:23–27).

Jesus' healings were not just some kind of protest against obeying Torah. Jesus promoted the validity of the Torah even while he gave priority of the kingdom and its requirements over Torah.[878] So his healings occur in the context of his proclamation of the kingdom and the Jubilean restoration of Israel (Isa 35:5–6). The kingdom is present, the time of salvation is here, so healing cannot wait. Jesus also asserts (in agreement with the Pharisees!) that human need has precedence over the law (Mark 2:27–28). He does not abrogate the law but fulfills its intent: it was given to keep the faithful close to God and his will. Community with God has been restored. When he heals on the Sabbath he justifies his behavior on the basis of the practice of every Jew and every Pharisaic teacher who would save an animal on the Sabbath.[879] Besides, the Sabbath meant being loosed from the bondage of labor and having a foretaste of the "rest" that came with the coming of the kingdom. The Jubilee had arrived. Now was the time of forgiveness, hospitality, binding up of wounds, sharing goods, and acceptance of the brother and echewing violence, especially toward Rome, and the willingness to turn the other cheek and go the extra mile.

"Son of man" is Jesus' self-designation (Mark 2:10) by which he identifies himself with humanity, with his own people, and with the weak and the humble. In this he was representative of the new Israel, the bearer of God's judgment, the presence of the kingdom, and the embodiment of forgiveness.

Far from abrogating the Torah, Jesus maintains it remains in force until the kingdom is fully established (Matt 5:17–20). However, because the kingdom is already present in his words and deeds and in the community it has established through him, the Torah must then submit to its sway and sovereignty. Under its gravity, people are healed on the Sabbath, sinners enjoy fellowship with God, and the Mosaic legislation on marriage and divorce must give way to the primordial state intended by God at the creation. The inclusion of women in Jesus' community of the end-time and their equality come under the same rubric.

The popular wisdom of the day assumed that when untoward events overtook someone, it was a punishment for sin. The great underlying support for this view was Israel's own history. The people were subject to exile for the sin of idolatry and the social sins of not caring for the least. Jesus contradicts this notion (slaughter of the Galileans, Luke 13:1–5). Pilate's slaying of pilgrims and the fall of the tower of Siloam taking the life of eighteen men were not to be thought of as the result of sin on their part. But such incidents were really a divine call to repent. They were a sign of the destruction that impended if Israel did not turn from its present violent course. Jesus used these incidents to warn that, if there were no turnabout in the attitude of the nation, which was becoming inured to violence, animosity, and hostility and trusting in the inviolability of the Temple and apocalyptic dreams of divine intervention, the nation would be destroyed. Jesus was countering a revanchism against Rome and even against such a man as Pilate in spite of his sadistic provocations. He was reminding Israel of the steadfast love of their God, his mercy, and his compassion. The people were to emulate him and save the nation by love of the enemy and forgiveness. Judgment would surely come when God's kingdom arrived.

The law as summarized by the double love commandment is universalized, extending it to the world of Gentiles.[880] Jesus vividly portrayed this universalism with the parables of the mustard seed and leaven in a lump.[881] Assenting to this commandment, however, does not gain one's entrance into the kingdom. Jesus tells the scribe that he is "not far" from the kingdom"— i.e., he's not yet in. The kingdom is not merely a mental matter of the understanding, the intellect, and reason, or even a matter of the "heart" (i.e., the will). It is a matter of one's "whole life" (the one element not repeated by the scribe in Mark 12:32). The whole person, including one's life in the world, is demanded: "If anyone would come after me, let him deny himself and take up his cross and follow me. For whoever would save his life will lose it; and whoever loses his life for my sake and the gospel's will save it" (Mark 8:34). Only by "losing oneself" will a person enter the kingdom. The scribe's distance from the kingdom comes from not being ready to dispossess himself of his goods and take up his cross and follow Jesus.

At the same time Jesus affirms the scribe's declaration that the double command is "greater than all holocausts and sacrifices." Implied in his affirmation is that the Temple sacrifices are superfluous and no longer required.[882] The Temple rather is to be a "house of prayer for all nations"

(Mark 11:17). The supersession of Temple sacrifices by the love commandment affirmed by Jesus refers also to the ultimate sacrifice of himself on the cross. The scribe is not yet in the kingdom. He lacks one thing: the giving of his whole life, which is precisely what Jesus will do on the cross as the beloved son. Jesus himself is the embodiment of the love commandment, which demands one's whole life. The cross is where Jesus' love for his people finds a climax. In it he achieves victory over evil. His love, especially of the Father, leads him to give himself, his very life, for others (Mark 10:45, Gal 2:20, Eph 5:2).[883]

Jesus asserts that his exorcistic activity was the binding of Satan (dispute about exorcism, Mark 3:22–30). The plundering of Satan's power would be fully effected with the arrival of the kingdom. The kingdom has invaded enemy territory. Satan's kingdom has begun to fall.

Like John, Jesus works with divine authority (the question on authority, Mark 11:27–33): John prepared the people for the coming kingdom, and Jesus prepares for and proclaims God's victory in the entry and cleansing narratives as he fulfills Zechariah's prophecy (Mark11:1–10, 15–17). The new age is dawning when God will establish his kingdom. The Gentiles will stream into Jerusalem and join in worship with the Jews in a great egalitarian feast of tabernacles. His interrogators in Jerusalem did not accept John's divine authority, nor did they believe that Jesus acted with that same authority. So he rhetorically deposes them from claiming that they function with God's authorization. In this he appears as a prophet who proclaims God's word that does "not return to me empty, but it shall accomplish that which I purpose, and prosper in the thing for which I sent it" (Isa 55:11).

Zacchaeus has the characteristics of a child, which Jesus finds as the proper way to relate to God and his kingdom. He's short of stature and so climbs a tree that he might glimpse Jesus in the crowd as it passes through Jericho. He enters the kingdom with a childlike trust, and the joy he finds in it leads him to show great mercy and make restitution far above what the law requires. That Jesus affirms that Zacchaeus has a right to enter the kingdom because he is a "son of Abraham" reflects an earlier stage in Jesus' ministry when he thought of his mission to be only to the "house of Israel" (Matt 10:6, 15:24), before his encounter with the Syrophoenician woman and the centurion whose servant was ill.

We find in the biographical pronouncement stories both positive and negative responses to Jesus. The story of Mary and Martha represents both possible responses to Jesus: Mary sits at his feet in repose and in the posture of a disciple,[884] which reflects her choice of the kingdom, while Martha is busy, although she is ostensibly concerned with being hospitable. However, Martha is also resentful and blames both Mary and Jesus that she "is left alone to serve." The kingdom is a matter of hearing and enjoying the respite of the kingdom, the eschatological Sabbath of rest.

This visit of Jesus with Mary and Martha (Luke 10:38–42) conjures up the whole of Jesus' ministry: table fellowship, the gathering of people to hear his teaching, and that the kingdom was already proleptically in the midst of the people. He emphasizes in his gracious chiding of Martha that the word of God takes priority over eating as it did in his temptation (Matt 4:3). To die by lack of physical sustenance is preferable to the death of the spirit, by a dearth of hearing the word of God. By Jesus' doubling of Martha's name, he evokes his own passion—such is the result of not listening to him. Listening was the foundation of his ministry. If he were heard, it would bring one into the kingdom; if the nation would listen, it would be brought into the kingdom and practice mercy and be saved from the terrible fate that loomed in the future.

There is another kind of "sitting" that must involve careful reflection. Jesus uses the request of James and John to sit by his side (i.e., share in his glory) in the kingdom as a teaching opportunity (Luke 18:31–33):[885] there is a fiery ordeal awaiting him and his disciples. He and they would go through the "birth pangs" that would precede the coming of the kingdom. Here we can glimpse the consciousness of his status as the beloved son: the judgment is coming, and he faces death, taking upon himself the end-time pangs. By rejecting him, the nation will reject their last chance to escape the national disaster that will ensue. He gives his life for his people and takes their sin upon himself to preserve them.

Another aspect of his status of beloved son occurs in the rejection that he experiences when he visits his hometown of Nazareth—and even more menacingly, Herod Antipas's intention to kill him. But his death will not occur until the time that God has set, and then his suffering will be on behalf of the whole people, who will not have to undergo the "messianic woes" of the end-times. Herod Antipas sought his life because he thought of him as John the Baptist redivivus, who had declared him an adulterer for unlawfully marrying his brother's wife. But for Jesus, Antipas is a mere "fox," without any real power because God is at work in Jesus' ministry and will bring it to completion in his own way and in his own time. That divine way is Jesus' death in Jerusalem, which will bring about raising him up, inaugurating the kingdom, and founding the new community. As Israel's representative, Jesus would restore her, and the exile would be conclusively ended. The Jubilee would dawn.

Jesus walking along the border between the Galilee and Samaria might expect to encounter a Samaritan, which he does in a group of ten lepers. His healing demonstrates that the power of the kingdom invades also the realm of disease and sin. The one returning to give thanks to Jesus for his healing recognizes a numinous quality in Jesus as he "falls on his face" in worship. That act elicits Jesus' affirmation that the Samaritan "has been saved"—that is, he is included in the kingdom of God. The Samaritan's thanksgiving indicates he acknowledges that the kingdom has found him, which brings forth the great joy that has overtaken him.

The healing of the ten lepers and the encounter with Zaccheus the toll collector (Luke 19:1–10) portray the kingdom in action: the one is healed; the other, though an abject sinner in the eyes of his countrymen, receives mercy and inclusion in the kingdom of the saved. In the first, the healing reintegrates the lepers into society, while the Samaritan who returns to give thanks indicates the much more important integration into the kingdom. In the psalms, thanksgiving is rendered by the psalmists based on the saving actions of God. Thanksgiving points to a personal relationship with God, which is what integration into the kingdom means. The kingdom means ethically showing mercy, which is a fundamental attribute of the God of Israel. Zaccheus's thanksgiving is reflected in his vow to give to the poor and return fourfold if he has defrauded anyone.

Both the leper and Zaccheus are like the man in the parable who found a treasure in the field, and both respond after they have experienced finding the treasure of the kingdom. Jesus himself stands at the center of these stories as the effective presence of the kingdom and its treasures.

Perhaps it was Shammaite Pharisees in some village square in Judea who dragged before Jesus a woman who had been caught in flagrante delicto and asked him to render the verdict that she be stoned as the Torah demanded. This was an obvious act of hoping to catch him in a clear-cut breach of Torah since his practice of receiving sinners had to have been well known. His provocateurs thought for sure they had him. But as in the discussion of the imperial tax (Mark 12:13–17), he turns the tables on them. Who could claim to be sinless? They were caught in their own judgment. Jesus reveals his identity with the God of Israel, who shows mercy.[886] It is mercy alone that will bring people to repentance. In the upside-down kingdom of God, mercy comes first and repentance later. He, by implication, nullifies the competency of the Temple authorities, who also would demand a strict application of the Law. He becomes the source of forgiveness and the mercy of God. In him the woman also has the right of access to the Temple. He includes her in the kingdom, and because she shares in that fellowship, she can go forward "forgetting what lies behind" (Phil 3:13) and repent of her sin and live a new life.

Regarding the half-sheqel Temple tax, Jesus declares that the kingdom renders a person free from that law. This freedom stands in contrast to the

Fourth Philosophy, which decreed that paying taxes to Caesar was tantamount to idolatry. But what does bind a member of the kingdom is not to use that freedom as a cause of offense. Jesus declares much the same as he does in the question concerning paying the imperial tax: if the kingdom frees one from paying the Temple tax, one should pay it to avoid giving offense. In the same way, one should pay the imperial tax (Mark 12:13-17).

Jesus was a public personality and hardly a secretive preacher who huddled with a few hearers in the corners of the villages. His fame spread far and wide.[887] His understanding of Torah was subsumed under the demands and character of the kingdom. That understanding, preached and practiced, challenged the absolute centrality of the Torah in the minds and hearts of the whole populace. He interpreted the Torah in a wholly new way. God's mercy and compassion were primary, and they played out in quite unexpected people and circumstances. He altered the way Israel was to look at the world and her own life in the world. The new covenant of Jeremiah was being inaugurated (Jer 31:31).[888] The old ordinances of circumcision, Temple, Jerusalem, and even the state itself were not essential because in the kingdom people will simply do what is right, living in the grace and mercy of God and in the forgiveness of sin.[889] In the kingdom, the exile is ended. The new time is here, and the Lord, through his servant Jesus, is directly involved, so the kingdom is already proleptically present. No intermediaries are needed such as Moses, prophets, priests, and an external code. In the kingdom one lives from God's love and mercy (Matt 9:13). Obedience is completely interiorized, and so exterior obedience follows naturally.[890]

On the other hand, Jesus was not critical of Torah as such but rather the nation's exclusive concentration on it to the exclusion of her cosmic mission. His real judgment was of the insurrectionist movements, which, prophetic-wise, he saw as leading to the demise of the nation. The twelve disciples in the eschaton would sit on thrones and judge the twelve tribes of Israel, while Jesus himself would judge the nations (the parable of the great Assize[891]).

Jesus tells a contrast parable that he places in the Temple. A widow, considered to be abandoned by God, and a rich man, considered to be blessed by God, go up to the Temple to donate their offerings. The widow offers only two lepta,[892] while the rich man deposits a large amount, perhaps as much as several hundred denarii. As in the parable of the tax collector and the Pharisee, Jesus turns the tables on the expectation of his hearers as to who would be looked upon favorably by God and who was the most devoted to God and his Temple. It is the widow who has offered her "whole life, all she had," witnessing to her total dependence on God and trust in him to provide.[893] She is the opposite of the rich man, who went away from Jesus sorrowfully because Jesus had told him to give all his riches away and follow him, which would have resulted in him having treasure in heaven (Mark 10:21). The poor widow has the heavenly treasure, whereas the rich man, by implication, does not. The widow has entered the kingdom, whereas the rich man has missed the boat. All the possessions of the world and its wisdom and knowledge are of no avail. Jesus illustrates this reality in his parable. She gives her whole life and therefore has treasure in heaven by her total reliance on God.

In the question on divorce (Mark 10:2–12), Jesus explicates yet another aspect of the kingdom: the kingdom restores the world to its original condition. Those who enter it are to live in accordance with its primordial order established by God, which has been built into the very structure of creation. Jesus speaks as the one greater than Moses and with sovereign authority. Marriage rests on God's own character. He is the faithful husband of his "wife" Israel and will never abandon her. In this discussion Jesus reveals his understanding of both Scripture and the nature of the kingdom. The primordial order of creation precedes and therefore takes precedence over the Torah, which had been introduced later. The kingdom is the restoration of that primordial, pristine creation of God at the beginning of the cosmos.

Jesus decided he had to go to Jerusalem for his final hour (Luke 13:33). It seems he came to the realization that the nation as a whole would not accept his proclamation of the kingdom so that he, as "son of man" and "beloved son," would have to take upon himself the end-time "messianic woes" and suffer in Israel's stead, thereby ransoming the nation from the threatened judgment of the coming kingdom.[894] That would mean the ultimate salvation of the nation and the world fulfilling the divinely appointed plan for terminating the exile and accomplishing Israel's redemption.

As Jesus approached Jerusalem, he paused at the top of the Mount of Olives and saw before and below him the Holy City and its Temple.[895] There he reflected on its future. The expectation for the gathering of the Gentiles had been disappointed. His ministry and proclamation were to have been the healing waters flowing from the Temple and preparing for the eschaton when the world would join with Israel in the worship of her God. But the nation as a whole had not heeded Jesus' call to enter the kingdom and eschew the way of violence and revolution. His understanding of the Temple and its function in God's eschatological plan had changed. He had witnessed the general rejection of his proclamation of the kingdom as well as his own personal rejection on the part of spiritual and political leaders. They had not accepted repentance and the way of the kingdom that eschewed violence, that positively regarded the enemy Rome in spite of its predations, and that practiced forgiveness. The demons of hostility, rivalry, revolution, and war had possessed the nation. The real enemy he revealed was not Rome but Satan and his minions, which had invaded the nation and infected it with a spirit of revanchism.[896]

By refusing the kingdom, Israel had chosen the way of destruction, which would include the city and the Temple. Jesus foresaw the result of the rejection of the kingdom in the coming catastrophe. He had called the nation to follow the way of peace and passive resistance to the outrages of their overlord as the way forward, even pray for the occupier, and live in forgiveness with one another. Because the nation could not accept the kingdom, its eyes were darkened, and it could not see the way of peace. The judgment that will come upon his beloved people causes him such sorrow that his eyes are filled with tears as he, representative of the whole people, weeps over the fate of Jerusalem.

As he enters Jerusalem, his followers, who have accompanied him, raise a shout of praise, which some Pharisees reprove concerned that Pilate might conceive of it as an uprising and, as was his wont in such situations, violently put it down. But Jesus, in his often hyperbolic style, says if they are silent, the very stones will cry out. That is, God will see that his "beloved son" is praised. God's divine approval rests on him.

Jesus also spoke explicitly about the coming destruction and that "not one stone would be left on another" and "in those days there will be such tribulation as has not been from the beginning of the creation which God created until now, and never will be" (Mark 13:2 and 13:19). The divine judgment was coming that would also vindicate Jesus' own proclamation and ministry.

The story of the cursing of the fig tree (Mark 11:12–14) corresponds to Jesus' prophecy of destruction. In this cursing he performs a prophetic action announcing that if Israel refuses the invitation, to bring forth the fruit of repentance God's judgment will come upon the nation, and it will be reduced to fruitlessness—that is, it will not enjoy the bliss of the eschaton.

The Gospels place the following two incidents in Jerusalem, which could well have been the place where they occurred, especially in the case where he is confronted by Sadducees. They portray the animosity that was directed toward him, which was a part of his encounter with those who found his words and activities provocative if not even subversive.

The first involves those who want to catch him in the question of whether to pay the poll tax with Tiberias's idolatrous coin, which claims his divine sonship (Mark 12:13–17). This story has apocalyptic overtones that pit Jesus against his antagonists, who are manifestations of Satan—that is, it is a conflict between God and anti-God, between God and Caesar. He vanquishes his opponents by a word. So he is intimately associated with the

Divine Warrior who overcomes the hostile forces of evil. He proleptically enacts God's ultimate victory. Jesus' "render to God" asserts the sovereignty of God over all worldly orders. Jesus' cross is intimated in the hostile intent of his interrogators. But it is in the cross that is imposed by Rome through Pilate that Caesar submits to God's will and by which God exercises his sovereignty over the world.

These antitheses reappear in Jesus' debate with certain Sadducees (Mark 12:18–27). In this case the antithesis is between God and not-God. The Sadducees' denial of resurrection denies God's fundamental character as the life-giver. The apocalyptists struggled with how God and the powers that subject history, the world, and the individual to death and corruption can coexist. So they asserted God would ultimately be victorious because he is a saving God, and life would be finally restored to the individual by the resurrection of the dead.

Jesus did not stand apart from the coming tribulation of the nation but perceived that his own death as the beloved son lay in the offing, which was a way of taking on the sins and suffering of the nation as a ransom. He interpreted the anointing in Bethany in the house of Simon the Leper as a prophetic action that signified the anointing of his dead body. So even in death, he identified with his beloved people. He would be the new Passover sacrificial lamb that bore their sins (John 1:29, 36). "She has done what she could; she has anointed my body beforehand for burying" (Mark 14:8).

Jesus, on his way to the cross, tells the women who weep for him to weep for themselves because of the coming catastrophe. If the Romans inflict the cross on Jesus the "green tree," what will they do to Israel "the dry tree," which has essentially rejected the life of the kingdom for the death that will ensue from opposition to Rome. Jesus' own death and the coming destruction are coordinated in the story of Simon, who bore Jesus' cross. Simon bears the cross of wood, but Jesus bears the cross of Israel's condemnation.

Jesus did not run some kind of protest movement, political program, or social movement. Although what he said and did was directed toward and had an impact on politics and social life, he was calling Israel back to life with God and his purposes for the nation. Everything he said and did was centered and comprehended in the reality of God's kingdom, his royal rule, and the coming Jubilee. Jesus was leading a political revolution but without politics: the nation, like Abraham, had to submit to God's will. But since it would not, he himself would submit as the beloved son and take upon himself the sins of the nation.

The Response Jesus Envisaged from the Nation

For the elites the kingdom meant practicing justice and not hoarding wealth.[897] Poverty and wealth loom large in Jesus' encounter with his society.[898] His understanding of the meaning of wealth diverged from the popular opinion, which thought of the wealthy as especially righteous and pious. Wealth for him meant inclusion in the kingdom and inauguration of the Jubilee by forgiving debts. It could even have meant divesting oneself completely of one's wealth and joining Jesus in his ministry (Mark 10:17-22).

He affirms the people's sense of exile, but instead of following the contemporary prophets who promised to effect the wondrous liberation of the past, he creates the community of the coming age where one is already at home with Israel's Father-God. But there is a martial aspect to Jesus' activity. He and his fellow workers are like men mustered into a holy war. Instead of martial aggression against the Roman overlord, however, they burst into Satan's "house" and bind him by their exorcisms so that they can "plunder his house" (Mark 3:27, 2 Cor 10:14).

Jesus' exorcisms were a replacing of anger with love even for one's enemies by refocusing feelings of aggression against the proper enemy, Satan and his minions. Such radical love, of course, is preternatural and flows directly out of a filial relationship with God. To enter the kingdom means being enmeshed in the net of God's love and forgiveness and throwing that same net far and wide to include both brother Jew and Roman stranger. Sublimating aggression in this manner also mitigates fear.

Jesus in some ways historicizes apocalyptic. As people respond to his proclamation and enter the kingdom, they are already being gathered into the divine granary. But those who reject him and the kingdom and choose to follow their own prescriptions for alleviating Israel's crisis are sure to experience the horrors of Roman retribution. However, the eschatological kingdom will arrive with its judgment of fire for those who eschew the kingdom.[899]

Like John, Jesus emphasizes it is not mere blood relationship—that is, being a descendant of Abraham and part of his family—by which one is included in the kingdom of God: it is hearing and doing God's will (Mark 3:35, Luke 11:28).[900] The kingdom is a dynamic not a static reality independent of how I live. It is not a claim that the individual can make but a divine designation. The marks of living in the kingdom are outlined in Luke's description of Jesus' declaration in Nazareth: it is initiating and celebrating the Jubilee, forgiving debts, having concern for the poor, and offering forgiveness. It is the time of the Lord's favor!

Essene-like withdrawal and standing in opposition to Jerusalem elites or the people in general were not the way of the kingdom. Jesus was intimately connected to and inextricably woven in the fabric of the daily life of the people as he journeyed from village to village. He participated in their lives and brought abundant gifts to the people. He took upon himself the concern for the poor, healed their diseases, drove out the vexing spirits, and sat at their tables. He was like a mobile temple bringing the forgiveness of sins and assuring the people they were incorporated into God's kingdom. If they were so gifted with their Father-God's love, care, and concern, they could live the Jubilee, reject hate and animosity, be generous, give up deceit, and have their fears abated. They were light, so now they could live as the light and be the nation that is a light to the Gentiles. The feast of the kingdom was among them.

For Jesus, fulfilling the prophetic summons of obedience to God's will as revealed in the Torah was important as per the Pharisees but not sufficient. If the Jubilee was to be enacted, forgiveness of debt and sins could run rampant. Healing did not have to wait, but the presence of the reign of the Jubilee demanded that the Sabbath could not interfere. The Jubilee recapitulated the time of the creation and its conditions, the reverence for the sanctity of marriage and its indissolubility.

God's beneficence includes the whole world of peoples. The universal character of wisdom emerges in Jesus as he integrates this personified attribute of God in his self-understanding and his interpretation of God's will. As wisdom, Jesus doesn't turn to his people objectively as just a teacher, or a provider of guidance, or an instructor in the way of salvation. He is a subject, a summoning "I." "Whoso finds me," says Dame Wisdom, "finds life" (Prov 8:35). And so Jesus. He is bidding his people to find life in and through him, in and through God's kingdom, which is present in his words and activity. Like Dame Wisdom, Jesus sits and eats with those who respond to the kingdom's call (Prov 9:1–6). Like her, Jesus reveals the hidden knowledge of God (Matt 11:27, cf., Prov 8:14–36).[901]

The Messenger

Jesus is embedded in the kingdom that he proclaims. Or to put it differently, he is utterly subject to God and his rule (i.e., his will and purposes). However, he does not quite speak as one of the classical prophets. His embeddedness in the kingdom makes him speak in a sovereign way: the Sabbath is subject to him, as are the demons. Obedience to the law does not qualify for existence in the kingdom. The scribe who affirms the double love command is "not far from the kingdom." Israel's leaders must also submit to his authority and the power of his pungent arguments. Because he cannot be trapped and meets the arguments of his opponents head-on, they are deprived of their authority and are reduced to attacking him with ad hominem arguments: he's demon possessed, he's a blasphemer, and he's obliquely judged as unclean and a sinner because he consorts with such people.

His speech and language are forthright. He doesn't mince words, and yet his words are not caustic or biting. He refuses to act as a judge and arbiter over the legalities connected with an inheritance (perhaps he wants to avoid the militant characteristics associated with a judge).[902] Although he rejects the popular equation of wealth and piety, he receives a rich man with "love." His capacious attitude is evident in his refusal to equate sin and untoward events: he observes that God's goodness is showered on both good and evil persons (Matt 5:45); he accepts those who do not follow him yet use his name to exorcise; he refuses to let his disciples call down judgment on those who refuse to accept him. That same commodiousness appears in his prohibition of divorce because it implies man and woman are equal in the kingdom (cf., Gal 3:28).

Because the kingdom is already present in Jesus' activities and his followers live in this new reality, fasting is inappropriate like pouring new wine into old, dilapidated skins or mourning at a wedding feast.[903] The real fast is establishing the Jubilee and bringing healing to the nation:

> Is not this the fast that I choose: to loose the bonds of wickedness, to undo the thongs of the yoke, to let the oppressed go free, and to break every yoke? Is it not to share your bread with the hungry, and bring the homeless poor into your house; when you see the naked, to cover him, and not to hide yourself from your own flesh? Then shall your light break forth like the dawn, and your healing shall spring up speedily; your righteousness shall go before you, the glory of the Lord shall be your rear guard (Isa 58:6–8).

So healing cannot wait until the morrow. This is the day of salvation (2 Cor 6:2). The Jubilee is here! Jesus is enacting the restoration while simultaneously rejecting the violent opposition to Rome, the competition between groups, the unconcern of the rich for the poor of the land, and the grasping of one's own in a limited good culture. Jesus is living out his baptismal call as the beloved son of God and as the one who heralds the divine call to the nation to "listen to him."[904]

Though already present, the kingdom will come in its fullness in the future, but it will be preceded by the woes of the end-time, its "birth pangs"

(Mark 13:8, ὠδίνων, ōdinōn). Jesus understands himself, though he doesn't use the terms of the suffering servant of Isaiah, as the one who takes upon himself the end-time woes. He speaks of his own "baptism" (suffering) as the "beloved son." In the Old Testament, God's love is connected with the covenant.[905] The covenant concerns exodus and God's election of Israel as his own people. God's love is selective, voluntary, spontaneous, and related to his righteousness, judgment, and forgiveness.[906] There is no explicit statement that the divine love extends to the nations.[907] However, Jesus did so perhaps most poignantly in the parable of the prodigal son.[908] "Beloved" is used of Israel (Pss 60:5, 108:6, Isa 5:1-2, Jer 12:7), which suggests that Isa 42:1-4 is being applied to Jesus.[909] The use of the same appellation in the baptismal scene and the transfiguration story again implies he is representative of the nation.[910] In this way he would have understood himself as recapitulating the people, their history, and their relationship to God.[911] This representational role is further suggested by the connection made between God's love and election (Col 3:12, Rom 1:7, 9:11-13, 11:28, Eph 1:4-5) and by the way he demands allegiance to himself (Matt 10:37-38) and to God (Matt 6:24, Mark 12:29-30). That allegiance is what the scribe in his affirmation of the double love command lacks.

Jesus sees himself, though he doesn't use the word, as a pioneer (Heb 2:10, 12:2) who is invading the kingdom of Satan, the "strong man," plundering his house (Mark 3:27) by his exorcisms, and ransoming "the many"[912] from satanic power. In a parallel way Jesus invades the world of sinners and sin and rescues the sinner from the threatening peril of sin when God comes in judgment. This consorting with sinners, whom Jesus has come to call (Mark 2:17), puts him in the place of the Lord who "instructs sinners" (Ps 25:8) and in the messianic role of returning sinners to the Lord's way (Ps 51:13).

In the first book of this series, I identified three models, ancient forms of Israel's political existence, that served as paradigms for any future renewal: prophet-king (messiah), priest, and judge.[913] Jesus explicitly eschews the role of judge. He overtly claims the prophetic role (Mark 6:4) and is so identified by others.[914] In his Temple cleansing he claims priestly authority to take charge of the temple precincts. Jesus' chosen title for himself is "son of man," which includes his identification with the suffering servant of Isaiah, the royal messiah, and the recapitulation of the nation. So Jesus as the agent of the Jubilee and inauguration of the kingdom of God identifies himself with the fullness of Israel's past and the expectations of God's saving help in the future. He is prophet, priest, and king. Above all, however, he is the beloved son who is "given" out of God's love for the nation and the world (John 3:16).

Epilogue

Retrospect and Prospect

This investigation delved deeply into Jesus' own self-consciousness by way of his baptismal experience, in which he was designated the "beloved son," a designation that is, as we have seen, fraught with deep biblical associations with Isaac and other beloved sons of the patriarchs who underwent symbolical deaths and resurrections. Jesus' life and ministry played out under the panoply of cross and restoration. He named himself "son of man" as the one who was in an intimate relationship with God and who, as the suffering servant embodying the nation, established the kingdom now and would return in the future to establish it in its fullness

I have made the point that Jesus and others saw where Israel was headed with its escalating and militant animosity toward Rome and the burgeoning divisions within Jewish society in the land of Israel. In the pronouncement stories, we encounter Jesus as he offered the alternative of the kingdom in specific situations. Was he imprudent and naïve in thinking that the nation would respond positively to his proclamation of a kingdom that seemed to overthrow all of Judaism's values by welcoming sinners, Gentiles, and people on the margins? Was he rash and unwise as he invited the nation into a kingdom where forgiveness reigned even for gross sins like adultery? Was it ill-considered and impulsive as he proclaimed a new order in which social relationships were inverted, the supposed God-blessed and pious wealthy were rejected, and adults were to become like children? Was he incautious and unsophistical as he challenged his hearers to love and pray for Rome, the oppressive enemy? Was he foolish and disingenuous as he taught and pursued a practice that claimed to be the reign of God but allowed the Torah to be broken for the sake of people who could just as well be rescued and healed on another than a Sabbath day and called divorce and remarriage adultery? Was he irresponsible and reckless as he relativized the family and brought, not peace, but division? We could well ask, like John the Baptist, "Are you the expected one or should we look for another?"

Jesus also proclaimed that the Jubilee, which had never been initiated, was now at hand, and so the kingdom meant the forgiveness of debts and freely giving to others, especially the poor. Magnanimous giving was at the root of the kingdom because it meant to have an unsullied trust in God as Israel's loving and compassionate Father. The overwhelming sense of being in exile in their own land had, he said, also ended by entering the kingdom. The Jubilee in its original conception applied to all residents in the land, whether Israelite or stranger. And so now. The unity of God and his people was restored when the people accepted the kingdom and lived according to its upside-down precepts, which opened the way for even Romans to be included.

Jesus and his close followers were like an army arrayed for battle, not against a material foe, but against a demonic one that had invaded Israel. They, as holy warriors, were set apart for a divine and priestly conflict as they assaulted the realm of Satan. Jesus was leading a kind of holy war, and so they were on the move continually, eschewed familial responsibilities and social relationships, and relied on village hospitality. In this way the movement constituted a new nonpatriarchal family that transferred the Jewish values of family, loyalty, care, and love to the community of the new age of the kingdom.

This new age was celebrated as Jesus sat at table with his motley crowd of adherents and partisans of the kingdom. Here the debilitating anger against Roman occupation and its hostility and flaunting of Israel's faith was defeated; the hatreds that worked for the destruction of the enemy, the fears that grew out of the desperation of victimhood, and the threat of going under were disabled; and the animosity toward one's own members of the covenant people was replaced with mercy.

Jesus was also met with a broad swath of rejection in his society: Herod Antipas sought to kill him, and his townsfolk did not accept him. Even his own family was arrayed against him as one who was out of his mind. He was accused of being in league with Satan and was confronted with hostility by leaders and others who perceived him as opposing the Torah. But he made clear he knew that as the beloved son he had a bitter cup to drink. In all of this, he was not arrayed against his own people, but he stood with them and among them and willingly would take their suffering upon himself. He wept in sorrow that his own beloved people would not be gathered under the wings of the kingdom like a mother hen gathers her chicks.

In the next volume of this series, I will analyze the "sayings" of Jesus (i.e., those without a context as distinguished from the pronouncement stories) and the miracle stories. Modern interpretation brackets out the possibility of miracles. Science postulates a "closed universe" that allows no events to be effected from the "outside" as it were. This stance of contemporary interpretation places miracles within the life of the church and how they function there. So scholarship understands them as community products, not historical reports and not a component of the life and ministry of Jesus. At most it vaguely bases them on some remembered activities of Jesus that in some way produced healing effects in his contemporaries.

I will deal with these questions and the evidence that Jesus performed deeds such as these, including exorcisms. These miracle stories, some of which I have dealt with in the present volume as pronouncement stories, are pervasive in the Gospels, and so minimally the interpreter must recognize that they are part of the ancient traditions handed down by the nascent church and therefore need to be taken into account as minimally a characteristic of Jesus' ministry.

Prepare for a lively discussion and a challenge to the so-called assured results of scientific conclusions, and be ready to learn how science has its limitations as I take a critical look at both the miracle stories and their contemporary interpreters.[915]

Chapter Endnotes

1. For a definition of these terms and a discussion about them, see Roemer, *Who in the World Was Jesus*, 72–6. See also Rodríguez, "Authenticating Criteria."
2. For that context, see Roemer, *World of Jesus*.
3. *The Journal for the Study of the Historical Jesus* over the years has included a number of articles discussing this thesis: Rodríguez, "Jesus as His Friends Remembered Him"; Kloppenborg, "Memory, Performance, and the Sayings of Jesus"; Crook, "Collective Memory Distortion and the Quest for the Historical Jesus"; Foster, "Memory, Orality, and the Fourth Gospel: Three Dead-Ends in Historical Jesus Research"; Porter et al., "Memory, Orality, and the Fourth Gospel: A Response to Paul Foster with Further Comments for Future Discussion"; reviews of Allison, *Constructing Jesus*, 12, 3 (2014); Allison, "Memory, Methodology, and the Historical Jesus: A Response to Richard Bauckham"; Bauckham, "The General and the Particular in Memory: A Critique of Dale Allison's Approach to the Historical Jesus"; Kirk, "Ehrman, Bauckham and Bird on Memory and the Jesus Tradition"; Goodacre, "Q, Memory and Matthew: A Response to Alan Kirk"; Le Donne, "The Problem of Selectivity in Memory Research: A Response to Zeba Crook"; Gregory, "Memory as Method: Some Observations on Two Recent Accounts"; Bauckham, "The Psychology of Memory and the Study of the Gospels"; Bryskog, "Memory and Narrative Time: Towards a Hermeneutics of Memory"; Le Donne, "Mnemonic Interplay: A Response to Bryskog, Bauckham, Zimmerman, and Schr`ter"; Schr`ter, "Memory, Theories of History, and the Reception of Jesus"; Zimmerman, "Memory and Jesus' Parables: J. P. Meier's Explosion and the Restoration of the 'Bedrock' of Jesus' Speech."
4. Allison, *Constructing Jesus*. But he had a precursor using memory studies. See Rodríguez, "Jesus as His Friends Remembered Him," 226.
5. Allison, *Constructing Jesus*, 9.
6. Allison, *Constructing Jesus*, 14.
7. This is opposed to the traditional "multiple attestation" that finds a particular tradition authentic if it occurs in more than one source. Allison, *Constructing Jesus*, 20.
8. Allison, *Constructing Jesus*, 304.
9. Allison, *Constructing Jesus*, 459.
10. Rodgíguez, "Jesus as His Friends Remembered Him," 238–40, wonders how the interpreter is to identify these themes if we are to give greater weight to the themes that emerge from the Gospels and not the details. He concludes "that the logic of recurrent

attestation is not so precise that it can be neatly quantified" and so could result in an "unbridled historical intuition (or 'commonsense')." He complains that whereas Allison identifies five "attested themes"—(1) Jesus as exorcist; (2) the apocalyptic nature of Jesus's eschatology; (3) Jesus's use of biblical traditions; (4) Jesus's understanding himself as the center of God's future activity; (5) Jesus's acceptance of his death.—he only analyzes in detail two of them (the second and fourth). He also does not deal with a number of other themes (e.g., parables, conflicts, Gentiles, the Temple, open commensality, the marginalized, and Jesus's own experience of God), which could have strengthened his idea of using "recurrent attestation" as a way of constructing his image of the Jesus of history.

11. Allison, *Constructing Jesus*, 20, himself admits that "recurrent attestation" is not sufficient in itself.

12. Rodríguez, "Jesus as His Friends Remembered Him," 243.

13. Rodríguez, "Jesus as His Friends Remembered Him," 243.

14. Rodríguez, "Jesus as His Friends Remembered Him," 244.

15. Foster, "Memory, Orality, and the Fourth Gospel," 195, critiques the application of memory studies to affirm the historicity of the materials in the Gospels because they rely on a circular argument that affirms that "recollective memory of eyewitnesses can be read out of the Gospel accounts and then see . . . such reliable eyewitness testimony as validating the Gospel accounts." He affirms (201) Allison's more nuanced understanding of the role of memory, who agrees with Sanders (*Jesus and Judaism*) that few traditions are verifiable and that one has to proceed by abduction, that is, to find a Jesus who makes the most sense of available facts and what we know of Judaism and Christianity. So memory, whether individual or corporate, does not guarantee reliability. Barber, "Did Jesus Anticipate," 198–9, also affirms Allison's approach, which relies on the gist and the "broad impressions" of the materials in the Gospels and his idea of "recurrent attestation." So even "manufactured stories" can be helpful in preserving the identity of Jesus.

16. For these points see Rodríguez, "Jesus as His Friends Remembered Him," 236–7. In n 63 he complains that Kelber, *The Oral and Written Gospel*, has not adequately explained how, if Mark had subverted the pre-Marcan traditions included in his Gospel, his audience "with conflicting, pre-established images of Jesus accepted Mark's narrative and its representations of Jesus." The answer is that each member of the Marcan community had a choice to accept or reject his Gospel and that their survival as a community of faith depended on that acceptance. Furthermore, before Mark they had no Gospel, no sense of how all of their traditions about Jesus related to one another. So Mark's Gospel made a compelling and persuasive impact. It literally became their authoritative Scripture. In my doctoral dissertation, *Giving the Vineyard to Others: A Form and Redactional Analysis of Mark 11 and 12*, I have shown how correct Kelber's thesis is: Mark did alter the traditions that appear in these chapters to help his community meet the traumatic and faith-challenging events connected with the destruction of the Temple and Jerusalem in AD 70, which also contributed to their acceptance of his Gospel.

17. On this perspective see Sanders, *Jesus and Judaism*.

18. I suspect that the three references to David in Mark (2:25–26, 11:10, and 12:35–37) come from his hand. Another example would be the woes against the Pharisees and lawyers (Matt 23:1–36, Luke 11:37–54). The core of this discourse derives originally from Q but has been expanded by Matthew. His expansions relate more to his time in the 80s and the controversy of his community with rabbinic Judaism. For a succinct description of the tradition history of these "woes" see Fuller, "Matthew," *Harper's Bible Commentary*, 975–6.

19. For instance, Matthew loves to double characters in many a tradition. He does this to stress that a true witness is established by two. Compare Mark 10:46-52 and Matt 20:29-34.

20. An example would be the autobiographical pronouncement story of the cleansing of the Temple (Mark 11:15-18). Mark has added vs 17b, "But you have made it a den of bandits," which changes the meaning of the cleansing from a renewal of the institution to declaring its ultimate destruction. See the exposition in chapter 2. Mark, in this way, has updated the pericope to reflect Jesus's later change in his attitude toward the Temple.

21. Brown, *Birth*, 34-5, who does not include this twelfth commonality.

22. McKnight, "Calling Jesus *Mamzer*," thinks otherwise. He cites Mark 6:3, where Jesus is called "son of Mary," which he finds to be "scurrilous" (77). See below for the disproof of this interpretation. He next refers to John 8:41, but one can only come up with this interpretation by reading illegitimacy into the text. The second-century accusations of illegitimacy are all secondary interpretations. Jesus was known to be and called the "son of Joseph" (Luke 4:22, John 1:45, 6:42). Jesus birth was "irregular," but Joseph, by marrying Jesus's mother, removed any stigma that may have been attached to her or to her son. His circumcision would have solidified his status as "an Israelite, descendant of Abraham" (Rom 11:1). McKnight honestly admits, "Jesus *may* [my emphasis] have been labeled by his contemporaries as a mamzer" (79). However, there is no evidence in the Gospels that Jesus was ever labeled as such. (Had he been so labeled the evangelists would doubtless have included it along with all the other accusations impugning Jesus's character that appear in the Gospels.) He also demonstrates that there was no clear and precise definition of *mamzer* until the Rabbis (86-91). He seeks a definition from the rabbinic sources and comes up with nine of them (89-97). He then acknowledges that if Joseph adopted Jesus, then Jesus grew up with absolutely "no stain against his classification" (97). He further concludes, quoting S. M. Passamaneck, "Some Medieval Problems in *Mamzeruth*," 124, "Clearly the Talmud did not exclude the *mamzer* from participating in many areas of Jewish life, and it is safe to assume that theoretically at least the *mamzer* led a normal life except for his limited marriage opportunities" (99). He finds Jesus's purported "antagonism" toward Temple authorities and his "cleansing of the Temple" as supporting Jesus's status as a *mamzer*. It is clear that Jesus opposed them on theological grounds because they denied the resurrection of the dead and rejected John's baptism. His "Temple cleansing" was a proleptic eschatological act based on Zech 14. So his antagonism had nothing to do with his social status. He also relates Jesus's concern for the marginalized to this status and his own experience of exclusion. This construal does not take into consideration the macro-social reality of Israel's position in the Graeco-Roman world: it was marginalized, despised, and disrespected (see Roemer, *World of Jesus*, 374-89). It was Jesus's mission to unify Israel under her compassionate Father-God and ultimately to include the whole Gentile world. However, I have to admit his identification with the marginalized is the strongest argument in favor of such a status.

23. There are possible accusations of illegitimacy early on in anti-Christian polemic. One of the earliest can be detected in John 8:39-41, "They answered him, 'Abraham is our father.' Jesus said to them, 'If you were Abraham's children, you would do what Abraham did, but now you seek to kill me, a man who has told you the truth which I heard from God; this is not what Abraham did. You do what your father did.' They said to him, 'We were not born of fornication; we have one Father, even God.'" Are Jesus's interlocutors saying, "We were not born illegitimate, but you were"? (There is an echo of the same accusation in 6:19.) McGrath, "Was Jesus Illegitimate," 91, asserts that scholars are reading illegitimacy into this text rather than actually finding it there.

In the second-century *Acts of Pilate*, 2, the accusation is explicit: "The elders of the Jews answered and said to Jesus, 'What should we say? First, that you were born of fornication.'" Also from the second century is the work of Celsus known from Origen's *Contra Celsus*, which accused Jesus of fabricating the story of the virgin birth while in reality his mother had been convicted of adultery with a Roman soldier by the name of Pantera. McGrath, "Was Jesus Illegitimate," 91, however, finds there are no precedents for an individual who is born out of wedlock to be referred to as being the son of a suspected father. Tertullian in the late second century mentions the charges against him by Jews that he was the son of a prostitute. The Talmuds also assert that a Pantera was the father of Jesus. A gravestone and statue were found of a Roman soldier named Pantera in Bingerbreck, Germany, in 1859. The inscription reads, "Tiberias Julius Abdes Pantera of Sidon, aged 62 a soldier of 40 years service of the 1st cohort of archers, lies here." He had died in the middle of the first century and came to Germany from Sidon. It is known that this particular cohort had been moved to Dalmatia in AD 6 and subsequently redeployed to Germany in AD 9. "Abdes" is an Aramaic name meaning "servant" (i.e., "servant of god"). For further details and pictures of the tomb and inscription see Tabor, *Jesus Dynasty*, 64–72. Tabor claims the name "Pantera" has been verified as extant in the Holy Land, having been discovered in a tomb on the Nablus road. He also speculates about the abrupt, unexplained, and unmotivated visit of Jesus to Tyre and Sidon in Mark 7:24 and 31 and the generally positive attitude toward Roman military personnel in the Gospel of Mark. But see Zeichmann, "Jesus 'ben Pantera.'" A careful investigation of the military involvement of the soldier Pantera and of the name itself refutes Tabor's claims and speculations. He concludes that the possibility that the man buried in the tomb was Jesus's father is remote: "the evidence adduced from the inscription means that the possibility that Pantera fathered Jesus, while remote, cannot be dismissed entirely; it is, of course, entirely conceivable that an entirely different soldier named Pantera was Jesus' biological father. However, many claims that have animated arguments favouring and opposing these possibilities have been untenable from military-historical and epigraphic perspectives" (154). The Mishnah in Yebamoth 4,13 reports that "Rabbi Simeon ben Azzai said: 'I found a family register in Jerusalem and in it was written "Such-a-one is a bastard through [a transgression of the law of] thy neighbor's wife," confirming the words of Rabbi Joshua.'" (The reference is to Lev 18:20.) The "such-a-one" is thought to originally have read "Jesus" but was replaced with a more generalized subject for fear of Christian reprisals. Some have argued that the designation of Jesus as "the *tektōn*, the son of Mary," in Mark 6:3 suggests his illegitimacy, which argument Brown, *Birth*, 537–42, lays to rest. (See also McGrath, "Was Jesus Illegitimate," 88–90). He concludes with regard to the whole question of a first-century Jewish charge of illegitimacy, "we simply do not know whether the Jewish charge of illegitimacy, which appears clearly in the second century, had a source independent of the infancy narrative tradition" (542).

24. McGrath, "Was Jesus Illegitimate," 83. He cites, e.g., Wis 3:16–19, "But children of adulterers . . . [e]ven if they live long they will be held of no account and finally their old age will be without honor." In the following I am relying on and surveying McGrath's analysis.

25. McGrath, "Was Jesus Illegitimate," 84.

26. McGrath, "Was Jesus Illegitimate," 97–8. He refers to other investigators who describe the social situation in which rivals to one's own power are denigrated because when the rival's power is increased, they are a social threat (n 61).

27. McGrath, "Was Jesus Illegitimate," 95.

28. McGrath, "Was Jesus Illegitimate," 96, observes that Justin Martyr was the first to try and reconcile virgin birth and Jesus's Davidic descent through Mary rather than

Joseph. In its historical context it would be impossible to be the son of an unknown father and assert Davidic descent through the mother. He does not accept that as a provable historical fact for "history abounds with examples of families that believed or claimed they had noble roots" (97). He finds that his Davidic descent, however, is at odds with the virginal conception witnessed by Matthew and Luke, which he discerns to be a later development than the son-of-David association.

29. McGrath, "Was Jesus Illegitimate," 100.
30. Matt 12:23, 15:22, 20:30, 21:9.
31. Paul's Galatian epistle was written in AD 55 or even earlier.
32. Levenson, *Death and Resurrection*, 100.
33. Bauckham, *Jesus and the God of Israel*, 199. In his chapter 6, "Paul's Christology of Divine Identity," he lists fifty-six Old Testament passages that Paul interprets Christologically as referring the divine name YHWH to Jesus (186–90).
34. In what follows I am surveying the arguments of McGrath, "Obedient Unto Death," 223–40.
35. Cf., also Rom 8:15–26, where Paul writes about the Spirit assisting prayer and referring to God as "Abba." McGrath, "Obedient Unto Death," 225–6.
36. McGrath, "Obedient Unto Death," 228.
37. Levenson, *Death and Resurrection*, 132, quoting GenRab 56,3. The rabbinic commentators, he notes, stress that Abraham and Isaac walk together to the place of sacrifice so that both are undivided in their obedience to God. So Jesus's death is also voluntary.
38. See Roemer, *Who in the World Was Jesus*, 74.
39. See Roemer, *Who in the World Was Jesus*, 73–4.
40. The narrative also assumes that in recalling this struggle of Jesus in the Garden of Gethsemane Mark's community would readily understand why God had chosen to sacrifice his son and demand that he undergo the passion. God's will is not capricious and arbitrary. His will that Jesus, his servant, suffer has a goal and objective. Rev 5:8–14 presents a parallel image: the exalted Christ as a Lamb is included with God in the worship of the whole of creation.
41. See below on the discussion of the "beloved son," which the voice at his baptism names him.
42. Mombray, "Why Did Jesus Surrender to the Cross?," affirms that Jesus freely chose to die but then endeavors to show he made that decision solely to save his disciples from a similar fate. He bases his thesis on the Roman practice of frequently only crucifying the leader of a revolt but not the followers, referencing the descriptions in Josephus, *Ant.* 17, 298, *War* 2, 75–78, and Tacitus 3, 74. So he understands the phrase λύτρον ἀντί πολλῶν (*lytron anti pollōn*, "as a ransom for many") of Mark 10:45 on the basis of such passages as Exod 21:28–33 as meaning "in place of" and saving someone from death by the payment of a penalty (250). So "ransom" is saving from death not sin. He finds the later interpretation of Jesus's death as saving from sin a post-Easter apostolic formulation as in 1 Cor 15:3. He restricts the meaning of πολλῶν to the disciples with whom Jesus is interacting in Mark 10:32–45. He further supports his contention with Caiaphas's judgment that one should die to save the nation rather than that the whole nation should perish (John 11:50) and with Jesus's action in the garden where he encourages his own arrest and demands that his followers be left alone (John 18:3–9). Finally (260–5), he supports his thesis on the basis of first-century Jewish understanding and the Hebrew Scriptures that God forgives repentant sinners (Deut 30:1–5) so that the cross is not needed to save sinners. Furthermore, he argues that Jesus himself preached repentance in the face of the coming kingdom of God, when God would reign as king on Mount Zion and bring peace, prosperity, and blessing and preside over a

general judgment. So Jesus's preaching of the "good news" (Mark 1:14) conformed to Jewish expectations with its judgment and belief that God forgives repentant sinners. He concludes that Jesus would not have preached repentance if he thought God would not meet it with forgiveness. Jesus's surrender to the cross for him, however, because it saved the lives of his disciples became the means whereby they could continue to call people to repentance for the forgiveness of sins. In all of this he has neglected the portrayal of Jesus as the "beloved son" (see below); that Jesus instituted a new covenant (Mark 14:22–25 and parallels) in which he became the sacrificial lamb by which the world is saved (Jesus establishing a new covenant by means of his sacrificial death and as the new Passover lamb is taken up by the apostolic witness proclaiming Jesus's cross as the means of salvation); that his parables of the wicked tenants (Mark 12:1–11), the great feast (Matt 22:1–10), the prodigal son (Luke 15:11–32), and the good Samaritan (Luke 10:30–37) limn Jesus's suffering as salvific, not to mention the Jewish sacrificial system that was understood to propitiate God for the sins of his people. To make the word "many" refer only to the disciples seems strained. Besides "many" is a Semiticism for "all." The saying parallels Isa 53:11–12, where the suffering servant "bears iniquities." In Mark 10:41–45 servanthood is also combined with Jesus's life given "for many." See the discussion in Taylor, *The Gospel According to Mark*, 443–6.

43. The usual posture for prayer was standing. See Roemer, *Who in the World was Jesus*, 323–30, and the parable of the Pharisee and tax collector. In regard to all of these intertextual resonances, McGrath, "Obedient Unto Death," 232, pointedly observes,

> Recent historiographical work, however, has consistently reminded us that we cannot hope to find a historical Jesus disconnected from notions of messiahship, a meaningful death, and theology, nor to completely disentangle Jesus' own views and interpretations from others that were subsequently overlaid onto the memory of him. In light of such work, the appropriate task of the historian is to note where new details are introduced over the course of time, to trace trajectories backwards, and to ask whether any of those trajectories may in fact connect us with the historical figure of Jesus, rather than representing a departure from him.

44. Jesus had used the "cup" metaphor previously when John and James asked to be seated at his left and right "in his glory" (Mark 10:38–39). The two pericopae mutually authenticate one another. "Cup" is a familiar symbol of a bitter fate (Pss 11:6, 75:8, Isa 51:17–22, Jer 25:15–28, Ezek 23:31–33) as well as one of weal (Pss 16:5, 23:5, 116:13).

45. McGrath, "Obedient Unto Death," 234.

46. See Roemer, *World of Jesus*, 418–27.

47. Mark 8:31, 9:31, 10:33, and parallels but Mark 10:38–39 above all!

48. McGrath, "Obedient Unto Death," 238. Although this commentator asserts that the historian cannot allow the importation of the "supernatural" into history and that miracles are "inherently unlikely" (237). However, he surely is correct that miracles "require a higher standard of evidence than is expected in the case of mundane and natural occurrences." He allows that Jesus "understood himself to be destined to suffer before becoming king, and that his disciples had trouble grasping this at the time." As will become clear in this study, Jesus came into conflict with his society, and was not successful in arousing the whole of his countrymen and nation to repentance in light of the coming kingdom and its ethics. Any observer of the day with even minimal insight could have easily predicted the outcome in the face of the rejection and highly charged accusations that were leveled against Jesus. See also Barber, "Did Jesus Anticipate," 200–202, who lists twenty-three passages that indicate Jesus knew of his fate and accepted it; six passages that depict Jesus knew of his fate; and eleven passage in which

Jesus was remembered as a willing victim.

49. When the Greeks and Romans talked about this or that god being the father of some eminent person, it did not mean that the person did not have an earthly father. C. S. Lewis, however, does find a comparability between it and the human being: how can the human being, a conglomeration of biochemistry, instincts, and sensory perception, "become the medium of rational thought and moral will which understand necessary relations and acknowledge modes of behavior as universally binding" Lewis, *Miracles*, 114-5. He finds this descent and ascent written all over the world: in reproduction, the death-like process of control and re-ascent to fully formed character, death and rebirth in nature (116).

50. Robinson, *Twelve More Studies*, 159.

51. See chapter 3, part 6, in *Who in the World Was Jesus*. About this story of the Syrophoenician woman, Robinson says, "under pressure Jesus comes through to a position he has apparently no intention of adopting at the outset." *Twelve More Studies*, 159.

52. See Hebrews 2:17, "He had to be made like his brethren," and 5:8, "he learned obedience." Cf., again the story of his prayer in the Garden of Gethsemane where he struggles to come to terms with God's will (Mark 14:36).

53. The rock opera *Jesus Christ Superstar* by Lloyd Webber again asks that question, speaking for each generation, "Who are you, what have you sacrificed?" and "Do you think you're what they say you are?"

54. Robinson, *Twelve More Studies*, 161.

55. See Roemer, *Who in the World Was Jesus*, 137-46, 154-7.

56. The verb here is *epiginōskō* (ἐπιγινώσκω), meaning "knowing," not in the sense of facts but in the sense of "recognize, to know a person." Arndt, Gingrich, *Lexicon*, 291a. The German *kennen* ("to know, be acquainted with, a person") is an accurate translation, which is how Luther translates it. Luke makes that even clearer by his "*who* the Son is" and "*who* the Father is" (Luke 10:22). This "knowledge" is grounded in the Old Testament idea of God's prevenient knowledge and covenant love. See Amos 3:2. Robinson, *Twelve More Studies*, 162.

57. But Robinson, *Twelve More Studies*, 163, insists that Matthew 27:11 does not necessarily indicate Jesus's consciousness of preexistence.

58. Robinson, *Twelve More Studies*, 165. In this he is relying on a lecture delivered by T. E. Pollard in 1964. Pollard concludes that Jesus is portrayed in John not as less human than the Jesus of the synoptics but rather as someone who "penetrates with deeper insight into the inner springs of the personality of Jesus." So John complements the synoptics and shows how to interpret them (165-6). See especially below on Jesus as the "beloved son."

59. The phrase "I have come" is often spoken by God or a divine messenger (Exod 3:8, Num 22:32, Dan 9:23, 10:20, 2 Esd 6:30, 7:2).

60. Robinson, *Twelve More Studies*, 166.

61. Robinson, *Twelve More Studies*, 167.

62. Which from a rabbinic perspective could mean being "as good as God." Robinson, *Twelve More Studies*, 168.

63. Robinson, *Twelve More Studies*, 169. The term "ground of being" comes from Paul Tillich and means that God is pure being and that he is the ground of all other being. We are "being" only in a derived sense because our existence is finite. God in this sense is the only one who truly exists, i.e., persists.

64. Robinson, *Twelve More Studies*, 170.

65. Matt 5:16, 45, 48, 6:1, 4, 6, 14, 10:32-33, 11:25-26, 12:50, 15:13, 16:17, 18:10, 14, 19:35, 26:39, 42. Designating God as "Father" is not often done in the Old Testament. In Judaism God was regarded as father of the individual only in postbiblical times, and

"my Father" is hardly ever employed by the Rabbis. It is not used much in Mark or Luke but most frequently in Matthew and John. "All of this clearly indicates that Jesus knew he had a special relationship to 'his Father' which was different from that of all other men." Schweizer, *Good News According to Mark*, 313. And how else would Paul, the Pharisee, have had the chutzpah to use those same words in describing Christian prayer (Rom 8:15) had he not taken them over from Jesus's own lips?

66. Scholarship must be cognizant, however, that the information we have about John is highly selective (by Christian tradents who would have had the tendency to emphasize Jesus's superiority over John) and that there is a limited amount of information about him in the Gospels. These considerations carry with them the implication that it is almost impossible to give a well-rounded picture of John and of his teaching and activities. So what follows in this section is a picture that is available to us on the basis of the limited and partial picture that is presented to us in the Gospels. Allison, "The Continuity between John and Jesus," 6–27, confronts this reality of the sources. He rightly questions whether our records preserve "all the major themes of John's repertoire . . . our Christian sources, even if one imagines them to be reasonably accurate, are not likely in their brief recaps to introduce us to *John in his entirety* [emphasis mine]" (12). So he insists on caution about going beyond the rather meager evidence we have for John and his ministry: "Extrapolating from what our all-too-brief sources fail to say about the Baptist is a risky business" (15).

67. Josephus, *War* 2, 129. Cf., CD 10, 12–3.

68. See Twelftree, "*Jesus the Baptist*," 106–7, who rightly compares this community of John not to a settled one like Qumran but more like Josephus's stay with the hermit Banus described in *Life* 2: he "lived in the desert, and used no other clothing than grew on trees, and had no other food than what grew of its own accord, and bathed himself in cold water frequently, both by night and by day, in order to preserve his chastity."

69. That is, they were a true "sect" as they saw themselves as the true Israel, and all others, outside of their community, were declared to be the lost "sons of darkness."

70. Richardson, *Word Book*, 280a.

71. First-century ritual bath installations or *mikvas* have been found all over the Holy Land. See Roemer, *World of Jesus*, 528.

72. Ninham, *Mark*, 57.

73. There is much discussion over whether Elijah was a forerunner of the Messiah in the Jewish expectation in the time of John and Jesus. Anthony Ferguson, "The Elijah Forerunner Concept as an Authentic Jewish Expectation," 127–45, concludes there is enough circumstantial evidence supporting that the idea did originate among the Jews.

74. It is difficult to understand why John would accuse his fellow Jews of thinking that mere descent from Abraham would constitute a true Israelite. Judaism of the time coordinated being of Abrahamic descent and obedience to Torah, however one understood it. See Sanders, *Judaism*, 262–78. It could be that he understood and included in the claim of Abrahamic descent Torah obedience and thought that both were insufficient without repentance and baptism and producing the fruits of a new life. Such an understanding of John's demand could point to his Essene background, which insisted that the Jews must become a member of their "new covenant" to be included in the "sons of light" and therefore saved. Apparently, John did not believe then that all Israelites would be included in the world to come.

75. See Sir 48:10, which refers to the return of Elijah who will restore the "tribes of Jacob." Targum Pseudo-Jonathan 40:10 says that Elijah will be "sent to the exiles" at the end of days. Even more striking is the Targum on Deuteronomy 30:4, which announces that Elijah will begin the work of gathering and the Messiah will complete it. Mark 9:11–12 evidently refers to a tradition of Elijah coming first. Ferda, "John the

Baptist," 172-3.

76. Although in this passage it is difficult to separate the messenger from the "lord" himself. Redditt, *New Century Bible Commentary*, 176.

77. For the full description of that crisis see Roemer, *World of Jesus*, particularly 228-63. For the various renewal movements see 391-442.

78. See the scriptural commentaries of Qumran in Vermes, *Complete Dead Sea Scrolls*, 429-504. The so-called *pesher* exegesis dominates these commentaries, meaning they apply the prophetic texts to the present circumstances of the community.

79. See Roemer, *World of Jesus*, 407-31.

80. See Isa 11:12, Mic 2:12-13, 4:6-8, Jer 23:3-8, 31:8-9, Ezek 11:17-20, 20:27-44, 28:25, Zeph 3:11-20.

81. Which was what the prophetic movements of the first century were enacting. See Roemer, *World of Jesus*, 407-17. For further references including postexilic literature see Ferda, "John the Baptist," 159-60.

82. See Mark 1:7-8, 6:16, Luke 3:3-14, 7:31-33, Matt 3:7-12, 11:10-18.

83. Ferda, "John the Baptist," 15-88. Ferda's analysis of John's understanding of his ministry in light of Isa 40 makes his use of it fairly certain, 174-6.

84. "Gathering" the scattered of Israel is a theme in 2 Isaiah: 40:11, 43:5, 49:18, 54:57, 56:8. The theme appears also in Mic 2:12-13, Jer 23:3, 31:8-9, Ezek 11:17, 27:33-44, 28:25.

85. The complexity of the issue is described by Ferda, "John the Baptist," 163-4.

86. The hope continues to echo through the later apocryphal scriptures: Bar 2:3-35, 2 Macc 1:25-28, Tob 13:5. Ferda, "John the Baptist," 159, n 15, cites Sanders, *Jesus and Judaism*, 95, who claims that the restoration theme is universal in the literature of the second Temple period.

87. Ferda, "John the Baptist," 164-5.

88. Ferda, "John the Baptist," 170.

89. See the previous page.

90. Ferda, "John the Baptist," 173, n 47.

91. The historicity of this event is firm perhaps primarily because of the embarrassment it enjoined, which I delineate in the following paragraph. Meier, *Marginal Jew*, 101, says the event may be questioned historically due to a reading back into the life of Jesus of Christian baptism. But in all of the occurrences of being baptized in the New Testament, there are none that connect it with the descent of the Spirit! Of course, he admits that the criterion of embarrassment ultimately triumphs.

92. I have also dealt briefly with the birth narratives in Roemer, *World of Jesus*, 168. See especially the notes to these paragraphs there.

93. E.g., in Matt 2:15 Jesus is compared with Moses when he applies the words of Hos 11:1 "out of Egypt I have called my son"; 2:20 quotes Exod 4:19; and as Israel, led by Joshua, went through the waters of the Jordan into the promised land, so Jesus now goes through the waters of baptism to lead his people into the new age of the kingdom (In 1 Cor 10:2 Paul makes the analogy with Israel going through the waters of the Red Sea as being "baptized into Moses").

94. Luke 3:21-22, my translation.

95. Fenton, *Matthew*, 59.

96. See Roemer, *Who in the World was Jesus*, 134-7, 198-201.

97. So the whole of the Old Testament resonates behind the baptismal text: Torah, Prophets, and the later (apocalyptic) writings.

98. Meier, *Marginal Jew*, 106-7, outlines the resonances with Old Testament texts: (1) the coming of the Spirit fulfills John's prediction; (2) the proclamation of sonship reiterates the words of Ps 2:7 addressed by the Lord to the messianic king; (3) the

"beloved" may, he says, allude to Isaac the "beloved one" of his father Abraham; (4) the phrase "with whom I am well pleased" suggests Isa 42:1's "the servant" upon whom God has placed his spirit; (5) the setting on the bank of a river, the opening of heaven, and the calling of a prophet recall Ezek 1:1 and the prophet's call; (6) the tearing open of the heavens carries "overtones" of Isa 64:1, whose context "ties in well with themes" of Jesus's baptism: redemption by passing though water, the Exodus, Moses the servant of the Lord, and God giving of his spirit to his people. He concludes that all of "this rich synthesis of OT prophecy and fulfillment reinforces a not-so-subliminal message: the person of whom all these things are true is obviously superior to John the Baptist," which means "we have a Christian composition interpreting the significance of Jesus' baptism." It's really the other way around. It is clear that Jesus thought of himself as the "beloved son," and the "cup" that he had to drink was a result of that rank and station (Mark 10:38, 14:36). He didn't make it up any more than the early church did. It was part of his baptismal experience.

99. The LXX translates "your only son" (Heb., YACHID) with ἀγαπητός (agapētos), "beloved." Notice that God does not demand the offering of the ram caught in the thicket as a substitute for Isaac, and when the angel commands Abraham to desist, it is not because the sacrifice of the child is offensive or that the ram is preferable. The reason is because Abraham's willingness to sacrifice his son verifies his fear and love of God (Gen 22:16-18). And Abraham is blessed with descendants only because he was willing to sacrifice his son. Levenson, *Death and Resurrection*, 13.

100. Levenson, *Death and Resurrection*, 59, whose central thesis is that the basic element of both Israel and the church lies in stories that are the narrative equivalent of these ritual substitutions. These narratives concern the beloved son who undergoes a symbolic death corresponding to the demand that the firstborn be sacrificed to God but who returns alive.

101. The birth order is not absolute. In the Jacob and Esau story God himself disregards the birth order and prefers the trickster over the firstborn. But Jacob experiences a symbolic death by his exile from the land of promise, his humiliation before his exaltation. Joseph experiences the same pattern of exile (symbolic death) and exaltation. God's favor for the late-born is portrayed not only in Abel, Isaac, Jacob, and Joseph but also in Levi, Judah, Ephraim, Moses, Eleazar, Ithamar, Gideon, David, and Solomon. Both the priestly and the royal dynasties trace their lineage through the late-born, but the blood lines remain intact along with God's freedom, which is proof of his grace and generosity. Levenson, *Death and Resurrection*, 70.

102. It is Abraham's obedience that is stressed, but that obedience is based on his faith in God (cf., Gen 15:6) contra Levenson, *Death and Resurrection*, 126. Job is like him in that his faith is tested. Both men pass the test, unlike Adam and Eve in the garden. If faith cannot withstand a test, it is no faith. That does not mean that Abraham thought somehow God would preserve Isaac's life. That would minimize the horror of God's command to sacrifice him, the mettle of his faith, and consequent obedience.

103. The word Paul uses here is φείδομαι (*pheidomai*, "spare"), the same word used in the LXX as a translation of the Hebrew word for "withhold" in Gen 22:12, 16 (*CHASAKH*). Levenson, *Death and Resurrection*, 25, refers to Turtullian's *Apology* where he discusses the god Saturn, who himself sacrificed his own son so expected the same of his devotees. In 2 Kgs 3:26-27 the Moabite King Mesha, because the battle with Israel was going poorly, sacrificed his firstborn after arraying his son in royal apparel, which implies that the son replaced the king himself. So the sacrifice ransoms the people and the king, the battle turns his way, and Israel is routed. This pattern of the sacrifice of the firstborn and beloved sons repeats itself over and over in the Old Testament history. Jacob, in effect, gives up his beloved son (Deut 33:12) Benjamin to save the family (Gen

43:11–13); when David's first son by Bathsheba dies, it brings relief from the threatened disaster occasioned by David's adultery. Solomon becomes the replacement of his dead brother. So David in effect gives his son as a sin offering. Levenson, *Death and Resurrection*, 29–30.

104. Exod 13:1–2, 11–16 outlines the law of the firstborn. The firstborn, even of their own sons, belongs to God, but in vs 13 he can be redeemed. However, in Exod 22:29 that demand for the firstborn son is absolute. It is clear from Jer 7:31 and Ezek 20:25–26 that Israel obeyed this command and practiced child sacrifice. (However, there is no textual or archaeological evidence for its widespread practice, which points to the fact that laws of the ANE were not prescriptive but rather expressed merely legal thinking. The law of the Jubilee is another example.) But it was practiced, and it was only late in Israel's history when it was considered idolatrous. Ezekiel actually affirms that it was God's will and that he commanded it, evil as it was, to accomplish good. Its aim was Israel's recognition and exaltation of God. Certainly, a difficult notion (but see also 1 Kgs 22:19–24). Mic 6:6–8 also witnesses to its practice but without censure. The prophet is apparently arguing from the lesser to the greater. Levenson, *Death and Resurrection*, 5–10. A valuable animal like a donkey could be redeemed from offering it in sacrifice by the sacrifice of a lamb (since donkeys were not an acceptable sacrificial animal). Even when God demanded of Abraham that he sacrifice Isaac, it was not merely an indiscriminate, tyrannical act of spite. Its goal was apparently to test the faith of Abraham. In Hebrew this story is called the "Aqedah," the "binding [of Isaac]."

105. ἔδωκεν (edōken, "he gave") is sacrificial language (cf., Ezek 20:31). Levenson, *Death and Resurrection*, 32–7, traces the law of the firstborn, Exod 13:2, back to a Canaanite myth of the god El. El is the father of gods, "creator of creatures," and "father of man." He is full of boundless wisdom and engages in prodigious sexual activities. In a time of crisis El hands over his son Baal for enslavement or death. El rejoices when his enslaved son is freed or his dead son is resurrected. All these elements of the myth find a place in the Joseph story: Jacob sends Joseph to his brothers knowing their enmity toward him. They plot his death, but he ends up in slavery. Jacob mourns his lost son but rejoices at their ultimate reunion. Notably there is no reference to a sacrifice. In Israel there was a continuity between El and YHWH (see Num 23:8). There is a polemic against Baal in Israel but not El. So in both the Canaanite and Israelite societies child sacrifice was practiced. But it was not an obligation. An animal could be substituted, but that did not replace child sacrifice. Levenson concludes that only in reference to the El myth can the origin and character of child sacrifice in Israel and in the church be understood. However, starkly different from the myth is the fact that the biblical narratives take place in history, and the troubled relationships between fathers and sons are unrelated to the myth. And of course, YHWH is utterly sovereign and has no wife or children. The law of the firstborn lived on in Israel, and circumcision, the paschal lamb, Levitical service, monetary ransom, and the Nazarite vow may all have been a sublimation of child sacrifice. Levenson, *Death and Resurrection*, 43–52.

106. But Jesus's resurrection is of a wholly different order although not completely unique. In 2 Kgs 4:8–37 Elijah raises the firstborn son of the widow from the dead. The story is told in the old pattern of the death of the beloved son (cf., 2 Kgs 13:20–21). Furthermore, resurrection was a central concept in first-century Judaism. Levenson, *Death and Resurrection*, 223–4.

107. Levenson, *Death and Resurrection*, 225. Paul implies that God's image is no longer mediated through Adam (Gen 1:26) but through Jesus, that is, not by natural procreation but by the supernatural regeneration mediated by Jesus's death and resurrection (221). For Paul then, because those who are in Christ are conformed to the "image of God's son," they receive more than all the blessings pronounced by the angel

in Gen 22:17–18: glorification and eternal life (Rom 8:20, 29). Levenson, *Death and Resurrection*, 174–99, also demonstrates that the story of the Aqedah had enormous importance for the Judaism of Jesus's time: the promise of descendants comes as a consequence of this near sacrifice, and the existence of Abraham's progeny depends on his obedience. So the Aqedah becomes a "foundational act:" Israel exists because of the patriarch's obedient faithfulness to God. Second Chron 3:1 identifies Mt. Moriah with the Temple mount, where countless sacrifices were offered. So because Abraham was met with divine favor there, so also Israel's sacrifices in the same place would be acceptable to God and "merit his good favor toward them." In the Chronicles passage the Rabbis found the idea that the Aqedah was the origin of the daily sacrifice of a lamb (for the "Tamid," see Roemer, *World of Jesus*, 549).

108. See Dunn, *Jesus and the Spirit*, 11–92, who presents an extensive discussion of Jesus's spiritual experience. He maintains that this experience was foundational to his understanding of himself and the ministry he ultimately pursues and is reflected in his understanding of God as his Abba, his robust consciousness of authority, his fulfillment of Isaianic prophecies, and his healings and exorcisms. While Dunn focuses on Jesus's consciousness of sonship through his charismatic activity, I understand that sense of sonship as emanating from his baptismal experience, and from that experience flowed the activity in his ministry. In other words, he is like the prophets of old whose prophetic activity derived from their call experiences.

109. The coordination between these texts is remarkable. Jesus clearly understood his status as "beloved son" was to be in terms of the offering of Isaac and the requirement that God had called him in his baptism to the sacrifice of his life. The parallelism between fire and baptism in the Lucan text coordinates Jesus's sacrifice of his life with the fire of eschatological judgment, God's wrath, and "the day of the Lord" (Isa 66:24, Mal 3:19). See Allison, "Continuity," 23. The implication is that Jesus's death would usher in the kingdom of God. In Mark 9:49 Jesus says, "for everyone will be salted with fire," an apparent reference to Lev 2:13, which commands that every sacrifice be salted (which is added to the text by a whole plethora of manuscripts and included in the KJV and Luther's translation; see Metzger, *Textual Commentary*, 102–3). To be "salted" suggests a sacrifice. Paul writes that in the judgment everyone's works will be tested by fire (1 Cor 3:13–15). Perhaps Jesus meant something like that too.

110. Jesus's consciousness of his role as beloved son is also expressed in his passion predictions (Mark 8:31, 9:31, 10:33–34) and underscores the historicity of those predictions. See Licona, "Did Jesus Predict," who affirms their historicity on the basis that they are early and multiply attested and fulfill the criteria of embarrassment and dissimilarity. One difficulty that seems to contradict their historicity is the disciples' inability to grasp and anticipate Jesus's resurrection. He meets this objection with the observation that the disciples held exalted expectations of the Messiah. A dying and rising Messiah did not fit their hopes and dreams. He also suggests that the disciples were perhaps thinking of the general resurrection, which would have included them. He further proposes that the predictions may have been vague and enigmatic in their original form and only later recalled and clarified in light of his actual resurrection. See also Zolondek, "The Authenticity of the First Passion Prediction," who asserts that "the most economical and comprehensive explanation as to the origin" of the passage is that Jesus foretold his death.

111. Joseph, "'I Shall Be Reckoned with the Gods,'" 222–5, would make Jesus a "mystic." He seemed to have implemented an ascetic program of instruction: he chose homelessness, celibacy, and a new kinship family within God's kingdom. Galilee, he points out, was also home to a rich history of charismatic men whose lives were driven by their spiritual experiences (Elijah and Elisha, the Hasidim, "the pious ones,"

of postexilic times, Honi the circle drawer, first century BC, and Hanina ben Dosa, first century AD, who was a healer and exorcist). Of course, "mystic" is not a biblical category; there was no such word in the biblical languages. Nor was this nomenclature used within Judaism. Hebrew and Aramaic use the word *RaZ* or *RaZah*, "secret," which is translated as "mystery" by the LXX in Dan 2. Paul and John in Revelation use the Greek *mysterion* (μυστήριον, "mystery"; e.g., see Eph 1–6, Col 1–2, 4, 2 Thes 2:7, 1 Tim 3:9, 16, Rev 1:20). In Daniel the "secret" is the meaning of Nebuchadnezzar's dream; in Paul "the mystery" is God's working salvation through Jesus and his cross; and in Revelation it is the hidden meaning of the images that appear there. It is the prophets who have experiences of the world of the spirit, e.g., Isaiah (Isa 6:1–9), Micaiah ben Imlah (1 Kgs 22:17–23), Exekiel (Ezek 1:1—3:13). In the case of Isaiah and Ezekiel these are prophetic call experiences. "Mysticism" and "mystic" seem to be particularly inept nouns to employ in a biblical context since they are understood, as Joseph points out, to refer to experiences in which one's own will is held in abeyance while the person is held by a supernatural power. These states are found in Hinduism, Buddhism, and Christianity. The experience has no specific intellectual content of its own and can be combined with all kinds of philosophies and theologies. Joseph notes that mysticism can then be made into a kind of universal religion and a timeless essence, and the various religions become different facets of the one God (227). That all stands in stark contrast to biblical prophets and their prophetic calls, which do not submerge the personality of the prophet, and, of course, their call is filled with specific content and a message for their time and place. Joseph finally arrives at a working definition of mysticism: "beliefs and practices associated with eliciting experiential contact with the divine" (231). However, as Joseph points out, there is an esoteric tradition within later Judaism, Merkavah, Halakot, and the later composition of the Zohar and Kabbalah (231-5). Paul's experience of a heavenly journey (2 Cor 12:2-4) must be understood within this Jewish tradition.

112. An expression of Sanders, *Judaism*, 262–75. The expression means the Jewish conviction that God by his grace elected them as his people, which required their joyful response of obedience to Torah.

113. Joseph, "'I Shall Be Reckoned with the Gods,'" 236. This experience of Jesus is graphically portrayed in Luke 5:1-11. See below, chapter 2. This is in contrast to many popular books that portray Jesus as a mystic. See Joseph's little bibliography in n 117, 237.

114. Joseph, "'I Shall Be Reckoned with the Gods,'" 236. He references McGinn, *The Foundations of Mysticism*, 62-83, who points out that Christian mysticism is not following Jesus's example but following an exegetical practice involved with reading, meditation, and preaching and teaching the biblical text. See also Quarles, "Jesus as Merkabah Mystic," who questions the existence of merkabah mysticism in the time of Jesus and concludes that the words and activity of Jesus differ from the tradents of this "chariot" mysticism.

115. Joseph, "'I Shall Be Reckoned with the Gods,'" 240–1, lists these characteristics to claim Jesus as a "mystic."

116. See Mark 4:11-12, Matt 11:25-27. But the people should be able to discern the nature of the times and the coming impending crisis since they're so good at predicting the weather (Luke 12:54-56). The prophets also spoke of revealing "hidden things" (Isa 48:6, Jer 33:3).

117. Joseph, "'I Shall Be Reckoned with the Gods,'" 239–41, insists that these characteristic of Jesus and his ministry place him in the mystic tradition. This thesis is contradicted by the fact that Jesus stood in the prophetic tradition (so he identifies himself and is often identified in those terms (Mark 6:4, 15, Luke 7:16). His ministry was one

of proclamation. The ancient prophets too stood as critics of the social, cultural, and religious norms of their societies. He understood his baptismal experience as a call to proclaim a message. This is not to deny that his baptismal experience was an experience of the world of the spirit and of the God of Israel, as were the calls of Israel's prophets of old. How else would Jesus interpret himself and his ministry except in Old Testament terminology and models?

118. Pss 60:5, 108:6, Isa 5:1–2, Jer 11:15, 12:7. Throughout the little book of the Song of Solomon, the absolute usage is applied to the man by the woman. He is also designated king and shepherd—i.e., he is the royal messiah who shepherds the people. (Throughout the New Testament the word "beloved" is applied to Christians.)

119. ἀνακεφαλαιώσασθαι (*anakephalaiōsasthai*, Eph 1:10).

120. Levenson, *Death and Resurrection*, 201. See also Kwon, *The Historical Jesus' Death*.

121. In Jub 17 a Job-like scene occurs in heaven as Mastema ("hostility, enmity") comes before God challenging him to test the faithfulness of Abraham. The figure of Mastema is a correlative of the Destroyer in the Passover narrative. So in the thought-world of first-century Judaism, Abraham's obedience becomes a proleptic defeat of the Destroyer and the origin of Passover. The salvation of the nation depended on a father's willingness to surrender his son. Levenson, *Death and Resurrection*, 176–9. Resonating here again is the story of Mesha of Moab (2 Kgs 3:27). Jewish literature identifies Isaac with the Paschal lamb and procures the deliverance of Israel's firstborn sons. The Targum Neofiti Lev 22:27 makes the most explicit identification of Isaac with the sacrificial lamb, the symbol of God's mercy. God will redeem those in affliction. God is implored to redeem Isaac's descendants when they invoke the memory of Abraham's and Isaac's obedience. It was thought that the Aqedah was hidden away in God's presence and that the daily offering of the lamb brought it to mind and established reconciliation, which then became universalized, opening God's grace to both Gentile and Jew. So the Aqedah had ongoing redemptive effects in Judaism. Levenson, *Death and Resurrection*, 183–5.

122. In his epistle to the Galatians Paul says that the blessings of Abraham are now extended to the Gentiles through Jesus and that the Gentiles can inherit descent from Abraham and the promises without the law and the adoption of Judaism.

123. Even the secular historiographer would find no problem with understanding this as a historical report. After all, Jesus would just be reporting a subjective experience, which, for such an interpreter, would have no objective referent.

124 Levenson, *Death and Resurrection*, 188–99, in his fourteenth chapter on the "rewritten Aqedah" presents a plethora of rabbinic and other sources that interpret Isaac as an active participant in his sacrifice and his binding as a sacrificial death, and because his blood was also on the doorposts of the liberated children of Israel, God choose Israel. Some of these sources speak of Isaac's ashes, his resurrection, that the death of the righteous atones for the sins of others, and by whose merit God will resurrect the dead. But Levenson also points out these ideas were not at the center of Jewish theology. The Aqedah had a high rank but shared honor with other stories like Sinai, the golden calf, and Moses's death (199). All of these ideas and concepts lay to hand as early Christians contemplated the meaning of the death of Jesus.

125. Levenson, *Death and Resurrection*, 37.

126. The relationship is, of course, metaphorical. They are not mythological descendants of a god. But it is also not purely figurative either. Kinship language in ancient Israel expresses relationships other than biological. The vocabulary of paternity is common in covenant texts (cf., 2 Kgs 16:7). YHWH is involved in the conceptions of the nation's fathers. Isaac is born not of natural desire but of God's covenant to make Abraham

"the father of a multitude of nations" (Gen 17:3). So the patriarchs are the firstborn of two fathers: filiation, consecration, and chosenness are all one reality and distinguish Israel from the nations (Deut 141–142). Levenson, *Death and Resurrection*, 39–42.

127. Cf., Ezra 6:10. Barber, "Did Jesus Anticipate," 215, n 114. He also refers to a plethora of texts from Qumran and the Pseudepigrapha, specifically 1 Enoch, Jubilees, the Sibylline Oracles, Psalms of Solomon, and the Testament of Moses (214, n 110).

128. Barber, "Did Jesus Anticipate," 216.

129. Barber, "Did Jesus Anticipate," 217–8. Furthermore, he notes that eschatological tribulation occurs in early Christian texts: Gal 4:19, 1 Pet 4:1–6. 12–19, 5:1, Rev 7:13–14, 1 Thess 3:4, Phil 2:17.

130. Barber, "Did Jesus Anticipate," 200–202, has a list of twenty-three references to logia, which indicates that Jesus knew of his fate and accepted it, six depictions indicating the same, and eleven that remembered Jesus as a willing victim. The cry of derelicition (Mark 15:34) and Jesus's prayer in the garden (Mark 14:32–42) may be contra-indicators, but in the case of the cry, the quoted Ps 22 ends with deliverance and the prayer with his acceptance of God's will.

131. Meier, *Marginal Jew*, 107–8. He rightly refers to a study that points out two key concepts that governed Jesus's ministry and activity: God as Father and the work of the Spirit. To assert that Jesus's baptism defined his call and supplied for him an identification of his person and work is not "psychologizing" but perceiving the underling unity between his self-understanding and his activity.

132. Meier, *Marginal Jew*, 109, by using that word denies he is "filling it with all the tired religious rhetoric and emotionalism that often plague the word in popular religion today" (189, n 33). Maybe not, but he is "psychologizing." A better word is "transformation," akin to what happened to Paul on the road to Damascus. Paul was not "converted" from one religion to another (he always thought of himself as an Israelite), from an immoral to a moral person, nor from irreligion to religion. His outlook was "transformed": he understood the God of Israel and his mighty acts in a totally new way. And it was no "decision" (a term freighted with revivalist overtones) but a transformation that came about from above.

133. The word is not to be translated merely as "carpenter." The *tektōn* was a woodworker in general and a builder. That is, the *tektōn* could be a wheelwright, construct ploughs and yokes, be a cabinet maker or carver, and also be involved in the construction of the wood frame for a building. He would also fell the trees himself that he used in his business (Isa 44:13–17). The best wood was that of the sycamore, which when properly treated could even serve as a plowshare. Cedar wood was the most expensive. Ordinary folk made do with the olive and cypress. So the *tektōn*'s shop had to be ready for the demand of all kinds of products: a plough, a chest, a kneading trough, jambs and lintels for doors. The tools were also varied: the axe, hatchet, saw, knives, adz, plane, square, hammer, clamps, nails, and bow-drill. Jesus surely has the *tektōn*'s shop in mind when he talks about specks and logs (Luke 6:41–42). Daniel-Rops, *Daily Life*, 241–3.

134. The close association between the spirit and wisdom is especially highlighted in Wisdom of Solomon 7:22–24:

> for wisdom, the fashioner of all things, taught me. For in her there is a spirit that is intelligent, holy, unique, manifold, subtle, mobile, clear, unpolluted, distinct, invulnerable, loving the good, keen, irresistible, beneficent, humane, steadfast, sure, free from anxiety, all-powerful, overseeing all, and penetrating through all spirits that are intelligent and pure and most subtle. For wisdom is more mobile than any motion; because of her pureness she pervades and penetrates all things.

135. Although early in Israel's history prophecy was a kind of ecstatic power that seized "holy men" (1 Sam 10:6, 19:23-24).

136. Other similarities include that they both conducted their ministry outside and gave their disciples special prayers (Luke 11:1-4). Jeremias, *New Testament Theology*, 48. Allison, "The Continuity between John and Jesus," 6-27, rightly emphasizes the relative paucity of information we have about John. However, even at that, it is possible, on the basis of the information we have, to see continuities and differences.

137. Except for the latter trait Paul also shared these characteristics. Of course, Paul had not known Jesus "in the flesh." However, that Jesus's ministry looked in some respects like John's does not imply that John was his "mentor." We would need to say the kingdom was the mentor of all three. Pace Meier, *Marginal Jew*, 124. Allison, "The Continuity between John and Jesus," 10, questions whether John spoke of the kingdom because the word is never used in the narratives about him, a curious observation since John spoke of the "harvest" (Luke 3:17), which is almost a synonym for the coming kingdom of God. Curious also is Allison's implication that John's proclamation didn't include social reform, which it obviously did (Luke 3:10-14).

138. It is possible that Jesus, in view of the irregularity of his conception, thought that he had to be cleansed from the taint of his mother's (alleged) sin (see Wis 3:16-19).

139. One could say this concern for the poor lay at the heart of Torah and prophetic witness. See, e.g., Exod 22:25, 23:6-11, Lev 19:10, 23:22, 25:25-47, Deut 24:12-15, Isa 3:14-15, 37:14. See also Pss 12:5, 37:14, Prov 13:23, Amos 2:7, 4:1, 5:11, 8:4-6.

140. See the parables of the mustard seed, leaven in a lump, the lost coin, and the lost sheep in particular. Roemer, *Who in the World Was Jesus*, 134-7, 198-201, 239-41, 154-7.

141. Meier, *Marginal Jew*, 110.

142. Jesus is constantly portrayed as teaching in the synagogues (Mark 3:1, 6:2, Luke 4:16).

143. See the parable of the Pharisee and the tax collector (Luke 18:10-14). Roemer, *Who in the World Was Jesus*, 323-30.

144. However, Jesus in his parables goes beyond this communal and collective guilt. It is because he stresses so much the inward and personal in parables such as the prodigal son, the Pharisee and the publican, the rich fool, and the rich man and Lazarus that Jesus also vividly portrays the personal sin. The prodigal confesses he has sinned not only against his father but against heaven (i.e., "God," Luke 15:18, 21); the rich man has personally sinned against Lazarus; the rich fool and the tax collector have sinned against the community. Of course, in each case the perpetrator was breaking the Torah: the prodigal transgressed the command to honor father and mother, and the others did not heed the Torah's command to have concern for the poor. In each case what is lacking is the inner change of heart that is determined by the love that Jesus said should permeate the heart and determine one's behavior toward others. This is very personal, particular, and even subjective.

145. Meier, *Marginal Jew*, 115, declares that the question of Jesus's sinlessness remains unclear. So he cannot determine from the baptismal narrative whether Jesus thought of himself as sinless. Of course, there's nothing in the Jesus tradition that depicts him as guilty of sin or thinking of himself as a sinner.

146 The Mandaeans of Iraq trace their gnostic religion back to John the Baptist. They practice frequent baptisms and stress knowledge as the way of salvation. Some scholars think their origin lies in pre-Christian times in the Holy Land, but there is no evidence of their origin earlier than the second century.

147. But then 4:2 contradicts these two verses, which assert that it was not Jesus himself who was baptizing. The language is found nowhere else in the Gospel and

suggests that the verse was inserted by a later redactor of the Gospel. Meier, *Marginal Jew*, 122–3, and n 73 and n 74, rightly finds embarrassment at work in this "correction."

148. A variety of manuscripts including the first hand of Sinaiticus read "Jews." But as Metzger, *Textual Commentary*, 205, notes, it is much more likely that the singular was changed to a "more customary" plural. Nestle, *Novum Testamentum*, 254, in his apparatus also includes the conjecture of some commentators that the original read "Jesus" instead.

149. That the Fourth Gospel included this historical relationship at all must point to the fact that these circumstances were just too well known in the evangelist's environment to be glossed over or denied. The critics see the hand of a final redactor of the Gospel in the denial that Jesus baptized (4:2) as a way of preserving the theology of the original author of the Gospel, who asserts that the Spirit had not been given during Jesus's earthly ministry (7:37–39) but only after the resurrection (20:22). To have Jesus baptizing and not also at the same time giving the Spirit would have been contradictory, and "the whole overarching process of the promise of the spirit [sic] during the public ministry and its bestowal in the death-resurrection is destroyed." Meier, *Marginal Jew*, 123 and 196, n 75.

150. Most scholars believe Jesus continued to baptize in his ministry, others not. Some hold he stopped baptizing, but there is no agreement on why he did. See Twelftree, "Jesus the Baptist," 104–5, for a taxonomy of views and their authors. Given that Jesus regarded John highly (see below) and there were continuities between them, his continuing to baptize is reasonable particularly in the light of John 4:1 and the practice of the church. See the discussion in Twelftree, "Jesus the Baptist," 118–22, who thinks that Jesus did initially baptize but gave up the practice, although it was not due to any break between Jesus and John.

151. Twelftree, "Jesus the Baptist," 105.

152. Jesus's demand that one "become as a child" to enter the kingdom (Mark 10:15, cf., John 3:3) echoes John's message to start over and go back to the beginning by insisting they not appeal to their Abrahamic descent and Torah obedience (see n 23 aove). Allison, "Continuity," 18.

153. However, these images seem to be common to biblical and Jewish imagery. See Allison, "Continuity," 20–2. But see Allison, "Continuity," 23, who identifies the synonymous parallelism in Luke 12:49–50, its Semitic coloring, and that it hints of Jesus's recoiling from the coming judgment, all of which speak for its authenticity. "Fire," he observes, is linked to God's wrath, eschatological judgment, and the "day of the Lord" (Isa 66:24, Mal 3:19).

154. Twelftree, "Jesus the Baptist," 113, who finds it an authentic account because it "too closely aligns John and Jesus for it to be a creation of John's followers or of Mark (or of other Christians before him)"

155. See Roemer, *World of Jesus*, 391–442.

156. Twelftree, "Jesus the Baptist," 123–4, who, on the basis of Luke 11:20, understands that Jesus saw the present arrival of the kingdom in his miracles and exorcisms.

157. Of course, we have such a restricted view of John because of the paucity of material in the Gospels that is devoted to him. We can hardly write a fulsome account of his persona, ministry, and teaching.

158. Meier, *Marginal Jew*, 127.

159. However, it is possible that John also taught in parables; we just do not have enough information about him to make a judgment in that respect. His metaphorical language points to his use of parable. After all, both he and Jesus lived in a storytelling society. In Jewish culture, narrative was the means of speaking of God's presence and activity in the world.

160. I have suggested one area of development in his thought in chapter 3, part 6, of the previous volume in this study, *Who in the World Was Jesus*. See also Meier, *Marginal Jew*, 125–6.

161. The reaction of his family who "went out to seize him" because he "had lost his mind" (Mark 3:21) at the very least exposes the radicalism of the break in Jesus's life from being a *tektōn* (Mark 6:3) to an itinerant preacher proclaiming that the kingdom was now already "among" the people (Luke 17:21).

162. But Jesus held John in high regard. In Mark 11:29–33 Jesus coordinates John's authority with his own. There is no particular break between him and John. As the discussion here makes clear, Jesus obviously understood John as the forerunner to his own ministry. John's death heightened the "eschatological tension" and was therefore a turning point in his own ministry. Twelftree, "Jesus and Baptist," 117.

163. See Matthew 13:44, 25:21, Luke 6:23, 10:17, 15:7.

164. Paul's baptismal practice may reflect Jesus's own. It apparently was not the center of his ministry either (1 Cor 1:14–17), not to say that it did not have a highly important function in his theology of the cross and his understanding of the Gospel (Rom 6:1–14).

165. Meier, *Marginal Jew*, 166–7. Meier finds this controversy dialogue authentic on the basis of embarrassment (it seems, according to him, to put John and Jesus on the same footing) and multiple attestation (it appears also in John 2:13–22 as in independent tradition).

166. Meier, *Marginal Jew*, 167–70.

167. Marsh, *Saint John*, 270.

168. Bultmann, *Das Evangelium des Johannes*, 300.

169. These two renditions of the same story have one difference. Luke does not have the saying about "taking the kingdom by storm" but places it in another context (Luke 16:16). Matthew is the great compiler (e.g., the Sermon on the Mount), so the saying probably was not part of the story in Q but included by Matthew since it dealt with John. Luke also does not have the reference to John in prison, but he has already referred to that in 3:20.

170. Which I have dealt with in the previous volume in this series. See Roemer, *Who in the World Was Jesus*, 292–4.

171. I.e., a saying of Jesus set within a brief narrative or description of the situation in which it was uttered. See the following chapter.

172. Pace Meier, *Marginal Jew*, 132, and especially 199, n 90, who judges the phrase in this manner. See Daniel 7:13, where one like a "son of Man" comes with the clouds of heaven and is given cosmic dominion.

173. The Palm Sunday entry narrative obviously has the psalm in mind. The acclamation in the entry narrative was a greeting for the one who was to fulfill these expectations and call on God to save by some transcendent action, i.e., to bring in the eschaton and establish his kingdom. That the psalm is intimately related to the entry narrative celebrating Jesus's arrival in Jerusalem (Matt 21:9, Mark 11:9, Luke 19:38, John 12:13) is demonstrated by the verbal resonances between the narrative and psalm: "save now, we implore" (vs 25, Hebrew HOSHI'H NA); "bind the festal procession with branches, up to the horns of the altar!" (vs 25). "Hosanna" occurs in Matthew, Mark, and John, and in each Gospel the crowd hails Jesus with branches cut from the trees. The "coming one" is associated in each Gospel with the royal messiah: "son of David" in Matt 21:9; "the king of Israel" in John 12:13; "the king" in Luke 19:38; and "the coming kingdom of our father David" in Mark 11:10.

174. It was a feast of harvest that included exuberant celebration and carnival indulgence. There were a great number of sacrifices (Num 29), greater than in all the

other feasts, which meant consuming great quantities of meat and drinking wine. Girls danced in the vineyard with the aim of seduction, which hints at many features of the feast having roots in Canaanite culture. It was an extended celebration and went on for seven days. It is not surprising that Gentiles connected it with their feast of Bacchus. Schuerer, *History*, 151.

175. There have been all kinds of psychological interpretations of John's state of mind that are inapposite because the Gospel traditions just were not concerned with such matters. But that doesn't mean we cannot perceive the basis of his apparent disappointment and the question he put to Jesus. Matthew, of course, is not interested in John but Jesus and his works, otherwise he would also have related John's reaction when his disciples returned with the answer they received from Jesus. Fenton, *Matthew*, 175.

176. John's question and Jesus's answer support the historicity of the scenario described by Matthew and Luke. One would expect an invented story to exalt Jesus as the expected eschatological figure, not question it, and to elicit John as the one who found in Jesus what he had expected. An invented story also would have Jesus answer with an explicit claim of some kind of dignified authority. Meier, *Marginal Jew*, 131.

177. These two references might have been added to 1 Isaiah from 2 Isaiah since they sound so much like the latter. However, just as likely, they show how closely connected were these two "Isaiahs."

178. Mark 9:43-49, Matt 5:22, 7:19, 13:50, 18:8-9, 25:41.

179. That Jesus is using the same language as John does not necessarily mean that he derived it from John. The association of the kingdom with a fiery judgment was a common conception. See Roemer, *World of Jesus*, 457-60.

180. Mark 9:49. Allison, "Continuity," 25.

181. E.g., Jubilees 1:29: "[on] the day of the new creation . . . the heaven and earth and all of their creatures shall be renewed according to the whole nature of earth . . . [a]nd all of the lights will be renewed for healing." Jubilees originated in the second century BC.

182. "Winnowing" is a metaphor for devastating judgment (Isa 21:10, 27:12, Jer 15:7, 51:2). Plants are metaphors all over the Old Testament for individuals and nations.

183. See Roemer, *Who in the World Was Jesus*, for the exposition of the parables of the prodigal son (241-7), treasure in a field (148-51), the lost coin (239-41), the lost sheep (154-7), and the Pharisee and the tax collector (323-30). There are parables that also promise judgment: the wicked tenants (137-46), the fishnet (151-4), the unforgiving servant (201-7), the guest without a garment (213-4), the talents (217-30), ten virgins (296-8), and the rich man and Lazarus (306-16).

184. Ackroyd, "Isaiah," 338a.

185. See particularly the parables of the mustard seed and leaven in a lump. Roemer, *Who in the World Was Jesus*, 134-7, 198-201. Cf., Meier, *Marginal Jew*, 135.

186. See Roemer, *Who in the World Was Jesus*, especially how Jesus encountered opposition, which he portrays in many a parable such as the sower (125-30), the mustard seed (134-37), leaven in a lump (198-201), two sons (207-9), and children at play (292-4).

187. See Matt 12:39-45, 16:4, 17:17.

188. Meier, *Marginal Jew*, 136.

189. Contra Twelftree, "Jesus the Baptist," 117.

190. See Roemer, *Who in the World Was Jesus*, and the parables of the lost sheep (154-7), the lost coin (239-41), treasure in a field (148-51), and the pearl of great price (294-6). This is not to minimize the similarities: people identified Jesus as the risen John (Mark 6:14, 8:28), the infancy narratives link the two, their message is the coming kingdom, and, most importantly, Jesus was baptized by John.

191. Meier, *Marginal Jew*, 139.

192. The "genitive absolute" in Greek casts the phrase in the genitive, which indicates that it is meant to be understood as an independent action from what precedes and follows it but closely connects the two in a temporal sequence. So we translate Matt 11:7 as "After (or when) [John's disciples] had left" and Luke 7:24 as "After (or when) the messengers of John had left."

193. See 3 Macc 2:22, where the divine punishment of Ptolomy IV (221–203 BC) is described. "He shook him on this side and that as a reed is shaken by the wind, so that he lay helpless on the ground and, besides being paralyzed in his limbs, was unable even to speak, since he was smitten by a righteous judgment." Cf., also 1 Kgs 14:15. The reed image is apt since John was baptizing in the lower Jordan near the Judean wilderness where reeds grew.

194. The first king of the separated ten northern tribes. His name became a byword for apostasy. See, e.g., 1 Kgs 16:26, 22:52, 2 Kgs 3:3.

195. Theissen, *Historical Jesus*, 101. His coins were in circulation only in the Galilee and Perea.

196. Neyrey, *Social World of Luke-Acts*, 55.

197. This sumptuousness is depicted in his birthday celebration at which Herodias plots successfully to have John the Baptist executed (Mark 6:21–29).

198. See the description of the Galilee and Galileans in Roemer, *World of Jesus*, 516–31.

199. Meier, *Marginal Jew*, 141, and Fenton, *Matthew*, 179.

200. Exod 23:20, 32:34, 33:2, 34:24, Deut 2:31, 6:19.

201. Caird, *Luke*, 113. The statement is included by Mark in his introduction of the Baptist (1:2) but not by Matthew (3:3) nor Luke (3:4) in their introduction of the Baptist. Luke also extends the Isaiah quotation (40:3) with some modifications in his rendition of Jesus's identification of John. The implication is that both Matthew and Luke found it in Q and that Mark knew of it and attached it to his introduction. The saying reads exactly the same in all three synoptic Gospels. That it doesn't appear in Q's version of the Baptist's activity (Matt 3:1–12, Luke 3:1–17) also suggests that Mark added it to his version (1:2–7). Both Hebrew and the LXX read not "before *you*" but "before *me*."

202. Cf., Micah 6:4: "For I brought you up from the land of Egypt, and redeemed you from the house of bondage; and I sent before you[r face (singular)] Moses, Aaron, and Miriam."

203. Robinson, *Twelve More Studies*, identifies four different uses of Scripture in the Gospels. He includes Matt 11:10 in his second usage under the category of "confirmatory use" and concludes this use "provides no criterion for distinguishing the usage of Jesus from that of the early church, and the strong probability must be that the claim to fulfillment . . . is read back onto his lips rather than the other way around" (38–9). But he finds his fourth category of "challenging use" (e.g., Mark 2:25, 12:10, 26) to be the "most characteristic and identifiable features of Jesus' teaching" (43). The other two usages he finds are the allusive (e.g., Jer 22:5 in Matt 23:38) and the argumentative (e.g., Matt 4:7–10).

204. See Roemer, *World of Jesus*, 409–10.

205. Meier, *Marginal Jew*, 207, n 127. Luke has Graecized the saying (7:28).

206. Literally "the smallest." The word occurs nowhere else in the New Testament and only in Gen 4:22 and Judg 6:15 in the LXX. The Syriac version also translates the word with זקורא (Z'ORA, "smallest").

207. See Roemer, *Who in the World Was Jesus*, and the parables of treasure in a field (148–51), the pearl of great price (294–6), the lost coin (139–41), and the prodigal son (241–7).

CHAPTER ENDNOTES 235

208. Meier, *Marginal Jew*, 144, recognizes the parallelism between John and Jesus: Jesus like John did not proclaim himself. John, however, insisted it was only though his baptism that one could escape "the wrath to come." So implicit in Jesus's declaration is a self-referential note that though he did not make himself the center of his proclamation, it was still in fellowship with him that one entered the kingdom.

209. Suggested by meaning 2b in Arndt, *Greek Lexicon*, 140a. They suggest translating the phrase with "everyone enters (or tries to enter) the kingdom with violence." It is also possible Luke meant to use the word βιάζομαι (*biadzomai*, "use force, force my way") in a positive sense such as in the parable of the great feast (14:23): "compel [ἀναγκάζω, *anankadzō*, "compel, constrain"] them to come in." Meier, *Marginal Jew*, 217, n 185. At least that may have been the way Luke, in his mild-mannered way, understood it.

210. My emendation of Meier, *Marginal Jew*, 162.

211. Roemer, *World of Jesus*, 409–17.

212. The prepositions "until" and "from the days of" describing John's activity can be either inclusive or exclusive. Meier, *Marginal Jew*, 218, n 199. So somehow John belonged to both the old and the new. He was a prophet but "more than a prophet."

213. See Roemer, *Who in the World Was Jesus*, and the parables of the mustard seed (134–7) and the unjust steward (247–59). John seems to have included the Gentiles also in the coming denouement of history.

214. Jesus's parables insist on the palpability of the kingdom and that it appears sometimes in the most unlikely of places and among the most unlikely of persons. See Roemer, *Who in the World Was Jesus*, and the parables of the mustard seed (134–7), treasure in a field (148–51), leaven in a lump (198–201), the unjust steward (247–59), the good Samaritan (303–6), and the Pharisee and the tax collector (323–30)

215. They identified the war with Rome as that battle, entered the fray, and were annihilated. See Roemer, *World of Jesus*, 391–442, which tells the story of individual revolutionary movements and personalities, and 265–389, for the devastating war with Rome.

216. Matthew's inclusion of 11:14–15 is clearly redactional on the part of the evangelist. A direct identification of John and Elijah appears elsewhere only in Mark 9:11–13 and in Matthew's version of it. See below.

217. Matt 17:1—18:6 follows Mark 9:1–48 except for the insertion of the discussion on taxes (Matt 17:24–27). Luke 9, on the other hand, does not include the discussion about Elijah after the story of the transfiguration in Mark 9. But he does identify John with the coming Elijah in 7:27. Brown, *Birth*, 276, opines the existence of traces of stages in Luke of two different viewpoints. The earliest stage would have identified Jesus with the Elijah-like prophet, and a later dominant stage, in the infancy narrative, stressed Jesus as God's Son. At any rate, Luke seems to have an ambivalent view of John.

218. m. Eduyoth 8,7. Danby, *Mishnah*, 436.

219. m. Sotah 9,15.

220. He also remains a popular figure of legend in which he opposes social ills. A place is always kept for him at the Passover Seder and at a circumcision since he is understood as the protector of children. Walsh, "Elijah," 465a.

221. Moore, *Judaism*, 360, referring to Justin Martyr's *Dialogue with Trypho*, 8,4, reports that was the belief of the Jews with whom Justin was acquainted.

222. See Brown, *Birth*, 279.

223. John has no such story at all. His cross is "the hour" of his confrontation with the "prince of this world" when he is exorcized (John 12:27–33) and Jesus draws everyone to himself.

224. Cf., also Sibylline Oracles 3:663, "the kings of the people will launch an attack

together against this land," and 2 Esdras 13:37-38, "he, my Son, will reprove the assembled nations for their ungodliness... and will reproach them to their face with their evil thoughts and the torments with which they are to be tortured... and will destroy them." The Jewish portion of the Oracles, the central sections of 2 Esdras, probably dates from around the early first century AD.

225. Levenson, *Death and Resurrection*, 154. Joseph then must be humiliated: he becomes a slave. But in that process, he learns to submit to God: he refuses the advances of Potiphar's wife, which leads to further humiliation as a prisoner in a dungeon.

226. Levenson, *Death and Resurrection*, 166. See also Roemer, *Who in the World Was Jesus*, and the parables of the lost sheep (154-7), the unforgiving servant (201-7), seats at a feast (215), the lost coin (239-41), the prodigal son (241-7), two debtors (299-303), the good Samaritan (303-6), and the Pharisee and the tax collector (323-30).

227. Levenson, *Death and Resurrection*, 167.

228. The LXX was an authoritative translation for Greek-speaking Jews. It was only after the rise of Christianity when it became the Bible of Christianity that this translation was abandoned by the Jews.

229. Meier, *Marginal Jew*, 271, n 1, relegates his understanding of the temptation narrative in this long endnote.

230. A biblical phrase meaning an extended period. In this case it reflects the forty-year period of the wilderness wanderings of the Israelites and the forty days Moses was with the Lord writing the ten commandments (Exod 34:28). Cf., also Gen 7:4, Exod 16:35, Num 13:25, Jud 3:11, 13:1, 1 Kgs 19:8, Ezek 29:12, Jon 3:4, Acts 1:3.

231. Meier, *Marginal Jew*, 271, n 1. In his argument he abandons his usual reliance on the multiple attestation criterion of authenticity (the occurrence of a given tradition in two or more sources) and contends that "since the heart of the temptation narrative concerns Jesus' struggle with a preternatural being in the desert, with no eyewitnesses present, that narrative does not belong to the Gospel material that is in principle open to verification by any and all inquirers... At best, one can argue that the attestation of both Mark and Q indicates that, immediately after his baptism, Jesus retired for a while in the Judean wilderness and there underwent an inner spiritual struggle in preparation for his public ministry [and one]... must also recognize that the entire tradition of Jesus' temptation by Satan... may be a symbolic representation of the apocalyptic struggle between God and the devil which was prophesied for the last days... which does not make it untrue or unreal, but it does withdraw it from the kind of examination... undertaken in this book." This judgment of his, of course, is to be expected since the story for him references the whole realm of the spirit that is bracketed out of any "scientific" historical inquiry. I deal with this question of the realm of the spirit in the arguments following.

232. Cf., Nineham, *Mark*, 63, "it was [sic] clearly nothing to do with the inner experience of Jesus." Contrast this understanding with Meier's in the previous footnote.

233. Caird, *Luke*, 79, who acquiesces to interpreting the Devil as a "mythological figure." But myth he says is a way of expressing truth that can't quite be so forcefully conveyed in any other way. He observes that evil is a reality that can take hold of people; it is personal; it is a distorted good and so masquerades as good; it is inimical to people. All well said, but it denies the experience of evil as a personal encounter.

234. One exception is Borg, *Jesus: A New Vision*. See also Roemer, *Who in the World Was Jesus*, 19, n 24.

235. The definitive study of this phenomenon is Moody, Jr., *Life After Life*. See also Glynn, *God The Evidence*. particularly 99-137. He writes,

... near-death research has produced an enormous body of data that no one honestly interested in rationally evaluating the likelihood of the existence of God can afford to ignore. It is difficult to analyze this evidence in depth and to come away with any other impression but that science has indeed stumbled on data of the soul. (136)

236. Glynn, *God The Evidence*, 22–3.

237. Called the "anthropic principle." Moody, *Life After Life*, 25. See pages 29–30 on the impossibility of a universe where some of the constants referred to were slightly different. To get around the seeming purposeful nature of the universe Stephen Hawking hypothesized the "multiverse"—i.e., that there are an infinite number of universes and by chance ours got all the numbers right and was then capable of producing life. But there is simply no proof for such a hypothesis and no way to verify it.

238. For example, it is the ideal distance from the sun that supports the existence of water in liquid form. (If it were closer water would boil away. If farther it would be permanently ice.) It is part of a planetary system that inhibits catastrophic encounters of our earth with meteors. (The giant outer planets absorb them). It is just the right size. (If it were smaller the atmosphere would dissipate.). The tilt of its axis makes the whole earth habitable. (There are even four species of penguins that live in Antarctica!). For its size the earth has a very large moon that stabilizes the tilt; the moon is at such a distance that in solar eclipses it perfectly and exactly covers the disc of the sun, enabling us to study our sun; the moon, also because of its size, causes the tides that contribute to biodiversity. Our solar system is in an ideal place in the Milky Way galaxy. (It is in a relatively star-free zone, which enables mankind to study the farthest reaches of the universe. If it were in a denser portion of the galaxy we would never know the full extent of the universe.)

239. See, e.g., Hall, *A Primer of Freudian Psychology*.

240. Glynn, *God: The Evidence*, 61–78.

241. Glynn, *God: The Evidence*, 139–40.

242. The preacher was Dr. Wilhelm Maurer (1900–1982), who was on the theological faculty of the Friederich-Alexander Universität, Erlangen, where he filled the chair of reformation history. He retired in 1967. The place was the little parish church of St. Luke in the small village just north of Erlangen called Bubenreuth where my wife and I lived during the first half of our stay in Germany. Several of the theological students at the university heard that he would be preaching at St. Luke's, so we went together to hear our professor's sermon. Maurer was denied a professorship during the war because he belonged to the Confessing church, a movement that opposed the Nazified, so-called German Christians. That opposition would have made him particularly cognizant of the evils of Nazism. He authored a large number of works including a commentary on the Augsburg Confession (1976), which was translated into English in 1986 four years after his death. In this same regard Luther reported an encounter with the Devil while he was at the Wartburg. There are many stories of such encounters reported on the internet. Caird, *Luke*, 79, rightly points out that evil is "real and potent" and a power that can grip human life and society; it is personal; it is distorted good; evil masquerades as good; and evil is the enemy.

243. Matthew further emphasizes Jesus as the new Moses by following the temptation with the Sermon on the Mount after gathering the nation by calling his disciples, proclaiming the kingdom, and healing, which causes his fame to spread through the Galilee ("Zebulon and Naphtali," Matt 4:15) and Syria (Matt 4:24). So the people gather to him on the mount as Moses had led the people to Mount Sinai. Here the "new law" is given the people.

244. See also Luke 10:41, 1 Cor 7:32–34, Bar 3:18, 2 Esd 2:27.
245. See Roemer, *World of Jesus*, 394–401.
246. Caird, *Luke*, 80.
247. Caird, *Luke*, 80.
248. See Roemer, *World of Jesus*, 560–1.
249. See Deut 13:17. Ps 145:9, Isa 14:1, 49:13, Lam 3:32, Hos 11:4–8, Mic 7:19, Zech 10:6. The Hebrew word is *RaChaM*, meaning to be soft, gentle, loving, affectionate, compassionate. The word also means "womb," a stunning association. God's love is like a mother's womb that holds her child, nourishes it, and brings it life. See Brown, *Hebrew and English Lexicon*, 933a.
250. A part of the corner of the pinnacle was recovered in 1968 by Benjamin Mazar in his early excavations of the southern wall of the Temple mount. On it was written, "at the place of trumpeting." The trumpeter stood at that place to blow the trumpet announcing the beginning of a feast or the Sabbath. In addition, Rosh Hashanah, the new year, was called the feast of trumpets (Lev 23:24–25, cf., Num 29:1–6). This pinnacle, I believe, was at the southwest corner of the Temple esplanade, which was some 250 feet above the street. See Ritmeyer, "Pinnacle."
251. See the apothegm of the rich man (Matt 19:16–29) in the following chapter and the question he put to Jesus.
252. Caird, *Luke*, 80.
253. "The world" as used in the New Testament refers to the world as it is in opposition to God.
254. See Roemer, *World of Jesus*, 445–457. So when it says that Satan is the "god of this world," it is not saying that he has ultimate authority. It is conveying the idea that Satan rules over the world in a specific way. In 2 Cor 4:4, the unbeliever follows Satan's agenda: "The god of this world has blinded the minds of unbelievers, so that they cannot see the light of the gospel of the glory of Christ." Satan's rule includes blinding the world to the truth of God's kingdom. Satan's work imprisons people, so they must be set free by the plundering of his kingdom by Jesus. New Testament eschatology sees the final dominion coming to Jesus so that in actuality the rulership of the kingdoms of this world belong by divine right to him (Ps 2:8–9, Rev 11:15) when "all things are put under his feet" (Ps 8:6) and God "is all in all" (1 Cor 15:28).
255. It is not unlike the one ring of Tolkien's *Lord of the Rings* trilogy: "One ring to rule them all, One ring to find them, One ring to bring them all and in the darkness bind them."
256. 1 Cor 15:20–28 is a virtual commentary on this temptation.
257. Caird, *Luke*, 80.
258. Which is certainly the view of the writer of the book of Revelation.
259. A new "Fourth Philosophy" that had its roots in the early first century AD asserted that paying taxes to Rome was tantamount to idolatry because it was tacitly recognizing the right of Rome's dominion over the people, thus usurping God's rightful dominion. This philosophy, no doubt, fueled much of the revolutionary spirit of the time.
260. For these various revolutionary movements see Roemer, *World of Jesus*, 401–37. The people involved in these movements were not secularists who were pursuing merely secular goals but deeply religious men who were seeking God's will and the establishment of his sovereignty over the Holy Nation.
261. Parables such as leaven in a lump and the unjust steward challenge the hearers to see that God's reign went far beyond the borders of the Holy Nation.
262. See Roemer, *World of Jesus*, 62–83.
263. Passive resistance was very much a part of Jewish ethos. See, e.g., the

confrontation between Pilate and the protesters of his illegal installation of Roman standards in Jerusalem, Roemer, *World of Jesus*, 235.

264. See "the Question to Jesus Concerning the Census" (Mark 12:13–17, Matt 22:15–22, Luke 20:20–26).

265. Caird, *Luke*, 81.

266. Nineham, *Mark*, 64.

267. Nineham, *Mark*, 64.

268. Mark is the only New Testament writer who rejects Jesus's Davidic sonship. His references to David in his Gospel are all due to his redaction. In 2:25 his citing of the story of David eating the bread of the presence erroneously includes his men being with him and anachronistically avers it was unlawful for a layman to eat the cultic bread. All of these anomalies indicate Mark's hand at work; in 10:46–52. Bartimaeus originally pleads for Jesus's succor by calling him "son of David," but once healed he refers to him as "Rabouni" (a heightened form of "my lord" or "my master"), in effect saying that the initial appellation used for Jesus by Bartimaeus was inadequate, which points to Mark's hand again at work by interpolating the reference to David. In 11:10 the crowd hails Jesus by identifying him with the "coming kingdom of our father David" (an appellation appearing in no other Gospel). The witness of the crowd in Mark is never reliable; and finally Mark brings his whole anti-son of David polemic to a head in 12:35–37, where he has Jesus himself assert that the Messiah cannot be the "son of David," which in its turn undercuts the earliest tradition that he was (Rom 1:3).

269. Like an Amos who had been herdsman and a dresser of sycamore trees but was made a prophet by the Lord's call (Amos 7:14).

270. God alone speaks in this way and then only in Exod 4:23, 6:29, Judg 7:4, Exek 2:8. The phrase occurs sixty-four times in the synoptic Gospels and twenty-seven times in John.

271. A characteristic continued by the apostles (2 Cor 11:7).

272. 2 Cor 6:2.

273. See 2 Cor 2:15–16.

274. Schweizer, *The Good News According to Mark*, 43.

275. Bultmann, *History*, 11–39

276. The other types will appear in the next volume of this study of the historical Jesus. Bultmann, *History*, 12–39, includes twenty-four controversy and scholastic dialogues and twenty biographical pronouncement stories. I deal with all of these but one (which I've included in my previous book on the parables) in this and the next chapter. Robbins, "Apophthegms," lists a number of interpreters and the number of units they consider to be included in this category: Dibelius, *From Tradition to Gospel*, includes twenty-two; Berger, *Formgeschichte des Neuen Testaments*, includes sixty-seven; Tannehill, "Introduction," includes eighty-five. Between these last two commentators one hundred units are discussed as pronouncement stories. I have chosen Bultmann's selections as an adequate representation of the form and of the tradition.

277. The word comes from the Greek ἀπόφθεγμα (*apophthegma*, "what is uttered, a terse saying"). There are other terms used for these brief narratives: paradigm, anecdote, and chreia. The latter term comes from the Greek word χρεία meaning "use, useful, need, or want." A chreia therefore was something shorter than a narration and often as short as a single sentence. It was attributed to a person and conformed to a few patterns beginning with "on seeing," "on being asked," or "he said." For example, "Aristeides, on being asked what justice is, said, 'Not desiring the possessions of others.'"

278. Bultmann, *History*, 39–69, maintains that the individual saying often precedes the context and that the context was added by the tradents. So the scenes in which the saying is embedded are "imaginary," although he finds the words of Jesus as historical.

He bases that judgment on the nature of the earliest church as a community of the end-time that produced prophets who would provide contexts and on the parallels found in the rabbinic forms. However, the rabbinic forms were produced by a community of legal scholars who were not eschatologically oriented. Quite the opposite, they were concerned with the preservation of the Jewish community and its ability to follow the law under the new circumstances of having been shorn of their Temple. The rabbinic stories look more like illustrations of an intracommunity dialogue—e.g., he cites a story in which Hillel was questioned by his students; or a Rabbi is questioned by a matron; or a Rabbi is questioned by another Rabbi; although he also cites examples where they are questioned by outsiders such as a philosopher or even the emperor; in this latter case it can well be asked if indeed a Rabbi were ever questioned by an emperor. But why would they have been remembered except that they may have been part of the academic discussions of the Rabbis who confronted theoretical questions regarding Israel's faith. So his conception of the origin of these stories locates them in the apologetics and polemics of the earliest church. He is more on the right track when he finds these discussions rooted in the oriental way of talking and discussing. Of course, Jesus himself was also embedded in such a culture. And Bultmann must admit when it comes to judging the historicity of a given story that he has no objective criteria, but one must depend on "taste and discrimination" (47)! So when I find these pronouncement stories are congruent with what we know of Jesus, his proclamation, and his teaching, I conclude they originated with him. In many cases with the rabbinic stories it is easy to see that the saying generated the scene (e.g., when the Rabbi is portrayed as conversing with the emperor). With many of the dominical pronouncement stories, however, even Bultmann has to judge that saying and narrative form such a close unity that the saying cannot be understood apart from the scene in which it is imbedded. He rightly deems irrelevant in terms of a unit's interpretation whether a given tradition was handed down orally or in written form. But he finds the church's voice at work defending its practice by appealing to their Lord when the disciples are attacked for their behavior rather than Jesus himself. However, in Mark 2:18 and 2:23 it is Jesus himself who is asked the question. (Although, see below. I too find the story of plucking grain on the Sabbath and the discussion of handwashing, Mark 7:1–23, a product of the church.) He also finds the stories that employ Scriptural quotations as deriving from the church. However, it would be peculiar if Jesus himself would not have made references to Scripture (which he admits, 49–50, particularly in Mark 10:2–9). Every Jew of the period would use Scripture to bolster his stand on a particular topic. He cannot gainsay that Jesus gathered disciples, taught something like a Pharisee, and engaged in disputations. So the controversy dialogues rightly portray Jesus "on the basis of historical recollection" (50). It is so, as he demonstrates, that there is a tendency within the development of the synoptic Gospels to turn a scholastic dialogue such as Mark 12:28–34 into a controversy dialogue by Matthew and Luke as well as the tendency to add Pharisees and Sadducees, which groups are conceived more and more as typical opponents of Jesus. It is difficult to see the church inventing dialogues to fulfill its need to justify its actions. Wouldn't it be the other way around that the church adopted its practices on the basis of Jesus's own teaching? He also finds most of the biographical pronouncement stories, although unitary, as ideal compositions—i.e., "they embody a truth in some metaphorical sort of situation," which gives them a symbolic character (56). He includes in this category "true kinsmen" (Mark 3:31–35), the "praising disciples" (Luke 19:39–40), "Mary and Martha" (Luke 10:38–42), "cost of discipleship" (Luke 9:57–62), "blessing of the children" (Mark 10:13–16), the "thankful leper" (Luke 17:11–19), the "widow's mite" (Mark 12:41–44), and "Zacchaeus the toll collector" (Luke 19:1–10). Although I think the story of the widow's mite was originally a parable for the others, see chapter 3 for my arguments regarding their authenticity. But Bultmann must admit a "historical reminiscence can be retained" in them. He compares them with the rabbinic stories, but there, as he observes, the teaching meant to be learned is placed first as the basis for repeating the story (57), so the Gospel stories do not follow that form. Furthermore, he recognizes that their origin is in the milieu of the land of Israel (60). As to their function in the church he avers, "apologetics and polemics, as well as edification and discipline must equally be taken into account as must scribal activity. But the biographical apothegms are best thought of as edifying paradigms or sermons. They help to present the Master as a living contemporary, and to comfort and admonish the church in her hope" (61). I conclude in my analysis that the biographical pronouncement stories reveal Jesus's character, his self-understanding, and his conception of the purpose of his ministry. So they are truly Christological and functioned in a way that undergirded the church's faith in him as Lord and Savior. In that case, the church did not invent them but remembered his words, which were part of the reason it had come to faith in him in the first place. It seems to me that Bultmann has turned the relationship between the church and these stories on its head. Just how did the church's faith arise? It arose because of the witness provided by the word proclaimed in these stories. First, it was the witnesses to the stories, then the faith of the church. This is underscored by his analysis that finds there are usually no reports on the response of the people to whom an action or word of Jesus is directed (63). Now it is certainly so that the evangelists have edited this material by expansions and the addition of other sayings. And this process continues in the manuscript tradition as the apparatus in the modern editions of the Greek New Testament give witness (e.g., see the expansion after Mark 11:24). Furthermore, the often included localization of the story witnesses to its historicity. However, it is so that typical groups like Pharisees are often brought in to substitute for what had not originally been specified. So the interpreter must be careful in how Pharisees are characterized. Their presence (see below) in the Galilee is highly suspect. And it is certainly possible that specific people who are named are a later specification (e.g., in Mark 14:3–9 those who murmur are unspecified; in Matt 26:8 they are disciples and in John 12:4 it is Judas who is named).

279. jShabbat 15d.

280. Josephus names three of this delegation of four—Jonathan, Ananias, and Jozar—as Pharisees. Their mission, at the instigation of Josephus's rival John of Gishala, was to remove Josephus as military general of the Galilee. It is notable that in Mark 3:22 the scribes "come down from Jerusalem"—i.e., they are not resident in the Galilee. Vermes, *Jesus the Jew,* 57, concludes, "Pharisaic opposition to Jesus in Galilee was mostly foreign and not local. Even assuming that the Pharisees had acquired some foothold in one or two Galilean cities . . . their authority was little noticed in rural Galilee, the main field of Jesus' ministry and success."

281. Finally, a further confirmation of this conclusion is to be found in the relative paucity of references to Jesus in the rabbinic tradition. It seems that few Pharisees encountered him, and they did not think their encounters memorable. As Horsley, *Archaeology,* 182, observes, this is no doubt due to the regional differences between Galilee and Jerusalem (and Judea) that were rooted in many centuries of separate historical development prior to the Maccabean victories. So it was only one hundred years before the death of Herod and the birth of Jesus that the Galilee was under Jerusalem's influence.

282. Bultmann, *History,* 28.

283. See, e.g., Matt 4:13–15, 8:24, 32, 13:1, 14:25, 15:29, Mark 2:13, 3:7, 4:1, 6:47, 7:31.

284. See Roemer, *World of Jesus,* 528–31, and the artist's rendering of the village, 586.

285. Isa 6:1–10. The designation of God as the "Holy One" occurs twenty-nine times in the Isaianic literature.

286. The Greek word θάμβος (*thambos*, "amazed") borders on the meaning of "terrified." See particularly Song 6:4, 10, implying an experience of the transcendent.

287. Danker, *Jesus and the New Age*, 65.

288. See particularly the story of the forgiven woman in which the parable of the two debtors is embedded (Luke 7:36–50). Roemer, *Who in the World Was Jesus*, 299–303.

289. The metaphor was well known in both the Jewish and Gentile world. Nineham, *Mark*, 72, who refers to Hab 1:15–17, Prov 6:26, Jer 16:16, Amos 4:2, and Ezek 19:4–5 and to Diogenes Laertius. However, it is used by them in a negative sense of catching people to take them off to divine judgment.

290. Nineham, *Mark*, 71. See Jer 16:16.

291. Schuerer, *History*, 171–2, who notes that the renaming must have occurred before 2 BC since Julia was banished by Augustus in that year to the island of Pandateria.

292. According to Josephus, *Ant*. 18, 2, 1, however, Phillip made of it a *polis* whose status was supported by the size of its population and by the grandeur of its architectural appointments.

293. See the narrative in chapter 12 of Theissen, *Shadow of the Galilean*, 109–16, "Men on the Frontier."

294. One could suspect that these witnesses changed the name to bring the two references into conformity.

295. See the pronouncement story of Luke 10:38–42 below.

296. There were, for example, the women who saw to his physical needs (Luke 8:3) and followers who remained settled in the villages.

297. Reynolds, *The Son of Man Problem*, is a recent collection of essays covering the years from 1950 to 2016. This collection does not come to any decisive solution to the meaning of "son of man" but represents the variety of conclusions that have been reached over the years. It is, of course, not exhaustive but gives a thorough overview of the various studies that have been pursued.

298. Ghnther Haufe, "Das Menschensohn Problem," 133, who finds seventy-one such occurrences: (1) the "parousia sayings" (total number twenty-eight, fourteen of which occur in Matthew, three in Mark, eleven in Luke); (2) the "suffering and rising sayings" (total number twenty-five, ten of which appear in Matthew, nine in Mark, and six in Luke); (3) the "present activity sayings" (total number eighteen, seven of which appear in Matthew, two in Mark, and nine in Luke). The occurrence in this text falls into the third category. Only two such sayings occur in Mark (here and in 10:45). Q contains only sayings from the first and third group.

299. See Kazen, "The Coming Son of Man Revisited," whose study avers that a collective interpretation of these sayings must be applied to them so that they reflect an eschatology not focused on an individual redeemer figure but on the community as it expressed the kingdom. I would suggest that if so, then Jesus also meant himself, as he realized in his words and actions the reality of the kingdom.

300. According to my count there are sixty-nine references to the "son of man" in the synoptic Gospels: twenty-seven occur in parousia sayings (thirteen in Matthew, three in Mark, and eleven in Luke); nineteen occur in sayings related to Jesus's present activity (eight in Matthew, three in Mark, and eight in Luke); twenty-three occur in sayings related to Jesus's sufferings and resurrection (nine in Matthew, eight in Mark, and six in Luke).

The following table shows how the "son of man" sayings are distributed among the three synoptic Gospels and when they are present in only one Gospel. The tables illustrates that all of Mark's sayings were adopted by the other two evangelists; that both

Matthew and Luke made extensive use of sayings that were known only to them; and that Q also provided a large number of such sayings but without any suffering-rising sayings, which is understandable since Q did not contain a passion narrative.

Source Saying Type	Mt	L	Q	Mk	Mk-Mt-L	Mk-Mt	Mk-L
Parousia	4	2	6[a]	3	5[d]	0	0
Present Activity	0	2	2[b]	3	4[c]	1	0
Suffering-Rising	1	3	0	8	6[e]	1	1
Total	5	7	8	14	15	2	1

301. [a] Matt 10:32 has changed the "son of man" in Luke 12:8 to "I."

[b] It appears that Matt 12:32 ("And anyone who says a word against the Son of man will be forgiven") and Luke 12:10 ("And every one who speaks a word against the Son of man will be forgiven") have substituted a Q version of the saying in Mark 3:28, which reads, "All sins shall be forgiven the sons of men." Mark's passive implies that the forgiving subject is God.

[c] Matt 13:37 has substituted "son of man" for Mark's "the sower" (4:14). Luke simply identifies the nature of the seed, "the seed is the word" (8:11). In Matt 16:13 Jesus asks, "Who do men say that the son of man is?" while Mark 8:27 has "Who do men say that I am?" and Luke 19:18 "Who do the crowds say I am?" Evidently Matt has added "son of man" to the passage. It can plausibly be asserted that Jesus's reference to "son of man" in Mark 2:27-28 means that human beings are masters of the Sabbath. Similarly, in Matt 12:32, Luke 12:10, cf., Mark 3:28-29, the comparison could have been speaking against people versus speaking against God's Spirit. However, in the context it seems that Jesus is referring to himself.

[d] Matt 16:27, which occurs in the context of saving and losing one's life, refers to the son of man coming with his angels to recompense people for their sins. In the same context Mark 8:38 and Luke 9:26 render Jesus's word in terms of the son of man being ashamed of those who are ashamed of him when he comes in the glory of his Father. Matt 16:28 refers to the son of man coming in his kingdom, while Mark 9:1 and Luke 9:27 refer only to the kingdom of God. "Kingdom of God" looks to be the original, and Matt has again added the "son of man."

[e] Matt 17:9 and Mark 9:9 both have a command of Jesus to be silent about the transfiguration until "the son of man was raised from the dead," while Luke 9:36 reports that the disciples kept silent about the vision. Both Matt 26:24 and Mark 14:21 repeat "son of man" twice, while Luke 22:22 refers to "son of man" only once. Both Luke 9:22 and Mark 8:31 refer to the son of man suffering, while Matt 16:21 does not refer to the son of man. Matthew seems to avoid coordinating "son of man" with suffering and rising.

In Matt 13:37, 41, the phrase occurs twice in the explanation of the parable of the enemy who sowed weeds in a field. I've judged the parable to be a Matthean construction. That judgment then applies also to the explanation of the parable in Matt 13:36-43.

302. For the sources of the Gospels see Roemer, *Who in the World Was Jesus*, 65-72.

303. An analysis reveals that an evangelist can change an original "son of man" to an "I." Luke can eliminate "son of man," smoothing out and Graecizing the language. Matthwe appears to avoid connecting "son of man" with suffering and rising (see "e" in n 301. So the evangelists can eliminate or add "son of man" according to their own

propensities. However, to emphasize once again: the occurrence of the locution across all of the sources indicates it was used by Jesus in the three contexts enumerated above. See also Elledge, *Use of the Third Person*: "Ancient Near Eastern texts contain many examples of direct speech of humans or deities who refer to themselves in the grammatical third-person, either using third-person verbal forms and third-person pronouns or denoting themselves with their distinctive names or epithets. This use of the third-person, which is known as illeism, is also widespread in the Bible. Good examples include, 'YHWH said to Satan, "YHWH rebuke you, Satan!"' (Zech 3:2), and 'Jesus said to them, "The Son of Man shall be delivered up"' (Matt 17:22). The phenomenon occurs only rarely in modern speech. This makes it confusing to present day Bible readers, who may wonder whether speakers are referring to others instead of themselves." Elledge contests the theory that the third-person self-references in Jesus's speech were inserted by the early church and prefers to approach them as an integral part of the transmitted text. He points out that Jesus's use of illeism conveys ambiguity. A good example is John 9:35, where Jesus asks, 'Do you believe in the Son of Man?' The addressee responds, "And who is he, sir, that I may believe in him?" However, Elledge rejects the idea that Jesus employed illeism to conceal his true nature, for fear of hostile authorities. This explanation is possible in only a few marginal cases. In general, Jesus's use of first-person pronouns in the near context shows clearly that the third-person references relate to Jesus himself. Further, Jesus speaks illeistically also when he addresses his intimates and when there is no reason to fear the reaction of the authorities. According to Elledge, the fundamental reason why Jesus uses illeism is pedagogical: by presenting himself from an external perspective he can more adequately portray his unique authority and divine status. Although there are correspondences with the illeism of biblical and ancient Near Eastern kings, the high quantity of Jesus's third-person self-references associates his illeism especially with the even more frequent illeism of God in the Old Testament. Elledge concludes that "by extensive use of illeism Jesus characterizes himself as God rather than as king." (The quoted material comes from a Society of Biblical Literature review by Paul Sanders of the Protestant Theological University.) The reviewer rightly questions if Jesus, by using the locution "son of man," is referring to his divine identity. More likely he took it up and filled it with his own content, all the while maintaining the historical associations it already encompassed.

304. See, e.g., Mark 8:27, cf., Matt 16:13 and Luke 12:8, cf., Matt 10:32.
305. Bruce, "Background," 51.
306. See Roemer, *World of Jesus*, 56–83.
307. Bruce, *Background*, 55, who suggests that this may be the background to Jesus' saying in Luke 12:32, "Fear not, little flock, for it is your Father's good pleasure to give you the kingdom." He further defines the "saints of the Most High" as the Hasidim, but that may be narrowing the application too much. See the references to the Hasidim in Roemer, *World of Jesus*, 630.
308. Bruce, *Background*, 56.
309. This section of the book is known as "The Book of Similitudes" (i.e., "parables") and is dated to the late second or early first century BC. See E. Isaac's introduction to the Enochic literature in Charlesworth, *The Old Testament Pseudepigrapha*, 5–12. Fragments of all the parts of 1 Enoch have been found at Qumran except the "Similitudes."
310. Nickelsburg, "Son of Man," 138b.
311. Nickelsburg, "Son of Man," 139b.
312. In the later additions to the Similitudes it is revealed that Enoch himself is the son of man!
313. This identification with Enoch is clear evidence that the Similitudes are not a Christian work. Bruce, *Background*, 68.

314. See Roemer, *Who in the World Was Jesus*, 65–7.

315. The author of the central section of this writing was a Jew living in the Holy Land near the end of the first century AD, that is, after the destruction of the Temple in AD 70. He wrote in either Aramaic or Greek. If it was originally written in Aramaic, it was later translated into Greek. Around AD 150 a Christian writer added chapters 1–2, and later another Christian added chapters 15–16. This work survives only in a number of Latin, Syriac, and Ethiopic versions, so we can only guess what the Semitic term was for "man." Bruce, *Background*, 69.

316. Qumran does not mention a "son of man" but does have a collective understanding of the "Suffering Servant" of Isaiah and the future Messiah. It thought of the "Council of the Community," which consisted of twelve men and three priests, as a collective and as embodying the suffering servant of Second Isaiah and the work of the coming Messiah: "[The Council's] work shall be truth, righteousness, justice, lovingkindness and humility. They shall preserve the faith in the Land with steadfastness and meekness and shall atone for sin by the practice of justice and by suffering the sorrows of affliction . . . who shall atone for the Land and pay to the wicked their reward" (1QS 8,2–7, "The Community Rule"). Vermes, *Dead Sea Scrolls*, 109. Mirrored here is the "Suffering Servant" of Isa 53 and the messianic descendant of David in Isa 11 who bears the spirit of the Lord and who judges the poor in righteousness and whose breath kills the wicked.

317. Bruce, *Background*, 70.

318. There are four approaches to understanding Jesus's use of the term "son of man" as outlined by Haufe, "Das Menschensohn Problem," 130–41. (1) the conservative solution: Jesus is understood to identify himself with the end-time "son of man," and all three of the groups of sayings are understood to have their root in his proclamation. (2) the radical critics: Jesus never spoke of an end-time "son of man." (3) the conservative-mediating position: Jesus knew himself and designated himself in a secret sense to be the "son of man" who in the last judgment would appear as witness. (4) the critical-mediating position: Jesus did refer to a coming "son of man" but never identified himself with him. He includes all the various commentators who subscribe to one or another of these various positions.

319. See n 303.

320. *paralellismus membrorum* means giving two or more parts of a sentence similar form so as to give the whole a definite pattern. This rhetorical device is used in biblical poetry:

> A wise son gladdens his father,
> But a foolish son grieves his mother (Prov 10:1).

321. Baldensperger, "Die neueste Forschung ueber den Menschensohn," 201, and Schmidt, "Recent Study," 326–8. See also Marshall, "The Synoptic Son of Man Sayings," 347–51. He concludes that Jesus at least spoke of himself as the future "son of man" because he wanted (1) to preserve a certain mystery regarding his person; (2) to give cautious expression to his own unique relationship with God as his son and agent of salvation; (3) to avoid the Messiah ascription because it designated an earthly figure of limited authority and was misleading because of popular notions; and (4) to use a current term that could be molded to fit his own ideas. "'Son of Man' was thus a perfect vehicle for expressing the divine self-consciousness of Jesus while at the same time preserving the secrecy of his self-revelation from those who had blinded their eyes and closed their ears."

322. Lindeskog, "Das Raetsel des Menschensohnes," 155. So it is not necessary to

postulate that certain sayings employing "son of man" originated with the church and then were read back into the mouth of Jesus. If that were so, why did the title not persist as a title in the church? It is more likely that it was a "taboo self-designation" of Jesus and so was passed on only within that context. See Stauffer, *Jesus: Gestalt und Geschichte*, 122. Stauffer points out that the title occurs in all the layers of the tradition (Q, the special material in Matthew and Luke, Mark, and the Johannine tradition) and then only in the mouth of Jesus and never used by others in his environment such as the disciples, his followers, those who question him, or his enemies. If it was read back into Jesus's mouth, why would not the church have placed it in the mouth of others? So there never was a "son of man" dogmatic in the church.

323. Perrin, *The Kingdom of God*, 99.

324. Contra Perrin, *Kingdom of God*, 90, who avers Jesus ethics were not directed to the general public. It is precisely Jesus's ethics that were meant to call the nation from revolutionary enthusiasm that would lead to its destruction.

325. Manson, *The Servant-Messiah*. That in the words of Jesus the son of man is associated with dying and rising even though it is not found anywhere in Jewish apocalyptic only emphasizes Jesus own appropriation of the term. The same may be said of the fact that preexistence and glorification motifs are not explicitly present in the synoptic Gospels. This contra Lindeskog, "Raetsel," 169–71, who maintains that the "son of man" Christology was "an original and independent creation of the primitive community" (translation mine) and that it somehow confessed Jesus as "son of man" but not in text or confession. That puzzle he is not able to solve!

326. See Roemer, *Who in the World Was Jesus*, and the parables of the fig tree (146–8), the doorkeeper (1958), the thief (214), building a tower and preparation for war (259–60), and the ten virgins (296–8). Even in the so-called Little Apocalypse (Mark 13), there is little apocalyptic material but rather a historical unfolding of events related to the destruction of the Temple. The only "apocalyptic" staging is the reference to cosmic events surrounding the coming of the "son of man" who will gather the faithful.

327. Parallel in Matt 10:32–33, where he substitutes "I" for "son of man" in the saying and eliminates "and my words." Mark does not have the "confessing" statement but prefaces the denying statement with a detailed description about following Jesus, taking up one's cross, and eschewing wishing to save one's life to gain it (Mark 8:34–37). These verses are included by Matt and Luke in other contexts (Matt 16:24–28, Luke 9:23–27). Luke does not parallel the confessing statement with the "son of man" in the denying statement but rather with a passive ("he shall be denied").

328. See footnote c in the table at n 301. See also Casey, *Solution*, 343, who finds that in the Aramaic language of Jesus's day it was an ordinary term for "man" and not a messianic title and that wherever it is used by Jesus it retains that general level of meaning. However, there is no clear support for this assertion in the Middle Aramaic of Jesus' day. He goes on to conclude that when it does not bear that meaning, it is an inauthentic saying. His rather rote application of his principle ultimately renders a Jesus who went around uttering general adages about the human condition.

329. A tendency in the history of the tradition is to supply identification of persons in traditional materials that were previously unspecified.

330. Matthew thoroughly eschatologizes the saying. Evidently, the marriage bond was too sacred to be broken or compromised even by Jesus's ministry or the later Christian ministry. See Acts 18:2, 24:24, and Paul's detailed discussion of marriage in 1 Cor 7 and especially Eph 5. That Peter and the disciples had "left everything" is somewhat of a hyperbole. Peter still had a house (Mark 1:29) and his boat (Mark 3:9). Nineham, *Mark*, 273, suggests that vs 30 was an "interpretive addition" to the previous verse made by early Christians whose experience was the loss of ties to home and possessions but

whose membership in the Christian community more than compensated for the loss. But the two verses are intimately tied to one another particularly because "father" does not appear in the list of vs 30, reflecting Jesus's own conviction that God was his Father. He is perhaps correct in eliminating "with persecutions" from the list since both Matt and Luke omit it, so it easily could have been an addition stemming from the experience of early Christians.

331. Danker, *Jesus and the New Age*, 124–5.

332 In 1 Cor 15:24–28 the Apostle employs the language of Ps 110 and Ps 8. Until he comes Christ is involved in the subjection of all things. First, he refers to Ps 110:1, "placing all things under his feet" (1 Cor 15:25), then repeats the language of Ps 8:6 (Cor 15:27). Ps 8:4 attributes all this to the "son of man." But in the Pauline passage the son returns all this authority to "God the Father," a designation for God consonant with the use of "son of man" in the Gospels (cf., Mark 8:38). See Nickelsburg, "Son of Man," 147b. That Paul was writing this epistle early in the 50s indicates that he was indeed repeating very early traditions that ultimately must rest on words of Jesus himself such as found in the passage under discussion.

333. Reed, "Burial," 474b. See also, e.g., Sir 38:16: "My son, let your tears fall for the dead, and as one who is suffering grievously begin the lament. Lay out his body with the honor due him, and do not neglect his burial. Let your weeping be bitter and your wailing fervent; observe the mourning according to his merit, for one day, or two, to avoid criticism; then be comforted for your sorrow." See also the story of Abraham purchasing a burial place in Gen 23 (cf., Gen 50:6). Not to be buried is to be cursed (Jer 14:16). The graves and their numbers at Qumran attest to this importance. In addition, during the first century, ossuaries came to be used in Judaism whereby bodies were placed in tombs and left to desiccate and the bones were then subsequently placed in boxes called ossuaries, which were often elaborately ornamented.

334. Danker, *Jesus and the New Age*, 125. "The dead" was used metaphorically for Gentiles and even the blind, leprous, the poor, and the childless. Lightfoot, Commentary, 94.

335. Bultmann, *History*, 28.

336. So Bultmann, *History*, 28–9, who finds the whole of the passage Luke 9:57–62 to be imaginary situations while maintaining that they reflect the truth that Jesus set his disciples free from every social obligation but required their surrender to himself alone.

337. Theissen and Merz, *Historical Jesus*, 214.

338. Theissen and Merz, *Historical Jesus*, 214. Further characteristics of Jesus's ministry were the free formation of tradition as contrasted with the Pharisaic memorizing of tradition and Jesus including women among his followers whereas the Pharisees included only men.

339. See Roemer, *World of Jesus*, 13–16, on the "holy war" and the further requirements that the military camp was to be kept holy so the individual soldier took on the quality of a holy person—i.e., one set aside for a divine action for YHWH was considered to be the general who led them into battle (see Deut 23:14). So the individual soldier was thought of as involved in a priestly action for the duration of the military campaign.

340. In other words, Jesus was not totally flaunting social norms. The military requirements of the holy war also made an exception to the usual demands of the norms of Israel's social life.

341. Further characteristics include participating in the charisma of Jesus' own ministry, healing and the authority to exorcize, the practice of an asceticism taking no bag for provisions and being dependent on the hospitality of villagers, and the participation in the eschatological promise. Theissen and Merz, *Historical Jesus*, 215–6.

342. Bultmann, *History*, 29.

343. This "interpolation" technique is one that Mark employs throughout his Gospel. See, e.g., Mark 11:12–24, where he has broken up the story of the cursing of the fig tree.

344. The verb is in the aorist tense, which suggests a permanent, irreversible condition! Similarly, two fourth- to fifth-century majuscules interpolate "scribes and others" for those who declared him to be "out of his mind."

345. Mary and Jesus' "brothers" gather with the disciples (Acts 1:14), and James, his brother, becomes a leader in the Jerusalem community (Acts 12:17, 5:13, 21:18, 1 Cor 15:7, Gal 1:19, 2:9, 12).

346. "Charismatic" refers to a quality in a person that goes beyond the everyday and shows itself in revelations and miracles. It is also a relational phenomenon. It has an irrational power to attract and fascinate others while simultaneously provoking opponents. Theissen and Merz, *Historical Jesus*, 190–1, refer in particular to Jesus's unique claim to authority and his readiness for conflict. Jesus' "holiness" was also not oriented to Torah and Temple but with mercy toward the marginalized "sinners" in Jewish society. In referring to one investigator they write that "Precisely by self-stigmatizing i.e., by the demonstrative adoption of outsider roles scorned by social morality, new values and orientations are established in society." See Zech 13:3–6, which indicates how prophecy involved frenzied activity by which the prophet became wounded and how prophecy itself had passed into disrepute. This frenzied behavior is perhaps what Jesus's family members thought of when they supposed he was "out of his mind" (see 1 Sam 10:6–11, 19:23–24).

347. See how Paul draws out this quality and values for the Christian community (e.g., Rom 12:9–16, 14:1—15:6). The earliest community continued this practice of care and concern for one another (see Acts 4:32 and the seven "deacons" appointed to help in this service, Acts 6:1–6).

348. Nineham, *Mark*, 123.

349. Contra Theissen and Merz, *Historical Jesus*, 218.

350. Schweizer, *Good News*, 87.

351. Theissen and Merz, *Historical Jesus*, 518.

352. Bultmann, *History*, 30. He thinks vs 27 presents an "imaginary situation," but then vs 28 is left out there dangling. Why shouldn't the tradents have preserved the memory of the setting in which it occurred? Besides, it is easy to visualize such a shout from the crowds that perennially surrounded Jesus as he moved from village to village.

353. Gk, σκύβαλα (*skybala*), "refuse, garbage, dung." See Phil 3:3–11. Cf., also Luther's Heidelberg Disputation Thesis 3: "Although the works of man always appear attractive and good, they are nevertheless likely to be mortal sins." Thesis 11: "Arrogance cannot be avoided or true hope be present unless the judgment of condemnation is feared in every work."

354. Mark 1:9, 24, 10:47, Matt 4:13, 21:11, Luke 4:34, 18:37, John 1:45–46, 19:19. And he is called the "Nazarene" in Matt 2:23, Mark 14:67.

355. It appears as Logion 31 in the Gospel of Thomas. It also appears in Papyrus Oxyrhynchus 1, a fragment of the Gospel of Thomas written in Greek covering Logion 26 to Logion 33. It was discovered by Bernard Grenfell and Arthur Hunt in 1897. The fragment is dated to the late third or early fourth century. It is housed in the Bodleian Library. The text was published by Grenfell and Hunt in 1898. The manuscript was written in the form of a codex and in a good-sized uncial hand. For a translation see Schneemelcher, *New Testament Apocrypha*, 104–0. The form of the Thomas logion is earlier than the synoptic versions. Theissen and Merz, *Historical Jesus*, 39.

356. Bultmann, *History*, 31, however, claims the early church was reading its

experience back into Jesus's experience in his hometown. But why would it do that? It would seem to be the other way around: the church comforted itself with its own experience by the experience of Jesus. If the church was reading its experience back into Jesus', why would it limit it to Jesus' visit to his hometown? From the book of Acts it does not look as if the church had that experience at all anyway.

357. The third-century Chester Beatty Papyrus (p45, a representative of the Caesarean text tradition that is thought to have originated in Egypt and been brought to Caesarea and used by Eusebius) along with the so-called family 13 manuscripts also read "the son of a woodworker." The more difficult reading is the one identifying Jesus as the "woodworker," the former having been interpolated into the text by copyists who were following Matthew or because they did not want to identify Jesus with that class of common workers. It was obligatory for a father to teach his sons a trade. Lightfoot, *Commentary*, 415, quotes the Tosephta of Kiddush 1, "It is incumbent on the father to circumcise his son, to redeem him, to teach him the law, and to teach him some occupation."

358. But this could be Mark's hand at work emphasizing that God was the Father of Jesus (Mark 8:38, 14:36, and Jesus is his son, 1:1, 11, 3:11, 5:7, 9:7, 12:6, 14:61, 15:39). The omission of "father" in 10:30 is for the same reason as already noted above in the discussion of that passage. The list of Jesus' brothers and reference to his sisters were later interpreted as his half-brothers and sister and children of Joseph by a former marriage (Epiphanius and Origen) because of the belief of the perpetual virginity of Mary. Jerome thought they were cousins. Tertullian defended the more natural interpretation. Nineham, *Mark*, 166.

359. This story would have been very precious to the early church because it underscored their experience of the majority of the Jewish nation not accepting the Gospel. Luke in his book of Acts, over and over again, reports the rejection by the Jews in the diaspora. On the other hand, this observation should not be exaggerated. The Pentecost story reports the large number of Jewish adherents of "the Way" including priests (Acts 6:7) and Pharisees (Acts 15:5, and Paul himself was a Pharisee). It can also be well imagined that those who became part of the church at Pentecost carried the faith back to their homelands, where they would have brought others to the faith.

360. The Haftarah, the reading from the prophets, occurred at the end of the synagogue service. These readings may have already been set in a lectionary by the first century. The exact word Jesus read cannot be precisely delimited since the reading is a composite of Isa 61:1, 58:6, and 61:2. No remains of a synagogue have yet been found in Nazareth. However, twenty-three tombs have been discovered and investigated. Of them, eighteen are of a type that was usually used between 140 BC and AD 150. Four of them were equipped with rolling stones, a practice used during the Roman period. Two of the tombs contained a variety of pottery, lamps, vases, and glass vessels that date from the first to the fourth century AD. This evidence makes clear Nazareth was an established but small village in the first century AD. For a description of the archaeology of Nazareth see Finigan, *Archaeology of the New Testament*, 43–65, and Theissen and Merz, *Historical Jesus*, 165. See Roemer, *World of Jesus*, 566–574, for a description of the organization of the synagogue and its appurtenances. As to the existence of a synagogue it could well be that the people met in the courtyard of some house in Nazareth. Such a gathering on the Sabbath could be called a "synagogue" (i.e., "assembly [of the people]").

361. Roemer, *Who in the World Was Jesus*, 247–59.

362. "Today" is used frequently in Luke's Gospel (12:28, 13:32–33. 19:5, 9, 42, 23:43).

363. Danker, *New Age*, 59.

364. Caird, *Luke*, 86.

365. Danker, *New Age*, 60.

366. Meier, *Marginal Jew* I, 270. Meier, as usual, is "wary" of any claim to Lucan historicity because of a "clear presence of Luke's redactional hand." However, Luke's vocabulary and style are everywhere in evidence and only point to his rendition of the tradition into his own style and syntax.

367. Bultmann, *History*, 32. But he must admit that vs 15 "finds symbolic expression in the setting of the story."

368. *Parallelismus membrorum* is used extensively in the Hebrew poetry of the psalms and proverbs. It coordinates independent clauses in complementary or contrasting extensions using the same grammatical elements for each side of the parallel. E.g., in Prov 1:5 we read, "A wise man will hear and increase in learning, and a man of understanding will acquire wise counsel."

369. Eunuchs would be included among people with physical defects and toll collectors and prostitutes among those with moral defects. See Matt 21:31 and Mark 9:43–48.

370. Matt 5:33–35, Luke 6:20–22. See also the parable of the rich man and Lazarus in Roemer, *Who in the World Was Jesus*, 306–16.

371. Theissen and Merz, *Historical Jesus*, 271.

372. Cf., how the prophets see God moving history for either the weal or woe of his people Israel. Urbrock, "Blessings and Curses," 755a.

373. Urbrock, "Blessings and Curses," 755b.

374. See how blessing and happiness are related in Luke 1:41–44.

375. Urbrock, "Blessings and Curses," 756b.

376. The subject of the verb is unspecified, so it could have been mothers, fathers, or even older children.

377. In Mark 9:33–37, Matt 18:2–4, and Luke 9:46–48 Jesus makes a child who is characterized by humility an example of greatness. In the Marcan passage, followed by Luke, it is a matter of one who, by "receiving" a child "in my name," also receives "the one who sent" Jesus. The commentators are befuddled by this collection of verses, whereas the Matthean version makes much greater sense. However, regarding this passage Taylor, *St. Mark*, 404, observes that "The teaching on true greatness (35), the indispensability of the attitude of childlike trust (Mt xviii.3), and the mind which esteems the lowly as in some sense Jesus Himself (37), are some of the most authentic and characteristic elements of His thoughts." He understands on the basis of vs 42 that Mark's use of "child" in vs 37 means one of the weaker members of Mark's community, one who has the greatest need of being served (405).

378. The word is used in Wis 5:22 to describe God's wrath against his foes. In the New Testament it is used in Matt 20:24 of the ten disciples who were angry at James and John, and it is used in Matt 21:15 and 26:8 of the Jewish leaders and their attitude toward Jesus.

379. See n 369.

380. See the LXX of Lev 7:18, 19:7, 22:23, 25. These verses refer to the so-called peace offering, on which see Roemer, *World of Jesus*, 25. If eaten after the second day of the sacrifice it would render the sacrifice unacceptable and incur sin on the part of the person who offered it. Any injured animal also was not acceptable as a "peace offering." Cf., Sir 35:16: "He whose service is pleasing to the Lord will be accepted, and his prayer will reach to the clouds."

381. See Luke 17:10, Matt 5:5, 23:12. So the two verses 14 and 15 are congruent.

382. Taylor, *Mark*, 424, quoting Bengel, *Plus fecit, quam rogatus erat*.

383. The words and action here are the sanction for and ground of infant baptism. See Nineham, *Mark*, 268–9.

384. Bultmann, *History*, 33.
385. Lohmeyer, *Das Evangelium des Markus*, 345.
386. Nineham, *Mark*, 334, and Dibelius, *Die Formgeschichte des Evangeliums*, 261.
387. Other parabolic features include that Jesus knew how much the people deposited and that he knew it was "all of her living" (vs 44). However, he could have heard the amounts that were called out by the priest in charge. The verb θεωρέω (*theōreō*, "see, look at") can be used in the sense of perceiving something that is heard (this word comes from the Marcan hand). Gingrich, *Lexicon*, 360b. Neirynck, "The Redactional Text of Mark," 144, 150–1, 157–61. But how could we know that it was used in that sense here? However, that the widow was "poor" could well have been seen by her dress.
388. Codex Bezae (D) has one of its "western non-interpolations" with the reading "he observed how the crowd deposited much." This "interpolation" could be due either to an attempt to align the story closer to Luke's version or to bring it into closer agreement with the tradition as the scribe of D or its prototype knew it.
389. Neirynck, "Redactional Text," 144, 150–1, 157–61.
390. The *quadrans* was the smallest Roman copper coin and was equal to two *lepta*.
391. Vs 41: "bronze" (employed only in these verses) and "rich" (occurs only here and in 10:25); vs 42: "widow" (occurs only here and in the previous passage); "poor" (occurs only in traditional contexts, 10:21, 14:5, 7); "cast" (occurs only in traditional context, e.g., 2:22, 4:26); vs 43: "more" (occurs only here), "truly I say to you" (occurs throughout the four evangelists in traditional contexts); vs 44: "abundance" (occurs only here in Mark), "life" (occurs only here in Mark), and "poverty" (occurs elsewhere only in Phil 4:11).
392. See Jer 7:6, 1 Kgs 17:20, Deut 14:29, Isa 1:17, Acts 6:1, Jam 1:27 and the provisions that were made for them in early Christianity (1 Tim 5:3–16).
393. The admonition not to judge by externals (Mark 7:18) and the call to deprive oneself of riches to follow Jesus (Mark 10:21).
394. Cf., the parables of the unjust steward (247–59) and the prodigal son (241–7) in Roemer, *Who in the World Was Jesus*. Grundmann, *Das Evangelium nach Markus*, 258. His observation here is apropos:

> [In her action] her love for God is visible. As Jesus saw demanded in the greatest of all commandments which sets free from the obligation to possessions, so the woman does not remain bound and captive to worry and so can give up everything, because she, in her love for God, trusts him to know how to care for her. [My translation.]

Cf., also Haenchen, *Weg Jesu*, 433,

> When a poor woman, who scarcely has anything to call her own, offers something of it, then it is clear that her heart participates in it. [My translation.]

395. Cf., the two parables referred to in the previous note.
396. The story resembles the parable of the toll collector and the Pharisee (Luke 18:10–14), where one expects the Pharisee to be made an example rather than the despised toll collector. The widow appears to be empty, a wasteland of want, but she turns out to be filled with faith and trust toward God. The toll collector was the sinner, but he was the one who was "justified," the one truly right with God. Both widow and toll collector exemplify the attitude of empty-handedness before God, which is what he requires. Cf., Sir 11:11–13:

> [T]here is a man who works, and toils, and presses on, but is so much the more in want. There is another who is slow and needs help, who lacks strength

and abounds in poverty; but the eyes of the Lord look upon him for good; he lifts him out of his low estate and raises up his head, so that many are amazed at him.

Its parabolic nature is underscored by the rabbinic example referred to by Bultmann, *History*, 59, from Lev. R 3:

> There was a woman who brought a handful of flour [as an offering]. The priest despised it and said, "Look what you bring! How much of that can be eaten [by the priest as his share]? And how much can be used for sacrifice?" Then the priest saw in a dream, "Do not despise her; for she is as one who has offered her life, her very self."

397. Lohmeyer, *Markus*, 345.
398. In Greek it would have read something like:

εἶπεν ὁ Ἰησοῦς τὴν παραβολὴν ταυτὴν»
τις πλούσιος καὶ χήρα πτωχὴ ἀνέβησαν εἰς τὸ ἱερὸν
βάλλειν τὰ δῶρα αὐτῶν εἰς τὸ γαζοφυλάκιον.
καὶ ὁ πλούσιος πολλὰ ἔβαλεν.
καὶ ἡ χήρα λεπτὰ δύο ἔβαλεν.
εἶπεν δὲ ὁ Ἰησοῦς, ἀμὴν λέγω ὑμῖν ὅτι
ἡ χήρα ἡ πτωχὴ πλεῖον τουτοῦ ἔβαλεν.
οὗτος γὰρ ἐκ τοῦ περισσεύοντες αὐτῷ ἔβαλεν.
αὕτη γὰρ ἐκ τῆς ὑστερήσεως αὐτῆς
πάντα ὅσα εἶχεν ἔβαλεν ὅλον τὸν βίον αὐτῆς.

399. Cf., also the saying in Luke 10:9 where having nothing is equated with "lacking nothing." The Corinthians, in spite of the fact that most of them were not "wise" or "powerful" or of "noble birth" (1 Cor 1:26) still were "not lacking any spiritual gift" (1 Cor 1:7). The same paradoxical quality is found elsewhere in Paul (1 Cor 4:8–13, 2 Cor 4:7–12, 8:14, Phil 4:12).

400. See note above.

401. Strack and Billerbeck, *Kommentar aus Talmud and Midrasch*, 46. Leviticus Rabbah originated sometime between the fifth and seventh century AD in the land of Israel and was based on older sources.

402. Mark has Jesus and his disciples sitting "opposite" the treasury. It's a loaded word. Jesus sits "opposite" the Temple mount in 13:3 and predicts its destruction—it is to be left without "one stone on the other" (13:2). So the widow has divested herself for a doomed institution. Just preceding the story Jesus refers to the scribes who "devour the houses of widows" (12:40) who then obviously are left bereft. So the widow is left bereft by giving all she had to the Temple, which has now "devoured" her goods. Her deed remains without effect and is consumed in the fate of the Temple. Mark retains, however, a certain ambiguity. He finds the faith-act of the widow commendable, but the identification of God with an institution abandoned by him leaves the devotee to it barren. The widow in her utter devastation is a symbol for the inner bankruptcy of the old order. But Mark doesn't gloat over its demise; he presents his "Gospel of Jesus Christ the Son of God" (1:1) as the new way of God in the world. Juxtaposed to the barren widow is she who anoints his body for burial (14:3–9). She is the true exemplar of giving: she gives to Jesus, the true Temple (John 2:19–21), and participates in his death. This woman who gives all to the living and true Temple gains a reward for what she has done for it "will be told in memory of her" as the Gospel is proclaimed in all the world (14:3–9). See Wright, "The Widow's Mites," 256–65.

403. There are a number of textual variants in the passage, none of which alter the sense. Some important ancient manuscripts read the more common word τυρβάζω (*tyrbadzō*, "trouble, confuse, stir up," and in the passive "to be in disorder, jumbled") for the word θορυβάζω (*thorybadzō*, "greatly disturbed"). The latter reading is supported by the most important ancient uncials, and because it is the more difficult reading it is therefore to be preferred. The most significant variant, however, is the substitution of "little is needed" for "one thing is needed" (vs 42) or the combination of both in the phrase "little is needed, or only one." Caird, *Luke*, 149, omits the whole phrase as an early gloss. The phrase is indeed omitted by a number of old Latin manuscripts and most importantly Codex Bezae (which usually includes a much fuller text so that when it does omit words or phrases textual scholars hold that as worthy of consideration as pointing to an original reading, which they call a "western non-interpolation"). Metzger, *Textual Commentary*, 154, however, judges the omission as "a deliberate excision of an incomprehensible" (referring to the double "little, only one thing is needful") reading, "if it is not a sheer accident, perhaps occasioned by homoeoarcton" (that is, the eye of the scribe, catching the reference to "Martha" in vs 41b, thought he had already included 41b-42 and so did not copy these verses, which he thought he had already reproduced in his manuscript). The "good part" finds a resonance elsewhere in Jesus's teaching. Cf., the parable of the rich fool (who didn't choose it); the unforgiving servant (who didn't practice it); the entrusted servant (who acts on it); the prodigal son (who finally chooses it); and the entrepreneur (who seeks the "Pearl of Great Price"). See Roemer, *Who in the World Was Jesus*, 165-8, 201-7, 215-7, 241-7, 294-6. Note that Luke places this little scene immediately after Jesus's parable of the good Samaritan. They form a unit that balances action with repose. Life in the kingdom is not a matter of unremitting action and doing but also involves quietude, listening, and learning.

404. The versions translate variously "desire to have you" (AV), "demanded permission" (NAS), "has got his wish" (NJB), "demanded to have you" (RSV). Arndt and Gingrich, *Lexicon*, 275a, give the definitions of "scrutinize, examine, inquire," and refer to its use as an "examination" particularly in a judicial process connected with torture. Satan is the prosecutor, the great accuser (Job 1:8—2:7, Zech 3:1).

405. Satan "demands the death penalty without recommendation to mercy [and] has asked to have [the disciples], as once he asked to have Job, confident that they too, in the midst of catastrophe, will learn to curse God who called them into the service of a lost cause." Caird, *Luke*, 240.

406. "Hear" occurs twenty times in Matthew, fifteen times in Mark, and twenty-three times in Luke!

407. On the Samaritans see Roemer, *World of Jesus*, 502-6.

408. "Giving thanks" occurs thirty-two times in the psalms. See, e.g., Pss 9:1. 28:7, 30:4, 12, 44:8. 54:6, 106:1, 47.

409. Jesus emphasizes over and over again that one's faith has saved from disease (Matt 8:10, 9:2, 22, 29, 15:28, Mark 2:5, 5:34, 10:52, Luke 7:50, 18:42). In this way Jesus preserves a person's autonomy and prevents himself from becoming some kind of guru on whom one becomes dependent. So no one is to call him or others of his entourage "father" (Matt 23:9).

410. That "must" is part of Jesus's ministry: he must preach the Gospel (Luke 4:43), he must suffer and die (Luke 9:22, 13:33, 17:25, 24:7, 26), he must loose from Satan's bondage (Luke 13:16), there must be rejoicing in the kingdom (Luke 15:32), and he must fulfill the Scriptures (Luke 22:37, 24:44). Danker, *New Age*, 191.

411. Danker, *New Age*, 192.

412. Fenton, *Matthew*, 333, interestingly suggests that Matthew here has used the story of David's intention to invade Jerusalem; the resident Jebusites, boasting of the

security of their citadel, then taunt him by saying the "blind and lame" could ward him off (2 Sam 5:6–7). David attacks and conquers the "lame and blind," to which the writer adds, "Therefore it is said, 'The blind and lame shall not come into the house.'" Matthew contrasts the messiah David with the messiah Jesus, to whom the blind and lame come and are healed. All of this points again to Matthew's massive reconstruction of the original narrative.

413. Or does he have in mind the stones strewn about the Mount of Olives, more or less imitative of John the Baptist and his reference to stones (Luke 3:8)?

414. See Roemer, *World of Jesus*, 235–7, for Pilate's irrational and egregious attacks on the Jews and the flaunting of their beliefs and practices.

415. Jesus is represented as traveling though Judea (Luke 13:32), in which case the insertion of this warning is out of place since Herod Antipas had no jurisdiction there. See below.

416. See Luke 5:30, 6:2, 7, 7:30, 11:42–43, 11:53, 12:1, 15:2.

417. The church would have preserved this saying because it understood it as a Christological expression about Jesus: the inert universe witnesses to his divine glory.

418. Luke may have understood that Jesus was speaking of the stones of the Temple, and so the divine sanctuary itself bore witness to him as the Son of God (Luke 4:1–12).

419. The coin in the mouth of a fish was widespread folklore in Judaism and the Hellenistic world. See the references in Bultmann, *History*, 35, n. 3.

420. See Roemer, *World of Jesus*, 395, concerning this tax. See also Exod 30:11–16, which required every Jew beginning at the age of twenty to pay this tax. The reference to the δίδραχμα (didrachma) refers to the temple tax. This Tyrian double drachma was the preferred currency to pay this tax. Harb, "Matthew 17.24–27," 256.

421. Harb, "Matthew 17.24–27," 266.

422. Harb, "Matthew 17.24–27," 268. She appeals (269) to Gerd Theissen's and Annette Merz's criterion of plausibility (*The Historical Jesus*, 116–22) whereby if the Jewish context and the "individual dimension" occur within a tradition, it is likely historical. A controversy about the Temple tax fits well within the time of Jesus, and Jesus's argumentation and his implied intimate relationship with God as his Father are uniquely his own. This tradition fits in the ideological continuity between Jesus's cleansing of Temple and his later prediction of its destruction. Here he asserts freedom from the tax, which underscores his initial attitude toward the Temple not as an economic institution of money making but the eschatological house of prayer for all nations.

423. The tax was collected in various centrally located places in the Galilee. Theissen and Merz, *Historical Jesus*, 176. See also their pages 232 and 439 for the latter two points.

424. Harb, "Matthew 17.24–27," 256. See also 257–9 on her brief history of the tax. Matthew would be interested in encouraging his community to pay the tax as Rome, after the war, had transferred the tax to its own fisc, calling it the *Fiscus Judaicus*. Nonpayment would then negatively exacerbate the relationship between his Jewish-Christian community and Rome. It is also possible Matthew wanted to preserve a relationship with the wider Jewish community and not offend it by the nonpayment of this tax (Harb, 261, cites Matt 10:6, 23:3). Payment of the tax also maintained Jewish religious freedom under Rome. Since Matthew's community consisted of both Jews and Gentiles and only the Jews had to pay the tax, he would be interested in the Gentiles paying the tax to preserve harmony within the community.

425. He applies the same principle to eating food offered to idols: "if food is a cause of my brother's falling, I will never eat meat, lest I cause my brother to fall" (1 Cor 8:13). Luther in his treatise "On Christian Liberty" expressed the same principle with the paradox that describes the Christian life: "The Christian is free subject to none and

slave to none. The Christian is also subject to all and slave to all."

426. Even Bultmann, *History*, 35, must admit that "we have here in the strict sense a piece of biographical material," although he and other scholars understand various pieces of it as originating with the editor.

427. Wright, *Victory of God*, 171-2, who labors mightily to find a modern model to illustrate Jesus's provocative, and one could say even incendiary, ministry: "he was more like a politician on the campaign trail than a schoolmaster; more like a composer/conductor than a violin teacher; more like a subversive playwright than an actor . . . He was issuing a public announcement, like someone driving through town with a [loudspeaker] . . . like a man with a red flag heading off an imminent railway disaster . . . like someone setting up a new political party and summoning all and sundry to sign up and help create a new world."

428. It is used in terms of a judicial decision in Mark 14:64 and Acts 25:21.

429. Wright, *Victory of God*, 171.

430. Bultmann, *History*, 35 n 5, remarks that in Judaism the fox was a pictorial description of an unimportant man, while an important one was a lion. Rienecker, *Sprachlicher Schlhssel*, 116, adds that the metaphor "functioned in Judaism as the type of a misdirected man who lacks real power" (my translation). Strack and Billerbeck, *Kommentar aus Talmud and Midrasch*, 200-1, cites examples associating the fox with slyness but says most of the associations are with an "unbedeutenden, niedriger Menschen, waehrend ein grosser bedeutender Mann mit einem Loewen verglichen ist" ("an unimportant and lowly person while a highly important man is compared to a lion"; translation mine).

431. The verb is τελειοῦμαι (*teleioumai*, present passive), which has a wide range of meanings: "complete, bring to an end, accomplish, finish, perfect, make perfect." It is used in the mystery religions "to be consecrated or initiated." The passive is difficult to translate with these definitions. So I find the suggestion of Arndt and Gingrich, *Lexicon*, 817, "bring to its goal," as the best translation and way of understanding what Jesus had in mind. Cf., KJV: "I shall be perfected"; NAS: "reach my goal"; NJB: "attain my end"; RSV: "finish my course"; NRSV: "finish my work." These varied translations witness to the difficulty involved in finding just the right words in English. Cf., Luther, "werde ich ein Ende nehmen" ("I will bring to an end").

432. See also Mark 9:12, 10:38-40, 14:27, 41, 49, Luke 12:49-50, 22:37.

433. Casey, *Aramaic Sources*, 193-4, reconstructs what he finds to be the original Aramaic of Mark 10:35-45, so the verses were probably not invented by the evangelist. See also Evans, *Mark*, 119-25, who provides a fulsome argument for the authenticity of the "ransom" saying.

434. Harb, "Matthew 17,24-27," 254-5, who references a study by Dieter Zeller.

435. Wright, *Victory of God*, 574-6. I will deal extensively with Jesus's death and its meaning in the final volume of this series.

436. In 56:1-8 the "orthodox" position regarding foreigners is challenged, and universalism is asserted. In chapters 60-62, which are the original nucleus of Trito-Isaiah, we find a stark contrast to Ezekiel. The latter's vision is based on mundane reality. The hierocracy consists of the anointed leaders who are in charge of rebuilding the Temple presented in his meticulous plans. These chapters have a visionary aspect to them: all are considered holy—i.e., all are priests, and the nations will bring in the materials and build the Temple (cf., Lev 16-17, Num 18, Ezek 44:5, 12, 15).

437. See also 57:1-7 and Hanson, *The Dawn of Apocalyptic*, 112. If Hanson is correct, these verses are an attack on the Temple, which equates it, in the most biting criticism, with a brothel. In 58:1-12 cultic technical terms are employed that refer to cultic inquiry and priestly ministrations at the altar. These terms characterize the oracles

as admonitory and challenging the legitimacy of the cultus in contrast to true cultic behavior. The cultus again figures in the background of 59:1–20, where it is judged as defiled and therefore ineffectual. The object of the complaint is the cult leaders. In chapter 65 the cultus and its ministers are once more the focus. The sacred activities in which they are engaged are portrayed as angering YHWH. Hanson understands this chapter as seminal in the developing of apocalyptic because of the nascent division of epochs between the present evil age and the world to come (157–9). Israel is no longer a unified entity seen as the object of YHWH's salvation but rent by schism between the corrupt and righteous as evoked by the image of the grape cluster (65:8).

438. Nickelsburg, *Jewish Literature*, 94.
439. Nickelsburg, *Jewish Literature*, 298.
440. Nickelsburg, *Jewish Literature*, 303.
441. Gaertner, *The Temple*, 16.
442. Gaertner, *The Temple*, 21.
443. Schrenk, "hieron," 239–40.
444. Clements, *God and Temple*, 105–6.
445. "P," one of the four sources combined into the five books of the Torah. The others are the Eloist ("E"), which originated in the north, the Yahwist ("J"), which originated in the south, and the Deuteronomist ("D").
446. Clements, *God and Temple*, 116.
447. Cf., von Rad, "Zelt und Lade," 109–29, who distinguishes between "dwelling temples" and "theophany temples." Jacob, *Theology of the Old Testament*, 73, interprets the Priestly Writers' concept of the cloud as an attempt to make YHWH's presence permanent in contradistinction to occasional. Koch, *Die Priestershaft*, understands the evidence as involving two interwoven concepts of the cloud. Clements, *God and Temple*, 119, speaks of a "sustained theophany."
448. Clements, *God and Temple*, 121. The critique is embodied in the narrative by the demand that everything must be anointed (i.e., nothing is holy in itself, Exod 22–33) and by the narrative element that Moses receives the instruction for the erection of the tabernacle directly from YHWH (Exod 25:8–9—i.e., true worship is known only to God).
449. Clements, *God and Temple*, 111
450. Ackroyd, *Exile and Restoration*, 153–217.
451. Hanson, *Apocalyptic*, 347. Ploeger, *Theocracy and Eschatology*, 101, relates the "pierced one" of 12:10 to the murder by the high priest Yohanan of his brother in the Temple (Josephus, *Ant*. 11, 7, 1) and suggests that the emphasis of the text is not so much on the murder itself but on the profanation of the Temple. But Dentan, *Mark*,, 1108, suggests, on the basis of Isa 53, that it may refer to a future martyred prophet of the messiah.
452. The "Divine Warrior" represents God as fighting alongside the nation's army in their conflict with pagan nations and as the determining factor in victory (see Exod 13:3–4). The ark was carried into battle as a concrete representation of the divine presence (Num 10:35-36, Josh 6, 1 Sam 4–7).
453. The MT text reads (*KeNa'aNY*, "Canaanite"), which cannot refer to a race of peoples but must refer to merchants since all the nations now have access to the holy mount. Mitchel, *A Critical and Exegetical Commentary*, 356.
454. Ploeger, *Theocracy*, 32–4, and Hanson, *Apocalyptic*, 273–5. For another opinion, cf., Stinespring, "Eschatology in Chronicles," 209–19.
455. See Roemer, *World of Jesus*, 22–31, 32–6, 549–57.
456. von Rad, *Wisdom in Israel*, 166.
457. Nickelsburg, *Jewish Literature*, 168. See the Epistle of Aristeas (84–99).

458. See 2 Macc 3:1-4, 24-30, 10:5, 3 Macc 1:10.

459. Schrenk, "ieron," 241, notes how highly Josephus prizes the Temple, a fact made clear by his historical presentation, which has everything culminating in its destiny. For him, the "right of free exercise of the cultus is more important that political freedom." He conceives the Temple as the οἰκητήριον τοῦ θεοῦ (*oikētēhieron tou Theou*, "dwelling place of God," *Antiquities* 8, 114, 131), but this conflicts with his "Greek sensibility that God cannot be localized" (*Antiquities* 3, 129). The Rabbis continue to share this attitude in that after the destruction, they look forward to the days of the Messiah when the Temple would appear again in greater glory. The description of this new construction is extravagant, reiterating much of the biblical imagery, particularly that of Zech 14: Eden offers its wood, the Temple abounds in precious metals, the holy objects lost since the first destruction return, God himself returns, the waters of life break forth from it, which dispenses healing and fruitfulness (Strack and Billerbeck, *Kommentar aus Talmud and Midrasch*, 885). However, the Rabbis are divided in their opinions concerning the return of the sacrificial system. In Pesiqta 79a, for example, it is said that only the thanksgiving sacrifice (see Roemer, *World of Jesus*, 25) would remain. Apparently, it was thought in messianic times there would no longer be any sin.

460. Black, *An Aramaic Approach*, 125-6. Mark uses this "redundant auxiliary verb" (Taylor, *Mark*, 48) to initiate a new action or a new stage in a discussion (cf., 1:45, 4:1). Each occurrence drives the action or discussion forward. So here, Mark indicates that a new stage of the entry into Jerusalem has begun.

461. "Money changers" is unique in Mark as is "seats," "over-turning," and "carry through." "Vessels" also appear in only one other context (3:27).

462. Pryke, *Horae Synopticae Electronicae*. Schmithals, *Das Evangelium nach Markus*. Neirynck, *Duality in Mark*, 144, 150-1, 157-61.

463. Hamilton, "Temple Cleansing and Temple Bank," 356-72.

464. Derrett, "Zeal of the House," 85

465. See also 2 Kgs 18:4-6, 22:3—23:25, 1 Macc 4:36-60, 2 Macc 10:1-8. Cf., Hiers, "Purification of the Temple, 86, and Nineham, *Mark*, 301.

466. On the whole economics of the Temple see Hamilton, "Temple Cleansing," 365-72.

467. Hamilton, "Temple Cleansing," 367.

468. Derrett, "Zeal of the House," 85.

469. See Derrett, "Zeal of the House," Hamilton, "Temple Cleansing," and Hiers, "Purification of the Temple." But none were particularly serious. Cf., Abrahams, *Studies in Pharisaism and the Gospels*, 82-9.

470. The accusation in that case would be "deriving profit from that which exists for the purpose of fulfilling a divine command." Derrett, "Zeal of the House," 82-3.

471. mBerakoth 9, 5: "One should not enter the Temple Mount with a staff, or with shoes on, or with a wallet, or with dusty feet; nor should one make it a short cut, all the more spitting [is forbidden]."

472. The portion of the yield of a Jewish farmer's harvests that was given to the priests (Num 18:8-10). See m. Shekalim 3,2:

> There were three chests of three seah each [about six gallons] in the treasury, marked alef, beth and gimmel. Rabbi Yishmael said they were marked with the Greek letters alpha, beta and gamma. The one who withdrew the funds was not allowed to enter the treasury wearing a garment with a hem, shoes or sandals, tefillin or an amulet (so that no one should suspect him of stealing funds and concealing them in these places). Without this precaution, if he became poor, people would think it was a Divine punishment for

misappropriating funds, and if he became wealthy, people would think it was because of his ill-gotten gains. It is important that a person please not only God but also other people as per Numbers 32:22, "You shall be innocent before God and Israel" and Proverbs 3:4, "find grace and good understanding in the eyes of God and man."

473. Ford, "Money 'Bags,'" 251.

474. "This is the House which [He will build for them in the] last days, as it is written in the book of Moses, *In the sanctuary which Thy hands have established, O Lord, the Lord shall reign for ever and ever* (Exod 15:17–8). This is the House into which [the unclean shall] never [enter, nor the uncircumcised,] nor the Ammonite, nor the Moabite, nor the half-breed, nor the foreigner, nor the stranger ever." Vermes, *Complete Dead Sea Scrolls*, 493. Such an attitude could rest on a literal interpretation of Zech 14:21 that would understand the *KeNaaNY* as "Canaanite" and therefore find justification for an outlook that would see the Temple mount as meant exclusively for Jewish visitation.

475. Roth, "The Cleansing of the Temple," 174–81.

476. The suggestion by Ford, "Money 'Bags,'" 250, that the vessels referred to receptacles for money lacks any supportive evidence.

477. Hamilton, "Temple Cleansing," 371. Cf., Isa 60:3. Isa 56:1–8 and 60–62 read like a commentary on Zech 14.

478. See Roemer, *World of Jesus*, 401–37.

479. Cf., Josiah's building activities and the reforms he initiated (2 Kgs 22). Simon the Maccabee was proclaimed high priest and leader who could then don "the purple robe and gold buckle" (1 Macc 14:44), the insignia of the high priesthood. The acclamation contained the proviso, however, "until a trustworthy prophet should arise who then would make clear, by divine oracle, whether the recognition of Simon and his descendants was legitimate or that some other arrangements in the leadership of the nation should be made." Roemer, *World of Jesus*, 79. In this way he was made the custodian of the Temple. First Macc 14:27–28 records that Simon was made "great high priest in Asaramel." The latter word is a Greek transliteration of the Hebrew "*Nasi 'am 'el*," i.e., "prince of the people of God." So it is a divinely appointed priest and prince who has charge of the Temple.

480. Wright, *Victory of God*, 494.

481. Hiers, "Purification of the Temple," 86: "there is enough evidence to suggest at least the possibility that Jesus went to Jerusalem in order to prepare that city and the temple for the coming of the kingdom."

482. Hiers, "Purification of the Temple," 87.

483. See the story of the healing of an official's household member below.

484. John says he was a βασιλικός (*basilikos*, a "royal official"), which would imply an officer in the service of Herod Antipas and therefore probably a Jew, although he might also have been a Gentile. "*Basilikos*" can also refer to the soldiers or troops (e.g., Josephus, *War* 1, 1, 5), so the terms "centurion" and "official" are not necessarily contradictory. See Meier, *Marginal Jew*, 721, on the title "centurion," who shows that even someone designated as "centurion" could be either a Jew or Gentile in Antipas's service. However, both Matthew and Luke make clear that he was a Gentile. Capernaum was near the border of Herod Antipas's Galilee and his brother Phillip's tetrarchy. There was a toll station nearby and a garrison of Herod stationed there. So when John refers to an official and Matthew and Luke to a centurion, such a person would be a natural part of the landscape of Capernaum.

485. Matthew refers to the person needing healing as παῖς (*pais*, "a male child, boy, son, a male slave, servant"). Luke refers to a δοῦλος (*doulos*, "slave"), although the

centurion also refers to him as "my servant" (ὁ παῖς μοῦ, *ho pais mou*). So Luke means by his use of *pais* his "boy" in the sense of "slave." John explicitly refers to the patient as his "son" (υἱός, *huios*) and then later as his παιδίον (*paidion*, "little boy") but also as his *pais*, by which he obviously means his "son." Perhaps the ambiguous *pais* stood in the tradition behind the various present forms of the story and then was interpreted variously as we find it in the three traditions. Meier, *Marginal Jew*, 724, suggests that the ambiguity traces back to an original Aramaic *talya*, which means "boy" in the sense of either "servant" or "son." That led to the Greek translation *pais*, which led to Luke's 'servant" and John's "son" and the various other words used in the three versions.

486. See Roemer, *Who in the World Was Jesus*, 365-7.

487. Meier, *Marginal Jew*, 725: "That two such diverse sources [i.e., John and Q], which otherwise have relatively little in common, should agree on the core of a miracle story is itself a striking datum."

488. Metzger, *Textual Commentary*, 220.

489. Under Rabbi Johanan ben Zakkai (post AD 70) the death penalty was no longer enforced. Understandably then, the Mishnah does not deal with the subject. (The Hillelite branch of Pharisaism, the more liberal of the two Pharisaic groups, became the majority after the destruction.) However, it became the duty of a husband whose wife was suspect to divorce her even if he was willing to overlook the offense in the case of a proven adultery. Moore, *Judaism*, 125. The Essenes upheld the punishment by stoning (Temple Scroll 66,1-9).

490. Contra Marsh, *John*, 685, who envisions Sadducees as Jesus's opponents.

491. Marsh, *John*, 686.

492. Thurman, *Disinherited*, 105.

493. Deut 29:19, 2 Macc 8:4, 12:42, and in the Pseudipigraphical works, Odes of Solomon 14:33, Enoch 99:2, and the Letter of Aristeas 252. Classically it meant "faultless" or "unfailing." In the Deuteronomy passage the LXX reads "lest they destroy the sinner and the innocent" in place of the Hebrew "bring disaster on the moist and dry alike" (NRSV). The LXX correctly interprets the meaning: the moist are the faithful and the dry the impenitent. See below on the words of Jesus to the weeping women of Jerusalem (Luke 23:31).

494. Suggested by Marsh, *John*, 688.

495. Bultmann, *History*, 36, and others who have followed him; see Wright, *Victory of God*, 348, n 113.

496. Wright, *Victory of God*, 349.

497. Nineham, *Mark*, 344, in agreement with Bultmann considers the question of the disciples in vs 1 as an obviously composed construction to elicit Jesus's prophecy concerning the destruction of the Temple. Whatever the situation in which Jesus uttered this prophecy, it is certainly authentic. It could have been borrowed from the following pronouncement story. At any rate the two belong together. And it is certainly not impossible that Jesus predicted the destruction of the Temple at different times and in different circumstances.

498. On the ideology of holy war see Roemer, *World of Jesus*, 13-6.

499. Jesus's ministry resembles that of Jeremiah, who called the nation to repentance and warned of its destruction. But he was only persecuted for his seemingly negative message. And the disaster did occur.

500. Wright, *Victory of God*, 493.

501. Josephus, *War* 6, 2, 99. See also Roemer, *World of Jesus*, 342.

502. The prophets had wept at the destruction of the Jerusalem Temple as did the people (Isa 22:4, Jer 9:1, 13:17, Joel 2:17). Earlier, when Titus had begun building the earthworks at the Fortress Antonia and the wall at Herod's palace in preparation for

breaking into the Temple and city, Josephus had addressed the defenders, declaring that he himself would be willing to die if only they would surrender and so save themselves, the Temple, and the Holy City (*War*, 5, 9, 5). See also Roemer, *World of Jesus*, 333–4. In like manner Paul in Rom 9:1–3 asserts his readiness to be "accursed and cut off from Christ" if it would lead to the conversion of his people.

503. See Roemer, *Who in the World Was Jesus*, and the parables of the rich fool (165–8), leaven in a lump (198–201), the unforgiving servant (201–7), a neighbor comes at midnight (230–4), the prodigal son (241–7), the unjust steward (303–6), the good Samaritan (247–59), and the returning demons (347–50).

504. See Roemer, *Who in the World Was Jesus*, 247–59, the parable of the unjust steward.

505. See below on the dispute about exorcism in chapter 3.

506. "Jerusalem" often stands as a metaphor for the whole people, e.g., Pss 122:6, 128:5, 147:2, 12, Isa 3:8.

507. I estimate that perhaps a million Jews lost their lives in the war with Rome.

508. Luke's story of a woman anointing him while he reclined at table (7:36–50) looks like a completely different incident, although the host bears the name "Simon" as in Mark's story, but he is a Pharisee not "the Leper." In Luke's account his name is only revealed when Jesus finally addresses him. There is no evidence that the other three evangelists thought of the woman as a prostitute, especially Mary in John. Luke does not refer to the anointing as Jesus's anointing for burial, and no one criticizes the woman for "wasting" the myrrh; rather she is held in contempt because of her sinful state. The anointing is of his feet (as in John). The point of Luke's account is the woman's extravagant way of showing her thankfulness for being forgiven (the point too of the embedded parable). So his account has little that aligns it with the other three accounts of Jesus's anointing, where the point is approving the woman's action as preparation for Jesus's burial. It would be difficult to show that Luke's accounts derived from the others or vice versa. For the exposition of Luke's account see Roemer, *Who in the World Was Jesus*, 299–303.

509. Nineham, *Mark*, 371.

510. Nineham, *Mark*, 372. He attributes the saying of preparation for his burial to the community that was "distressed" that this usually respectful treatment of the dead was omitted.

511. Fenton, *Matthew*, 412, suggests that the saying of Jesus could be rendered, "when God's angel announces the victory of God to the whole world, this also what she hath done, shall be spoken of (before God's throne, in the last judgment) that God may mercifully remember her." It would resemble Nehemiah's appeal to God to remember his deeds in a favorable way (Neh 5:19). In that case the saying could well be authentic, reflecting Jesus's own proclamation of the kingdom.

512. Cyrene had a large Jewish population. Simon was probably in Jerusalem to celebrate the Passover. Cyrene was located in Lybia, the oldest and most important of the five Greek cities in the region. It gave eastern Libya the classical name *Cyrenaica* that it has retained to modern times. Located nearby is the ancient Necropolis of Cyrene. The city was named after a spring, Kyre, which the Greeks consecrated to Apollo.

513. Later in the early second century, gnostic groups claimed that Simon changed places with Jesus and was crucified in his stead. Gnosticism conceived the only-begotten One of God to be incorporeal and incapable of death, least of all able to suffer crucifixion. Irenaeus, *Adversus Haereses* 1, 24, 4, describes their beliefs:

> the Father without birth and without name . . . sent his own first-begotten *Nous* (he it is who is called Christ) to bestow deliverance on them that believe

in him, from the power of those who made the world. He appeared, then, on earth as a man, to the nations of these powers, and wrought miracles. Wherefore he did not himself suffer death, but Simon, a certain man of Cyrene, being compelled, bore the cross in his stead; so that this latter being transfigured by him, that he might be thought to be Jesus, was crucified, through ignorance and error, while Jesus himself received the form of Simon, and, standing by, laughed at them. For since he was an incorporeal power, and the Nous (mind) of the unborn father, he transfigured himself as he pleased, and thus ascended to him who had sent him, deriding them, inasmuch as he could not be laid hold of, and was invisible to all.

Referred to by Nineham, *Mark*, 422.

514. "Simon" (Shimon) was the most frequently used Jewish name for males in the Galilee and Judea, followed by Joseph, Lazarus, Judas, John, Jesus, Ananias, Jonathan, and Matthew. These nine names were borne by about half of the men. yeshuaincontext.com.

515. Gen 25:29, 30:16, 34:7, Exod 23:16, Deut 14:22, 1 Sam 11:5, Luke 17:7. But Arendt and Gingrich, *Lexicon*, 13b, find that it also means "country" as opposed to a city or village. They cite the Codex Bezae, reading "on a journey" with "arrived from the country" (παρίστιν ἀπ' ἀγροῦ, *paristin ap' agrou*) in Luke 11:6. That seems to be the extent of examples for the meaning "country."

516. The English versions (KJV, NAS, NJB, NRS, RSV) translate "from the country." Luther, however, "der kam vom Felde," "who came from the field."

517. The Roman military had the right to impress citizens to carry their barrage and other paraphernalia for a mile (Matt 5:41). Luke substitutes ἐπιλαβόμενοι (*epilabomenoi*, "to seize, lay hold of") and omits the references to Alexander and Rufus, which persons had no meaning for him and for Theophilus, for whom he was writing.

518. Bultmann, *History*, 37. Yet he still considers them as originally Christian apologetic.

519. Strack and Billerbeck, *Kommentar aus Talmud and Midrasch*, 263, gives a number of parallels. MQ 25b Rab Aschi: "What did you say at that day [of the funeral lament]? He answered, 'When the cedar falls in the flame what will the hyssop on the wall do? When Leviathan is drawn up on the hook what will the fish in shallow water do? When in the flowing stream the hook falls what will the water of the cistern do?'" Seder Eliz R 14,65: "The learned have said, 'When fire seizes the damp what should the dry do?'" GenRab 65, 42a:

> As Jose ben Joezer was led off to his crucifixion his nephew also road next to him and mocked, "Do you see the steed on which my lord allows me to ride and look at your steed [the cross beam] on which your Lord [God] lets you ride." He answered, "If such is for those who vex God what then will to be for those who do his will?" He [the nephew] answered, "Is there anyone who has done his will more than you have? If such a death is for those who do his will what will happen to those who vex him?" [my translation]

Evidently, these pithy sayings were prevalent in Judaism and are examples of arguments from the lesser to the greater (*a minore ad maius*). Cf., Matt 6:24–34 for a series of examples of this argument.

520. I'm following Caird, *Luke*, 249, here.

521. Caird, *Luke*, 250.

522. Nineham, *Mark*, 110. Matthew's version is clearly parallel to Mark's, but he introduces the saying of the legality of rescuing animals on the Sabbath (Matt 12:11)

as a counterargument to his unnamed interlocutors who ask an apparently accusatory question of whether it is lawful to heal on the Sabbath. He further adds the saying about human beings being of more worth than animals, apparently a variant of a similar saying about sparrows (Matt 10:29–31).

523. The Essenes, on the other hand, did not allow even the rescue of an animal on the Sabbath. Damascus Document XI, 13. Fragment 7, I, 6. Helping a person who fell into water on the Sabbath was allowed, but an instrument could not be used, only his garment.

524. The Jubilee year is described in Lev 25:8–17 and involves the proclamation of liberty and freedom from oppression, recognizing that they are the people of God. The language of Isa 61:1–3, to which Jesus himself refers in the Lucan passage, is redolent with the vocabulary associated with the Jubilee, particularly "liberty" or "emancipation" (Hebrew, *DeRoR*). C. J. H. Wright, "Jubilee," 1028b.

525. The passage was probably originally part of Second Isaiah's prophecy.

526. See the justice that is required in economic transactions and the return of leased land to the owner in the Leviticus description of the Jubilee.

527. See Roemer, *World of Jesus*, 571–3, on the synagogue personnel.

528. Cf., Judg 3:14, 10:8, 1 Kgs 7:15, 2 Kgs 25:17. The number appears in the previous passage in Luke, being the number upon whom the Tower of Siloam fell.

529. Contemporary Jews who take the prohibition against work on the Sabbath seriously have caused stove manufacturers to install a "Sabbath setting" on their stoves that eliminates having to turn it on so that one may avoid work by kindling a fire on the Sabbath. See mBethzah ("Festival Days") 4,7: "They may not produce fire [i.e., bring into existence what was not previously made ready] out of wood [i.e., by rubbing two sticks together], stone [i.e., creating friction with metal], or water [by filling a glass container with water and setting it in the hot sun, which makes the glass so hot it can ignite a wick]."

530. Damascus Document XI, 15–16: "But should any man fall into water or [fire], let him not be pulled out with the aid of a ladder or rope or [some such] utensil." "Falling into water" apparently refers to falling into a cistern.

531. Again the argument from the lesser to the greater comes to the fore. If God does not forget the lives and the fate of sparrows, how much more is he concerned with human life.

532. Danker, *The New Age*, 159, notes that the Sabbath was the climax of God's creative activity and a day of blessing. The Sabbath was a protection against exploitation, so it is entirely apropos that the woman be healed and be freed of any further exploitation by Satan.

533. The same word is used in Luke 9:22 expressing the divine necessity of the cross. See Caird, *Luke*, 171.

534. Caird, *Luke*, 171.

535. Bultmann, *Synoptic Tradition*, 13.

536. John reports the same accusation in 8:48, 52, 10:20.

537. Nineham, *Mark*, 120.

538. It is God's finger that wrote the ten commandments on the stone tablets (Exod 31:18, Deut 9:10).

539. Nineham, *Mark*, 120, suggests that the "strong one" may have been used to describe the eschatological deliverer and was therefore a primitive eschatological title for Jesus. See Mark 1:7.

540. See m. Sanhedrin 10:1:

> And these are they that have no share in the world to come: he that says that there is no resurrection of the dead . . . and that the Law is not from Heaven, and an Epicurean. R. Akiba says: also he . . . that utters charms over a wound.

"Epicurean" does not mean the Greek philosophy but those who are licentious and skeptical. Danby, *The Mishnah*, 397, n 4.

541. E.g., Bultmann, *Synoptic Tradition*, 15. He lists the interpreters, both pro and con, to his position in n 1. He would trace this "interpolation" back to the Palestinian church to justify her right to forgive sins. It seems that the exact reverse is the case! Jesus is explicitly represented as conferring that right to the church (Matt 18:18, John 20:22). John makes it a word of the resurrected Lord. Matthew may have retrojected that back into the pre-Easter life of Jesus.

542. Of course, this latter pericope was a piece of free-floating tradition and not originally a part of John's Gospel as witnessed by the oldest manuscripts. Some manuscripts place it at the end of the Gospel or after Luke 21:38, which provides a context for the surrounding material in each case. sHowever, it appears to be an authentic piece of tradition that somehow was not included in any of the Gospels.

543. It appears that Jesus is not inside a house (which could hardly accommodate a crowd) but in the common courtyard of several houses. A house had a rather thick covering of mud, straw, and clay, which would have rained down a shower of debris if it were "dug through." The courtyard, however, had a covering of thatch, which would have been easily removed and produce only a little falling debris. The courtyard also would have accommodated many more people than a house. These insights were provided by a docent at the Museum of the Bible in Washington, D.C., in the section where a mockup of a Galilean village is located, which I visited with my grandsons in August 2019.

544. The parallel in Luke 20:26 reads, "they marveled and were silent."

545. The term frequently occurs in the Gospels as an expression of Jesus himself. If it is a self-designation of Jesus in this pericope it expresses his identity with humanity and especially his own people, with the weak and humble and as the "representative of the new Israel and bearer of God's judgment and kingdom." Caird, *Luke*, 94.

546. "Forgiveness is a prerogative of God which he shares with no other and deputes to none." Moore, *Judaism*, 535. The sacrificial system, of course, provided a means for forgiveness (see Lev 5). And God is the compassionate one who himself forgives (Pss 65:3, 85:2, Jer 31:34, 33:8, 36:3).

547. Gk. σάββατον ὁδός, *Sabbaton hodos*, "Sabbath journey." The distance has been generally reckoned as 2000 cubits (3000 feet) or approximately two-thirds of a mile. Acts 1:12 is the only place where the phrase occurs in the Bible and specifies its length as the distance from Mt. Olivet to Jerusalem. (From the eastern gate of Jerusalem to the present site of the Church of the Ascension on Mt. Olivet is slightly over one-half mile.) The regulation perhaps had its origin in the Mosaic period in the injunction to the Israelite not to leave camp to collect manna on the Sabbath (Exod 16:29). In the Targum the command reads: "Let no man go walking from the place beyond 2000 cubits on the seventh day." Another origin of the idea is the provision that the area belonging to the Levitical cities included land that extended from the wall 2000 cubits on every side (Num 35:5). Still another is the supposed distance that separated the Ark and the people both on the march and at camp (Josh 3:4). The specific regulation, however, applied only to leaving the city, the prescribed distance being measured from the city gate. Within the city proper, no matter how large it might be, there was no such limitation. The original intent of the provision was to ensure that the day was given over to God, to emulate him in his resting on the seventh day (Gen 2:22–23), and to keep

it holy, preserving it from profane activities. It did, however, permit exceptions. For example, if one were caught at a distance on a journey, he might travel to the nearest shelter for safety.

548. Most commentators agree that the story is a composite. See Beare, "The Sabbath Was Made for Man?," 130. However, this attachment formula occurs both in the tradition and in Marcan redaction.

549. Caird, *Luke*, 98.

550. The story of David is found in 1 Sam 21:1-6 and the ritual placing of the loaves in Lev 24:5-9. In the Judaism of the time the figure of David functioned as the embodiment of the aspirations of Israel for renewal and vindication, as an instrument by whom the light of the knowledge of God would go out to all the nations, and that through him there were to be a renovation of worship and the defeat of the power of evil. Kee, "The Function of Scriptural Quotations," 165-88. The Dead Sea Scrolls, 4QpIsd 1-8, 4QFlor 1.1, 10-14, and Patriarchal Blessings 1-6 describe the universal dominion of the Branch of David that will occur. The "branch" is identified as the Messiah of righteousness in the latter named writing. So the figure of David was a living symbol in Judaism and connected with the eschatological renewal of Israel. Mark interpolates the reference to make a statement about Jesus that thoroughly fits his theological point of view. But Mark is not asserting that Jesus is "son of David," but he is like David who is effecting, as David did, a turning point in the kingdom. There is no organic connection between the two. In 12:35-37 Mark decisively rejects that Jesus is "son of David." Mark is asserting that in Jesus the kingdom is turning but not from one earthly kingdom to another but to the kingdom of God (1:14-15). This new kingdom will bring about the abandonment of the old leadership and the turning over of his vineyard to a new leadership (12:1-12). The new founder is rejected by the leadership of the old, but his election is of God (12:11). Thus, the shape of Mark's version of the pericope has to do with rejection and election, destruction of the old and foundation of the new, with a subtle premonition of the cross that is the exaltation and enthronement of this new king who founds the kingdom of God. Mark also appears to make a mistake by his reference to Abiathar because it was his father, Ahimelech, who was the actual high priest at the time (but Abiathar was taken under David's protection and shared the high priesthood with Zadok during his reign, 2 Sam 20:25). In addition, there was nothing unlawful about laymen eating the bread of the presence. Ahimelech's only concern was that David and his men were ritually pure. Apparently, Mark is reflecting contemporary conditions concerning the bread of the presence in the Temple of his day (see Josephus, *Ant.* 3, 10,7).

551. Origin of this commentary probably in the third century AD.

552. Mark may have understood it as a reference to Jesus himself. Nineham, *Mark*, 106, regards it as a "Christian comment . . . added before Mark's time—'expressing the conviction that Jesus is Lord of all that belongs to man, including the Sabbath.'"

553. Bultmann, *Synoptic Tradition*, 17-18: the basis of the whole is to be found in vss 1-8, which he styles as a community product since Jesus is defending the behavior of the disciples. Mark then added additional dominical sayings in vss 9-13 with the attachment formula "and he was saying to them" (derived from the polemic of the early church) and vss 14-15, another saying from the tradition (vs 16 is a gloss not supported by the best manuscripts). Following these additions, he appended the commentary of vss 18b-19, inserting the transition provided by vss 17-18a. Meanwhile the "Pharisees and scribes" of 7:1 disappear from the scene. The final verses again are linked by an attachment formula "and he was saying," which could also mean "he meant thereby." Because they are a catalogue of vices, he judges them as coming from a Hellenistic milieu.

554. See Roemer, *World of Jesus*, 468-83. This adoption of the oral law, interpreted

as going back to Moses and participating in the divinity of the written Torah, made the Pharisees very popular with the people.

555. Others occur, e.g., in 5:41 and 13:14.

556. The translation of the Hebrew by the RSV reads, "And the Lord said: 'Because this people draw near with their mouth and honor me with their lips, while their hearts are far from me, and their fear of me is a commandment of men learned by rote.'"

557. However, Jesus does not say their intention is to deliberately disobey the written Torah as Nineham, *Mark*, 189, avers. The text reads, "How well you reject the commandment of God in order to observe your tradition" (my translation). Jesus means that their oral law supersedes that of the written.

558. Quoted in Sanders, *Jewish Law*, 54, from Philo, *Hypothetica* 7, 3.

559. See Roemer, *World of Jesus*, 480–1. mEduyoth 5, 1–4 refers to a whole list of rulings in which they differ.

560 And see the discussion in mNedarim ("Vows"). Listed in 1–2, for example, are various circumlocutions for vows that the Rabbis said one could not evade performing.

561. Nineham, *Mark*, 190.

562. I suspect, as I've frequently stated, that Jesus's conflicts with the "Pharisees" reported in the Gospels were with the School of Shammai, the more strict Pharisaic school.

563. Sanders, *Jewish Law*, 57.

564. Literally Mark 7:3 reads, "For the Pharisees and all the Jews except they wash the hands by the fist [Gk., πυγμή, *pygmē*] they do not eat." It has been variously translated. Most translate simply "wash the hands," but NJB renders it with "washing their arms as far as the elbow." The regulations in the Mishnah suggest it means "up to the wrist."

565. m. Hagigah ("the Festival Offering") 3, 5. The hands had to be ritually clean to make a valid heave offering (*Terumah*), i.e., the portion of the harvest that had to be given to the priests (Num 18:8–9, Deut 18:4). Because of its sanctity it was susceptible to uncleanness, so the hands that offered it had to be ritually cleansed. A cooking pot full of heave-offering liquid are both made unclean by ritually unclean hands, mTebul Yom ("One Who Immersed Himself on That Day") 2, 2.

566. See Roemer, *World of Jesus*, 25.

567. mYadaim ("Hands") 1, 1.

568. mKelim ("Vessels") 25, 7–8.

569. mTohoroth ("Cleannesses") 4, 11.

570. Sanders, *Jewish Law*, 40.

571. Nowhere in the Gospels is Jesus represented as visiting Tiberias. Sanders, *Jewish Law*, 40. See the discussion above on corpse impurity in the exposition of the parable of the good Samaritan in Roemer, *Who in the World Was Jesus*, 303–6, and in Roemer, *World of Jesus*, 475. In the parable, Jesus by implication criticizes the priest and the Levite for ignoring the man beaten almost to death by bandits. Jews had the obligation to at least bury the dead of their own people.

572. It is not clear in whose house the meal takes place. It could have been in the house where Jesus stayed and that he was the host. Luke, however, clarifies it by saying explicitly that Levi hosted a feast. Levi was obviously at the tollbooth that divided Herod Antipas's Galilee from Phillip's tetrarchy. He technically then was not a tax collector, but the stigma of a collaborator would still have clung to him. He was in regular contact with Gentiles. The toll collector would also have been involved in extortion. All of these tax men were looked upon as traitors, and no respectable Jew would involve himself with such employment. They were banned from the synagogue.

573. Matt 9:11 refers only to "Pharisees," and Luke 15:2 makes it "the Pharisees and the scribes." Both these readings witness to the text of Mark.

574. Sanders, "Jesus in Historical Context," 440, concludes that Antipas was overall thoroughly Jewish, as were his governors and magistrates, the courts, and the law that governed the land. (Most of the Gentiles lived in Scythopolis and the territory that belonged to it.) To be inferred from this study is the presence of Jewish scribes all over the Galilee who were well versed in the law.

575. See the description of scribes in Roemer, *World of Jesus*, 417.

576. On the identity of this "Levi" see Nineham, *Mark*, 99.

577. See Roemer, *World of Jesus*, 528–31, for a description of first-century Capernaum and for a reproduction of how the town probably looked in the first century, including contemporary photographs of the ruins of Peter's house and the tenements in which Jesus probably made his home.

578. See Roemer, *World of Jesus*, 394–8, on taxes and toll collectors.

579. So God himself is represented as a healer who obviously must deal with the people's uncleanness. See also 2 Chr 7:14, Job 5:18, Isa 57:14–21, Hos 7:1, 14:4.

580. Nineham, *Mark*, 97, who engagingly presses the medical metaphor: the average person will not deal with contagious people, but the doctor and his agents, the nurses, must come and deal with the patient.

581. Oprah Winfrey is quoted as saying, "Surround yourself with only people who are going to lift you higher." Jesus surrounded himself only with people whom his culture said could pull one down by potentially leading one to adopt their manner of life. Nineham, *Mark*, 95.

582. See Hgg 2:11–13.

583. The great eighth-century prophets Amos, Hosea, Isaiah, and Micah condemned the concern for proper ritual in the Temple, which was associated with sheer injustice (Amos 5:21–24). They all showed a marked bias in favor of the poor. They identified justice as true righteousness.

584. See, e.g., Deut 10:18, 14:29, 16:11–14, Pss 10:18. 82:3, Isa 1:17, Jer 5:28.

585. E.g., at the time of a death (John's?). There were days of fasting connected with the new year (mRosh Ha Shannah 3,4) and special days of fasting, for example, if there was no rain (mTaanith 2,3). The practice had been systematized in Judaism and valued for its own sake. The Pharisees apparently voluntarily fasted twice a week (Luke 18:12). Early Christianity continued the practice (Acts 13:2–3, 14:23, Didache 8:1.

586. Ninham, *Mark*, 103, agrees with the commentators that the reference to the Pharisees was added and was perhaps a deduction from the sayings themselves. Bultmann, *History*, 19, opines that Mark added the metaphors of vss 21–22.

587. E.g., even if a bridegroom appeared to have leprosy, he was exempt from priestly inspection for the seven days of the wedding feast. mNegaim 2, 2.

588. Jeremias, *Gleichnisse*, 117, who cites also Rev 19:7, 21:2, 9, 22:17.

589. Ninham, *Mark*, 101.

590. See also Jer 16:19, 33:11, 1 Macc 1:27. Cf., Rev 18:23

591. See Acts 13:2–3 and 14:23.

592. See also Rev 19:7, 21:2, 9, 22:17. And the Song of Songs was interpreted as applying to God in his relationship to his people.

593. Jeremias, *Gleichnisse*, 117. "Repair a rag with expensive material? Pour fermenting wine into worn-out, dilapidated wineskins?" Luke 5:36, however, destroys the realism of the imagery of the patch by having the patch torn from a new garment to repair an old one, something no one would do.

594. Jeremias, *Gleichnisse*, 118. Similarly, in the parables of the guest without a garment (Matt 22:11–13) and the prodigal son (Luke 15:11–32) the festal garment is an image of the time of salvation. Cf., also the story of Joseph (Gen 41:42), who is adorned in garments of "fine linen" and then ushers in a time of salvation for the whole world.

See also Eth Hen 62:15–6: the righteous "shall wear the garments of glory. These garments of yours shall become the garments of life from the Lord of the Spirits. Neither shall your garments wear out, nor your glory come to an end before the Lord of the Spirits." Cf., Rev 3:4–18.

595. Jeremias, *Gleichnisse*, 118.

596. Matthew adds to the end of the passage "so both are preserved," asserting that Judaism is not abolished but both it and Christianity continue side by side until the coming of Christ at the end of the age. Fenton, *Matthew*, 140.

597. Contra Dibelius and Bultmann. Hultgren, *Adversaries*, 73.

598. Hultgren, *Adversaries*, 73.

599. Mark is the source used by both Matthew and Luke in their respective renditions of these narratives.

600. Only Matt 21:5 makes that explicit. The entry narrative has associations with the feast of tabernacles: the carrying of branches, the reference to Ps 118, and the eschatological coloring. In addition, there were water rites associated with the feast when water was brought from the Pool of Siloam and libations conducted at the altar. Exuberant joy and celebration accompanied the feast. The reading of Zech 14 might have already been attached to the feast in the first century. Many of the rites associated with tabernacles were transferred to the new feast of Hanukkah initiated in Maccabean times. The Haphtarah (prophetic reading) associated with this feast was Zech 3:1—4:7, which contains a number of remarkable resonances with the entry narrative: Joshua, the high priest, is informed he will rule YHWH's house and have charge of his courts. Zechariah is informed of the establishment of a new age in which everyone will live in peace and prosperity in what appears to be the worship of God in a perpetual autumnal festival (Ackroyd, *Exile and Restoration*, 191). Zechariah sees a lampstand, which is associated with light-giving and the restoration of the Temple. In this regard, Zerubbabel, the Davidide, is told the great mountain, the symbol of all opposition, will be leveled before him. The completion of the rebuilding of the Temple is indicated by the promise that Zerubbabel will bring forth the headstone.

601. Water issuing from the temple is a traditional element; see Ezek 47, Pss 46:4, 65:9, Isa 33:21, Joel 3:18. Clements, *God and Temple*, 72, notes that these waters:

> may have been identified with the spring Gihon which played a part in the Jerusalem festivals, but its real significance is to be found in the mythological belief in the river which fructified the garden of paradise, where God's dwelling was situated. The idea of this river is vitally related to the belief in the presence of God, for just as in paradise a life-giving river was thought to flow, so Jerusalem was looked upon as a paradise on earth, a place where God's presence was to be found [which idea] . . . enjoyed its greatest prominence in connection with the Autumn Festival.

602. Rowley, *Worship in Ancient Israel*, 202.

603. John 2:14–18 supports this unity. "The Judeans" immediately after his cleansing of the Temple ask him for a sign to corroborate his actions.

604. Elsewhere in Mark's tradition as he received it, the word "authority" is related to the disciples' authority to exorcise (3:15, 6:7).

605. Cranfield, *St. Mark*, 43.

606. Shae, "The Question on the Authority of Jesus," 18.

607. Zech 14:16–21. With the destruction of Jerusalem and the Temple, however, all of these hopes were dashed. Mark's community had put their hopes and trust in this apocalyptic scenario and no doubt understood Jesus's resurrection as a confirmation of its fulfillment. One of the ways Mark deals with this tragedy, which had the potential

for destroying the faith of his community, is his reorienting the tradition and interpreting the cleansing as a proleptic destruction of the Temple. He accomplished this by the addition of Jeremiah's words about making the temple a "den of bandits" (7:11), which is set in the context of the Lord's words that he would destroy the Temple as he had the temple at Shiloh. In addition, he interpolates the cleansing into the middle of the story of the cursing of the fig tree that becomes "withered to the roots" (Mark 11:20; the Temple's destruction is then made explicit in Mark 13:2). His Gospel then reorients the Jesus tradition in the direction of Jesus's salvific death and resurrection. As it is said, "the gospels are passion narratives with long introductions." See Telford, *Barren Temple*, 1–38. Munderlein, "Die Verfluchung des Feigenbaumes," 92–4. Giesen, "Verdorrte Feigenbaum," 95–111.

608. Nineham, *Mark*, 306. The phrase "from heaven" was the usual circumlocution for "from God" reflecting the Jewish reverence for the divine name and avoiding trespassing the second commandment.

609. The commentators latch onto the word "believe" in vs 31 as a Christian point of view. E.g., Bultmann, *History*, 20, Nineham, *Mark*, 308. However, "believe" occurs twenty-seven times in the Old Testament. The story of Moses at the bush (Exod 4) is particularly apropos; Moses has a dialogue with God and complains that he will not be believed even though he performs wonders. See also Deut 1:32, Ps 78:32. It is the prophet's experience that he or she is not believed.

I have dealt with the "sinful woman at table" and the parable it contains in the previous volume *Who in the World Was Jesus*, 299–303.

610. Taylor, *Mark*, 424–5.

611. Nineham, *Mark*, 273. It is in fact applied to persons in the Old Testament. See 1 Sam 29:6–9, Mal 2:17, Eccl 2:26, 7:26. Brown, *Lexicon*, 373b. Jesus himself refers to good and evil persons in Matt 5:45.

612. Taylor, *Mark*, 426a.

613. Taylor, *Mark*, 427b.

614. Cf., Matt 6:21 and the parables of treasure in a field, the rich fool, and the rich man and Lazarus in Roemer, *Who in the World Was Jesus*.

615. See the parables of treasure in a field and the pearl of great price in Roemer, *Who in the World Was Jesus*.

616. Bultmann, *History*, 22. Taylor, *Mark*, 430, affirms that these sayings are so closely related to the former narrative "so as to be almost a part of it."

617. See Matt 7:3–5. The "miniscule 13" (i.e., written in lowercase letters as all modern editions of the Greek New Testament; the lowercase was invented during the ninth and tenth centuries AD) manuscript reads κάμιλος (*kamilos*, "a rope or ship's cable") instead of κάμηλος (*kamēlos*, "camel"), a change of only one letter. The reading was thus an endeavor to mitigate somewhat the severe metaphor of Jesus. The manuscript 13 is the lead manuscript in a group known as Family 13 (designated by the siglum *f*13). This group now contains thirteen manuscripts. It is also called the Ferrar Group. This family of manuscripts varies in date from the eleventh to the fifteenth century and display a distinctive pattern of variant readings. For example, they place the story of Jesus and the woman taken in adultery in the Gospel of Luke, rather than in the Gospel of John; the text of Luke 22:43,44 is placed after Matt 26:39; and the text of Matt 16:2b-3 is absent. These manuscripts are all thought to derive from a lost majuscule (written only in capital letters as all of the oldest and most ancient manuscripts). On the basis of palaeographical analysis, it appears that most of these manuscripts (with the exception of minuscule 69) have been written by scribes trained in Southern Italy. The same change is made in Matthew and Luke by several later witnesses. Metzger, *Textual Commentary*, 169, notes that the two words later began to be pronounced alike.

618. See Trueblood, *Humor of Christ*, who finds thirty humorous passages in the synoptic Gospels.

619. Job being the quintessential example of virtue and piety being rewarded with wealth. For Judaism wealth was no barrier to the divine favor but, to the contrary, a sign of it. In these sayings of Jesus therefore, differing as they do from Judaism's understanding of wealth, we hear the very voice of Jesus.

620. See Ps 1:3. The Torah observant man "is like a tree planted by streams of water, that yields its fruit in its season, and its leaf does not wither. In all that he does, he prospers."

621. Nineham, *Mark*, 272. Matthew, on the other hand, takes a different tack. One must go beyond the keeping of the law. To achieve perfection (Matt 19:21) the man would have to sell all he has, give to the poor, and then follow Jesus.

622. Peter has more individuality in the Gospels than the other disciples, but he appears always with the twelve in the background. Bauckham, *Jesus and the Eyewitnesses*, 168.

623. Nineham, *Mark*, 273. "For the sake of the gospel" in vs 29 is Marcan. This phrase is actually omitted by Codex Alexandrinus (fifth century) and the first hand of Vaticanus (fourth century) and a few late miniscules. Taylor, *Mark*, 434a.

624. E.g., note the repetition of the dreams of Pharaoh in Gen 41.

625. The final vs 31, however, is free-floating tradition that becomes appended to many a context in the Gospels and is therefore surely a Marcan addition.

626. Taylor, *Mark*, 435a.

627. Mark seems to have had available several historical reports such as is suggested here. Others can be found for example in 1:21–38 and 5:22–43.

628. Haenchen, *Weg Jesu*, 413.

629. Bornkamm, "Das Doppelgebot der Liebe," 89. Because of this rationalistic cast Bornkamm finds the passage's provenance in the Hellenistic milieu as well as because Philo (*de spec leg* II, 63) makes a similar coordination between one's duty to God and others. See also Donahue, "Neglected Factor," 563–94.

630. The Rabbis did make a distinction between the law (Torah) and the precept (*Mizwah*). By the precept they meant some special rite like circumcision, the use of phylacteries, or the observance of Sabbath. The scribe may have had in mind the question whether these precepts were the greatest and if so which among them were the most important. Lightfoot, *Commentary*, 437.

631. Donahue, "Neglected Factor," 578, n 51, lists scholars who concur with this assessment, adding that there is a "growing consensus that the double command took shape in an environment strongly influenced by Hellenistic wisdom." The Rabbis sought Scripture passages that expressed comprehensively the law. For example, Rabbi Simlai (3rd Century AD) found eleven in Ps 15, six in Isa 33:15, three in Mic 6:8, one in Amos 5:4, and one in Hab 2:4. In mAboth 1,2 Simeon the Just (third century BC) declared "by three things is the world sustained: by the Law, by the [Temple] Service, and by deeds of loving kindness." Rabbi Akiba (first century AD) announced "You shall love your neighbor as yourself" to be the most comprehensive rule in the Torah (Sifra on Leviticus 19:18). So the question of the "greatest commandment" was a completely unsettled topic. Moore, *Judaism*, 85.

632. Von Rad, *Theology*, 227, 230.

633. See Roemer, *World of Jesus*, 594–617.

634. Thomas, "Liturgical Citations," 209.

635. As noted below, the Marcan structure is amorphous. However, there is a parallelism between the answer of Jesus and the repetition of it by the scribe and also between the positive affirmation by the scribe at the beginning who evaluates Jesus'

answer to the Sadducees in the preceding passage as "well done" and Jesus' declaration at the end that the scribe is "not far from the kingdom."

636. Quoted in Moore, *Judaism*, 86.

637. Donahue, "Neglected Factor," 578.

638. Thomas, "Liturgical Citations," 209–10, finds the scribes' citation in Mark 12:33 to be based on the Septuagintal text form found in Codex Alexandrinus (fifth century) and Ambrosianus (five manuscripts dating from the fifth to eleventh centuries) where σύνεσις (*synesis*) has replaced ψυχή (*psychē*) and where ἰσχύς (*ischus*, "strength") is used for δύναμις (*dynamis*, "power, force, I can, I am able"). These are stylistic changes made to avoid the repetition of Jesus's words. Mark has apparently intervened redactionally into the scribe's answer. The quotation as attributed to Jesus in 12:30 rests on the same Septuagintal text except for the addition of διάνοια (*dianoia*) after ψυχή (*psychē*). This addition either was a result of Mark finding it in the tradition because it was a highly regarded variant appearing in the text tradition of Codex Vaticanus (fourth century) or was a gloss adopted later by the Marcan text. Cf., also Schweizer, *Mark*, 250: "the unique character of vs. 34 together with the scarcity of parallels to vss. 28–31 favors [the passage] being the record of an incident in the life of Jesus."

639. Stern, "Jesus' Citation," 312–6. Jesus does the same in Mark 12:26 when he refers to the story of Moses "at the bush."

640. Schweizer, *Good News*, 252.

641. See Num 27:8–11 concerning the lines of inheritance and Deut 21:15–17 for protecting the right of the firstborn in case of multiple wives.

642. The Mosaic Torah included without distinction moral, civil, religious, and criminal law. How familiar this situation is where heirs fight over their inheritance and bring endless lawsuits to the courts!

643. The Mishnah deals extensively, exhaustively, and in great detail with the rights of inheritance. Some examples: Baba Kama ("First Gate") 9,10 states that a (first) son may still inherit from his father if the father had declared *Korban* (dedicated as sacred) any "benefit the son would have from him" but not so if the father had added "and at my death" to his declaration. In the latter case the son would have to restore the benefit to the father's other sons or the father's brother. In mBaba Bathra ("Last Gate"), 8,5 says that a father may apportion his property in various sizes including making all equal to the first son's inheritance. See especially this latter tractate sections 8–9 on all the ways property and its inheritance are to be disposed. mBekoroth ("Firstlings") 8,9 allows the firstborn to receive a double share of the father's property but does not allow him to share in the increased value made before the division of the property.

644. See Roemer, *World of Jesus*, 401–6. These bandits were like Robin Hoods who stole from the rich and gave to the poor. In contrast Jesus brought the riches of the kingdom with its forgiveness, healing, and mutual support. The Greek word *lēstēs* (λῃστής) is incorrectly translated in the versions as "robber." The word means "bandit" and should be so translated. So Barabbas was a bandit as were the two who were crucified with Jesus.

645. Neyrey, *The Social World of Luke-Acts*, 34.

646. See Roemer, *World of Jesus*, 235–7.

647. Lightfoot, *Commentary*, 138.

648. The Pool of Siloam is mentioned in 2 Kgs 20:20 (cf., Isa 8:6), and a pool is mentioned in the inscription found in Hezekiah's tunnel. Josephus seems to indicate it was outside the city wall (*War*, 5, 4, 2), and he refers to it as a fountain or spring, which means he may have been thinking of the water that poured out of the tunnel into the pool. Finegan, *Archaeology of the New Testament*, 190–1.

649. Lightfoot, *Commentary*, 139, thinks that the tower might have been built over

the porticoes of the pool.

650. See Roemer, *Who in the World Was Jesus*, and the parables of the unforgiving servant (201–7), the prodigal son (241–7), on the way to the judge (291–2), the good Samaritan (303–6), the Pharisee and the tax collector (323–30).

651. See the discussion of the baptism in chapter 1.

652. Pace Bultmann, *History*, 23–4.

653. He was in the Fortress Machaerus some five miles east of the Dead Sea in Herod Antipas's territory of Perea. It had been built by Alexander Jannaeus in the second century BC. It was destroyed by Gabinius but refortified by Herod the Great. See Roemer, *World of Jesus*, 197–8.

654. Matt 3:11–12, Luke 3:16–17, cf., Joel 2:28, 1 Cor 3:13. The account comes from Q, written within a few years of the events it records. Obviously, neither Matt nor Luke are interested in the psychology of John. If that were so they or their Q source would have included John's response to the report that was brought to him by his disciples. The focus is on Jesus.

655. Of course, the experience of Pentecost reinterpreted Joel's prophecy as being fulfilled in that event. John also apparently did not have the Christian understanding of the "Holy Spirit" as shown by Acts 9:2. The phrase "the holy spirit and fire" also may be a hendiadys and mean "with the fire of the spirit" as Caird, *Luke*, 74, suggests.

656. Caird, *Luke*, 112.

657. See below in the summary characterizing the messenger Jesus.

658. See Roemer, *Who in the World Was Jesus*, 148–51.

659. Bultmann, *History*, 24.

660. Nineham, *Mark*, 279.

661. The word in Greek is συνέχω (*synechō*, "pressed from every side, afflicted, suffering from, urged, impelled, compelled"). The Luther translation has "*es ist mir so bange*," meaning "alarmed, afraid, anxious, worried."

662. Caird, *Luke*, 167–8.

663. Nineham, *Mark*, 280.

664. The word "ransom" does not occur often in the New Testament, only in 1 Rom 2:6, Rev 5:9, but the cognates "redemption" and "redeem" occur frequently and even more often in the Old Testament.

665. See chapter 1.

666. In an encomium of the mother and her seven sons martyred by the decrees of Antiochus who threw herself into the flames so that no pagan would touch her, it is said, "These, then, who have been consecrated for the sake of God, are honored, not only with this honor, but also by the fact that because of them our enemies did not rule over our nation, the tyrant was punished, and the homeland purified—they having become, as it were, a ransom for the sin of our nation. And through the blood of those devout ones and their death as an expiation, divine Providence preserved Israel that previously had been afflicted" (4 Macc 17:20–22). Nineham, *Mark*, 281, remarks that "there is no precise verbal parallel to this passage . . . in Paul."

667. Cf., Isa 53:10: "Yet it was the will of the Lord to bruise him; he has put him to grief; when he makes himself an offering for sin."

668. "Jesus therefore intended not only to share Israel's sufferings, but to do so as the key action in the divinely appointed plan of redemption for Israel and the world." Wright, *Victory of God*, 603.

669. Bultmann, *History*, 245.

670. Did Matthew compose the passage on the basis of people who used the name of Jesus as a magical incantation such as is depicted in Acts 19:13–17?

671. See Roemer, *Who in the World Was Jesus*, and the parables of the mustard seed

(134-7, leaven in a lump (198-201), the unjust steward (247-59), the good Samaritan (303-6), and the Pharisee and the tax collector (323-30).

672. Bultmann, *Jesus*, 78-9, solves the idea of reward as opposed to grace. "[Jesus] promises reward to those who are obedient without thought of reward."

673. See Roemer, *World of Jesus*, 401-42.

674. See Roemer, *Who in the World Was Jesus*, and the parables of treasure in a field (148-51), leaven in a lump (198-201), and the pearl of great price (294-6).

675. Nineham, *Mark*, 298-9. Munderlein, "Die Verfluchung des Feigenbaumes," 92-94, lists the various interpretations and their representatives.

676. Bundy, *Jesus and the First Three Gospels*, 425. So there were various attempts made to explain it away—e.g., Haenchen, *Weg Jesu*, 381, who maintains, "Nichts deutet darauf hin, dass Markus diese Geschichte . . . mit dem Schicksal Jerusalems irgendwie verbunden hat" ("nothing points to Mark combining in any way this story with the fate of Jerusalem"), whereby he completely ignores its rather pointed relationship with the Temple cleansing and the words of Jesus that follow in the eschatological discourse of Mark 13.

677. Munderlein, "Verfluchung," confirming Bundy's basic insight underscores the symbolical character of the action. See Bundy, *First Three Gospels*, 425, n 121. Giesen, "Verdorrte Feigenbaum," building on Munderlein's work has demonstrated the high probability of his thesis. Telford, *Barren Temple*, in this exhaustive examination has all but proved its certainty.

678. See Smith, "No Time for Figs"; Munderlein, "Verfluchung," 91; Giesen, "Verdorrte Feigenbaum," 95.

679. Mark makes of this incident a symbol for the destruction of the Temple.

680. Munderlein, "Verfluchung," 100-101.

681. Telford, *Barren Temple*, 195.

682. Telford, *Barren Temple*, 195

683. Referenced in Telford, *Barren Temple*, 198.

684. See Isa 25:6, 34:6-8, Jer 46:10, Zeph 1:7, 1 Enoch 62:14, 2 Enoch 42:5, bShab 153a, Luke 14:15, 22:30, Rev 2:7, and Behm, ἐσθίω (*esthiō*), 691.

685. Munderlein, "Verfluchung," 97.

686. Giesen, "Verdorrte Feigenbaum," 104. See Matt 5:6, Amos 8:11, Sir 24:21. Note too that Jesus alone is hungry.

687. Munderlein, "Verfluchung," 97; Giesen, "Verdorrte Feigenbaum," 107. Both assert the story, as they have reconstructed it, is a report from the life of Jesus

688. Codex Bezae (fifth-sixth centuries), Cyprius (ninth-eleventh centuries), Γ (ninth-tenth centuries), and the miniscules (lowercase) known as the Family 1 group of manuscripts. These all represent what is known as types of the "Western text" tradition. The chief characteristic of these manuscripts is their fondness for paraphrase and the expansion of the text of the New Testament as we find it in this passage. The text without this addition is supported by the most important manuscripts of the fourth century.

689. See Roemer, *World of Jesus*, 502-11, on the origin, development, and religion and culture of the Samaritans.

690. The hostility between Jews and Samaritans is strikingly portrayed by Josephus, who relates the story of how some Samaritans actually killed some Jewish pilgrims who were on their way to ("had set their face toward") Jerusalem to attend a festival. See Roemer, *World of Jesus*, 404.

691. In fact, a whole group of manuscripts insert into the brothers' request "as also Elijah did."

692. See Roemer, *Who in the World Was Jesus*, and the parables of the lost sheep

(154–7), the lost coin (239–41), the prodigal son (241–7), and the unfruitful tree (169–70).

693. The tax referred to was a poll tax payable since AD 6 by all of Judea, Samaria, and Idumea. At the time of its imposition a revolt broke out, and a "new philosophy" was born that stated to pay the tax was tantamount to idolatry because it was, in effect, recognizing the divine claims of Caesar and his reign rather than Israel's only true king, God alone. See Roemer, *World of Jesus*, 394–8, 433, Acts 5:37, and Josephus, *War* 2,8,1.

694. Klemm, "De Censu Caesaris."

695. Donahue, "A Neglected Factor," 572.

696. Already beginning with Octavian, popular sentiment greeted his rule as a marvel of divine manifestation, particularly in the East. His acceptance of the title "Augustus" indicates his simultaneous acceptance of the idea that his position was one of incomparable loftiness. Although his successors Tiberius and Claudius refused divine honors, Caligula and Nero abandoned all reserve. Caligula's image was minted on coins with the halo of the sun god Helios, and Nero represented himself as Apollo.

697. Stauffer, "Story," 126–7. The coin's inscription read *Ti[berius] Caesar Divi Aug[usti[F[ilius] Augustus* ("Tiberius Caesar of the divine Augustus son of Augustus"— i.e., he claims to be "son of god").

698. However, the commentators, except for Klemm, "De Censu," have focused their attention on the meaning of Jesus' pronouncement and its biblical or historical background, e.g., Giblin, "Things of God," 524–6, who finds Isa 44:5 and Jesus's question concerning the image and inscription on the denarius as the key to understanding the pronouncement, viz., that it refers to man's actions before God as they are expressed in moral conduct; or Stauffer, "Story," 128–33. He makes the historical points that the coinage is the emperor's in the "triple legal sense of majesty, guarantee, and property," and by using the coin one recognizes a legal subservience to Caesar and the legal obligation to pay it back. However, Jesus stresses not only this legal obligation but also the moral and theological duty based on a prophetic and apocalyptic theology of history, as is expressed in Jer 27:5–7, and just as concrete, he understands the second half of Jesus' pronouncement that "rendering to God" meant the payment of the "tithes, first fruits, vows, sacrifices, and the half-sheqel annual tax into the temple treasury." But these obligations stand superior to the monetary tax in that the *imperium Caesaris* is pronounced as the "way of history" and the *imperium Dei* as the "goal."

699. Robinson, *Problem of History in Mark*, 44–6. He found similarity in terms of the Marcan presentation—but the words ἐκθαυμάδω (ekthaumadzō) and θαυμάδω (thaumadzō) are traditional and evoke the sense of how Jesus was meant to be understood.

700. Robinson, *Problem of History in Mark*, 33–42.

701. Russel, *Jewish Apocalyptic*, 276.

702. Russel, *Jewish Apocalyptic*, 277–9, notes that the anti-God or anti-Christ is sometimes a human figure who subdues men, makes himself equal to God, and tramples on the saints. His identity can easily change. Russel finds the earliest reference to the anti-Christ in Dan 11:40–42, where the figure is to be identified with Antiochus. In the Asum Mos 8:1–3, the figure refers either to Antiochus or Herod the Great; in Pss of Sol 2:29, he is Pompey; in Sib Or III, 63–5, he is Simon Magus or perhaps Nero.

703. See Roemer, *World of Jesus*, 445–57, Russel, *Jewish Apocalyptic*, 220–1.

704. Hanson, *The Dawn of Apocalyptic*, 387. The analysis of Zech 14 that follows depends on Hanson, 369–401.

705. This division is also clearly made in the parable of the wicked tenants in Mark 12:1–12, where the leaders of the nation are distinguished from the nation itself.

706. Lohmeyer, *Das Evangelium Des Markus*, commenting on the passage, notes

that the phrase "you are true" is usually made only of God.

707. The encounter between Jesus and his questioners may well have been an extended narrative filled with details much like the parables, which are a precis of what were probably short stories. The scribal elements of Mark's community then took that old story and turned it into a concise and rhetorically sophisticated passage Mark has preserved for us. As it is, it certainly represents the gist of that encounter.

708. See Caird, *Saint Luke*, 22–3, Nineham, *Mark*, 326. Taylor, *St. Mark*, 480, presents a good summary of this point of view: "The reply does not mean that the world of politics and religion are separate spheres, each with its own governing principles. Jesus held that the claims of God are all embracing, but He does recognize that obligations due to the State are within the divine order. In particular, the acceptance and use of Caesar's coinage implicitly acknowledges his authority and therefore the obligation to pay taxes . . . this duty is not in conflict with, nor merely parallel to, the requirement to pay back to God all that is due to Him."

709. Theissen, *Shadow of the Galilean*, 157. In his narrative reconstruction of the Jesus of history he puts these words into the mouth of Pilate as he discusses Jesus' words about rendering to Caesar and God with the narrative's protagonist.

710. Mark enhances the association with the cross, by which he provides the hermeneutic with which he intends this passage to be read. For Mark, Jesus submits in the cross to the dominion of Caesar. It is Caesar's cross imposed by his representative Pilate, who, acquiescing to the Jewish leadership, arrays himself against God's beloved. It is thus in the cross that Caesar submits to the will of God, and God in the cross exercises his sovereignty over the whole world. So it is in the cross that Mark deprives the state of humanity's absolute allegiance and makes it subject to God's sovereign reign. Although the cross is not explicitly present in this passage, the reference to the plot against Jesus in 11:18 and 12:12, the death of the "son" in 12:8, and the intent of the leadership groups to ensnare Jesus in 12:13 all point to apprehending this pericope in the context of Jesus's death on the cross.

711. Donahue, "Neglected Factor," 574, suggests vss 26–27 have a less clear relationship to the old tradition. Schweizer, *Good News According to Mark*, 246–8 concurs. He sees two sets of answers here. One in vs 25 directed against Pharisees who ask what the resurrection will be like and a second in vss 26–27 against those who do not believe in the resurrection. Cf., Nineham, *Mark*, 322, who opines that Mark replaced an original acclamation at the end with vss 26–27. Downing, "The Resurrection of the Dead," 45–6, feels that vs 25 is the intruding verse inserted by Mark or the community and is a "bit of stock apocalyptic speculation." Bultmann, *Synoptic Tradition*, 26, regards the whole as coming from the church's own internal debate; when formulating this narrative they choose the Sadducees as foil since they were known as those who denied the reality of the resurrection.

712. Nineham, *Mark*, 319.

713. Russel, *Jewish Apocalyptic*, 220–40.

714. *Theological Dictionary*, II, 293. The following discussion is drawn from this article on δύναμις (*dynamis*, "power, force").

715. Bultmann, *Synoptic Tradition*, 27.

716. See Roemer, *World of Jesus*, 480–1 on the schools of Hillel and Shammai.

717. The fact that the questioners are described as "tempting" or "putting to the test" (vs2) could mean that they have in mind Herod Antipas's taking his brother's wife illegally and thus, in effect, committing adultery and getting Jesus to make a pronouncement about it and so, like John the Baptist, put himself in jeopardy.

718. The Mishnah is quite clear about causes. Of course, it also reflects the diverse attitudes between the school of Shammai and Hillel. Both sages were older

contemporaries of Jesus. mYebamoth ("Sisters-in-Law") 14,1: "a husband can put away his wife only with his own consent" (as compared to a wife). Gittin 9,10: "The School of Shammai say: A man may not divorce his wife unless he has found unchastity in her, for it is written, *Because he hath found in her* indecency *in anything* (Deut 14:1). And the School of Hillel say: [He may divorce her] even if she spoiled a dish for him, for it is written, *Because he hath found in her indecency in* anything." Danby, *Mishnah*, 240, 321. So Shammai refers the Scripture to only acts of unchastity, while Hillel (the more liberal of the two) takes it to mean any failure on the part of the wife. Nineham, *Mark*, 260, notes that Mal 2:13–16 does not affect the discussion. This passage, he avers, is too obscure to offer any commentary on determining just causes for divorce.

719. His exception clause, it has been argued, is a correct interpretation of Jesus' understanding since Deut 22:22 had already dealt with adultery. Nineham, *Mark*, 261. However, that Jesus would, according to Matthew, agree with the Shammaites immediately makes this Matthean "exception" suspect. I have suggested elsewhere that the Shammaities were probably Jesus' Pharisaic antagonists.

720. See note above. Paul builds his sexual morality on these words of Jesus in 1 Cor 7:10–15, which corroborates them as authentic. However, he does not say whether a Christian man or woman can remarry in the case of an unbelieving spouse who leaves the marriage. One may assume that Paul himself assumed that, on the basis of the remarriage prohibition he annunciated (1 Cor 7:10), they would understand that in such cases they were not to remarry.

721. Thanks to Montefiore, *The Synoptic Gospels*, 239, for this taxonomy.

722. Although such a case occurred when Salome, the sister of Herod the Great, "wrote a bill of divorce" divorcing her husband Costobar. Josephus, *Ant*. 15, 7, 10. Josephus notes that it was only lawful for a man to do so. However, in the Graeco-Roman milieu a woman could initiate divorce. Mark is apparently writing in such an environment. Mark may have had in mind Herodias, who simply left her husband and married Herod Antipas. See Roemer, *World of Jesus*, 195–9.

723. Montefiore, *Synoptic Gospels*, 239.

724. The argument resembles Mark 7:6–13, where Jesus quotes Scripture and then contrasts it with the Pharisaic tradition, which, in effect, nullifies a clear divine commandment.

725. "Nowhere more than here does Jesus go nearer to denying the absolute divinity, permanence and perfection of the law." Montefiore, *Synoptic Gospels*, 237–38.

726. The command is beyond dispute and absolutely certain.

727. Meier, *Marginal Jew* IV 123.

728. See LXX Deut 10:16, which reads literally, "Circumcise your *hardness of heart*"; Jer 4:4 (again literally): "Circumcise yourselves to the Lord, remove the *hardness of your hearts*, O men of Judah and inhabitants of Jerusalem; lest my wrath go forth like fire, and burn with none to quench it, because of the evil of your doings."

729. Meier, *Marginal Jew* IV, 122.

730. From the time of Hosea God's relationship with his people Israel was expressed in terms of the love bond of marriage (Hos 2:19–20, Isa 54:5, Ezek 16). Then in the church the metaphor was continued in terms of Christ's relationship with his church (Eph 5:23–33, Rev 19:7–9, 21:2, 9, 22:17). Richardson, *Word Book*, 140b.

731. By citing Deut 6:4–5 Jesus could be affirming the whole law. However, he does not focus on the legal fulfillment of individual commandments because he saw their fulfillment in the law of love (Rom 13:10).

732. Wright, *Victory*, 566.

733. Wright, *Victory*, 607.

734. See Roemer, *Who in the World Was Jesus*, and the parables of the mustard seed

(134–7), treasure in a field (148–51), lost sheep (154–7), leaven in a lump (198–201), the shameless neighbor (230–4), the lost coin (239–41), the unjust steward (247–59), the good Samaritan (303–6), and the Pharisee and the tax collector (323–30).

735. See Roemer, *World of Jesus*, 401–6.
736. See the previous chapter, which discusses Jesus' baptism.
737. See Exod 34:10, 27–28, 24:1–11, Amos 3:2, 7:15.
738. Richardson, *Word Book*, 132a, who notes that earlier traditions avoided the use of "beloved" perhaps due to its association with the pagan fertility cultus. Later it was widely used. God's love has its origin in the depths of his being.
739. However, it is hinted at in Amos 9:7, Isa 19:19–25, 42:1–6, 49:6, and the books of Ruth and Jonah. Richardson, *Wordbook*, 133a.
740. See John 3:35, 5:20, 15:9, 17:23.
741. In Isa 49:1–3 the prophet announces that his call began before his birth and that God calls him his servant, whom he identifies as "Israel." So the prophet recapitulates the nation in his call. Jesus, similarly identified as God's servant, replicates the ancient prophet's call and identity.
742. The word "beloved" occurs most frequently in the Song of Songs, where it is applied almost exclusively by the maiden to her lover. The Song of Songs was employed in the Passover liturgy, which interpreted it as the love relationship between Israel and her God. The apostle picks up this imagery in Eph 5:23–32, taking the love between man and wife as image of the relationship between Christ and his church.
743. A Hebraism meaning "all," Fenton, *Matthew*, 325.
744. The context of Jesus is thoroughly explicated in the first volume of this series, Roemer, *World of Jesus*.
745. See Roemer, *World of Jesus*, on the "holy war," 13–6.
746. See Deut 31:7–8, Josh 10:40–42, and Roemer, *World of Jesus*, 65. Judah slaughtered all the Gentiles within the city of Bozra.
747. See Roemer, *World of Jesus*, 62–83.
748. See Roemer, *World of Jesus*, 12–3.
749. See Roemer, *World of Jesus*, 3–13.
750. You can hear these longings voiced in Luke's canticles, the Magnificat (1:54–55) and the Benedictus (1:68–75).
751. See Roemer, *World of Jesus*, 9–17.
752. Matt 1:2, 11:9, 21:26, Mark 1:2, 11:32, Luke 1:76, 7:26, 13:33, 24:19.
753. See Roemer, *World of Jesus*, 409–17.
754. See Roemer, *World of Jesus*, 17–31.
755. Josephus, *Ant.* 17, 10, 7–8.
756. I quote this psalm extensively in *World of Jesus*, 424–6. This book of eighteen psalms was composed in the first century BC responding to the Roman conquest in the year 63. It could be of Pharisaic provenance. Its authors were pious adherents of the Torah who longed for a righteous, independent state under the guidance of a Davidic king.
757. Which I analyze in *World of Jesus*, 418–23.
758. Pss of Solomon 17:24.
759. Josephus, *Ant.* 20, 8, 10, says the name derived from the crooked daggers they used that resembled the "Roman *sicae*, sickles."
760. Josephus, *War* 2, 13, 3.
761. See Roemer, *World of Jesus*, 325–6.
762. See Roemer, *World of Jesus*, 468–502.
763. See Roemer, *World of Jesus*, 168.
764. See Sanders, *Judaism: Practice and Belief.*

765. See Ps 119:39, Isa 9:3–7. The Lord's zeal is the salvation of his people (Isa 26:11).

766. See Roemer, *World of Jesus*, 431–5, for a detailed description of the concept and its adherents.

767. Roemer, *World of Jesus*, 436.

768. A characterization of Thurman, *Jesus and the Disinherited*. He found a parallel between the life situation of the Black population of the United States and the peasants of Jesus' time and therefore, in the face of criticism for embracing Christianity given the persecution that African Americans experienced under a so-called Christian culture, found a solidarity with Jesus, who inhabited the condition of the disinherited.

769. See Roemer, *World of Jesus*, 394–401.

770. Roemer, *Who in the World Was Jesus*, 306–16.

771. See Roemer, *World of Jesus*, 483–88.

772. For details of procuratorial government and Pilate's antagonistic administration see Roemer, *World of Jesus*, 229–33, and 235–7. One of his hostile actions, which is not described by Josephus, is referenced in Luke 13:1–5, the slaughter of some Galileans "whose blood Pilate mixed with their sacrifices" (see above, chapter 3).

773. See Roemer, *World of Jesus*, 195–9.

774. Luke 13:31–33. See above, chapter 2.

775. See the two tables in Roemer, *World of Jesus*, 442, 512.

776. However, see Fiensy, "Large Estates." He argues that these estates were of modest size and had no significant impact on the economy of the Galilee.

777. Roemer, *Who in the World Was Jesus*, 160–5.

778. See Roemer, *World of Jesus*, 402–6.

779. Josephus, *War* 1, 16, 2–4.

780. Roemer, *World of Jesus*, 405. Josephus, *Ant.* 18, 1, 6, revealingly describes them as having "an invincible passion for liberty" and having "God as their only leader and Lord."

781. This hatred was vividly on display at the outbreak of the war when the Gentile majorities in various cities attacked and murdered their Jewish neighbors. Where the Jews were a majority, they wreaked the same fate upon their Gentile neighbors. See Roemer, *World of Jesus*, 268–9.

782. See Roemer, *World of Jesus*, 200–214.

783. I deal extensively with Herod the Great in *World of Jesus*, 134–73; for Archaelaus see 193–5.

784. On apocalyptic see Roemer, *World of Jesus*, 443–63.

785. See n 769 above. Howard Thurman mirrored the ministry of Jesus. He could have found a comfortable academic position but chose to be a pastor. He co-founded the Church for the Fellowship of All Peoples, the first interracial church in the United States by design. His context was Jim Crowism, the constant threat of lynchings, and the indignities suffered by African Americans. He was not known for marching in the streets or for blistering speeches deriding injustice and racism. Rather, he emphasized the spiritual, the inner life, and a personal encounter with the divine. He insisted that the individual could best come to know the self in relationship with others. He stressed the interconnectedness of all people and so could not be at rest while some were imprisoned, treated as inferiors, or relegated to a lower class. For a fuller treatment of Thurman's character and story see Tisby, "Howard Thurman," 176–184. Of course, there were Jews who were ready to accommodate their faith with Graeco-Roman culture and religion. See Roemer, *World of Jesus*, "Hellenization as Prelude to War," 52–6.

786. See Pss of Solomon 17.

787. Smith, "'Low in the Well,'" 197.

788. Thurman, *Jesus and the Disinherited*, 74–88. The whole of volume 17, 3 of the

Journal for the Study of the Historical Jesus is devoted to Thurman and his work, which has contributed to my understanding of Thurman's achievement. The endnotes indicate the contributions of Thurman and the authors of the various studies in this issue of the *JSHJ* to the analysis which follows.

789. Thurman, *Disinherited*, 36–57.

790. See the history of the procurators, Roemer, *World of Jesus*, 228–56.

791. Smith, "'Low in the Well,'" 193.

792. As Josephus reports the land was overrun with bandits. War, 1, 16, 2–4. Although he is describing Herod the Great's actions against them in 45 BC, it scarcely could have been different in Jesus's day, when all kinds of revolutionary movements were active. The two bandits crucified with Jesus also point in this direction. See Roemer, *World of Jesus*, 401–6, and Horsley, *Bandits, Prophets, and Messiahs*, 67. Herod the Great was able to effectively eliminate these movements during his reign, having inaugurated what amounted to a totalitarian police state.

793. Horsley, *Bandits, Prophets, and Messiahs*, 50.

794. In this regard see Wurmbrand, *Tortured for Christ*. Wurmbrand was imprisoned for fourteen years by the Communists in Romania after the war, during which he was tortured to get him to reveal the names of people in the "Underground Church" (a designation he invented to describe the house churches that met in secret to avoid Communist persecution). The Communist regime beat him, scarred him with burning pokers, broke his bones, and all but starved him. He, however, was convinced that God would judge him not on how much torture he could take but rather on how well he could love his torturers! In that way he was able to convert even some of them to Christianity.

795. Cf., especially the story of the Gerasene demoniac (Mark 5:1–20). Human bodies can function as metaphors for the body politic. The demoniac embodies the social reality of living under an occupying power: he is occupied by a legion of demons; the demons enter pigs (the Roman Tenth Legion was stationed in the land during the war, and its emblem was the boar); it is not possible to bind the demoniac (v 3), and the numerous attempts (v 4) to do so point to the overwhelming strength of the Roman occupation; the demons exhort Jesus "not to send them out of the country"—i.e., they recognize their subordination to Jesus but still want to limit his power and defend their occupation of the land. The word "send" has military associations and means dispatch as when a commanding officer dispatches spies (Josh 2:1) or military forces (Josh 8:3). In this way the demon legion recognizes Jesus's authority as a military officer but seeks to secure its own interest, power, and authority; the same motif is expressed in the legion wanting to be sent into the pigs: to preserve control over the land's production. The request to "let us enter them" or "go into them" also has sexual connotations. So the demon legion's request seeks to maintain imperial control over the land and its production and projects military occupation and the violence associated with war including rape; entering into the swine they rush into the sea and drown, just as Pharaoh's army perished in the Red Sea, utterly deprived of their power. See Carter, "Cross-Gendered Romans and Mark's Jesus."

796. E.g., during the 60s a movement called the sicarii emerged in Jerusalem who carried small daggers in their clothing (from which their named derived) and who would murder people they singled out as collaborators. They were clearly urban terrorists. When it became obvious that the Roman siege of Jerusalem would be successful, they left the city and settled at Masada, where they engaged in raids on the caravan traffic in the area. The Romans besieged Masada in 74, but before they finally stormed the top of this butte, all its defenders committed suicide, depriving the Romans of a military victory. See Roemer, *World of Jesus*, 368–71, 435.

797. Thurman, *Disinherited*, 74.

798. Thurman, *Disinherited*, 85.

799. So even though there was many a Gentile who adopted Judaism, the so-called God-fearers, and who positively regarded the Jews (like the description of the centurion in Luke 7:4–5, Acts 10:1–2), a revolutionary could see them as exceptions against the background of a mighty Rome that held the Jew in contempt.

800. See n 797 above.

801. See Roemer, *World of Jesus*, 153. Herod's action stands in contrast to the behavior of the man in Jesus's parable of the rich fool who hoarded for himself the great harvest he enjoyed. The parable illustrates that such behavior was not uncommon in the world of Jesus.

802. The most egregious examples of this occurred some years earlier during the reign of the Maccabee Alexander Jannaeus (103–76 BC). At the feast of tabernacles the people taunted him as unworthy to serve as high priest, and he let loose his soldiers on them and slaughtered six thousand. Later, during a rebellion when he captured a village into which the rebels had retreated, he crucified eight hundred and had the throats of their wives and children slit in front of them as they hung on their crosses. See Roemer, *World of Jesus*, 101–5. That violence, animosity, and rage were endemic to these times. Read the story of the war with Rome, its beginnings, execution, and bloody denouement in Roemer, *World of Jesus*, 265–354.

803. Thurman, *Disinherited*, 39.

804. Thurman, *Disinherited*, 40.

805. Primarily somatic anxiety is marked by events such as stomachache, headache, muscle tension, muscle aches, increased heart rate, rapid breathing, hyperventilation, sweating, shaking, and nausea. In some cases the anxiety can cause symptoms that are unusual such as nerve symptoms, trouble swallowing, feelings of lumps, unusual pains, and more. Anxiety can have an intense effect on the body, possibly leading to issues that create further anxiety. On the other hand, primarily cognitive anxiety implies that the above physical symptoms are present to a lesser degree and that mental symptoms of anxiety happen most often without concurrent physical effects. The cognitive symptoms of anxiety include unease, repetitive negative thoughts, difficulty concentrating, confusion, and depersonalization. Both types of symptoms may be present, but it is thought that in most cases one or the other type of symptom is predominant. In addition, it should be noted that somatic symptoms can cause cognitive symptoms and vice versa. For example, an anxiety headache might lead to further negative thinking creating possible reasons why the headache is there in the first place. This can lead to further somatic symptoms such as sweating or shaking, causing a potential panic attack. https://www.calmclinic.com/anxiety-treatments/somatic

806. Thurman, *Disinherited*, reads too much of the experience of Black people living under the devastating racist regime of Jim Crow in the post–Civil War era into the first-century Jewish experience, as should be clear from what I have described of the circumstances of the Jewish peasant in the Holy Land of that time. Differences include racism, that the Jewish peasant was not alienated from Israel's heritage, that violence was not a constant threat, that the people could move about freely, guaranteed by the *Pax Romana* (think of Paul's missionary journeys), that they were free of being conscripted into the Roman armies, and that the practice of Torah and Temple worship was in no way proscribed.

807. See the stories of Jacob's deception of his father, Isaac (Gen 27:1–29) and the Gibionites' deception (Josh 9:1–27). The latter story more closely resonates with the deceptions practiced by oppressed people undermining their overlords. See also Thurman, *Disinherited*, 58–73.

808. Cf., Job 27:4, Ps 32:2, Prov 20:17, Isa 57:4, Jer 23:26, Rom 1:29, Wis 1:5, Sir 19:26.

809. Thurman, *Disinherited*, 69.

810. Perhaps even more horrifically and limning the loss of all morality, one woman desperate for food and "driven mad by hunger" killed her own baby and, after roasting it, ate it. See Roemer, *World of Jesus*, 345.

811. Thurman, *Disinherited*, 71. Cf., Ps 139.

812. Roemer, *Who in the World Was Jesus*, 241–7.

813. See particularly Dan 7–12 and Zech 8–14 with their powerful promises of the victory of YHWH. Apocalyptic literature extended, of course, far beyond the biblical apocalypses. Charlesworth, *The Old Testament Pseudepigrapha*, contains nineteen apocalyptic writings and eight "testaments" containing often apocalyptic sections. The Essenes had their own apocalyptic writing. The sheer volume of this literature witnesses to a widely held belief in the soon-to-occur intervention of God that would bring judgment on the world and vindication of his people.

814. See the discussion above on his occupation as a woodworker in the pronouncement story of the rejection in the hometown. He was part of a village and its life and relationships.

815. He had a "hometown" inhabited by his mother and "brothers" who had a house where he grew up and called home.

816. See the parable of the unjust steward, Roemer *Who in the World Was Jesus*, 247–59. My interpretation of this difficult parable suggests that passive resistance is a powerful tool in the hand of the poor and that subterfuge can produce the in-breaking of the kingdom, one aspect of which is the forgiveness of debt and the liberty of the Jubilee (Lev 25:10).

817. "But truth endures and is strong forever, and lives and prevails forever and ever. With it there is no partiality or preference, but it does what is righteous instead of anything that is unrighteous or wicked. Everyone approves its deeds, and there is nothing unrighteous in its judgment. To it belongs the strength and the kingship and the power and the majesty of all the ages. Blessed be the God of truth! When he stopped speaking, all the people shouted and said, 'Great is truth, and strongest of all!'" (NRSV).

818. Levenson, *Death and Resurrection*, 188–99.

819. Mark 1:12–13, Matt 4:1–11, Luke 4:1–13.

820. 2 Sam 15:13—16:14, David's "via dolorosa." See also Roemer, *World of Jesus*, 420.

821. 1 Cor 1:25, 2 Cor 11:30, 12:9, 13:4, Heb 11:34.

822. The ministry of Jesus is replete with evidence that he thought of himself as wisdom. See Roemer, *Who in the World Was Jesus*, 15–17, which summarizes Witherington, *The Jesus Quest*.

823. Roemer, *Who in the World Was Jesus*, 148–51, 294–6.

824. Roemer, *Who in the World Was Jesus*, 165–8, 306–16.

825. See the story of Jesus weeping over Jerusalem above in chapter 2, Isa 53:10, and 4 Macc 17:20–22.

826. See n 788 and Roemer, *World of Jesus*, 443–63.

827. In the long discussion that ensues from the Baptist's question to Jesus sent via his disciples while he was in prison (Matt 11:2–19, Luke 7:18–35).

828. In John 3:30, John declares Jesus must "increase" and he must "decrease." This saying is another way of expressing John's greatness in the period leading up to Jesus but his decrease in the period of the dawning kingdom brought by Jesus.

829. Roemer, *Who in the World Was Jesus*, 292–4.

830. See, e.g., Gen 49:28, Exod 24:4, 39:14, Num 7:84–87, Josh 4:8, 1 Kgs 18:31, Rev 7:5–8, 21:12–22.

831. Cf., also the story of Nathaniel (John 1:45–49), who is also overwhelmed by this numinous aspect of Jesus.

832. John's chronology sees Jesus active in the Galilee, where he calls disciples, and doing the first of his signs in Cana, turning water into wine.

833. That particular text would have hummed in Jesus's mind as well as in the minds of the people, as it was quite probably read in the synagogues during the most popular of all the feasts, Sukkoth. The feast was redolent with egalitarian ideas and Israel's liberation.

834. For the Sadducees the prophetic writings were of no account. Their "Scripture" was the Torah and nothing else. They were more or less hidebound traditionalists whose thought world never moved beyond the literal interpretation of Torah. Of course, that all redounded to their exalted economic position.

835. As he did of the peaceful and unarmed demonstration of the Samarian prophet. See Roemer, *World of Jesus*, 409–10.

836. See Roemer, *World of Jesus*, 228–56. The last procurator, Gessius Florus (64–66), was an obvious anti-Semite and seemed to have the very intention to so offend the people to foment an uprising that Rome could then violently put down. He succeeded!

837. Horsley, *Bandits, Prophets, and Messiahs*, 161–72. Roemer, *World of Jesus*, 409–10. See n 836.

838. See Roemer, *Who in the World Was Jesus*, and the parables of the mustard seed (134–7), treasure in a field (148–51), lost sheep (154–7), leaven in a lump (198–201), the shameless neighbor (230–4), the lost coin (239–41), the unjust steward (247–59), the good Samaritan (303–6), and the Pharisee and the tax collector (323–30).

839. Arnal, *Jesus and the Village Scribes*, 198.

840. The Torah was full of exhortations regarding how one should act toward the neighbor. Cf., Exod 18:16, Lev 19, Deut 19, Pss 12:2, 15:3, 101:5, Prov 11:12, 14:21, 24:28, Isa 41:6, Jer 22:13, Zech 3:10. In the following discussion on love of enemies I am surveying the chapter on love in Thurman, *Disinherited*, 89–109.

841. Roemer, *Who in the World Was Jesus*, 303–6.

842. It was well known that they extorted more than required because they were allowed to add to the required tax a surcharge that they exacted as payment for their work. That it was exorbitant was reflected in their wealth.

843. Thurman, *Disinherited*, 93.

844. This affirmation is repeated over and over again in the Scriptures: Num 14:18, Neh 9:17, Pss 86:5, 103:8, 145:8, Joel 2:13, John 4:2. Mercy is emphatically an attribute of the God of Israel and concretized in the "mercy seat" on the ark (see, e.g., Exod 25:22).

845. Thurman, *Disinherited*, 94.

846. See Roemer, *World of Jesus*, "Procutorial Government," 229–33.

847. Thurman, *Disinherited*, 97.

848. E.g., when Pilate inexplicably brought Roman standards into Jerusalem in direct violation of Roman policy, he was met by a contingent of Jewish representatives in his palace in Caesarea Maritima, where he conspired to physically attack them. When his soldiers brandished their weapons, they, to a man, bared their necks willing to die for the integrity of the Holy City. This passive resistance worked. This was a social encounter based on a ruler with power and powerless suppliants, the weak and the strong, the privileged and the underprivileged. See Roemer, *World of Jesus*, 235, and Thurman, *Disinherited*, 97. Referring to the relationship between races in the Jim Crow era, Thurman illuminates lucidly the situation between Jew and Roman in the first century and in particular the encounter that I have just described. He writes, "There is a great intimacy between whites and Negroes, but it is usually between servant and served, between employer and employee. Once the status of each is frozen or fixed, contacts are

merely truces between enemies—a kind of armistice for purposes of economic security. True, there are times when something great and dependable emerges, and the miracle takes place even though the status has remained, formally. But during such moments status is merely transcended; it is not broken down . . . but in a very tragic sense, the ultimate fate of the relationship seems to be in the hands of the wider social context."

849. In the healing of the official's household member, the "centurion" apparently recognizes this prohibition of entering a Gentile's house (Matt 8:8, Luke 7:6, and cf., the story of Cornelius in Acts 10).

850. Thurman, *Disinherited*, 100.

851. Thurman, *Disinherited*, 102. With this mindset the official in Luke 7:4–5 could be considered an "exception" because he loved Israel and built the synagogue.

852. Thurman's term, *Disinherited*, 102.

853. As in the parable of the Pharisee and the tax collector (see Roemer, *Who in the World Was Jesus*, 323–30). In contradistinction to the Pharisee in the parable, the centurion does not place himself above Jesus but puts himself on the same level and appeals to Jesus as one man to another. It is an experience of human universality. Jesus expresses his surprise that he has not even found such faith in Israel. He, in effect, is saying, "This man has found the kingdom. Would that all my countrymen could!" As I have suggested, this experience and that of the Syrophoenician woman profoundly affected Jesus and his understanding of the kingdom.

854. Wright, "Jubilee," 1025b.

855. The name in Hebrew is "the year of the ram's horn." Josh 6 distinguishes between the ram's horn and the ordinary trumpet. The former has greater sanctity and divine effect. It was blown only by the priest. The legislation connected with the Jubilee (Lev 25) is part of the so-called Holiness Code (Lev 17:1—26:46; see Roemer, *World of Jesus*, 29–30; its roots go back to pre-exilic times, but its redaction was exilic). In the book of Jubilees (second century BC) the Jubilee has become only a period of time as the largest unit of time reckoning and consists of a period of forty-nine years. So the Jubilee was a theoretical construct, which lent to its becoming eschatologized and its prescriptions becoming eschatological realities.

856. It is noteworthy that the prophets never appeal to the Jubilee. So historically, the Jubilee, if it was ever practiced, one would have to surmise, fell into disuse because of social disruption as more and more people were uprooted and dispossessed of their land (Mic 2:2). In this scenario the conclusion would have to be that after generations, there was simply no memory of lost ancestral lands and no basis for any claim. The rabbinic discussion of the Jubilee with regard to real property is totally theoretical since the Mishnah was written when Israel did not live in the land. See, e.g., mRosh ha-Shanah 1,1, mKiddushin 1,2, mBekhoroth 8,10.

857. Lev 25:39–43 makes clear that even in the case of a total economic breakdown of a family and its members entering the bonded service of the next of kin, they are not to be treated as slaves but rather employees, which status is to continue only until the Jubilee, at which time they are to be emancipated, recover their property, and have a new beginning.

858. Wright, "Jubilee," 1026a.

859. Lev 25:13–17 makes clear that the sale of land was really only a sale of use. The purchaser was only buying a number of harvests until the Jubilee, when the land was restored to the original owner. Wright, "Jubilee," 1026b.

860. Wright, "Jubilee," 1028a.

861. I don't think Matt 6:25–32 is directed exclusively toward the Sabbath year in exhorting the people not to be anxious. Much more it is directed to the daily life of the peasant who was constantly faced with the possibility of scarcely being able to provide for

himself and his family's ongoing needs. Contra Yoder, *The Politics of Jesus*, 61. Of course, Jesus's words would apply with even greater force during the fallow Sabbatical year.

862. Cf., the German "*Schuld*," which word also has meanings of both guilt and debt.

863. See Roemer, *Who in the World Was Jesus*, 201–7.

864. Roemer, *Who in the World Was Jesus*, 247–59.

865. Yoder, *Politics of Jesus*, 64.

866. Hillel approached the problem of the forgiveness of debt, which was supposed to occur during the Sabbath year (i.e., every seven years). As the Sabbatical year approached creditors stopped lending simply because they could not recoup the debt in the Sabbatical year, which provoked a hardship for many a small landowner. He inaugurated the so-called *prosboul* (from the Greek, πρὸς βουλή, *pros boulē*, "to the council"), which, by a legal fiction, shifted the ownership of the debt to a council, which was not forbidden to collect on a debt in the Sabbatical year. This was a practical solution that relieved the quotidian difficulties of the small landowner while simultaneously avoiding transgressing the Torah. The *prosboul* also demonstrates that the Sabbatical release of debts was actually practiced. See Roemer, *World of Jesus*, 424, 477.

867. Theissen, *Shadow of the Galilean*, 157.

868. The parable illustrates how intermediate functionaries worked. They added an arbitrary surcharge to the collection of the debt. The debtors would have had no recourse because the masters permitted them the accumulation of wealth in this manner. But in the process they lost the honor and respect of the people. Yoder, *Politics of Jesus*, 67. See also the parable of a neighbor comes at midnight, Roemer, *Who in the World Was Jesus*, 230–4.

869. Yoder, *Politics of Jesus*, 66

870. See no 849 above.

871. Yoder, *Politics of Jesus*, 60.

872. See Mark 10:9. And it was the practice of the apostles to be accompanied by their wives (1 Cor 9:5). "Leaving all" did not include one's wife (Mark 10:2–9).

873. E.g., Lev 27:30–32, Num 18:21–26, Deut 12:17, 14:22–28. Roemer, *World of Jesus*, 394–8. The Pharisees would also be concerned that the food they purchased and consumed would come from tithed produce; otherwise it would be unclean to them. See Roemer, *World of Jesus*, 476.

874. Vermes, *Jesus and the World of Judaism*, 47.

875. Jesus may have had in mind here Isa 1, which criticizes Israel for externally observing the requirements of the Temple cultus but then practices injustice. So Israel must then wash herself by removing wickedness. Only then will she be "pure" (Isa 1:16). Danker, *Jesus and the New Age*, 143–4. Israel's connecting cultic practice and morality was unique to the ancient world.

876. There is a certain justice rendered by offering the tithe. The tribe of Levi had no land inheritance and therefore no means of supporting themselves. Their survival depended on the tithe.

877. Jesus emphasizes this unsullied trust and dependence on God's mercy in his parable of the Pharisee and the tax collector, Roemer, *Who in the World Was Jesus*, 323–30.

878. The two cities of the Galilee, Sepphoris and Tiberias, are never mentioned in the Gospels, which suggests that Jesus did not conduct his ministry in these places. Both cities contained Gentiles and perhaps even Gentile installations. So Jesus's avoidance of them reflects his concern for Torah. The only mention of Tiberias in the Gospels is John 6:1, which says that boats came from there to where Jesus had performed the miracle of loaves.

879. Indeed, it is a principle of Judaism that every law can be suspended where life

is at stake.

880. By citing Deut 6:4–5 Jesus could be affirming the whole law. However, he does not focus on the legal fulfillment of individual commandments because he saw their fulfillment in the law of love (Rom 13:10).

881. Roemer, *Who in the World Was Jesus*, 134–7, 198–201.

882. Wright, *Victory*, 566.

883. Wright, *Victory*, 607.

884. The root of the word means "learner." Cf., Ezek 33:31 for the posture of one sitting to learn.

885. To "sit with" frequently involves a king, which means sharing their character, sharing the power of their position, enjoying their favor, or succeeding them (1 Sam 2:8, 20:5, 1 Kgs 1:17).

886. In this Jesus aligned with the more liberal Hillelite Pharisees who rejected the harsh demands of Torah to stone an adulteress.

887. The evangelists do not make a big point of this, but Matthew and Mark do allude to Jesus's growing celebrity and reputation (Matt 4:24, 9:31, 14:1, Mark 1:28).

888. Jesus understood that a new covenant would be inaugurated by his death and celebrated in the meal he instituted (Luke 22:20, 1 Cor 11:25. Cf., also 2 Cor 3:6, Heb 8:8, 13, 9:15, 12:24).

889. See Ezek 26:24–28, Num 11:26–29, Joel 2:28–29.

890. For Jeremiah and Hosea the covenant is based on love and mercy symbolized by marriage. It is the divine gift of a new heart and a new spirit (cf., Ezek 11:20, 18:31, 36:26, Isa 59:21).

891. Roemer, *Who in the World Was Jesus*, 350–6.

892. Two lepta were about one-sixty-fourth of a denarius (a day's wage)—i.e., if a laborer worked twelve hours, he earned two lepta in about eleven minutes.

893. One could think here of the poor widow who was ready to have her last meal and die when Elijah, sent by God, showed up and saved her and her son from starvation (1 Kgs 17:8–16).

894. See the story of Jesus weeping over Jerusalem above in chapter 2., Isa 53:10, and 4 Macc 17:20–22.

895. The summit of the Mount of Olives is some 150 feet taller than Mount Zion, on which Jerusalem and the Temple were built.

896. See the parable of the returning demons, Roemer, *Who in the World Was Jesus*, 347–50.

897. Cf., the parable of the rich man, Roemer, *Who in the World Was Jesus*, 165–8.

898. See above chapter 2 the widow's mite and Zaccheus the toll collector and wealth and the kingdom and the dispute over an in heritance in chapter 3. Related is the question in the story of Jesus concerning the census in chapter 3.

899. The threat of judgment is very real in the proclamation of Jesus (Matt 5:22–30, 10:28, 18:9, 23:33, Mark 9:43–47, Luke 12:5).

900. A familiar prophetic theme. Piety and ethics were inextricably linked in Judaism (Ps 15). Jesus justifying his concern for the toll collector Zacchaeus by saying that he too was "a son of Abraham" only emphasizes Jesus's call to the whole nation, not the grounds of his inclusion in the kingdom (Luke 19:9).

901. Witherington, *The Jesus Quest*, 185, points out other associations with wisdom in the ministry and person of Jesus: his healing, exorcisms, never using the prophetic declaration "Thus says the Lord," using parables and aphorisms, gathering disciples, appealing infrequently to Torah but rather to the created order, infrequent engagement with halakhic discussions, and claiming that something greater than Solomon was present in him and his activity.

902. See Roemer, *World of Jesus*, 401–6.

903. "Fasting" meant a total abstinence from food and would be undertaken during mourning (1 Sam 31:13) or as a part of performing an act of repentance (1 Kgs 21:27). There were set fasts. Pharisees apparently fasted twice a week (Luke 18:12). John's disciples, as we have seen, fasted (Mark 2:18–22). Apparently, people in general fasted, but Jesus enjoined them to do it "in secret" (Matt 6:18). There is no evidence, however, in the New Testament that regular fasts were part of church life (but see Acts 13:2, 14:23, 2 Cor 6:5, 11:27). See Richardson, *Word Book*, 79a–80b.

904. See chapter 1, which discusses Jesus's baptism.

905. See Exod 34:10, 27–28, 24:1–11, Amos 3:2, 7:15.

906. Richardson, *Wordbook*, 132a, who notes that earlier traditions avoided the use of "beloved" perhaps due to its association with the pagan fertility cultus. Later it was widely used. God's love has its origin in the depths of his being.

907. However, it is hinted at in Amos 9:7, Isa 19:19–25, 42:1–6, 49:6, and the books of Ruth and Jonah. Richardson, *Wordbook*, 133a.

908. Roemer, *Who in the World Was Jesus*, 241–7.

909. See John 3:35, 5:20, 15:9, 17:23.

910. In Isa 49:1–3 the prophet announces that his call began before his birth and that God calls him his servant, whom he identifies as "Israel." So the prophet recapitulates the nation in his call. Jesus, similarly identified as God's servant, replicates the ancient prophet's call and identity.

911. The word "beloved" occurs most frequently in the Song of Songs, where it is applied almost exclusively by the maiden to her lover. The Song of Songs was employed in the Passover liturgy, which interpreted it as the love relationship between Israel and her God. The apostle picks up this imagery in Eph 5:23–32, taking the love between man and wife as image of the relationship between Christ and his Church.

912. A Hebraism meaning "all," Fenton, *Matthew*, 325.

913. Roemer, *World of Jesus*, 1–16.

914. Matt 14:5, 21:11, 21:46, Mark 6:15, Luke 7:16, 13:33, 24:19, John 4:19, 6:14, 7:40, 9:17, Acts 3:22, 7:37.

915. In this regard you may want to read Sullivan, *The Limitations of Science*. It is, of course, a little dated in terms of the developments and discoveries that have occurred since its writing, but the author's analyses are still apropos. Here's a little taste of the author's argument:

> We have seen that the scientific account of our universe appears clearest and most convincing when it deals with inanimate matter. Here we feel that the account is relatively satisfactory because it does, on the whole, meet the kind of interest we take in these phenomena. The age, position, size, velocity, chemical constitution of a star is, for instance, the kind of information we want about a star. And to be told that matter consists of little electrified particles arranged with respect to one another in certain ways makes us feel that our curiosity about matter has very largely been met. But when we come to the sciences dealing with life, the state of affairs is less satisfactory. Many of the questions that seem to us quite fundamental have not been met. What, for instance, makes us regard a living organism as a whole, and not merely the sum of its parts? What does this vague notion of "wholeness" or "individuality" really amount to? Even if every bodily activity of the animal was explained in terms of physical and chemical changes, we should still feel that our question was unanswered unless what appears as the *purposive order* of those changes was also accounted for. But "purpose" is not a scientific notion. (125)

Bibliography

Abraham, Micah. "Somatic Anxiety—Treating the Body vs. the Mind." https://www.calmclinic.com/anxiety-treatments/somatic

Abrahams, Israel. *Studies in Pharisaism and the Gospels*. Vol. 1. Cambridge: Cambridge University Press, 1917.

Ackroyd, Peter R. "The Book of Isaiah." In *The Interpreters One-Volume Commentary on the Bible*, edited by Charles M. Laymon 329–371. Nashville: Abingdon, 1971.

———. *Exile and Restoration: A Study of Hebrew Thought of the Sixth Century B.C.* Philadelphia: Westminster, 1968.

Aland, Barbara, et al. *Novum Testamentum Graece*. Stuttgart: Deutsche Bibelstiftung, 2012.

Aland, Kurt, ed. *Synopsis Quattuor Evangeliorum: Locis parallelis evangeliorum apocryphorum et partum adhibitis edidit*. Stuttgart: Whrttembergische Bibelanstalt, 1967.

Allison, Jr., Dale C. *Constructing Jesus: Memory, Imagination, and History*. Grand Rapids: Baker Academic, 2010.

———. "The Continuity between John and Jesus." *Journal for the Study of the Historical Jesus* 1, 1 (2005) 6–27.

———. "Memory, Methodology, and the Historical Jesus: A Response to Richard Bauckham." *Journal for the Study of the Historical Jesus* 14, 1 (2016) 13–27.

Arendt, William F., and F. Wilber Gingrich. *A Greek-English Lexicon of the New Testament and Other Early Christian Literature*. Chicago: The University of Chicago Press, 1952.

Arnal, William E. *Jesus and the Village Scribes: Galilean Conflicts and the Setting of Q*. Minneapolis: Fortress, 2001.

Bailey, Kenneth E. "Informal Controlled Oral Tradition and the Synoptic Gospels." *Asia Journal of Theology* 5 (1919) 34–54.

———. "Middle Eastern Oral Tradition and the Synoptic Gospels." *The Expository Times* 106 (1994–1995) 363–67.

Baldensperger, W. "Die neueste Forschung über den Menschensohn." *Theologische Rundschau* 3, 6 (1900) 201–210.

Barber, Michael Patrick. "Did Jesus Anticipate Suffering a Violent Death?" *Journal for the Study of the Historical Jesus* 18, 3 (2020) 191–219.

Bauckham, Richard. "The General and the Particular in Memory: A Critique of Dale Allison's *Approach to the Historical Jesus*." *Journal for the Study of the Historical Jesus* 14, 1 (2016) 28–51.

———. *Jesus and the Eyewitnesses: The Gospels as Eyewitness Testimony*. Grand Rapids: William B. Eerdmans, 2006, 2017.

———. *Jesus and the God of Israel*. Grand Rapids: William B. Eerdmans, 2008.

———. "The Psychology of Memory and the Study of the Gospels." *Journal for the Study of the Historical Jesus* 16, 2–3 (2018) 136–55.

Beare, F. W. "The Sabbath Was Made for Man?" *Journal of Biblical Literature* 79, 2 (1960) 130–36.

Behm, Ernst. "esthio[set mackron over o]." In *TDNT* 2:691.

Berger, Klaus. *Formgeschichte des Neuen Testaments*. Heidelberg: Quelle & Meyer, 1984.

Black, Matthew. *An Aramaic Approach to the Gospels and Acts*. Oxford: At the Clarendon Press, 1946.

Borg, Marcus J. *Jesus: A New Vision*. San Francisco: Harper & Row, 1988.

Bornkamm, Günther. "Das Doppelgebot der Liebe." In *Neu Testamentliche Studien für Rudolf Bultmann zu seinem siebzigsten Geburtstag*, edited by Walter E. Hester, 85–93. Berlin: Alfred T`pelmann, 1957.

Brown, Francis, S. R. Driver, Charles Briggs. *A Hebrew and English Lexicon of the Old Testament: With an Appendix Containing the Biblical Aramaic*. Oxford: Clarendon, 1976.

Brown, Raymond E. *The Birth of the Messiah*. Garden City: Image, 1979.

Bruce, F. F. "The Background to the Son of Man Sayings." In *Christ the Lord: Studies in Christology Presented to Donald Guthrie*, edited by Harold H. Rowden, 55–70. Leicester: Inter-Varsity, 1982.

Bryskog, Samuel. "Memory and Narrative Time: Towards a Hermeneutics of Memory." *Journal for the Study of the Historical Jesus.* 16, 2–3 (2018) 108–72.

Bultmann, Rudolf. *Das Evangelium des Johannes*. Göttigen: Vandenhoeck & Ruprecht, 1964.

———. *Jesus*. München und Hamburg: Siebenstern Taschen Verlag, 1965.

Bundy, W. E. *Jesus and the First Three Gospels*. Cambridge, Massachusetts: Harvard University Press, 1963.

Caird, G. B. *The Gospel of Saint Luke*. Middlesex, England: Penguin, 1963.

Carter, Warren. "Cross-Gendered Romans and Mark's Jesus: Legion Enters the Pigs (Mark 5:1–20)." *Journal of Biblical Literature* 134, 1 (2015) 139–55.

Casey, Maurice. *Aramaic Sources of Mark's Gospel*. Cambridge: Cambridge University Press, 1998.

———. *The Solution to the "Son of Man" Problem*. Library of New Testament Studies 343. New York: T&T Clark, 2007.

Charlesworth, James H. *The Old Testament Pseudipigrapha: Apocalyptic Literature and Testaments*. Vol. 1. Garden City: Doubleday, 1983.

Clements, R. E. *God and Temple*. Philadelphia: Fortress, 1965.

Cranfield, C. E. B. *The Gospel According to St. Mark*. Cambridge: Cambridge University Press, 1971.

Crook, Zeba A. "Collective Memory Distortion and the Quest for the Historical Jesus." *Journal for the Study of the Historical Jesus* 11, 1 (2013) 53–76.

Danby, Herbert. *The Mishnah: Translated from the Hebrew with Introduction and Brief Explanatory Notes.* Oxford: Oxford University Press, 1933.
Daniel-Rops, Henri. *Daily Life in the Time of Jesus.* Ann Arbor: Servant, 1962.
Danker, Frederick W. *Jesus and the New Age, According to Luke: A Commentary on the Third Gospel.* St. Louis: Clayton, 1972.
Dentan, Robert C. *Mark.* Interpreters Bible 6. Nashville: Abingdon, 1968.
Derrett, Duncan M. "The Zeal of the House and Cleansing of the Temple." *Downside Review* 95 (1977) 79–94.
Dibelius, Martin. *Die Formgeschichte des Evangeliums.* Thbingen: J.C.B. Mohr (Paul Siebeck), 1919.
Donahue, John R. "A Neglected Factor in the Theology of Mark." *Journal of Biblical Literature* 101, 4 (1982) 563–94.
Downing, F. Gerald. "The Resurrection of the Dead: Jesus and Philo." *Journal for the Study of the New Testament* 5, 15 (1982) 42–50.
Dunn, James D. G. *Jesus and the Spirit: A Study of Religious and Charismatic Experience of Jesus and the First Christians as Reflected in the New Testament.* Philadelphia: Westminster, 1975.
Elledge, Roderick. *Use of the Third Person for Self-Reference by Jesus and Yahweh: A Study of Illeism in the Bible and Ancient Near Eastern Texts and Its Implications for Christology.* Library of New Testament Studies 575. London: T&T Clark, 2017.
Ellis, E. Earle, and Erich Graesser, eds. *Jesus und Paulus, Festschrift: W. G. Kümmel.* Göttingen: Vandenhoeck und Ruprecht, 1975.
Eusebius. *Ecclesiastical History.* Translated by Kirsopp Lake. 1926. Cambridge, Massachusetts: Harvard University Press, 1926.
Evans, Craig A. *Mark 8:27–16:20.* Word Biblical Commentary. Grand Rapids: Zondervan, 1988.
Fenton, J. C. *The Gospel of Saint Matthew.* Middlesex, England: Penguin, 1963.
Ferguson, Anthony. "The Elijah Forerunner Concept as an Authentic Jewish Expectation." *Journal of Biblical Literature* 137, 1 (2018) 127–45.
Fiensy, David A. "Did Large Estates Exist in Lower Galilee in the First Half of the First Century CE?" *Journal for the Study of the Historical Jesus* 10, 2 (2012) 133–53.
Finegan, Jack. *Archaeology of the New Testament: The Life of Jesus and the Beginning of the Early Church.* Rev. ed. Princeton: Princeton University Press, 1992.
Florentino, Garcia Martinez. *The Dead Sea Scrolls Translated: The Qumran Texts in English.* The Netherlands: E. J. Brill, 1996.
Ford, J. M. "Money 'Bags' in the Temple." *Biblia* 57 (1976) 251.
Foster, Paul. "Memory, Orality, and the Fourth Gospel: Three Dead-Ends in Historical Jesus Research." *Journal for the Study of the Historical Jesus* 10, 3 (2012) 193–212.
Gaertner, Bertile. *The Temple and the Community of Qumran and the New Testament.* SNTSMS 1. Cambridge: Cambridge University Press, 1965.
Giblin, Charles H. "'The Things of God' in the Question Concerning Tribute to Caesar." *Catholic Biblical Quarterly* 33 (1971) 510–14.
Giesen, Heinz. "Der Verdorrte Feigenbaum-eine Symbolishe Aussage? Zu Markus 11:12–14." *Biblische Zeitschrift.* Neue Folge 1 (1976) 95–111.
Glynn, Patrick. *God: The Evidence.* Rocklin: Forum, 1997.
Goodacre, Mark. "Q, Memory and Matthew: A Response to Alan Kirk." *Journal for the Study of the Historical Jesus* 15, 2–3 (2017) 224–33.

Gregory, Andrew. "Memory as Method: Some Observations on Two Recent Accounts." *Journal for the Study of the Historical Jesus* 16, 1 (2018) 52–61.
Grundmann, Walter. *Das Evangelium nach Markus*. 3rd ed. Berlin: Evangelische Verlagsanstalt, 1965.
Haenchen, Ernst. *Weg Jesu*. Berlin: Walter de Gruyter, 1968.
Hall, Calvin S. *A Primer of Freudian Psychology*. New York: Harper & Row, 1982.
Hamilton, Neill Q. "Temple Cleansing and Temple Bank." *Journal of Biblical Literature* 83, 4 (1964) 365–72.
Hanson, Paul. *The Dawn of Apocalyptic*. Philadelphia: Fortress, 1975.
Harb, Gertraud. "Matthew 17.24–27 and Its Value for Historical Jesus Research." *Journal for the Study of the Historical Jesus* 8, 3 (2010) 254–74.
Haufe, Günther. "Das Menschensohn Problem in der gegenw@rtigen Wissenschaftlichen Diskussion." *Evangelishe Theologie* 26, 3 (1966) 130.
Hiers, Richard. "Purification of the Temple: Preparation for the Kingdom of God." *Journal of Biblical Literature* 90, 1 (1971) 82–90.
Horsley, Richard. *Archaeology, History and Society in Galilee: The Social Context of Jesus and the Rabbis*. Valley Forge: Trinity, 1998.
——— et al. *Bandits, Prophets, and Messiahs: Popular Movements in the Time of Jesus*. San Francisco: Harper & Row, 1985.
Hultgren, A. J. *Jesus and His Adversaries*. Minneapolis: Augsburg, 1979.
Jacob, Edmond. *Theology of the Old Testament*. London: SPCK, 1957.
Jeremias, Joachim. *Die Gleichnisse Jesu*. Göttingen: Vandenhoeck & Ruprecht, 1965.
———. *New Testament Theology*. New York: Scribner, 1971.
Joseph, Simon J. "'I Shall be Reckoned with the Gods'": On Redescribing Jesus as a First-Century Mystic." *Journal for the Study of the Historical Jesus* 18, 3 (2020) 220–43.
Josephus: *Contra Apion*. Vol. II. Translated by William Whiston. 1737. Reprinted, Grand Rapids: Baker, 1974.
Kazan, Thomas. "The Coming of the Son of Man Revisited." *Journal for the Study of the Historical Jesus* 5, 2 (2007) 155–74.
Kee, Howard Clark. "The Function of Scriptural Quotations and Allusions in Mark 11–16." In *Jesus und Paulus: Festschrift für Werner Georg Kümmel zum 70. Geburtstag*, edited by E. Earle Ellis and Erich Graesser, 165–188. Göttingen: Vandenhoeck und Ruprecht, 1975.
Kelber, Werner H. *The Oral and the Written Gospel: The Hermeneutics of Speaking and Writing in the Synoptic Tradition, Mark, Paul, and Q*. Philadelphia: Fortress, 1983.
Kirk, Alan. "Ehrman, Bauckham and Bird on Memory and the Jesus Tradition." *Journal for the Study of the Historical Jesus* 15, 1 (2017) 88–114.
Kittel, Gerhard, and Gerhard Friederich. *Theological Dictionary of the New Testament*. Translated and edited by Geoffrey W. Bromiley. 1964. Grand Rapids: Wm. B. Eerdmans, 1964.
Klemm, Hans G. "De Censu Caesaris-Beobachtungen zu Ducan M. Derretts Interpretation der Perikope Mk 12:13–17 Par." *Novum Testamentum* 224 (1982) 147–8.
Kloppenborg, John S. "Memory, Performance, and the Sayings of Jesus." *Journal for the Study of the Historical Jesus* 10, 2 (2012) 97–132.
Koch, Klaus. *Die Priestershaft von Exodus 25 bis Leviticus 15*. FLANT 71. Göttingen: Vandenhoeck und Ruprecht, 1959.
Kwon, Jong Hyun. *The Historical Jesus' Death and Forgiveness of Sin*. Wissentshaftlicher

Untersuchung des Neun Testaments 2, 467. Thbingen: Mohr Siebeck, 2018.

Le Donne, Anthony. "Mnemomic Interplay: A Response to Bryskog, Bauckham, Zimmerman, and Schr`ter." *Journal for the Study of the Historical Jesus* 16, 2–3 (2018) 173–82.

———. "The Problem of Selectivity in Memory Research: A Response to Zeba Crook." *Journal for the Study of the Historical Jesus* 11, 1 (2013) 77–97

Levenson, John D. *The Death and Resurrection of the Beloved Son*. New Haven: Yale University Press, 1993.

Lewis, C.S. *Miracles: A Preliminary Study*. New York: Macmillan, 1947.

Licona, Michael R. "Did Jesus Predict His Death Vindication/Resurrection?" *Journal for the Study of the Historical Jesus* 8, 1 (2010) 47–56.

Lightfoot, John. *A Commentary on the New Testament from the Talmud and Hebraica: Matthew-1 Corinthians*. Vol. III. Peabody: Hendrickson, 1989.

Lindeskog, G`sta. "Das Rätsel des Menschensohnes." *Studia Thelogica* 22 (1968) 149–76.

Lohmeyer, Ernst. *Das Evangelium des Markus. Kritisch-exegetish Kommentar über das neuen Testament*. Vol. 3. 2nd ed. Goettigen: Vandenhoeck & Ruprecht, 1951.

Manson, T. W. *The Servant-Messiah: A Study of the Public Ministry of Jesus*. Cambridge: Cambridge University Press, 1953.

Marsh, John. *The Gospel of Saint John*. Middlesex, England: Penguin, 1968.

Marshall, I. H. "The Synoptic Son of Man Sayings in Recent Discussion." *New Testament Studies* 12 (1966) 347–51.

Mays, James L., ed. *Harper's Bible Commentary*. San Francisco: Harper & Row, 1988.

McGinn, Bernard. *The Presence of God: A History of Western Christian Mysticism: The Foundations of Mysticism: Origins to the Fifth Century*. New York: Crossroad, 1991.

McGrath, James F. "Obedient Unto Death: Philippians 2:8, Gethsemane, and the Historical Jesus." *Journal for the Study of the Historical Jesus* 14, 3 (2016) 223–40.

———. "Was Jesus Illegitimate?" *Journal for the Study of the Historical Jesus* 5 1 (2007) 81–100.

McKnight, Scot. "Calling Jesus *Mamzer*." *Journal for the Study of the Historical Jesus* 1, 1 (2003) 73–103.

Meier, John P. *A Marginal Jew: Rethinking the Historical Jesus: the Roots of the Problem and the Person*. Vol. I. New York: Doubleday, 1991.

———. *A Marginal Jew: Rethinking the Historical Jesus: Mentor, Message, Miracle*. Vol. II. New York: Doubleday, 1994.

———. *A Marginal Jew: Rethinking the Historical Jesus: Law and Love*. Vol. IV. New Haven: Yale University Press, 2009.

Metzger, Bruce M. *Textual Commentary on the Greek New Testament*. London: United Bible Societies, 1971.

Mitchel, Hinckley. *A Critical and Exegetical Commentary on Haggai and Zechariah*. ICC. New York: Charles Scribner Sons, 1912.

Montefiore, C. G. *The Synoptic Gospels*. Vol. I. London: Macmillan, 1909.

Moody, Jr., Raymond A. *Life After Life*. New York: Bantam, 1976.

Moore, George Foote. *Judaism in the First Centuries of the Christian Era: The Age of the Tannaim*. Vol. II. New York: Schocken, 1971.

Münderlein, Gerhard. "Die Verfluchung des Feigenbaumes." *New Testament Studies* 10 (1963) 92–4.

Neirynck, Franz. *Duality in Mark: Contributions to the Study of the Marcan Redation.* Bibliotheca Ephemeridum Theologicarum Lovaniensium 31. Leuven: University Press, 1968.

———. *The Redactional Text of Mark.* Bibliotheca Ephemeridium Theologicarum Lovaniensium 57. Leuven: University Press, 1981.

Neyrey, Jerome H., ed. *The Social World of Luke-Acts: Models for Interpretation.* Peabody: Hendrickson, 1991.

Nickelsburg, George W. E. *Jewish Literature between the Bible and the Mishnah.* Philadelphia: Fortress, 1981.

———. "Son of Man." In *ABD* 6:137–50.

Nineham, D. E. *The Gospel of Mark.* Middlesex, England: Penguin, 1969.

Passamaneck, S. M. "Some Medieval Problems in *Mamzeruth*." *Hebrew Union College Annual* 37 (1966) 121–45.

Perrin, Norman. *The Kingdom of God in the Teaching of Jesus.* London: SCM, 1963.

Philo. *De Specialibus Legibus.* Vol. I. Translated by F. H. Colson. Loeb Classical Library 320. Oxford: Harvard University Press, 1937.

Pliny. *Natural History* 5, 73. Translated by H. Rackham. Loeb Classical Library. Cambridge, Massachusetts: Harvard University Press, 1938.

Ploeger, Otto. *Theocracy and Eschatology.* Oxford: Basil Blackwell, 1958.

Porter, Stanley E., et al. "Memory, Orality, and the Fourth Gospel: A Response to Paul Foster with Further Comments for Future Discussion." *Journal for the Study of the Historical Jesus* 12, 1–2 (2014) 143–64.

Pritchard, James. *The Ancient Near East: An Anthology of Texts and Pictures.* Vol. I. Princeton: Princeton University Press, 1958.

Pryke, E. J. *Horae Synopticae Electronicae. Word Statistics of the Synoptic Gospels.* Society for Biblical Literature Source for Biblical Study 3. Missoula: Scholars, 1973.

Quarles, Charles L. "Jesus as Merkabah Mystic." *Journal for the Study of the Historical Jesus* 3, 1 (2005) 5–22.

Redditt, Paul L. *New Century Bible Commentary: Haggai, Zechariah and Malachi.* Grand Rapids: William B. Eerdmans, 1995.

Reed, W. L. "Burial." *IDB* I, 474–6.

Reynolds, Benjamin E., ed. *The Son of Man Problem: Critical Readings in Biblical Studies.* London: Bloomsbury, 2018.

Richardson, Alan. *A Theological Word Book of the Bible.* New York: Macmillan, 1960.

Rienecker, Fritz. *Sprachlicher Schlüssel zum Griechischen Neuen Testament.* Giessen-Basel: Brunnen-Verlag, 1960.

Ritmeyer, Leen. "The Pinnacle of the Temple." https://www.ritmeyer.com/2010/12/07/the-pinnacle-of-the-temple.

Robbins, Vernon K. "Apophthegms." In *ABD* 1:307–9.

Robinson, James M., ed. *The Nag Hammadi Library.* San Francisco: Harper & Row, 1977.

———. *The Problem of History in Mark.* Studies in Biblical Theology 21. London: SCM, 1957.

———. *Twelve More Studies.* London: SCM, 1984.

Rodriguez, Rafael. "Authenticating Criteria: The Use and Misuse of a Critical Method." *Journal for the Study of the Historical Jesus* 7, 2 (2009) 152–67.

———. "Jesus as His Friends Remembered Him." *Journal for the Study of the Historical Jesus* 12, 3 (2014) 224–44.

Roemer, Carl E. *Giving the Vineyard to Others: A Form and Redactional Critical Analysis of Mark 11 and 12*. PhD diss., The Lutheran School of Theology at Chicago, 1990.

———. *What Was the World of Jesus?: A Journey for Curious Pilgrims*. Bloomington: True Directions, 2014.

———. *Who in the World was Jesus?: An Encounter for Brave Hearts*. Lanham: Hamilton, 2019.

Roth, Ceci. "The Cleansing of the Temple and Zechariah 14:21." *Novum Testamentum* 14 (1960) 174–81.

Rowley, H. H. *Worship in Ancient Israel*. London: SPCK, 1969.

Russel, D. S. *The Method and Message of Jewish Apocalyptic*. Philadelphia: Westminster, 1964.

Sanders, Edward Parish. *Jesus and Judaism*. Philadelphia: Fortress, 1985.

———."Jesus in Historical Context." *Theology Today* 50, 3 (1993) 429–48.

———. *Jewish Law from Jesus to the Mishnah: Five Studies*. London: SCM, 1990.

———. *Judaism: Practice and Belief, 63 BCE–66 CE*. London: SCM, 1992.

Schmidt, N. "Recent Study of the Term 'Son of Man.'" *Journal of Biblical Literature* 45, 3/4 (1926) 326–49.

Schmithals, Walter. *Das Evangelium nach Markus: Kapital 1–9:1*. Ökumenisher Taschenbuchkommentar zum Neuen Testament 2. Würzburg: Echter-Verlag, 1979.

Schneemelcher, Wilhelm, ed. *New Testament Apocrypha I: Gospels and Related Writings*. Philadelphia: Westminster, 1963.

Schrenk, Gottlob. "hieron." In *TDNT* 3:239–40.

Schröter, Jens. "Memory, Theories of History, and the Reception of Jesus." *Journal for the Study of the Historical Jesus* 116, 2–3 (2018) 85–107.

Schuerer, Emil. Revised by Geza Vermes et al. *The History of the Jewish People in the Age of Jesus Christ*. Vol. III. Edinburgh: T & T Clark, 1986.

Schweizer, Eduard. Translated by Donald H. Madvig 1970 *The Good News According to Mark*. Atlanta: John Knox, 1952.

Shae, Gam Seng. "The Question on the Authority of Jesus." *Novum Testamentum* 16, 1 (1974) 1–29.

Smith, Abraham. "'Low in the Well': A Mystic's Creative Message of Hope in *Jesus and the Disinherited*." *Journal for the Study of the Historical Jesus* 17, 3 (2019) 185–200.

Smith, Charles W. F. "No Time for Figs." *Journal of Biblical Literature* 79, 4 (1960) 315–27.

Stauffer, Ethelbert. *Jesus: Gestalt und Geschichte*. Bern: Francke Verlag, 1957.

———. "The Story of the Tribute Money." In *Christ and the Caesars*, 112–137. London: SCM, 1955.

Stern, Jay B. "Jesus' Citation of Deut 6:5 and Lev 19:18 in the Light of Jewish Tradition." *Catholic Biblical Quarterly* 28, 3 (1966) 312–6.

Stinespring, W. F. "Eschatology in Chronicles." *Journal of Biblical Literature* 80, 3 (1961) 209–19.

Strack, Herman L., and Paul Billerbeck. *Kommentar zum neuen Testament aus Talmud und Midrasch II: Das Evangelium nach Markus, Lukas, Johannes, und Apostelgeschichte*. Mhnchen: C. H. Beckische Buchhandlung Oskar Beck, 1924.

Sullivan, J. W. N. *The Limitations of Science: A Creative Scientist's Approach to the Unknown*. New York: Viking, 1933.

Tannehill, Robert C. "Introduction: The Pronouncement Story and Its Type." *Semeia* 21 (1981) 1–13.

Taylor, Vincent. *The Gospel According to St. Mark*. 2nd ed. London and Basingstoke: MacMillan, 1966.

Telford, William R. "The Barren Temple and the Withered Tree." *Journal for the Study of the New Testament*, Supp. 1. Sheffield: JSSOT, 1980.

Theissen, Gerd. *The Shadow of the Galilean: The Quest of the Historical Jesus in Narrative Form*. Philadelphia: Fortress, 1986.

———, and Annette Merz. *The Historical Jesus: A Comprehensive Guide*. Minneapolis: Fortress, 1998.

Thomas, Kenneth J. "Liturgical Citations in the Synoptics." *New Testament Studies* 22, 2 (1976) 205–14.

Thurman, Howard. *Jesus and the Disinherited*. Boston: Beacon, 1976.

Tisby, Jemar. "Howard Thurman: Spiritual Activist and Mystic of the Movement." *Journal for the Study of the Historical Jesus* 17, 3 (2019) 176–84.

Tolkien, J. R. R. *Lord of the Rings*. London: Folio Society, 1977.

Trueblood, Elton. *The Humor of Christ*. New York: Harper & Row, 1964.

Tucker, S. Ferda. "John the Baptist." *Journal for the Study of the Historical Jesus* 10, 2 (2012) 154–88.

Twelftree, Graham H. "Jesus the Baptist." *Journal for the Study of the Historical Jesus* 7, 2 (2009) 103–25.

Urbrock, William J. "Blessings and Curses." In *ABD* 1:755–61.

Vermes, Geza. *The Complete Dead Sea Scroll in English*. Allen Lane: Penguin, 1998.

———. *Jesus and the World of Judaism*. Philadelphia: Fortress, 1984.

———. *Jesus the Jew: A Historian's Reading of the Gospels*. Philadelphia: Fortress, 1973.

Von Rad, Gerhard. *Old Testament Theology: The Theology of Israel's Historical Traditions*. Vol. I. New York: Harper & Row, 1962.

———. *Wisdom in Israel*. Nashville: Abingdon, 1972.

———. "Zelt und Lade." In *Gesammelte Studien zum Alten Testament*, 135–164. Munich: Christoph Kaiser, 1959.

Walsh, Jerome T. "Elijah." In *ABD* 2:463–66.

Witherington, Ben. *The Jesus Quest: The Third Search for the Jew of Nazareth*. Downers Grove: InterVarsity, 1995.

Wright, Addison. "The Widow's Mites: Praise or Lament? A Matter of Context." *Catholic Biblical Quarterly* 44, 2 (1982) 256–65.

Wright, Christopher J. H. "Jubilee, Year of." In *ABD* 3:1025–30.

Wright, N. T. *Jesus and the Victory of God*. Minneapolis: Fortress, 1996.

Wurmbrand, Richard. *Tortured for Christ*. Bartlesville: Living Sacrifice, 1967.

yeshuaincontext.com.

Yoder, John Howard. *The Politics of Jesus*. Grand Rapids: Eerdmans, 1972.

Zeichmann, Christopher B. "Jesus 'ben Pantera': An Epigraphic and Military-Historical Note." *Journal for the Study of the Historical Jesus* 18, 2 (2020) 141–55.

Zimmerman, Ruben. "Memory and Jesus' Parables: J. P. Meier's Explosion and the Restoration of the 'Bedrock' of Jesus' Speech." *Journal for the Study of the Historical Jesus* 16, 2–3 (2018) 156–72.

Zolondek, Michael Vicko. "The Authenticity of the First Passion Prediction and the Origin of Mark 8:31–33." *Journal for the Study of the Historical Jesus* 8, 3 (2010) 236–53.

Index

Abba, 7, 8, 12, 21, 52, 218, 225
action prophets, 185
Ancient of Days, 62
Antiochus IV Epiphanes, 62
Apocalypse of Abraham, 90
apocalyptic ideas, 169
apocalyptic viewpoint, 148
apothegm, 57
Aqedah, 177
Archaelaus, 169
attitude toward outsiders, 158
attitudes toward the Temple in Late
    Antiquity, 89
authenticity, 1

banditry, 173
bandits, 40, 168
baptism, 29
baptizing, 27
beloved son, 8, 19, 20, 21, 22, 44, 50,
    52, 53, 54, 56, 160, 177, 200,
    201, 204, 205, 206, 209, 210,
    218, 219, 220, 223, 224, 225,
    226
Bethsaida, 60
binding of Satan, 155, 200
Biographical Pronouncement Stories
    Blessing of Mary, 70
    Cost of Discipleship, 66
    Foretelling the Destruction of the
        Temple, 103
    Healing of the Ten Lepers, 81
    Herod Antipas Threatens Jesus, 86
    Jesus Blesses the Children, 74
    Jesus Weeps over Jerusalem, 104
    Anointing of Jesus at Bethany, 105
    Mary and Martha, 80
    On the Way to the Cross
        Simon of Cyrene, 107
    Paying the Temple Tax, 85
    Rejection in the Hometown, 70
    The Calling of Disciples, 59
    The Cleansing of the Temple, 89
    The Disciples' Praises, 84
    The Healing of an Official's
        Household Member, 98
    The Widow's Mite, 76
    The Woman Taken in Adultery,
        100
    True Kinsmen, 68
    Zaccheus the Toll Collector, 82
    Lamenting Women, 107
birth narratives, 4
birth pangs, 157
Blessing, 75
Book of Jubilees, 90
breaking of the Sabbath, 115

Capernaum, 53, 59, 60, 72, 98, 99, 100,
    121, 183, 260, 267
chaff, 34
chiasmus, 146

children, 12, 30, 41, 42, 55, 74, 75, 103, 105, 140, 197, 216, 217, 225, 228, 233, 235, 241, 250, 251, 281
Christ Hymn, 7, 180
classical prophets, 159
coming one, 31
common meals, 29, 55
Controversy And Scholastic Dialogues
    Divorce and Celibacy, 152
    Eating with Tax Collectors and Sinners, 121
    Healing of the Crippled Woman, 111
    Healing of the Man with a Withered Hand, 109
    Plucking Grain on the Sabbath, 115, 117
    The Chief Commandment, 131
    The Cursing of the Fig Tree, 142
    The Dispute about Exorcism, 112
    The Dispute Over an Inheritance, 134
    The Healing of a Paralytic, 114
    The Inhospitable Samaritans, 144
    The Man with Dropsy, 110
    The Presence of the Kingdom, 141
    The Question of John and James, 138
    The Question of John the Baptist, 136
    The Question on Authority, 125
    The Question on Fasting, 123
    The Question to Jesus Concerning the Census, 145
    The Rival Exorcist, 140
    The Sadducees and the Question of the Resurrection, 149
    The Slaughter of the Galileans, 135
    Wealth and the Kingdom, 127
Copernicus, 46
coram Deo, 174
corruption, 35
Cost of Discipleship, 66
covenant, 15, 16, 17, 18, 24, 25, 26, 87, 97, 148, 160, 165, 191, 210, 219, 220, 222, 228, 287
covenantal nomism, 20, 165
creation story and divorce, 153
crisis, 15, 36, 54, 75, 163, 166, 176, 192, 198, 207, 222, 224, 227
cross, 107, 157
Cyrus's edict, 16

Dame Wisdom, 208
Darwin, 46
day laborers, 168
deception, 173
demon possession, 173
demonic possession, 172
dependent hieratic state, 163
descendant of David, 6
Devil, 45
disciples of John, 123
dispensing with familial obligations, 68
divine claims of the emperor, 148
Divine Warrior, 148, 206
divinity, 7, 9, 10, 12, 52, 180, 266, 277
double love commandment, 156
dove imagery, 18
"Dream Visions" of Enoch, 90

ecological divisions, 169
economic inequality, 168
Elijah, 14, 15, 41
Elisha, 67
elites and their retainers, 163
end of exile, 36
Enoch, 63
entry into the kingdom, 26
eschatological fire, 33
Essenes, 13, 15, 40, 96, 112, 165, 169, 260, 263, 282
ethics of the kingdom, 155
evil has a personal dimension, 47
exile, 87, 170
Exodus-conquest tradition, 17
exorcisms and the Jubilee, 194
Ezekiel's living creatures, 53

faith and reason, 46
family of the kingdom, 69
fasting, 160
fear, 172
Feast of Tabernacles, 88
fence around the law, 165

figs as symbols, 143
filial piety, 66
firstborn, 19
fishers of men, 60
forgiveness, 115
Fourth Philosophy, 165, 203
Freud, 46
fruit as symbol, 143

gathering of the Gentiles, 204
Gaulanitis, 60
Gentiles, 10, 13, 28, 29, 42, 54, 61, 72, 94, 99, 100, 112, 114, 120, 127, 155, 156, 163, 182, 184, 188, 193, 195, 199, 200, 208, 215, 228, 232, 235, 248, 255, 267, 278, 286
go the extra mile, 50
God, land, and people, 170
God's faithfulness, 178
God's gratuitous favor, 54
God's kingdom, 87
going the extra mile, 136
Greek Apocalypse of Baruch, 90

half-sheqel tax, 85, 202
hand washing, 117
hand washing not Pharisaic, 119
Healings, 33
Hellenistic Judaism, 132
Herod Antipas, 13, 14, 16, 37, 41, 60, 86, 121, 167, 169, 173, 196, 201, 255, 259, 267, 272, 276, 277
high priests, 166
holiness as contagious, 123
Holy Land as buffer state, 169
holy war, 162, 196
hospitality, 28, 40, 48, 52, 54, 69, 104, 157, 158, 175, 181, 184, 186, 188, 195, 197, 248
human memories, 3
hyper-patriotism, 174

"I am" sayings, 11
Identifying John with Elijah, 41
illegitimacy, 5
inclusion of women, 159

inner disposition, 120
invasion against Satan, 186
Isaiah's vision, 52
Isaianic prophecies, 54
Israel
    as transcendent reality, 56
    a light to the Gentiles, 191
    as God's beloved people, 22
    itinerant ministry, 66, 175, 184, 196

James and John, 60, 138, 145, 157, 186, 201, 251
Jesus,
    "I" utterances, 11
    abandoning social connections, 68
    a martial aspect to his activity, 207
    ad hominem arguments against him, 160
    agreement with the Pharisees, 198
    and open commensality, 192
    and the Jubilee, 191
    as a bridegroom, 124
    as a pioneer, 161
    as hungering, 144
    as inverse priest, 123
    as perverter of Israel, 70, 197
    as prophet, 156
    as prophet, priest, and king, 210
    as representative of Israel, 160
    as self-promoting pretender, 71
    as Servant of the Lord, 50
    as socially prominent person, 134
    as Son of David, 6
    as son of man, 155
    as stumbling block, 183
    as the messenger and his hearers, 159
    as the end-time prophet, 125
    as the new Adam, 50
    as the pioneer, 138
    as traitor, 187
    as wisdom, 42
    baptism, 18, 29
    baptizing, 27
    calls for the absolute forgiveness, 193
    claims royal prerogatives, 185

298 INDEX

    concerned with inner disposition, 135
    counters a revanchism against Rome, 199
    total filial self-awareness, 12
    healings, 155
    his "homelessness," 175
    his call to forgive debts, 192
    his emphaasis on interiority and purity of intention, 196
    his filial relationship with God, 176
    his identity, 180
    his regard for the Torah, 155
    his setting in the Holy Land of the first century, 162
    his suffering as a baptism, 139
    his table practice and the Jubilee, 195
    his understanding of the meaning of weaalth, 207
    historicizes apocalyptic, 207
    identification with sinful Israel, 53
    inner life of, 10
    like a mobile temple, 208
    like a new Moses, 50
    not a "judge," 181
    numinous aspect, 184
    power over unclean spirits, 9
    prayer in Gethsemane, 7
    recapitulating Israel's history, 50
    relationship with John, 27
    religious experience, 20
    reverses Adam's defeat by Satan, 51
    self-consciousness, 9
    sense of sonship, 23
    temptation, 43
    reverses Adam's defeat by Satan, 51
    visit to Nazareth, 71
Jewish faith, 170
Johanna, the wife of Chuza, 196
John, fulcrum of history, 40
John the Baptist, 164
John's baptism, 125
John's vision of the resurrected Lord, 53
Jordan, 13, 14, 19, 27, 36, 223, 234
Joseph story, 44
Josephus, 13, 40, 58, 94, 103, 104, 164, 168, 169, 218, 221, 241, 242, 257, 258, 259, 261, 265, 272, 274, 277, 278, 279, 280, 293
Jubilee, 72, 110, 111, 155, 189, 190, 191, 196, 197, 198, 201, 206, 207, 208, 209, 210, 224, 263, 282, 285, 297
judges, 163, 171
judges called bandits, 164

kashrut, 121
kenosis, 9, 176
Kingdom
    corruption, 35
kingdom is God, 40
kingdom of God, ii, 14, 15, 19, 21, 25, 31, 33, 34, 38, 39, 40, 41, 52, 53, 62, 64, 65, 68, 74, 75, 86, 97, 100, 103, 112, 113, 120, 124, 137, 140, 144, 153, 168, 170, 175, 177, 179, 184, 185, 195, 196, 197, 202, 207, 210, 219, 226, 229, 244, 265
Korban, 117, 155

Leprosy, 82
Letter of Aristeas, 94
Levi, 59, 60, 61, 121, 184, 223, 267, 286
love for enemies, 136, 158
    Jesus' visit to Nazareth, 72

Maccabean revolt, 162
mamzer, 5
manna, 47
Marriage, 159
martyr's death, 22
Massah, 49
materialist mode of modern historiography, 45
merged quotation, 37
messianic movements, 40
Micaiah ben Imlah, 52
mightier one, 39, 137

near death experiences, 45
neighbor, 187
new covenant, 203
new creation, 19
new family of the kingdom, 156

new Passover covenant, 177
nonspatial love, 187
nonviolent passive resistance, 171
numinous experience, 59

one flesh, 153
oral law, 117
order of creation, 153

parable of a widow and a rich man, 203
parables, 3, 25
Parables
    a neighbor comes at midnight, 111
    children at play, 183
    Children at Play, 42
    Lazarus and the rich man, 156, 181
    leaven in a lump, 199
    pearl of great price, 79, 156
    prodigal son, 35
    returning demons, 105
    Rich Man and Lazarus, 48
    seats at a feast, 111
    the binding of the "strong man, 33
    the door, 110
    the good Samaritan, 111, 134, 186
    the great Assize, 141
    the great feast, 110
    the lost sheep, 10, 134
    the mustard seed, 156, 199
    the patient vinedresser, 145
    the Pharisee and toll collector, 84
    the returning demons, 114
    the rich fool, 111, 130, 134, 156, 181
    the rich man, 79
    the rich man and Lazarus, 130, 134, 166
    the tax collector and the Pharisee, 203
    the thief, 110
    the two debtors, 111
    the unforgiving servant, 111, 115, 134, 192
    the unjust steward, 192, 194
    the wicked tenants, 88
    the widow's mite, 194
    the workers in the vineyard, 168
    treasure in a field, 79, 82, 138, 156

    the lost sheep, 230, 233, 236, 274
    treasure in the field, 202
    wicked tenants, 10
paralellismus membrorum, 64
passion predictions, 23
Passover, 22
Passover liturgy, 143
patriarchy, 197
persecutions, 131
Peter, 10, 59, 60, 79, 81, 130, 192, 247, 267, 270, 290
Pharisees, 6, 15, 58, 68, 84, 86, 101, 110, 114, 115, 116, 117, 119, 120, 121, 123, 131, 152, 155, 165, 169, 196, 202, 208, 215, 241, 242, 248, 250, 266, 267, 268, 276, 286, 287
Philip the Tetrarch, 121
Philo, 118
Pilate, 167
plant imagery, 143
political injustice, 169
population density, 169
power of hatred, 172
procurators, 167, 169
prodigal son, 35
prophets, 14, 15, 16, 21, 23, 25, 26, 28, 38, 39, 40, 53, 54, 93, 97, 132, 163, 170, 185, 207, 208, 225, 226, 227, 240, 250, 251, 261, 267, 285
prosbul, 194
psychological effects of Roman occupation, 171

Qal VaChomer, 110
quietism, 171
Qumran, 90

rabbinical principle re: the sabbath, 116
reality of this world of the spirit, 45
reconstituted Israel, 183
recurrent attestation, ii
religious competition, 169
remembered Jesus, i
remnant, 65
rendering the hands clean, 118

repentance, 14, 16, 17, 18, 24, 25, 26, 28, 30, 38, 42, 59, 69, 83, 84, 87, 102, 114, 122, 136, 143, 144, 158, 176, 202, 204, 205, 219, 220, 222, 261, 287
restoration, 14, 16, 17, 19, 31, 32, 34, 51, 54, 89, 90, 92, 95, 105, 110, 112, 114, 137, 148, 152, 176, 183, 185, 190, 191, 198, 204, 209, 222, 269
reverence for persons, 189
revolution, 49
revolutionary activity, 171
ritual purity, 119
Roman occupation, 16, 17, 33, 48, 80, 163, 164, 171, 172, 195, 280
Rome's accommodations with Jewish law, 163
royal messianic claimants, 163
ruler of this world, 49

Sabbath, 80, 116
sacrificial language, 9
Sadducees, 15, 97, 101, 163, 166, 169, 185, 193, 205, 206, 241, 260, 271, 276, 283
salted with fire, 33
Samaritan, 81, 82, 201, 219, 235, 236, 254, 261, 267, 272, 273, 277, 283
Samaritan prophet, 164
Satan, 5, 33, 44, 45, 47, 49, 50, 55, 81, 105, 110, 112, 113, 114, 141, 148, 158, 177, 178, 181, 183, 198, 205, 207, 210, 236, 238, 244, 254, 263
schools of Hillel and Shammai, 117
Scribes, 121
Sepphoris and Tiberias, 87
service, 157
Shammaites, 102, 152
sharing of goods, 157
Sibylline Oracles, 94
Sicarii, 165
Similitudes of Enoch, 64
Sin, 25
sitting as reflection, 201
social tensions, 168

son of man, 61, 115, 178
sovereignty of God, 158
spirit of God, 24
Suffering and sin, 136
Sukkoth, 31, 126, 148
Syriac Apocalypse of Baruch, 90

Taheb, 164, 185
Targums, 117
tax collectors, 6, 33, 61, 187, 188
Teacher of Righteousness, 15
Temple, 199
Temple as "house of prayer," 185
Temple cleansing, 88
    inviolability, 157
the ban, 162
the binding of the "strong man, 33
the chaos monster Leviathan, 147
the cross, 149
the danger of riches, 129
the Gerasene demoniac and the Jubilee, 194
the Jordan and Holy History, 182
the kingdom as yoke, 180
the kingdom's critique, 70
the land as Israel's heritage, 190
The Martyrdom of Isaiah, 90
The Rewards of Discipleship, 130
the treasury, 77
the wealthy, 166
the world as enemy occupied territory, 113
Tiberias an unclean city, 119
tithe, 190, 196
toll collector, 82
Torah, 6, 9, 14, 15, 16, 21, 22, 25, 26, 29, 42, 49, 56, 58, 62, 72, 87, 91, 93, 101, 112, 117, 118, 119, 120, 122, 123, 125, 132, 134, 145, 150, 152, 154, 159, 165, 166, 167, 169, 170, 174, 186, 188, 192, 194, 195, 196, 198, 202, 203, 204, 208, 222, 223, 227, 230, 231, 248, 257, 266, 270, 271, 272, 278, 282, 283, 286, 287
traitor, 188
True kinsmen, 197

True Kinsmen, 68
twelve disciples, 54, 183

unity of God, land, and people, 191
universe designed, 46
universe is not random, 46

validity of the Torah, 155, 198
via dolorosa, 8
vicarious atonement, 21
violence, 173
virgin birth traditions, 6

water for cleansing, 14

way of "weakness," 178
wedding celebrations, 123
widow, 78
wild beasts, 51
wilderness wanderings of Israel, 47
Wisdom, 93, 181
wives, 66, 272, 281, 286
women, 28, 107

Yohanan ben Zakkai, 58
yoke of the kingdom, 65, 133

zeal, 166
Zerubbabel and Joshua, 93

www.ingramcontent.com/pod-product-compliance
Lightning Source LLC
Chambersburg PA
CBHW070231230426
43664CB00014B/2266